Failing Forward

Failing Forward

THE RISE AND FALL OF
NEOLIBERAL CONSERVATION

Robert Fletcher

UNIVERSITY OF CALIFORNIA PRESS

University of California Press
Oakland, California

© 2023 by Robert Fletcher

Library of Congress Cataloging-in-Publication Data

Names: Fletcher, Robert, 1973– author.
Title: Failing forward : the rise and fall of neoliberal conservation / Robert
    Fletcher.
Description: Oakland, California : University of California Press, [2023] |
    Includes bibliographical references and index.
Identifiers: LCCN 2022031921 (print) | LCCN 2022031922 (ebook) |
    ISBN 9780520390683 (cloth) | ISBN 9780520390690 (paperback) |
    ISBN 9780520390706 (ebook)
Subjects: LCSH: Conservation of natural resources. | Neoliberalism. |
    Environmental policy. | Economic development—Environmental aspects.
Classification: LCC GF75 .F58 2023 (print) | LCC GF75 (ebook) |
    DDC 333.72—dc23/eng20221205
LC record available at https://lccn.loc.gov/2022031921
LC ebook record available at https://lccn.loc.gov/2022031922

32 31 30 29 28 27 26 25 24 23
10 9 8 7 6 5 4 3 2 1

To Julia, for bringing me home

CONTENTS

List of Illustrations   ix
Acknowledgments   xi
Abbreviations   xv

Introduction: Capitalism on Trial   1

1 · Conceptualizing Neoliberal Biopower   17

2 · Conjuring Natural Capital   38

3 · Imagining the Market   67

4 · The Neoliberal Ecolaboratory   91

5 · The Anti-regulation Machine   117

6 · How to Fail Forward   146

7 · Neoliberal Conservation in Ruins?   172

8 · There Is No Alternative to Degrowth   190

Conclusion: Traversing the Neoliberal Fantasy   210

Notes   231
Bibliography   249
Index   289

ILLUSTRATIONS

FIGURES

1. The 2016 World Conservation Congress, Honolulu, Hawai'i   *2*
2. Illustration for "The Emperor's New Clothes"   *22*
3. The triple bottom line   *56*
4. The new economics of nature   *57*
5. The mitigation hierarchy   *80*
6. Teak plantation enrolled in Costa Rica's PSA program   *105*
7. A classic illustration of the Jevons Paradox   *138*
8. Opening ceremony at the 2012 World Conservation Congress, Jeju Island, South Korea   *163*
9. The Yasuní-ITT initiative   *176*
10. Degrowth   *194*
11. The streetlight effect   *230*

TABLE

1. Environmental market-based instruments (MBIs)   *78*

MAP

1. Map of Costa Rica   *93*

ACKNOWLEDGMENTS

The full irony of this book's title became clear to me as I began writing the third version, the first two having received such searing critique that it paralyzed me for some time. Yet, as I explain in subsequent chapters, I believe that persevering through obstacles should be distinguished from repeatedly beating one's head against an unyielding wall. Achieving the former rather than the latter, as I hope I have, would not have been possible without the support of a great many people. Darren Applegate first led me to Costa Rica, where a community centered on the whitewater paddling industry warmly embraced me and helped me find my feet, resulting in enduring friendships with Alex Fernandez, Viviana Chavez, and Marianela Jimenez, among others. Years later, at the University for Peace, Rolain Borel, Mahmoud Hamid, Jan Breitling, and Jürgen Carls welcomed me back to the country and the Department of Environment and Development that became my home for many years. Conversations with all of these colleagues, along with fellow newcomer Guntra Aistara and resident iconoclast Ross Ryan, helped shape the initial phase of the project. The arrival of Brian Dowd-Uribe several years later further enriched my intellectual landscape. But it was primarily through ongoing conversations with Jan Breitling, on the benches in front of our office or over beers at Zompopas, that this project started to take its present shape. Informant confidentiality prevents me from singling out the countless individuals who facilitated my actual research on the ground. Suffice it to offer a warm collective thank-you here for accommodating my intrusion into your lives.

The project was also shaped though exchanges with countless colleagues at professional conferences on the global academic circuit where I presented various aspects of it over the years. A panel at the American Anthropological

Association (AAA) meetings in Philadelphia in 2009 organized by Katja Neves and Jim Igoe snowballed into a cascade of subsequent events, including the Society for Conservation Biology (SCB) conference in Edmonton in 2010; American Association of Geographers (AAG) meetings in Seattle and New York City; more AAAs in New Orleans, Montreal, and San Francisco; Society for Applied Anthropology (SfAA) meetings in Merida and Baltimore; and several others, culminating in the heady Nature Inc. conference in The Hague in 2011, then Grabbing Green in Toronto in 2013, then the series of conferences organized by the rapidly expanding Political Ecology Network (POLLEN). While particular contributors to these various sessions are far too numerous to name, enough cannot be said for continued support and inspiration from members of POLLEN and associated researchers, including inter alia Adeniyi Asiyanbi, Bill Adams, Zach Anderson, Tor Benjaminsen, Jevgeniy Bluwstein, Sarah Bracking, Dan Brockington, Bram Büscher, Lisa Campbell, Noel Castree, Connor Cavanagh, Ariadne Collins, Ben Colombi, Catherine Corson, Jessica Dempsey, Sierra Deutsch, Wolf Dressler, Rosaleen Duffy, Liza Grandia, Noella Gray, Violeta Gutiérrez Zamora, Nora Haenn, Tobian Haller, David Hoffman, George Holmes, Amber Huff, Jim Igoe, Jerry Jacka, Ilan Kapoor, Kariuki Karigia, Larry Lohmann, Jens Lund, Ken MacDonald, Kate Massarella, Kathy McAfee, Marcos Mendoza, Jesse Montes, Ben Neimark, Adrian Nel, Katja Neves, Nancy Peluso, Scott Prudham, Chris Sandbrook, Neera Singh, Sian Sullivan, Erik Swyngedouw, Lerato Thakholi, Lisa Trogisch, Paige West, Peter Wilshusen, and Japhy Wilson. Other important interlocutors include fellow researchers on Costa Rica Bill Durham, Carter Hunt, Kate Fischer, Emily Hite, David Lansing, Brett Matulis, Franklin Paniagua, Alonso Ramírez Cover, and Gaby Stocks. In my previous association with American University, Judy Shapiro, Ken Conca, Garrett Graddy-Lovelace, Simon Nicholson, and Paul Wapner were all influential. Questions and critical analysis from students in my various courses at the University for Peace deepened the project significantly. My new colleagues and students at Wageningen University have since challenged me to broaden and hone my perspective. Finally, my editor Stacy Eisenstark from University of California Press and two anonymous reviewers have been invaluable in patiently guiding my initially cumbersome manuscript into this far more coherent final form.

On a more personal note, acknowledgments go first to my family for love and support and for tolerating my endless coming and going over the years. Inca and Rainer Rumold have been enthusiastic backers as always, while

Claudia made it all possible by agreeing to turn her life upside down for an ill-fated move to Costa Rica. In addition to also suffering this dislocation, my lovely and amazing first child, Tenaya, accompanied me on several whirlwind trips through the country, enduring such trials as sunburn, near death on the Costa Rican highways, a night on the floor of the Denver airport, and the monotony of numerous academic conferences. Luin Goldring and Peter Vandergeest bridged the gap between personal and professional spheres, offering encouragement and advice as well as food and shelter when I periodically passed through Toronto. My mother, Hasanna, has been a wonderful source of unconditional love, support, and guidance throughout my life. My sister Raina and brother Simon have always graciously welcomed me home amid my wanderings. My spritely second child, Lori, arrived toward the end of this project to enrich the whole experience enormously. Finally, I cannot fully express the depth of my love and gratitude to Julia Hoffmann, for everything.

This book draws on a wider body of research previously published in a series of articles and book chapters, thoroughly revised and updated for inclusion herein. Chapter 2 contains material from my articles "Neoliberal Environmentality: Towards a Poststructuralist Political Ecology of the Conservation Debate," *Conservation and Society* 8(3): 171–181, and "Capitalizing on Chaos: Climate Change and Disaster Capitalism," *ephemera* 12(1/2): 97–112. Parts of chapter 4 were originally published in "Market Mechanism or Subsidy in Disguise? Governing Payment for Environmental Services in Costa Rica," *Geoforum* 43(3): 402–411. Acknowledgments to Jan Breitling, my coauthor on this article, for graciously allowing me to reproduce text here under my name alone. Chapter 4 also contains material from my chapters "Between the Cattle and the Deep Blue Sea: The Janus Face of the Ecotourism-Extraction Nexus in Costa Rica," in *The Ecotourism-Extraction Nexus: Political Economies and Rural Realities of (un)Comfortable Bedfellows*, edited by Bram Büscher and Veronica Davidov (London: Routledge, 2013), and "Making 'Peace with Nature': Costa Rica's Campaign for Climate Neutrality" in *Climate Change Governance in the Developing World*, edited by David Held, Charles Roger, and Eve-Marie Nag (London: Polity Press, 2013). Chapters 2, 5, and 6 contain passages from "Decoupling: A Key Fantasy of the Post-2015 Sustainable Development Agenda," *Globalizations* 14(3): 450–467, coauthored with Crelis Rammelt (who also graciously agreed to its reproduction here). Chapter 6 contains material from my article "How I Learned to Stop Worrying and Love the Market: Virtualism,

Disavowal and Public Secrecy in Neoliberal Environmental Conservation," *Environment and Planning D: Society and Space* 31(5): 796–812. Chapter 7 contains passages from "Neoliberal Conservation" in the *Oxford Research Encyclopedia of Anthropology*, edited by Mark Aldenderfer (New York: Oxford University Press). Finally, parts of chapter 6 and the conclusion were originally published as "Beyond the End of the World: Breaking Attachment to a Dying Planet" in *Psychoanalysis and the GlObal*, edited by Ilan Kapoor (Lincoln: University of Nebraska Press, 2018).

ABBREVIATIONS

AbC	accumulation by conservation
AI	artificial intelligence
(BI)NGO	(big international) nongovernmental organization
CBC	community-based conservation
CBD	Convention on Biological Diversity
CCS	carbon capture and storage
CCT	conditional cash transfer
CEE	collaborative event ethnography
CI	Conservation International
CIFOR	Center for International Forestry Research
CPR	common property regime
CSR	corporate social responsibility
FCPF	Forest Carbon Partnership Facility (World Bank)
FONAFIFO	Fondo Nacional de Financiamiento Forestal (National Forestry Finance Fund)
FORESTA	Forest Resources for a Stable Environment
FUNDECOR	Fundación para el Desarrollo de la Cordillera Volcánica Central (Foundation for the Development of the Central Volcanic Mountain Range)

GEF	Global Environment Facility
GOD	Grow or Die
GTZ	Deutsche Gesellschaft für Technische Zusammenarbeit GmbH (German Agency for Technical Cooperation)
ICDP	integrated-conservation-and-development project
ICE	Instituto Costarricense de Electricidad (Costa Rican Electricity Institute)
IFI	international financial institution
IMF	International Monetary Fund
INBio	Instituto Nacional de Biodiversidad (Costa Rican National Biodiversity Institute)
IPBES	Intergovernmental Science-Policy Platform for Biodiversity and Ecosystem Services
IPCC	Intergovernmental Panel on Climate Change
IPCM	Inflection Point Capital Management
IRP	International Resources Panel (UNEP)
IUCN	International Union for the Conservation of Nature and Natural Resources
KfW	Kreditanstalt für Wiederaufbau (German Development Bank)
LEDS	low emissions development strategy
MBI	market-based instrument
MINAE	Ministerio de Ambiente y Energía (Ministry of Environment and Energy)
MNC	multinational corporation
MRV	monitoring, reporting, and verification
NCC	Natural Capital Coalition
NCP	Natural Capital Project
NFT	non-fungible token
OPEC	Organization of the Petroleum Exporting Countries

OPF	Osa Productos Forestal
PA	protected area
PES	payment for environmental/ecosystem services
PSA	Pago por Servicios Ambimentales
REDD+	Reduced Emissions from avoided Deforestation and forest Degradation
SAP	structural adjustment program
SDGs	Sustainable Development Goals
SINAC	Sistema Nacional de Áreas de Conservación (National System of Conservation Areas)
TEEB	The Economics of Ecosystems and Biodiversity
TEK	traditional ecological knowledge
TFCA	Tropical Forest Conservation Act
TNC	The Nature Conservancy
TSC	Tropical Science Center
UBI	universal basic income
UN	United Nations
UNEP	United Nations Environment Programme
UNFCCC	United Nations Framework Convention on Climate Change
UNWTO	United Nations World Tourism Organization
US	United States
USAID	United States Agency for International Development
VCO	voluntary carbon offset
WAVES	Wealth Accounting and Valuation of Ecosystem Services
WBCSD	World Business Council for Sustainable Development
WCC	World Conservation Congress
WCS	Wildlife Conservation Society

WFNC	World Forum on Natural Capital
WRI	World Resources Institute
WSDE	worker self-directed enterprise
WWF	World Wildlife Fund (also World Wide Fund for Nature)

Introduction

CAPITALISM ON TRIAL

> It is both an indictment of neoliberalism and testament to its
> dogged dynamism, of course, that laboratory experiments do not
> "work." They have nonetheless tended to "fail forward," in that
> their repeated manifest inadequacies have—so far anyway—
> repeatedly animated further rounds of neoliberal intervention.
>
> JAMIE PECK, *Constructions of Neoliberal Reason* (2010a: 6)

In September 2016, I was in Honolulu, Hawai'i, along with other environmentalists from around the globe who had converged there for the World
Conservation Congress. This was the sixth in a series of such events organized every four years by the International Union for the Conservation
of Nature (IUCN), an umbrella organization for some thirteen hundred
environmental groups worldwide that bills itself as "the largest global environmental network" and its Congresses as the world's most significant
forums for promotion of biodiversity conservation. Sheltered within the
Honolulu Convention Center from the sweltering tropical heat, more than
nine thousand delegates met for ten days to chart the future of conservation policy and practice around the world. The myriad events occurring during this time included a self-styled "High Level Dialogue," chaired by then
IUCN director general Inger Anderson, to discuss "Private Finance for the
Public Good." Participants included representatives from the nongovernmental organization Conservation International (CI), the World Bank, the
United Nations Environment Programme (UNEP), the Global Environment Facility (GEF), the US government, and the German Development
Bank (KfW). Also represented were the Leonardo DiCaprio Foundation,
the investment firm Credit Suisse, and bankers JPMorgan Chase.

Current public funding, all participants agreed, was far less than that required to support effective conservation action globally. Consequently, they
concluded, enhanced private-sector engagement was desperately needed

FIGURE 1. The 2016 World Conservation Congress, Honolulu, Hawai'i. SOURCE: IISD/ENB Diego Noguera.

to make up the shortfall. In explaining the potential for this engagement, Fabian Huwyler, then representing Credit Suisse, highlighted "an increasing interest of investors in investments in nature that generate returns for both environment and economy."[1] Camilla Seth explained of JPMorgan's newfound interest in environmental issues that "the health of ecosystems and the predictability of the services that they provide are of growing concern and engagement across the bank." In order to attract private investment, Seth continued, "a big challenge for the conservation community is in learning to recognize where conservation opportunities provide cash flows. If you want to get private investment into these transactions you have to understand where the revenue is, where the cash flows are." Christy Goldfuss, then managing director of the White House Council on Environmental Quality, emphasized that the US government had concluded that "we're never going to have enough public money to address the conservation challenges we have," and hence a key question had become: "How can we set up the policies that really establish the markets and the predictability that we've learned so much that the private sector needs?" Responding to all of this, Lynn Scarlett, then CI's global managing director for public policy, asserted, "I think the big question in the room now . . . is how do we move beyond 'early days' so that five years hence what we have is a robust and routine private sector conservation investment marketplace?" In order to realize this intention, Anderson announced at the end of the session, all of these organizations and others had decided to come together in a newfound Coalition for Private Investment in Conservation (International Institute for Sustainable Development [IISD] 2016) (see Figure 1).

ENCOUNTERING NEOLIBERAL CONSERVATION

This is the new face of the global conservation movement: an increasingly interconnected network of actors representing international financial institutions, bilateral lenders, national governments, nongovernmental organizations, and private-sector firms from around the world, all increasingly focused on transforming conservation into the basis of profitable enterprise. The conservation movement has always enjoyed a complex set of interconnections among civil society, governmental, and private-sector players. Yet these connections and the network they have engendered have expanded dramatically in recent years. In the course of this expansion, some conservation organizations have become quite large, wealthy, and influential. The Nature Conservancy (TNC), headquartered in Arlington, Virginia, employs more than 4,150 people, works in 72 countries and controls assets totaling more than $7 billion (The Nature Conservancy [TNC] 2020), while the World Wildlife Fund, based in Amsterdam, runs over 1,300 projects in more than 100 countries, drawing on assets of almost $800 million (World Wildlife Fund [WWF] 2020).

In and through this global ascendance, however, the conservation movement's dominant strategies have changed dramatically. Long gone is what Naomi Klein calls the "golden age of environmental legislation," in which the main aim of most organizations concerned with ecological sustainability was to "ban or severely limit the offending activity or substance and where possible, get the polluter to pay for the cleanup" (2014: 203). In the realm of biodiversity conservation, this approach translated into a global campaign to create and maintain "protected areas" throughout the world, predominantly managed via a strongly state-centered "fortress" strategy (Brockington 2002; Igoe 2004).[2]

All of this changed with the rise, beginning in the 1970s, of the global political-economic program of neoliberalism.[3] The increasingly hegemonic influence of neoliberalism within the global conservation movement can be identified in a variety of trends, including the growing prominence and power of nonstate actors such as big international nongovernmental organizations (NGOs) like TNC, WWF, and CI (the so-called "BINGOs") (Chapin 2004) and increasing alliances among these BINGOs and multinational corporations as well as international financial institutions like the World Bank and GEF to generate funding (Levine 2002; Chapin 2004). This has been complemented by the proliferation of privately owned and operated nature reserves (Langholz 2003; Palfrey et al. 2021) as well as widespread devolution of resource control to nonstate actors like NGOs and a corresponding decline of state-based environmental regulation. It has also entailed creation of markets for trade in natural resources, privatization of resource control within such markets, and commodification of resources to facilitate their trading through creation of so-called market-based instruments (MBIs) including ecotourism, payment for environmental services (PES) programs, and biodiversity and wetlands banking, as well as a variety of creative newer initiatives described in later chapters.

For the past two decades, I, as part of a growing network of international researchers and activists, have been documenting this trend as the rise of "neoliberal conservation."[4] Despite increasing promotion of this approach by a growing range of actors from public, private and civil society sectors alike, however, more than five years on from the Honolulu World Conservation Congress (WCC) the "robust and routine private sector conservation investment marketplace" Scarlett and others envisioned there remains elusive. Indeed, available evidence demonstrates that the "market-based" initiatives around which neoliberal conservation revolves have thus far largely failed to create the profitable markets they pursue nearly anywhere in the world. And even when such initiatives do take root, they tend to quickly deviate—often quite dramatically—from the market logic they originally sought to implement, instead promoting forms of intensified state regulation of the very type they claimed to render obsolete. Moreover, the rise of right-wing authoritarian populism in a number of societies in recent years threatens the future of the neoliberal conservation initiatives that do continue to be implemented even in mutated form. As a component of this populism, indeed, we have instead witnessed a resurgence of intensified resource extraction in order to re-stimulate accumulation in the wake of the 2008 economic crisis, accompanied by rising levels of violence exercised by states and other actors to suppress resistance to this activity.

Rather than provoking critical self-reflection concerning the essential viability of a market-based strategy, however, all of these daunting obstacles in the face of neoliberal conservation's success have thus far tended merely to spur introduction of even grander initiatives aiming to intensify market logic still further as the great future promise for global conservation efforts. Consequently, as Jessica Dempsey (2016: 255) observes, the strategy currently "exists in an entirely paradoxical situation. It is at once a totalizing mainstream discourse and one that exists on the margins of political-economic life, on the outside of many flows of goods, commodities, and state policies."

Yet neither Dempsey nor anyone else has yet convincingly explained why this is so. The present book aims to account for this paradoxical situation, which I, following Jamie Peck (2010a), term neoliberal conservation's pervasive tendency to "fail forward." As Peck describes in this chapter's epigraph, this can indeed be viewed as the essential tendency of neoliberal policies more generally. But while this pattern is widely documented, how and why it occurs is less clear. Bloch points out in his endorsement of Peck's text, indeed, that "most critics of neoliberalism leave the reader mystified as to how such flawed ideas could ever have become so powerful" (Peck 2010a: back cover). The purpose of this book is to explain exactly this with respect to neoliberal conservation in particular.

TRACKING A GLOBAL PROCESS

As previously noted, this project is the culmination of nearly two decades of research. This began with my doctoral dissertation, a multi-sited ethnographic study of the promotion of ecotourism as a strategy for integrating conservation and development within a neoliberal framework that led to my first monograph *Romancing the Wild* (Fletcher 2014a). Relocating to Costa Rica in 2008 to teach at the United Nations University for Peace, I expanded my focus to investigate other efforts to harness conservation as an economic development strategy, including sustainable agriculture, forestry, and PES. This research also comprised multi-sited ethnography, moving between the capital city, San José, where environmental policies were generally formulated, and several rural field sites in the south of the country where such policies were put into practice. In the course of this research, I conducted participant observation and semi-structured interviews with a wide variety of actors involved in environmental work at both national and local levels, including state officials, representatives of NGOs both domestic and international, private ecotourism operators and reserve owners, conservation biologists, and local residents in numerous communities.[5]

In addition to this more conventional field research, during my time in Costa Rica I also began to participate in what has come to be called "collaborative event ethnography" (CEE): studying how environmental policy is formulated and negotiated at key international meetings (see especially Corson et al. 2014; Fletcher 2014b). In this effort, I participated in the Fifth World Conservation Congress on Jeju Island, South Korea, in 2012; then continued this research after moving to the Netherlands in 2014 by attending the World Parks Congress (another IUCN event held once per decade) in Sydney, Australia, in that year; then the Honolulu WCC in 2016; and finally (in virtual form) the Seventh WCC held in September 2021 (after being postponed twice due to COVID-19 restrictions) in Marseille, France. In addition to this empirical research, I have conducted an extensive review of published literature from organizations and individuals central to developing and promoting the neoliberal conservation project. Combining this investigation of high-level policy discussions with exploration of both policy deliberation in the Costa Rican capital and its implementation in rural parts of the country has, I believe, afforded me a unique and productive vantage point to understand the rollout of neoliberal conservation at multiple scales as well as the interconnections among these.[6] In this book, I have sought to synthesize the results of my own empirical study with a larger body of research engaging similar issues in other contexts to develop a more comprehensive analysis of the global neoliberal conservation project than my individual research could provide.[7]

EXPLAINING "FAILURE"

Why so many planning efforts, in international development and elsewhere, have so often "failed" in their intended aims has long been a central concern for a wide range of critical analysts, who have offered a variety of different explanations to account for this reality.[8] The most prominent theoretical perspectives informing such analysis are Marxism and poststructuralism, respectively. For orthodox Marxists, ostensible "failure" of this sort is generally not considered failure at all, since the explicit intentions of planners are commonly seen as merely an ideological smokescreen obscuring a more fundamental objective to facilitate accumulation by capitalist elites. David Harvey is paradigmatic of this stance in his popular critique of neoliberalism, which asserts: "It has been part of the genius of neoliberal theory to provide a benevolent mask full of wonderful-sounding words like freedom, liberty, choice, and rights, to hide the grim realities of the restoration or reconstitution of naked class power, locally as well as transnationally, but most particularly in the main financial centres of global capitalism" (Harvey 2005:119).[9]

Yet such explanations are commonly contested by those working in a poststructuralist tradition, who tend to ascribe less duplicitous motives to most actors.[10] Taking policy makers at face value, poststructuralists thus offer an alternative set of explanations for project "failure." Much of this points toward the pervasive presence of a fundamental mismatch between the narrow vision planners usually bring to their work and the complex local realities they confront.[11]

What is seen to be most overlooked as a consequence of such myopia differs among analysts. For some, it is the essential discrepancy between inevitably simplified interventions based on blueprint plans and the dynamic contexts within which such interventions manifest.[12] For others, it is the essentially political nature of development projects and the contexts in which they occur, which are commonly denied through efforts to prescribe mere "technical" interventions (Ferguson 1994; Li 2007). Still others highlight how institutional politics also shapes interventions in ways counterproductive to successful project outcomes.[13]

While both Marxist and poststructuralist approaches offer some help in explaining the dynamics investigated in this book, there are other important aspects for which they cannot so convincingly account. It is clear, for instance, that few of the countless neoliberal conservation initiatives in development around the world produce any actual profit, let alone enough to attract serious elite investors (Dempsey 2016; Dempsey and Suarez 2016). On the contrary, most require continual injections of new capital from which no returns are ever earned. Hence, it is difficult to argue that a logic of accumulation actually drives such initiatives (even if pursuing this is indeed often the aim for at least some actors involved). Poststructuralists, meanwhile, have difficulty explaining why, if failure results from how the context-specific complexities of local realities stymie simple plans, neoliberal conservation initiatives tend to fail in such similar ways, and display such similar patterns of transformation away from market logic toward state-centered regulation, in such different contexts throughout the world.

To address unresolved issues such as these I offer my own analysis, which both builds on and departs from these others in important ways. With Marxists, I agree that neoliberal conservation is indeed often inspired by a quest for new forms of accumulation even if these frequently fail to materialize. With poststructuralists, I agree that such failure is partly due to the inevitable mismatch between abstract plans and concrete realities. Yet I contend that there is also something about the fundamental strategy informing neoliberal conservation interventions that helps to account for their widespread failure to create actual markets, for their tendency to instead morph into forms of intensified state regulation, as well as for the common tendency of proponents to deny these dynamics and paradoxically promote more intensified market-based engagement instead. It is this dimension of neoliberal conservation that previous research has failed to adequately capture, and that I seek to elucidate herein.

EXPLAINING FAILURE TO ACKNOWLEDGE "FAILURE"

Equally pervasive as documentation of project "failure" is the documentation of the widespread failure to acknowledge and act to correct such "failure," as Peck's quotation in the epigraph again makes clear.[14] How does one explain this common, paradoxical tendency of such far flung programs to "fail forward"? Different researchers, again, offer different answers to this question.

For orthodox Marxists, there is actually little to explain here, given their deep suspicion that interventions are even intended to function at face value.[15] Again, however, attribution to planners of such duplicitous motives is contested by poststructuralists. As Mosse states explicitly, "There is no suggestion of duplicity" in his analysis of development interventions' shortcomings (2004: 657). Rather, from this perspective, failure to acknowledge "failure" is explained through exploration of how discourse works to obfuscate or rationalize evidence of ostensive deficiency. Exemplary of this approach is Michel Foucault himself, whose prescient analysis of neoliberalism interprets its tendency to explain away "failure" in terms of the discourse's fundamental logic in asserting: "Nothing proves that the market economy is intrinsically defective since everything attributed to it as a defect and as the effect of its defectiveness should really be attributed to the state" (2008: 116).

Others, likewise, highlight how evaluation of development outcomes influences how these outcomes are interpreted and framed, such that evidence of "failure" is frequently ignored or explained away. Some researchers point, again, to pressures from institutional politics that tend to inhibit acknowledgment of "failure."[16] In a similar spirit, still others highlight how the common need to secure organizational funding creates pressure to emphasize project success in order to keep finances flowing from donors discouraged by failure.[17] In this way, savvy marketing of success can form the basis of value creation in its own right, regardless of how projects actually function in practice (Igoe et al. 2010; Büscher 2014). All of this, Mosse maintains, demonstrates how "development projects work to maintain themselves as coherent policy ideas" (2004: 254) by consistently interpreting outcomes to reinforce original policy visions.

While all of these explanations again undoubtedly hold some truth, there remain important dynamics for which they cannot account. Marxists have difficulty appreciating the fact that many proponents of neoliberal conservation are clearly quite committed to the project for its own sake (Dempsey 2016)—and indeed, may actually sacrifice other more lucrative opportunities in the process. Poststructuralists, meanwhile, have trouble explaining that many proponents' reflections on neoliberal conservation's past track record demonstrate less wholesale denial of "failure" than a more ambivalent dynamic in which such "failure" is in fact acknowledged to some degree even as the overarching project moves forward with increased intensity (Watt 2021). Moreover, as we will see, much of the ostensible "reasoning" underlying assertions of neoliberal conservation's potential is in fact so flimsy and incoherent that it is difficult to account for it as a cogent explaining (away) of anything in particular. Drawing on Lacanian psychoanalysis, my analysis therefore complements dominant Marxist and poststructuralist approaches by explaining neoliberal conservation's perennial tendency to "fail forward" as a *fantasy structure* promising an eventual success that is continually deferred into the future. More on this below.

AN ANTI-REGULATION MACHINE

I have placed the word *failure* in quotations throughout the preceding discussion in appreciation of Mosse's important caution that "'success' and 'failure' are policy-oriented judgements that obscure project effects" and hence risk impeding a measured analysis of "how things actually happen" (2004: 662).[18] Following Mosse's example, therefore, in this book I also go beyond simple diagnosis of success and failure to explore the *instrument-effects* that neoliberal conservation interventions produce in and through their "failure."[19] Chief among such instrument-effects, I find, is a pervasive tendency to expand state regulation under the pretext of rolling this back.

This has indeed been documented as a tendency common to neoliberal programming more broadly.[20] While identifying this tendency, however, most previous researchers have not explained why it occurs, given neoliberalism's explicit aim to reduce the regulation it paradoxically expands. The exception is Ray Kiely, who identifies as "the neoliberal paradox" the reality that neoliberalism "must always rely on the state to carry out this political project" of establishing ostensibly free markets (2021: 337; see also Kiely 2018). In other words, far from embodying a hands-off laissez-faire approach, as many critics assert, neoliberal governance in fact require states to construct and maintain the "free market," albeit indirectly from the margins rather than intervening within markets to directly allocate resources (Foucault 2008). Consequently, when neoliberal mechanisms fail to produce intended aims (as I argue must inevitably occur due to essential contradictions in their design, see below), the state must continually re-intervene within the market to attempt to make these mechanisms function as intended, as well as to address problems left unresolved in the process. Within the overarching economy, at the same time, states must increasingly intervene to sustain accumulation as the basic contradictions of capitalist development inevitably intensify. This means that, over time, efforts to replace direct state regulation with market mechanisms—in the realm of conservation as elsewhere—paradoxically produce their opposite: an intensification of the very direct state regulation that was intended to be replaced. Following Ferguson's (1994) classic characterization of international development as an "anti-politics machine" that claims to be apolitical while in fact politicizing everything it touches, I argue that neoliberal conservation can thus be understood as an "anti-regulation machine" purporting to reduce state regulation while actually expanding it at every turn.

At its extreme, I contend, this dynamic leads directly to the type of violent authoritarianism we have witnessed on the rise in a number of societies around the world in recent years. This authoritarian turn is often interpreted as a decisive departure from the neoliberalism previously prevailing in most of these societies. Yet one could argue that it was precisely the failure of neoliberal conservation—as a component of a wider "progressive neoliberal" program promoted since the 1990s among others by the US Democratic Party (Fraser 2017)—to establish itself as an effective basis for renewed, ecologically sustainable accumulation in the wake of the 2008 economic crisis that partly precipitated a resurgence of heavy-handed autocracy to instead jumpstart accumulation via resort to the intensified resource extraction neoliberal conservation initiatives were intended to replace (Kiely 2018; Brown 2019). There is, I therefore suggest, a direct lineage from Reagan and Thatcher to Trump and Bolsonaro, with Clinton and Obama as logical stepping-stones in between.

Analysis in these terms contributes to ongoing debate concerning precisely *how* neoliberal conservation mechanisms actually are in practice. In response to early research characterizing such mechanisms as neoliberal in both theory and practice, other researchers have, as previously noted, since pointed out that many mechanisms deviate substantially from their initial design in the course of implementation, instead commonly undergoing extensive state direction and regulation contradicting core neoliberal dictates. Yet an understanding of the essentially paradoxical nature of neoliberal policy suggests that such mechanisms can still be considered neoliberal in their aim to enact an overarching vision of the world in which all aspects of social life, including state processes themselves, operate as markets, even if they do not actually realize this ideal vision in practice.

CAPITALISM ON TRIAL

My analysis suggests, in short, that it is the very design of neoliberal conservation initiatives that causes them to fail to produce the profitable markets they intend. This is, most fundamentally, because the way that the capitalist mode of production that such initiatives seek to harness produces profit runs contrary to the social and environmental sustainability these initiatives also pursue. Profit within capitalism is produced precisely by offloading social and environmental problems onto others—what economists euphemistically call creating "externalities." To the extent that such problems are instead internalized, which must occur for neoliberal conservation to succeed in its own terms, the capacity to extract profit is similarly diminished. There is, in other words, a fundamental contradiction within the capitalist economy between demands of "people, planet, and profit" that neoliberal conservation claims can all be achieved simultaneously. But the problem is more essential even than this, for the quest to maintain sustainable profit irrespective of environmental and social aims is futile in and of itself in the long run. This means that the goal to maintain (environmentally, socially, and economically) sustainable profit within a capitalist system is impossible, and hence that neoliberal conservation—like pursuit of "green" capitalism more generally—is a dangerous illusion.

Going further, I argue that neoliberal conservation is not merely about supporting conservation, but that the project in fact signifies a much larger campaign to render the global capitalist system, as a whole, sustainable in the face of mounting critique concerning the pervasive negative social and environmental impacts commonly produced by capitalist development. This is because neoliberal conservation seeks to transform the global economy from reliance on the resource extraction that has fueled accumulation since capitalism's outset to a new model that could instead potentially harness natural resources' non-use—conservation—as the basis for economic growth. In this sense, neoliberal conservation can be understood as essentially testing the hypothesis "that capitalist markets are the answer to their own ecological contradictions" (Büscher 2012: 29; see also Swyngedouw 2010, 2011). Or as U2 front man turned celebrity development pundit Bono explains of his endorsement of social-impact investment, "Capitalism is going up on trial, and I think that it's clear that putting profit before people is a nonsustainable business model" (Sorkin 2016). The neoliberal conservation project can thus be understood as central to this effort to defend capitalism's potential to become sustainable and thus acquit it in the court of public opinion.

This is intended to occur, most fundamentally, via "decoupling": the divorce of economic growth from resource use and impact by "dematerializing" the economy (United Nations Environment Programme [UNEP] 2011a). Such dematerialization in reality denotes increased financialization, by means of which the basis of capital accumulation shifts from the conventional M-C-M' model of commodity production to an M-M' strategy that bypasses commodity production entirely and instead relies on investment in financial markets as the basis for accumulation.[21] This movement from commodity production to financialization is evidenced in the evolution of neoliberal conservation over time, and especially in the decoupling it promises, which stands central to the Sustainable Development Goals (SDGs) agenda currently promoted as the new great hope for redemption of the capitalist system generally.

The story of neoliberal conservation's rise and fall thus holds important lessons for the global pursuit of sustainable development writ large. It demonstrates, in essence, that achieving sustainability is impossible within the context of a capitalist economy. Capitalism depends on continual growth to overcome internal contradictions, and this growth relies on both resource extraction and exploitation of human labor to proceed. This growth imperative is particularly central to neoliberal capitalism, which disdains redistribution and hence must rely on growth as social policy too (Foucault 2008). Consequently, for capitalism to sustain itself it must paradoxically cannibalize the social and biophysical environments that sustain it. Neoliberal conservation offers the potential to overcome this paradox through reliance on non-consumptive accumulation, yet this potential is illusory, exposing capitalism's essential unsustainability once more. The only viable alternative capable of realistically pursuing both environmental sustainability and social equity simultaneously, I conclude, is thus a concerted program of "degrowth" grounded in post-capitalist principles.

TOWARD A PSYCHOANALYTIC POLITICAL ECOLOGY

To develop my analysis, as previously noted, I integrate Lacanian psychoanalysis with the Marxism and poststructuralism on which I also draw.[22] In focusing on the affective and psychic mechanisms operating at both individual and societal levels, Lacanian psychoanalysis offers a useful complement to Marxist and poststructuralist approaches that have difficulty accounting for the ways that discourses and practices are internalized and structured so as to obscure essential contradictions.

Psychoanalysis has been relatively marginal thus far within the growing body of literature addressing neoliberal conservation, which has, as earlier explained, been largely investigated from the perspectives of Marxism and/ or poststructuralism. There is, however, a fairly long tradition of drawing on psychoanalytic approaches to explore aspects of environmentalism more generally.[23] Recently, a small but growing body of research has also applied psychoanalysis to the study of international development policy and practice too.[24] Neoliberalism writ large has been subject to investigation from different psychoanalytic perspectives as well.[25] Meanwhile, a handful of recent psychoanalytic studies have sought to address particular aspects of neoliberal environmentalism specifically.[26] My analysis here builds on all of this to offer the first sustained Lacanian analysis of the neoliberal conservation project as a whole.

In so doing, it seeks to advance a psychoanalytic perspective more centrally within the broader intellectual landscape in which it is grounded, namely the interdisciplinary field of *political ecology*. This field began with an effort to apply a Marxian critique of political economy to environmental politics, an approach that was subsequently complicated by introduction of a poststructuralist perspective seeking to deconstruct forms of discourse also shaping environmental policy. More recently, Escobar (2010) argues that these first two "generations" of political ecology research have been complemented by a third, advancing a variety of "post-constructivist" or "post-representational" approaches, to which the growing prominence of feminist and decolonial perspectives should also be added (Sultana 2021).

With notable exceptions, however, psychoanalysis has received little attention within the field thus far. This book can therefore be understood as aiming to integrate a psychoanalytic approach more centrally into the political ecology toolkit. It seeks to bring this approach together with more conventional Marxist and poststructuralist approaches (while also dialoguing with aspects of post-constructivism) in pursuit of a novel synthesis. While there are of course key differences among these various perspectives, in recent years a number of researchers have sought to reconcile them in different ways, suggesting potential points of articulation, for instance, between Foucault and Lacan (Butler 1997), Marx and Foucault (Bidet 2015), and Marx and Lacan (Tomšič 2016). Here, I build on the approach outlined in my previous work on ecotourism (Fletcher 2014a) to apply this synthetic perspective to the neoliberal conservation project more generally.[27]

What a fusion of Marx and Foucault offers most productively, for my purposes here, is a balanced consideration of both material and discursive dimensions of a given political-economic process.[28] What Lacan contributes to this mix is appreciation of the affective, embodied elements of such processes that neither Marx nor Foucault provide much guidance in understanding (see Fletcher 2013a). Key to Lacanian political analysis, as explained further in chapter 1, is an appreciation of the role of fantasy in suturing what is considered the essential gap between an impossible Real that lies forever beyond signification and the latter's (inevitably distorted) representation within the symbolic universe (Žižek 1989; Stavrakakis 2007). Fantasy, here, is to be understood not merely as a projection of future fulfilment but as also offering an explanation for why that fulfilment is not achieved. In this way, Slavoj Žižek explains, "fantasy is a means for an ideology to take its own failure into account in advance," constituting "the frame through which we experience the world as consistent and meaningful" and obscuring the symptoms signifying the "irreducible excess" of the Real disrupting our symbolic quest for order and coherence (1989: 142, 138). One of fantasy's principal functions is to structure desire, giving form to the raw libidinal force Lacan called *jouissance*—usually translated as "pleasure" but more properly a mixture of pleasure and pain in equal measure or an ambiguous "excitement" (Fink 1995)—and channeling it in pursuit of objects (what Lacan called *objets petit a*) that promise the satisfaction fantasy proffers. Hence, Žižek explains, "In the fantasy-scene desire is not fulfilled, 'satisfied,' but constituted"; rather, "through fantasy, *jouissance* is domesticated" (1989: 132, 138). Or as Stavrakakis puts it, fantasy should be seen "not only as a screen which promises to fill the lack in the Other, but also as what 'produces' this lack" (2007: 241).

With respect to neoliberal conservation specifically, what a merger of Marx and Foucault provides is appreciation of the ways that the project can be understood as both a particular form of capitalism and a particular governmentality (see chapter 1) without reducing one to the other or privileging either. What Lacan adds to this mix is an explanation of why the project remains so "sticky" (Stavrakakis 2007), so resistant to critique despite such copious evidence of its deficiency in practice. Combined, the three perspectives afford the "expanded understanding" of neoliberalism in "cultural, psychological, libidinal, as well as economic and ecological" dimensions that Bakker (2010: 728) advocates, and thus provide a powerful conceptual foundation for the analysis undertaken here. From this synthetic perspective, I describe neoliberal conservation as simultaneously a particular mode of capitalist accumulation, the expression of a particular governmentality, and a fantasy structure disavowing both the Real of capital as an inherently descriptive force (Wilson 2014a) and the Real of nature as imposing fundamental biophysical limits on the potential for economic growth (Stavrakakis 1997a, 1997b).[29]

STRUCTURE OF THE BOOK

The remainder of the book develops my analysis step by step. Chapter 1 elaborates the psychoanalytically informed understanding of "power" and its application underpinning the rest of the discussion. Based on this, I argue that neoliberal conservation should be understood as embodying and enacting a form of *neoliberal biopower* in particular. Chapter 2 then begins my empirical analysis by describing the historical development of the global neoliberal conservation project and the singular vision it champions. Chapter 3 focuses specifically on one of neoliberal conservation's central aims: to create voluntary markets for trade in "natural capital" and "ecosystem services." Chapter 4 turns to a case study of Costa Rica—one of the first and most intense foci of neoliberal conservation initiatives—to explore how these initiatives have played out in practice. Chapter 5 then pulls back again to place this case study in the context of neoliberal conservation's overarching trajectory, demonstrating that one of the project's most pervasive effects has been to paradoxically extend and expand the very state-centered regulation it intended to diminish. Chapter 6 explains the logic by which this reality is obfuscated in preserving the project's zombie-like forward momentum. Chapter 7 describes newfound challenges to neoliberal conservation posed by the rise of right-wing authoritarian populism and its no-holds-barred embrace of intensified resource extractivism. Shifting to the essential question of what is to be done in the face of the analysis developed in previous chapters, chapter 8 then argues that a truly sustainable future demands a shift from the growth imperative of "sustainable" capitalism to a program of concerted "degrowth." And this, the conclusion asserts, necessitates traversing the fantasy of sustainable capitalist development entirely in pursuit of a post-capitalist social order grounded in post-fantasmatic desire.

ONE

Conceptualizing Neoliberal Biopower

Power is tolerable only on condition that it mask a substantial part of itself. Its success is proportional to its ability to hide its own mechanisms.

MICHEL FOUCAULT, *History of Sexuality:*
An Introduction (1978: 86)

The central question of how neoliberal conservation "works" (or does not) explored in this book inevitably raises the issue of "power" and how to understand this much-contested concept. How, in other words, has the neoliberal conservation project managed to enroll actors and organizations within its campaign? And more importantly, how does it sustain this campaign in the face of the string of largely disappointing outcomes it has demonstrated thus far?

Power has long been one of the key terms of contention within social science generally, with various theoretical traditions defining and operationalizing the concept in quite divergent ways (see Lukes 2004; Fletcher 2007). Despite the centrality of questions of power within the field of political ecology in particular, however, explicit conceptualization of the term in relation to these discussions has been relatively limited thus far (cf. Svarstad et al. 2018). This chapter addresses this issue by outlining ongoing discussion concerning the nature and purpose of power as the basis for fleshing out the theoretical framework grounding the rest of the book's analysis. Anchored in on this discussion, I will argue that the neoliberal conservation project is fundamentally supported by a particularly *neoliberal form of biopower* sustaining the project's essential claim that biodiversity must be valued in economic terms in order to convincingly justify the need for its conservation. In the next section, I begin to develop this argument by describing the different ways that the central term of contention—power—has been defined and debated.

In an important intervention within social scientific discussions of power, Lukes (2004) outlines what he calls three "dimensions" embodied in different understandings of the term. What Lukes calls a "one dimensional" definition views power as directing the outcome of decisions, as causing one set of interests to prevail over another. A "two-dimensional" view, on the other hand, understands power as controlling both decisions and the framework within which decisions are deliberated. In this way, one's overarching aims can prevail whichever specific decision is ultimately reached. In contrast to both of these, Lukes outlines his own "three-dimensional" perspective, in terms of which power is seen to control both decisions and the decision-making framework as well as serving to direct actors involved in the decision-making process toward the pursuit of ends contrary to their "true interests." Power, in this sense, is understood as the "capacity to make another do what they wouldn't otherwise" (Lukes 2004: 25).

This three-dimensional approach is tantamount to the orthodox Marxist concept of "ideology" conceived as a form of false consciousness that inhibits subjects from understanding the true nature of the reality they confront. This function of ideology is also often described as "hegemony," following Gramsci's (1971) famous introduction of this concept in his poignant *Prison Diaries*. Yet like power, how hegemony should be understood remains contested as well, given that Gramsci seemed to define it in different ways himself (Femia 1975). This ambivalence has come down through the scholarly literature in the form of a common division of the term into two distinct forms, which Femia (1975) calls "strong" and "weak" versions and Scott (1990) "thick" and "thin." The distinction is between an understanding of hegemony as demanding wholesale "consent" on the part of its subjects and one that merely requires "compliance" but not necessarily ideological buy-in, respectively (Williams 1977; Comaroff 1985). A strong/thick hegemony, in other words, is seen to impose "an all-embracing domination upon the ruled ... reaching down to the very threshold of their experience, and implanting within their minds at birth categories of subordination they are powerless to correct" (Thompson 1993: 87). Weak/thin hegemony, by contrast, is understood merely to "define for subordinates what is realistic and what is not realistic, and to drive certain aspirations and grievances into the realm of the impossible, of idle dreams" (Scott 1990:73).

In both of these perspectives, subjects are seen to succumb to a false consciousness that compels them to submit, and the picture these stances evoke is of a power "held" by one group of people (elites) and "exercised" over another (subordinates/subalterns). Power's function, in this sense, is primarily negative, serving to obfuscate subalterns' understanding of the domination to which they are subject (or at least, in a thin/weak hegemony, of their capacity to resist this domination). Yet this perspective on power as constraining ideology was contested by Foucault, who in *Discipline and Punish* famously asserted, "We must cease once and for all to describe the effects of power in negative terms: it 'excludes,' it 'represses,' it 'censors,' it 'abstracts,' it 'masks,' it 'conceals.' In fact, power produces; it produces reality, it produces domains of objects and rituals of truth" (1977: 194). In this way, Foucault replaces a Marxist focus on ideology with what he calls "discourse" understood as a productive constellation of power/knowledge[1] (Foucault 1977, 1980). Power, from this perspective, does not simply obstruct or disguise one's "true interests" but actually constructs those interests too. Power's function in this scenario is thus both negative and positive. Furthermore, Foucault asserts, power cannot be "held," it can only be "exercised," in concrete "relations between individuals" (Foucault 1983: 217). Moreover, power may be exercised from the "bottom up" as well as "top down."

While these different understandings of power are often understood as starkly opposed, subsequent theorists have sought to bring them together as part of a larger effort to unite Marxist and poststructuralists perspectives more generally within a more holistic conceptual framework (see especially Bidet 2015). At times, this effort draws on Gramsci's hegemony as a potentially more conducive complement to Foucault's discourse than Marx's original ideology (Li 2007). As Svarstad et al. (2018) describe, these different understandings are, respectively, the main ways (including through their attempted synthesis) that the power concept has been employed within political ecology discussions specifically as well thus far.[2]

FROM POWER TO RESISTANCE

These divergent approaches to analyzing power also shape researchers' understandings of how and why power is contested, a dynamic commonly glossed as "resistance" (Scott 1990; Fletcher 2007). Given Marxists' characteristic framing of power as a negative constraint, they also tend to view power and resistance as diametrically opposed, with the latter understood as something existing outside of power that cuts through the false consciousness that ideology imposes.[3] Resistance, in this sense, is seen to provide privileged access to a realm of truth beyond power's censorship.

Foucault's more constructive notion of power contests this characterization, instead viewing resistance as a function of power itself. Foucault (1978: 95) described this approach as asserting that "resistance is never in a position of exteriority in relation to power." From this perspective, then, the conventional Marxist dichotomy between power and resistance disappears; what we call resistance is merely a particular exercise of power, opposite of and opposed to that which is resisted.

Even in this understanding, however, resistance is seen to exist to some degree outside of the particular exercise of power it contests. Yet Bell (1992), following Gramsci, suggests that a given structure of power may in fact encompass its own avenues for (limited) dissent, thereby also internalizing— even prescribing—a certain mode of resistance. She terms this dynamic "redemptive hegemony," suggesting that in this way subjects' sense of having effectively resisted a dominant ideology can paradoxically keep them bound within it by inhibiting them from pushing further for more transformative ends. Moreover, both Marxist and Foucauldian approaches to power/ resistance share a common assumption that subjects will adhere to one or another perspective unambiguously, while in reality it is clear that actors are often quite ambivalent in their convictions, subscribing to multiple conflicting perspectives simultaneously (Gal 1995).[4]

ENTER PUBLIC SECRECY

Anthropologist Michael Taussig further complicates this discussion in highlighting another dynamic that confounds conventional understandings of power and resistance as previously outlined. Fundamental to the exercise of power, Taussig asserts, is a phenomenon he calls "public secrecy," defined as "that which is generally known but cannot generally be articulated" (1998a: 246).[5] Secrecy is commonly understood as something private and hidden (Merten 1999), a "purposive hiding or masking" (Simmel 1950: 330), or what Deleuze and Guattari (1987) describe as "the contents in a box or envelope" (in Bratich 2006: 494). In this framing, the secret is dissipated by opening the container and revealing its contents to the collective gaze.

Taussig's *public* secret, by contrast, describes something that is in fact readily available—even explicitly presented—for all to see, yet which nonetheless retains an aura of obscuration as all involved sustain the fiction that there is a secret to be hidden. It is, he explains, a "magnificent deceit in whose making all members of a society, so it would seem, conspire" (1992: 132). As in Hans Christian Anderson's classic fairytale "The Emperor's New Clothes" (Figure 2), all profess ignorance of a reality that is actually evident to everyone. Far from passive ignorance, however, this entails an "active not-knowing" or "knowing what not to know" (Taussig 1999: 6, 7). Consequently, Taussig maintains that there is in fact "no such thing as a secret"; rather, the notion of a secret "is an invention that comes out of the public secret" (6, 7). Stated differently, the construction of a public secret supports the idea that there is in fact something hidden, when in fact "the secret of the public secret is that there is none" (6).

Unlike in Anderson's fairytale, however, in Taussig's analysis a public secret is often not dispelled but paradoxically strengthened through revelation. Taussig (1998a: 222) thus contends, "The mystery is heightened, not dissipated, by unmasking. . . . Power flows not from masking but from an unmasking which masks more than masking does." In fact, Taussig suggests that what he, following Deleuze and Guattari (1987), calls "secretion of the secret" is itself integral to public secrecy, for "part of secrecy is secreting" and therefore "revelation is precisely what the secret intends" (1998a: 242). This is because revelation confirms the perception that there is in fact something to hide, and therefore to reveal, thus paradoxically reinforcing the public secret it ostensibly reveals. It is, after all, impossible to discover something that is already known, and "this is what will always resist the wedge of truth no matter how interested, or persistent . . . the wedge may be" (Taussig 1998a: 242). Hence, Taussig concludes that "it would seem that such a phenomenon has built-in protection against exposure because exposure, or at least a certain modality of exposure, is what, in fact, it thrives upon" (1999: 216).

Taussig asserts that public secrets are pervasive in social life, explaining, "Much social knowledge is of this sort and perhaps most of most important knowledge is too. Like families and universities, all institutions breed such secrecy" (1998b, 226). Indeed, Taussig maintains that the significance of public secrecy is such that "what we call doctrine, ideology, consciousness, beliefs, values and even discourse, pale into sociological insignificance and

The Emperor walked under his high canopy in the midst of the Procession.

FIGURE 2. Illustration for "The Emperor's New Clothes," in Hans Andersen, *Fairy Tales and Legends*, published by Cobden-Sanderson, 1935. SOURCE: Rex Whistler. With kind permission of Salisbury Museum.

philosophical banality by comparison" (1999: 3), and hence that "without such shared secrets any and all social institutions ... would founder (1999: 7). Public secrecy, Taussig concludes, thus "lies at the core of power" itself (1999: 7).[6]

POWER, DISAVOWAL AND DESIRE

Both Marxist and Foucauldian analyses of power and resistance have difficulty accounting for ambiguous dynamics like redemptive hegemony and public secrecy. Drawing on Lacanian psychoanalysis, however, Žižek advances an alternative perspective that offers potential to illuminate dynamics such as these. Žižek's perspective is grounded in Lacan's iconic triad positing an interconnection among three distinct ontological spheres: Imaginary—Symbolic—Real. In this model, the *Real* is a placeholder name for that which subverts signification, exhibiting a dual character as "both the hard, impenetrable kernel resisting symbolization and a pure chimerical entity which has in itself no ontological consistency" (Žižek 1989: 190). By contrast, the *Symbolic* designates our attempts to represent the Real and impose order upon it. Due to the very nature of the Real, however, such representation inevitably falls short of its aim. The Real, as Lacan famously asserted, is thus "impossible," incapable of representation; it is "the rock upon which every attempt at symbolization stumbles" (Žižek 1989: 190).

Consequently, there is invariably a gap between the Real and its Symbolic representation, with the Real comprising an "irreducible excess" beyond our illusions of order and coherence. This excess, denied within the symbolic order, manifests as "symptom," the "return of the repressed" (Žižek 1989: 57) via which the Real ruptures and undermines symbolic attempts to create coherence. A symptom is thus "the point at which the immanent social antagonism assumes a positive form, erupts on to the social surface, the point at which it becomes obvious that society 'doesn't work,' that the social mechanism 'creaks'" (143). A symptom therefore indicates a fundamental antagonism or inconsistency in the social order; it is a "surplus-object" or "the leftover of the Real eluding symbolization" (51).

The *Imaginary*, the third element in Lacan's triad, represents our efforts to conceal this essential disjuncture by means of fantasy, which Žižek calls the "screen concealing the gap" (1989: 132) between Real and Symbolic. Fantasy thus "constitutes the frame through which we experience the world as consistent and meaningful," obscuring the fact that the Symbolic order is in fact "structured around some traumatic impossibility, around something which cannot be symbolized" (138). Together, the Imaginary—Symbolic—Real triad thus leads to an understanding of ideology as "a totality set on effacing the traces of its own impossibility" (50).

Contesting the conventional Marxist understanding of power as obscuring ideology, Žižek's perspective thus comes closer to Foucauldian discourse in asserting that ideology is "not simply a 'false consciousness,' an illusory representation of reality, it is rather this reality itself which is already to be conceived as 'ideological'" (1989: 15). Yet he goes further than Foucault in suggesting that ideology, defined in this way, can actually encompass some questioning of its own basic parameters. In particular, Žižek argues that ideology is characteristically supported by what philosopher Peter Sloterdijk (1988) calls "cynical reason," in terms of which "an ideological identification exerts a hold on us precisely when we are aware that we are not fully identical to it" (Žižek 1997: 21). As Žižek explains:

> The cynical subject is quite aware of the distance between the ideological mask and the social reality, but he nonetheless still insists upon the mask. The formula, as proposed by Sloterdijk, would then be: "they know very well what they are doing, but still, they are doing it." Cynical reason is no longer naïve, but is a paradox of an enlightened false consciousness: one knows the falsehood very well, one is well aware of a particular interest hidden behind an ideological universality, but still one does not renounce it. (1989: 25–26)

Similar to Taussig's discussion of the importance of secretion in public secrecy, therefore, Žižek asserts that, for ideology also, "the laying bare of its mechanism, functions as a fetish which conceals the crucial dimension of [its] form" (1997: 102). Like Taussig's claim that there is in fact no secret at the heart of a public secret, Žižek asserts that "fantasy is basically a scenario filling out the empty space of a fundamental impossibility, a screen masking a void," and that ultimately "there is nothing 'behind'" this mask and that "fantasy masks precisely this nothing" (1989: 141). In other words, what is hidden is "precisely the fact that there is nothing to hide. What is concealed is that the very act of concealing conceals nothing" (219).

In Žižek's analysis, the psychic mechanism that sustains this paradoxical situation is "fetishistic disavowal," which, like Taussig's public secret, Žižek describes as a simultaneous admission and negation of the phenomenon in question. As Žižek phrases it, disavowal operates according to the general formula: "I know very well, but still . . ." (1989: 12). Unlike outright denial, disavowal is thus an ambivalent dynamic, in which "reality is more accepted, but its significance is minimized" (Weintrobe 2013b: 7). As a result of this essential ambivalence, Weintrobe suggests, disavowal "is a more serious and intractable form of denial," in that "disavowal . . . can be highly organized at an unconscious level and can become entrenched. It distorts the truth in a variety of artful ways. Disavowal can lead us further and further away from accepting the reality. . . .This is because the more reality is systematically avoided through making it insignificant or through distortion, the more anxiety builds up unconsciously, and the greater is the need to defend with further disavowal" (2013b: 7).

Žižek's Lacanian perspective offers another important contribution to analysis of power in its focus on the role of *desire* in power's exercise (see also Butler 1997). Neither Marx nor Foucault are able to do justice to this crucial dimension of power. Members of the Frankfurt school (particularly Herbert Marcuse) sought to compensate for this in relation to Marx by merging Marxism with Freudian psychoanalysis (see especially Marcuse 1966; Jay 1996). Yet this strategy remains fraught due to the deeply problematic essentialized (and gendered) subject Freud endorses (Weedon 1987; Butler 1997), which Foucault sought specifically to undermine in his various analyses (Foucault 1972, 1978) and hence remained "notoriously taciturn on the topic of the psyche" (Butler 1997: 18).

Žižek's Lacanian perspective offers a potential way out of this impasse by proposing a non-essentialized subject, understood as an unknowable void defined precisely as that "which resists 'subjectivation'" (Žižek 1989: 236). As an infinite void, this subject is characterized by a fundamental lack, which it seeks to fill through pursuit of *jouissance*, which adheres to fantasies that subjects therefore desire to fulfil. Such fantasies thus sustain a commitment to particular ideologies and states of being by promising potential for pleasure. For Lacanians, consequently, "Ideology isn't simply imposed on ourselves. . . .We enjoy our ideology" (Žižek 2012a).

Yet *jouissance*, by definition, is unattainable, offering merely a pale taste of the real Thing (what Lacan called the illusory *object petit a* to which it refers) that lies forever beyond one's grasp. In this sense, fantasy serves not only to compel a quest for the *object petit a* and the *jouissance* it promises, but also to explain why neither is actually attained. Consequently, fantasy's promise to deliver the desired satisfaction at some future point conceals the impossibility of this promise, the Real-Symbolic gap it obscures, and the symptoms that signals this disjuncture as well.

In its dual focus on disavowal and desire, Lacanian psychoanalysis thus offers tools for analysis of "psychopower" (Stiegler 2010; Han 2017) that can complement exploration of the discursive power to which Foucault's studies were devoted. Despite the important ways that this perspective complicates the more conventional understandings of power outlined earlier, however, its discussion within political ecology research has been quite limited thus far.[7] Integrating analysis of desire and disavowal, Žižek proposes, entails two "complementary procedures": "One is *discursive*, the 'symptomal reading' of the ideological text bringing about the 'deconstruction' of the spontaneous experience of its meaning.... The other aims at extracting the kernel of *enjoyment*, at articulating the way in which—beyond the field of meaning but at the same time internal to it—an ideology implies, manipulates, produces a pre-ideological enjoyment structured in fantasy" (1989: 125, emphasis in original).

A DIALECTIC OF POWER AND VIOLENCE

Yet there is a further dynamic to be integrated into this discussion. Social theorists commonly distinguish power from exercise of direct, physical violence (Han 2018). According to Williams (1977: 108), "Gramsci made a distinction between rule and 'hegemony,'" with the former referring to exercise of coercive force to compel subjects' compliance. Similarly, Foucault asserts that power should not be understood as the direct application of force to bodies, but rather as "an action upon an action" intended "to structure the possible field of actions of others" (1983: 220, 221). Consequently, he maintains, "power is exercised only over free subjects, and only insofar as they are free" (221). "Where the determining factors saturate the whole," he goes on to explain, "there is no relationship of power" (221). Thus, there is "not a power relationship when man is in chains"; rather, this is instead "a question of a physical relationship of constraint" (221).[8]

In this understanding, violence may well provide support for power (in the sense that the threat or example of its use may function as an action influencing a subject's subsequent action), but it is not the exercise of power per se. Yet, even in this distinction, power and violence remain intimately related. Just as Foucault asserts an inherent connection between power and knowledge, Graeber (2015) suggests a similar relationship between *violence* and *ignorance*, observing that when one resorts to direct violence all of the complex machinations needed to gain the knowledge requisite to effective exercise of (indirect) power become irrelevant. As he phrases it, "Violence may well be the only way it is possible for one human being to do something which will have relatively predictable effects on the actions of a person about whom they understand nothing" (Graeber 2015: 67–68). One can simply hit one's target over the head with a stick to ensure compliance without knowing anything about their motives or intentions.[9] In this sense, violence can be understood as one of the main strategies employed to enforce compliance when power fails in this aim.[10]

Often underappreciated by social theorists concerned to understand power, in this respect, is the extent to which the effective exercise of power (as indirect action upon action to compel compliance without need for physical force) may actually rely on an earlier or underlying threat of direct violence. This is something that Graeber (2015) is at pains to emphasize. He labels this dynamic "structural violence," defined as "forms of pervasive social inequality that are ultimately backed up by the threat of physical harm" (57).[11] Graeber asserts that structural violence, defined in this way, is pervasive in social life, given that society essentially comprises "institutions involved in the allocation of resources within a system of property rights regulated and guaranteed by governments in a system that ultimately rests on the threat of force" (58). He observes, "It is curious how rarely citizens in industrial democracies actually think about this fact, or how instinctively we try to discount its importance" (58). Echoing both Taussig and Žižek, Graeber thus suggests that this situation entails a certain disavowal, what he calls "willful blindness" (57), in that "everyone concerned colludes to downplay the fact (perfectly obvious to those actually running the system) that all of it ultimately depends on the threat of physical harm" (58). Consequently, Graeber concludes, "what we talk about in terms of "belief" are simply the psychological techniques people develop to accommodate themselves to this reality" (59).

From this perspective, power and violence can be seen to exist in a dialectical relationship, with each functioning as simultaneously opposite and constitutive support of the other.

BIOPOWER

This dialectic of power and violence takes particular shape in one of Foucault's most popular forms of analysis, namely his exploration of what he terms "biopower" or "biopolitics."[12] In his earlier work, Foucault described "Western" societies as moving historically from an emphasis on sovereign power to disciplinary power to biopower (with each new form building on rather than wholly superseding the former). Yet it is the contrast between sovereign power and biopower on which he focuses most extensively. The sovereign power dominant in premodern Western societies, Foucault claims, rests on its prerogative to "let live or make die," while modern biopower claims the opposite capacity to "make live or let die" (Foucault 2003: 241). Rather than the "might makes right" approach grounding sovereign power, exercise of biopower is thus legitimized by its claim to nurture and sustain the population, to make subjects (on the whole) better, healthier, and stronger than they would be otherwise. As Foucault phrases it, biopower thus concerns itself with "generating forces, making them grow, and ordering them, rather [than] impeding them, making them submit, or destroying them" (1978: 136). Disciplinary power, he claims, is how biopower is implemented with respect to the individual bodies who make up the population to be regulated, entailing tactics intended to compel subjects to internalize norms and values such that they will self-regulate in socially desirable ways, thereby minimizing the need for direct physical force to ensure compliance (Foucault 1977). This is, of course, Foucault's (1977) famous "Panopticon" model of modern power. In this way, disciplinary power and biopower go hand in hand. While sovereign power has recourse to direct physical violence to enforce rule, therefore, the disciplinary techniques through which biopower is enacted rely more on subjects' own acquiescence to and embrace of these techniques (as well as on the structural violence, in Graeber's understanding, that supports these).

Foucault then introduces another crucial dynamic into this mix, namely his prolific concept of "governmentality." Defined as the "conduct of conduct," Foucault initially introduced the term governmentality in a 1977 lecture, situating it within his famous "triangle, sovereignty-discipline-government, which has as its primary target the population and as its essential mechanism the apparatuses of security" (1991a: 102). Despite the clear opposition between discipline and governmentality within this initial formulation, however, the wealth of subsequent research building on it has predominantly depicted governmentality as enacting a form of disciplinary power in its own right. And although he does not mention biopower specifically in this lecture, it seems clear that Foucault understood governmentality as the means through which biopower is enacted, as the set of strategies aiming to conduct the conduct of target populations in conformance with biopower's life-enhancing aims.[13] This equation of biopower with governmentality reinforces the sense that the latter was indeed intended to refer to the disciplinary power that he was busy fleshing out in other works during the same period (e.g., Foucault 1977, 1978).

Yet while Foucault's initial formulation of governmentality generated a torrent of subsequent research (Rose et al. 2006), in subsequent lectures over the next two years he continued to rework this inchoate term, eventually resolving his initially monolithic concept into a series of distinct governmentalities that, he claimed, "overlap, lean on each other, challenge each other, and struggle with each other" (Foucault 2008: 313) within particular contexts and institutions. There exist, Foucault asserted, four primary forms of governmentality, which he defined as "art of government according to truth, art of government according to the rationality of the sovereign state, and art of government according to the rationality of economic agents, and more generally according to the rationality of the governed themselves" (313). In this new formation, then, sovereignty and discipline cease to be opposed to governmentality but become instead particular forms of governmentality in their own right (Foucault's "rationality of the sovereign state" and "rationality of the governed themselves," respectively). Within this refined typology, biopower becomes similarly variegated, pursued in different ways depending on the particular governmentality through which it is operationalized. In this sense, biopower is less a mode of power per se than a particular way of legitimizing the exercise of power distinct from the sovereign "might makes right" justification to which Foucault contrasts it.

This more variegated understanding of biopower has intriguing implications for analysis that are only beginning to be explored (see, e.g., Fletcher 2018b; Fletcher et al. 2019). How biopower is approached by different theoretical traditions constitutes another interesting focus of attention. While Foucault's approach to power generally was strongly opposed to a Marxist perspective, as previously described, it is clear that he understood biopower as not only a method of population governance but also as a key support for the development of capitalism. As he explained, "bio-power was without question an indispensable element in the development of capitalism; the latter would not have been possible without the controlled insertion of bodies into the machinery of production and the adjustment of the phenomena of population to economic processes" (Foucault 1978: 140–141). Federici (2004: 16) goes even further to assert that "the promotion of life-forces turns out to be nothing more than the result of a new concern with the accumulation and reproduction of labor-power."

Approaching biopower from a Lacanian perspective, moreover, Dean introduces another element of complexity into the discussion in asserting that "Foucault's concept of biopolitics is best understood in terms of [the psychoanalytic notion of] drive" (2010: 13). Lacan suggested that when the *object petit a* of desire is considered unattainable, desire instead turns inward and becomes "drive," propelled by the inability to mourn for the loss of the object, which causes attachment to turn from the object to the *experience of loss itself.* As a result, this very experience of loss becomes the object perpetually pursued. In this way, drive becomes a vicious cycle in which one endlessly repeats a self-destructive behavior while disavowing this dynamic.

This shift from desire to drive, Žižek claims, describes the trajectory of contemporary capitalism as a whole, whereby desire for *jouissance* promised by increased consumption in an "economy of enjoyment" is increasingly replaced by the endless repetition of a failure to attain enjoyment, instead becoming attached to this failure itself. In this way, drive "turns crisis into triumph, generating enjoyment, not from success, but repeated failure" (Kapoor 2015: 66). As with desire, it is the "libidinal kick (*jouissance*) which accompanies drive that helps explain capitalism's continued obstinacy and endurance" (67). In this way, desire and drive have come to complement one another as twin "drivers" of capitalist development operating on different registers. While desire grips us as particular "consumers, as subjects of desire, soliciting in [us] ever new perverse and excessive desires (for which it offers products to satisfy them) . . . drive inheres to capitalism at a more fundamental, *systemic* level: drive is that which propels the whole capitalist machinery, it is the impersonal compulsion to engage in the endless circular movement of expanded self-reproduction" (Žižek 2009a: 61, in Kapoor 2015: 69). Dean (2010) identifies this dynamic of drive within the exercise of biopower too. She describes the "historical emergence of biopolitics as the byproduct, the effect, of political sovereignty's confrontation with an economic demand, that is, with the appearance of the market as a site of truth beyond the reach of sovereign power" (2010: 4). Bridging, in a sense, Foucauldian and Marxist approaches to biopower, Dean thus contends that "biopolitics is best understood not as a mode of governance that takes life as its object but rather as the unintended byproduct of the clash between sovereign power and capitalist economics" (2–3).

Yet in its function as drive, Dean identifies a self-destructive dialectic, for in "taking possession of life, biopolitics provides a particularly dangerous and murderous supplement to classical sovereignty's right of life and death" (2010: 5–6, 7). Echoing the dialectic of power and violence outlined earlier, Dean thus concludes that biopower should be understood as "the coincidence of an ostensibly vital and energetic domain of productive life with a stagnant, deadened, and deadly terrain of sovereign political action" (Dean 2010: 2). This resonates with Mbembe's (2003) important assertion that biopower is always necessarily complemented by the exercise of "necropower" in terms of the (sovereign) use of direct violence to kill those considered threats to the population in question.

NEOLIBERAL POWER

One of the particular governmentalities Foucault identifies in his refined typology—his "art of government according to the rationality of economic agents"—is a specifically *neoliberal* one. As he further describes, this is "an environmental type of intervention instead of the internal subjugation of individuals" (2008: 260); "a governmentality which will act on the environment and systematically modify its variables" (271). In this way, Foucault directly opposes this approach to a disciplinary governmentality concerned precisely with the "internal subjugation of individuals." In Foucault's conception, by contrast, neoliberal governmentality dispenses with concern for subjects' internal states and instead "seeks merely to create external incentive structures within which individuals, understood as self-interested rational actors, can be motivated to exhibit appropriate behaviours through manipulation of incentives" (Fletcher 2010a: 17).

From this perspective, neoliberalism can be understood as advancing a particular form of power distinct from both the sovereign and disciplinary modes that proceeded it historically. Byung-Chul Han (2017) contends that this distinctive neoliberal power is characterized by the way it mobilizes freedom in the interest of subjection. Under neoliberalism, he asserts, "Power need not exclude, prohibit or censor. Nor does it stand opposed to freedom. Indeed, power can even use freedom to its own ends" (Han 2017: 13–14). Han views this dynamic as quite different from disciplinary power, which, he contends, "is still commanded by negativity. Its mode of articulation is inhibitive, not permissive" (14). The shift from disciplinary to neoliberal power, Han suggests, is related to how capitalism changes under neoliberalism as well: while "nineteenth-century capitalism . . . operated by means of disciplinary constraints and prohibitions," neoliberalism "places its stock in voluntary self-organization and self-optimization" (2015: 16).

In this way, Han explains, neoliberalism has discovered the psyche as a new realm in which to exercise power, and hence represents the introduction of "psychopower," having "discovered the psyche as a productive force" (2015: 25).[14] Yet while Han sees only neoliberalism as productively mobilizing freedom in the interest of power, one could argue that disciplinary power, in Foucault's formulation, does this too. Foucault's general characterization of (disciplinary) power as "exercised only over free subjects, and only insofar as they are free" (1983: 221) makes this quite clear. By the same token, disciplinary power can also be understood to encompass a certain form of psychopower, as Foucault's various analyses of how the pursuit of psychological knowledge has been instrumental in the exercise of modern power demonstrate (e.g., Foucault 1972, 1977, 1978).

What Han's analysis does point to, most centrally, is the *particular way* that neoliberal power seeks to mobilize freedom in relation to the psyche. Different modes of power—of governmentality—also prescribe particular forms of subjectivity (Miller and Rose 2008; Fletcher 2020b). In Han's (2017) analysis, both sovereign power and disciplinary power produce an "obedience-subject" while neoliberalism produces what he calls a novel "achievement-subject." Yet one could argue that Foucault understands disciplinary power as producing less an obedience-subject than what we might call a *self-regulating subject* that seeks to discipline itself to societal norms rather than following commands from an external authority. Like Han's achievement-subject, this disciplinary subject endeavors to "act on [itself] so that power relations are interiorized" and hence to become a *"panopticon of itself"* (Han 2015: 61, emphasis in original).

Even with this qualification, however, Han clearly identifies a novel relationship with the psyche that neoliberal power introduces. He describes the neoliberal achievement-subject as bent on "compulsive achievement and optimization" (Han 2017: 1), as (following Foucault) "an entrepreneur of the self practising self-exploitation" (61). Indeed, Han sees neoliberalism as shifting emphasis from understanding selves as "subjects" at all to instead becoming *projects* who are "always refashioning and reinventing ourselves" (1). These new achievement-subjects are fashioned through a variety of new techniques including "self-management workshops, motivational retreats and seminars on personality or mental training [that] promise boundless self-optimization and heightened efficiency" (29).

This shift, Han contends, effects a fundamental change in the nature of the self, particularly with respect to the function of the superego. Under disciplinary power, the superego is primarily "repressive. It mainly voices prohibitions" (Han 2018: 36). Under neoliberalism, by contrast, the superego instead enjoins the self to pursue unlimited excess. Žižek (2008) points to a similar dynamic in observing that within neoliberal society the superego shifts from trying to domesticate enjoyment to instead commanding the subject to enjoy as much as possible, such that the main source of guilt shifts from concern about whether one is enjoying correctly or in excess to worry, conversely, that one is not enjoying *enough*. As Han (2017) phrases it, the disciplinary injunction *should* is thus replaced by the neoliberal *can*. In this way, he asserts, neoliberalism "proves so effective because it does not operate by means of forbidding and depriving, but by pleasing and fulfilling" (14).

Consequently, neoliberalism embodies a unique approach to desire, exploiting "emotion in order to influence actions on this pre-reflexive level" (Han 2017: 48). This is a far cry from the coolly rational *Homo economicus* researchers—Foucault included—have usually identified at the heart of the neoliberal project (see Fletcher 2010a). Brown (2019) also contests this common characterization of the neoliberal subject, highlighting how key architects of the neoliberal project such as Hayek emphasized the need to cultivate a particular moral orientation in order to direct subjects' cost-benefit calculation in appropriate directions. Yet Han, like both Layton (2009) and Dean (2008), goes beyond a focus on how such disciplinary tactics support neoliberal governance to highlight the visceral, affective forces—the "irrational exuberance"—that also influence the seemingly rational calculation such governance purports to promote.

While Han asserts that only neoliberalism develops such a positive strategy for stimulating desire as a technique of power, however, Foucault also saw this as one of disciplinary power's functions. In countering the "repressive hypothesis" commonly identified in Western approaches to regulating sexuality, for instance, he argued instead that modernity has actually sought to stimulate desire for sexual fulfilment in manifold ways (Foucault 1978). Yet while disciplinary power seeks primarily to channel desire into particular socially acceptable avenues for (sublimated) fulfilment, neoliberalism aims to liberate desire from all constraints.[15] This, Han (2018: 90) maintains, produces an "orgy of liberation, deregulation, dissolution of boundaries, and deritualization."[16]

BIOPOLITICS AND PSYCHOPOLITICS

This novel neoliberal power, Han argues, signals a shift away from biopower altogether.[17] He suggests that Foucault's inability to recognize that the rise of neoliberalism signaled the end of biopolitics was due to the fact that Foucault died right at the moment when neoliberalism exploded onto the world stage. Hence, when developing the biopower concept, "Foucault evidently did not appreciate that biopolitics and population—which represent genuine categories of disciplinary society—are unsuited to describing the neoliberal regime. Consequently, he failed to do what the circumstances actually called for: to make the turn to psychopolitics" (Han 2017: 23).

Rather than viewing biopower and psychopower as diametrically opposed, however, one can argue, as I have above, that different modes of (bio)power also enact psychopower in different ways (see also Dean 2010). Hence, one can understand neoliberalism as mobilizing its own distinctive mode of biopower. Foucault, indeed, intimated just this at the end of *The Birth of Biopolitics*, stating, "What should now be studied, therefore, is the way in which the specific problems of life and population have been posed within a technology of government which, although far from always having been liberal, since the end of the eighteenth century has been constantly haunted by the question of liberalism" (Foucault 2008: 324).

Foucault's untimely death left this investigation unrealized, and subsequent analysis has yet to pursue it systematically. In an earlier work, I have speculated concerning what analysis in such terms would look like:

> How would the exercise of biopower in terms of a neoliberal governmentality differ from a disciplinary approach? First, a neoliberal perspective would likely focus less on subjects' internal states than on the external structures within which they act. Second, interventions would be framed less in terms of morality than cost-benefit characteristics. Third, a neoliberal governmentality would likely place less emphasis on nurturing and sustaining life directly than on supporting economic growth, which Foucault calls neoliberalism's "one true and fundamental social policy" (2008: 144). In neoliberal discourse, in other words, economic growth is the chief mechanism through

which the aims of biopower are pursued. Limiting economic growth is implicitly construed as a threat to human life, and thus to the exercise of biopower as well. (Fletcher 2010a: 175)

While elements of this speculative outline remain compelling, and indeed have been empirically substantiated to some degree in subsequent research (Fletcher et al. 2019), Han's (2017, 2018) work makes it clear that this characterization overlooks the ways that subjects' internal states can indeed become central to neoliberal biopolitics in terms of mobilizing desire as part of the incentive structures motivating subjects' actions.

CONCLUSION

The preceding discussion of the various dimensions and contestations concerning the nature of "power" forms the basis of the analysis developed throughout the rest of the book. There are several key take-away messages from this discussion that I want to highlight before delving into this analysis. First, this discussion importantly highlights the ways that power can be exercised not merely through cultivating subjects' wholesale buy-in to an ideology but rather through (stimulating) their ambivalence and skepticism concerning this ideology itself. Indeed, as I have shown, active questioning of an ideology can at times paradoxically strengthen allegiance to it, via dynamics such as public secrecy, disavowal, and cynical reason previously outlined.

This is explainable by the insight a Lacanian perspective affords concerning how power inheres within subjects, a topic that neither Marx nor Foucault provide significant guidance in addressing.[18] For Lacan, such ambivalent attachment to power is explained by the way desire for *jouissance* (itself a highly ambivalent state) motivates subjects' attachment to an ideology promising provision of this enjoyment. As Stavrakakis explains, "By taking into account emotion, affect, and passion one may be able to reach a more thorough understanding of 'what sticks': both what fuels identification processes and what creates discursive fixity" (2007: 165). Affective attachment compels subjects to maintain allegiance to an ideology even when it does not appear to function in the ways intended—or, indeed, even foils attainment of the promised enjoyment—via ideology's promise to correct course in the future. Consequently, subjects are able to (half-consciously) engage in a process of disavowal, allowing them to convince themselves (and others) that success is indeed possible, even while they may simultaneously doubt this same possibility—a doubt that is then denied or explained away by refocusing on positive future potential. In this way, ideology can persist in failing forward in the face of critique both external and internal. This ambivalent lurching forward despite persistent doubt, skepticism, and disavowal is, as I will show, precisely how the neoliberal conservation project has developed over time.

A Lacanian perspective can thereby mediate between Marxist and poststructuralist positions concerning the key question of whether or not to take subjects' expressed allegiance to a particular project at face value. With poststructuralists, Lacan permits us to assume that subjects indeed believe what they claim while also looking beyond their conscious proclamations to explore the potential presence of less-than-conscious reservations that may conflict with or contradict explicit pronouncements. This intermediate position thus allows us to "not dismiss the people involved in" developing neoliberal conservation, as Dempsey (2016: xii) asserts, while at the same time still affording critique of the "ideas . . . knowledges and tools" (xii) they bring to their work, as Büscher (2018) advises in a review of Dempsey's work.

In addition to contributing to discussions of power in political ecology by advancing this Lacanian perspective to complement Marxist and poststructuralist approaches currently dominant in the field, this chapter has also developed an original conceptualization of a specifically neoliberal form of biopower as the basis for understanding the neoliberal conservation project in particular. This neoliberal biopower analytic allows us to further synthesize Marxist, poststructuralist, and psychoanalytic perspectives, all of which take biopower as a focus of attention, albeit in different ways. This synthetic approach enables us to understand biopower as a function simultaneously of accumulation, of governance and securitization, and of the psychic process of drive.

At its core, Dean (2010) contends, biopower can be understood as a dialectic of freedom and security, as an ongoing effort to strike the appropriate balance between state control and individual autonomy that, she suggests, precipitates its own inversion in paradoxically compelling progressive governmentalization in the interest of preserving freedom and in this way cannibalizing the very freedom biopower aims to preserve. The transition to neoliberalism, Dean suggests, merely "intensifies and extends biopolitical processes and mechanisms" (10) in this regard. This perspective resonates with the recognition that neoliberal governance tends to extend the very forms of direct state regulation it ostensibly seeks to minimize discussed in the introduction (and again in chapter 5).

As well as illuminating this paradoxical element of neoliberal governance, the concept of neoliberal biopower helps to explain the particular preoccupation with economic growth as the basis of the population support that biopower prioritizes under neoliberalism. In this neoliberal framing, the biopolitical imperative to "make live"—and a given entity's right to be included within the population receiving this support—must be justified through evaluation and demonstration of life's "value" understood in economic terms. Within this cold cost-benefit calculation, conversely, one must "let die" entities unable to demonstrate possession of sufficient value within the context of the finite planet containing scarce resources that forms the essential basis of the economists' worldview (Farber et al. 2002; Kallis 2019a), a worldview in which "hard choices" (McShane et al. 2011) must be made concerning where to direct scarce resources to achieve optimal "return on investment." This particular neoliberal biopolitical logic aiming to "defend life by demonstrating its 'profitability' and hence right to exist" (Fletcher et al. 2019: 1068) is satirically captured in a political cartoon by Seppo Leinonen, in which a suit-clad consultant surrounded by endangered wildlife points to a graph of the global economy and explains that "these species are unprofitable, so they will be laid off" (Leinonen n.d.).

It is from this vantage point of a peculiarly neoliberal biopolitics, I argue, that the neoliberal conservation project must be understood. The next chapter begins my analysis in these terms by outlining the historical development of this project and biopolitical logic underpinning its approach.

TWO

Conjuring Natural Capital

> In speculative enterprises, profit must be imagined before it can
> be extracted; the possibility of economic performance must be
> conjured like a spirit to draw an audience of potential investors.
> The more spectacular the conjuring, the more possible an invest-
> ment frenzy.
>
> ANNA TSING, "Inside the Economy of Appearances" (2000: 118)

In February 2020, British Petroleum (BP) created a media stir by announc-
ing the intention to become "a net zero company" (i.e., to become totally
carbon neutral across its suite of operations) by 2050 (British Petroleum
[BP] 2020).[1] As the company explained:

> BP's new ambition to be a net zero company by 2050 or sooner covers the
> greenhouse gas emissions from its operations worldwide, currently around 55
> million tonnes of CO_2 equivalent ($MteCO_2e$) a year, and the carbon in the
> oil and gas that it produces, equivalent currently to around 360 $MteCO_2e$
> emissions a year—both on an absolute basis. Taken together, delivery of
> these aims would equate to a reduction in emissions to net zero from what is
> currently around 415 $MteCO_2e$ a year (BP 2020).

Within this pronouncement, "net zero" was defined as "zero GHG [green-
house gas] emissions, after deduction of sinks, removals or reductions and
as determined in accordance with BP's methodologies." Achieving this, the
company explained, would entail five key objectives:

1. Net zero across BP's operations on an absolute basis by 2050 or sooner.

2. Net zero on carbon in BP's oil and gas production on an absolute basis
   by 2050 or sooner.

3. 50 percent cut in the carbon intensity of products BP sells by 2050 or
   sooner.

4. Install methane measurement at all BP's major oil and gas processing sites by 2023 and reduce methane intensity of operations by
   50 percent.

5. Increase the proportion of investment into non-oil and gas businesses over time.

As Bernard Looney, the recently appointed CEO responsible for the plan's development, explained at the time:

> BP needs to continue to perform as we transform. As committed as I am to making transformation happen, I am equally committed to some fundamental principles that have served us well. Safe and reliable operations will always underpin all we do, and we remain committed to meeting the promises we have made to our shareholders. We can only reimagine energy if we are financially strong, able to pay the dividend our owners depend on and to generate the cash to invest in new low and no-carbon businesses.

Looney also reassured investors that BP would safeguard the eight billion dollars paid out in shareholder dividends every year by becoming "a force for good as well as a provider of competitive returns" (BP 2020).

While the plan was (and remains) short on specific measures to achieve these ambitious aims, as critics quickly pointed out, it did include at least one concrete commitment: "The net zero strategy will require BP to cut or offset around 360m tonnes of greenhouse emissions created by the oil and gas it produces every year through measures such as tree-planting, and carbon capture technologies" (Ambrose 2020).

CONDITIONS OF POSSIBILITY

How is it possible for a company whose business model is fundamentally based in the extraction of fossil fuels so that they can be burned to create energy, emitting substantial greenhouse gasses in the process, to assert its potential to fully neutralize these same emissions while maintaining profitability? Some critics have, understandably, reacted quite suspiciously to this announcement, suspecting it of being mere opportunistic "greenwashing."[2] While sharing this skepticism concerning the plan's potential, here I follow the poststructuralist approach of instead taking it seriously as a genuine proposal that earnestly aims to achieve what it claims. From this perspective, in this chapter I explore what Foucault (1970) calls the "conditions of possibility" for this extraordinary claim: the system of ideas that allow the proposal to be presented and received (at least by some) as a plausible proposition, whereas from a critical perspective it appears quite ludicrous.[3] It would be one thing for BP to assert that it could achieve carbon neutrality by dramatically refocusing and reducing its business and hence also diminishing the return to investors it offers; it is quite another to insist that neutrality can be attained without compromising such returns in the slightest (or even enhancing them). How is it possible to make such a claim, and for it to be taken seriously by a range of industry and media pundits? I explore this key question in the following.

I argue that BP's claim is only credible within the context of the neoliberal conservation project on which this book focuses. In other words, it is the neoliberal biopolitical vision underpinning this project that forms the condition of possibility for BP's plan. This chapter outlines this vision and the growing network of actors and organizations that have organized around it. While there is of course substantial divergence among the views promoted by the various actors within this diverse network (see Dempsey 2016), there is also sufficient commonality and cross-fertilization of perspectives that they can also be understood to comprise a relatively coherent "discourse coalition" (Hajer 1993).[4]

Analysis of the discourse this coalition espouses is based primarily on my reading of a large corpus of texts produced by the set of interconnected actors and organizations comprising it, as well as my research—collaborative event ethnography—at several international meetings in recent years where these players have met to present, discuss, and align their positions. I focus here on outlining the overarching patterns of thought within these texts and discussions that form the core elements of a generally shared vision.[5] I begin by charting the origins of a neoliberal perspective and the coalition promoting it within conservation circles in the global crisis moment of the 1970s.

ASSEMBLING NEOLIBERAL CONSERVATION

The rise of neoliberal conservation can be understood, in substantial part, as a response to several forces that converged in the late 1960s and early 1970s to challenge the hegemony of the Keynesian, state-centric political-economic paradigm dominant until that point. First, widespread social unrest in both high- and low-income societies raised fundamental questions about the distribution of wealth in the world and the capacity of the dominant economic development model to address these. Second, environmental social movements called into question the ecological implications of a Keynesian strategy grounded in the imperative to stimulate growth in response to recession, which came at the expense of both increased resource extraction and the pollution resulting therefrom due to the demand to continually expand both production and consumption. All of this was exacerbated by the global economic crisis precipitated by the OPEC (Organization of the Petroleum Exporting Countries) oil embargo in 1973, which trained further attention on issues of development, environment, and the relationship between these.

The combined consequence of these converging forces was to put dramatic obstacles in the face of continued capital accumulation globally by increasing the costs of production in order to both internalize environmental "externalities" and raise wages for workers in high-income societies, on the one hand, and on the other to challenge the capacity of state-centric capitalist production to sustain adequate growth. From a Marxist perspective, this could be seen as a crisis of accumulation, while for poststructuralists it can equally be viewed as what Habermas (1975) at the time labeled a "legitimation crisis" of the state-centered governance model that neoliberals would subsequently deride as "command-and-control." These twin crises spurred a quest both to roll back the newfound obstacles to continued accumulation in high-income societies and to expand production into low-income ones where both wages and environmental restrictions were typically much reduced. In this way, as Harvey (2005) describes, the rise of neoliberalism provided a series of "fixes" to restimulate expanded accumulation on a global scale while at the same time legitimizing a new form of governance as a corrective to the diminishing credibility of the welfare state.

As Klein (2007) demonstrates, the 1973 recession provided the convenient crisis that Milton Friedman had foreseen as necessary for "ideas that are lying around" to gain traction, such that a neoliberal project in gestation since the end of World War II could now assert its relevance in resolving the crisis and restoring conditions for continued accumulation.[6] Responding to both social and environmental movements, neoliberals asserted, essentially, that both issues could be redressed without the global socioeconomic transformation called for by activists. Quite to the contrary, they claimed, it could be done by giving the capitalist economy even more free reign and thus allowing the "invisible hand" of supply and demand to efficiently optimize resource allocation. With the institutionalization of neoliberalism as the basis for governance, first in the high-income societies of the United States, United Kingdom, and elsewhere, then via structural adjustment programs

(SAPs) throughout most of the rest of the world too, both social and environmental safety nets erected by welfare states under Keynesianism were progressively dismantled in an initial "roll-back" phase (Peck and Tickell 2002). At the same time, reduced restrictions on international capital mobility allowed greatly expanded access to markets in lower-income societies, facilitating an intensified wave of globalization via outsourcing of production and proliferation of transnational conglomerates (Harvey 2005).

In the environmental realm, roll-back neoliberalism facilitated increased access by private sector firms to a range of natural resources that had previously been off-limits due to these resources' nationalization within some societies and state-created restrictions on their exploitation within others (Heynen et al. 2007). The result in many places was, initially, a dramatic increase in environmental degradation from the expanded production unleashed by these changes. At the same time, however, and partly in response to this very problem, plans were already being laid for the creation of a new array of global environmental governance institutions grounded in neoliberal principles—what Peck and Tickell (2002) label "roll-out" mechanisms—to replace state-centered structures in the process of roll-back.

This newly neoliberalized environmental governance was produced and championed by a growing convergence among a number of disparate groups. First, conservationists were facing growing critiques of the state-centered "fortress conservation" paradigm, prevailing previously, on the grounds that it tended to unfairly displace and disadvantage local people while also often failing to adequately conserve resources due in part to resistance by these same local groups (see Brockington 2002; Igoe 2004). This resulted in promotion of a "new" strategy seeking to combine resource preservation with social development under the label of "community-based conservation," implemented via so called integrated-conservation-and-development projects (ICDPs) (see Wells and Brandon 1992; Mulder and Coppolillo 2005). This novel approach received its first widespread public endorsement in the 1980 World Conservation Strategy spearheaded by the International Union for the Conservation of Nature (IUCN), which established the foundation for the strategy's diffusion as a global policy platform to be further developed through the series of World Conservation Congresses (WCCs) held periodically thereafter.

Meanwhile, among international development planners, growing discussion of potential "limits to growth," first popularly articulated by the influential 1972 Club of Rome report (Meadows et al. 1972), highlighted a pressing need to explicitly incorporate environmental concerns within development considerations too. Attention to this issue grew throughout the 1980s, crystalizing in the famous 1987 UN Bruntland Commission report *Our Common Future* (World Commission on Environment and Development [WCED] 1987) that drew directly on the 1980 World Conservation Strategy to articulate a new global agenda for pursuing "sustainable development."

At the same time, a growing school of self-styled ecological economists had begun to establish themselves as a distinct field of inquiry separate from an overarching environmental or natural resource economics perspective grounded explicitly in neoclassical theory. Led by budding luminaries including Herman Daly, then with the World Bank, and prolific author Robert Costanza, ecological economists argued not merely for submission of environmental concerns to conventional economic logic but instead for a profound reformulation of our understanding of the overarching economy as itself merely a component of a larger ecosystem and hence to place environmental concerns at the center of economic considerations generally (see especially Costanza et al. 1991).

This was complemented by the rise of "complex systems theory" in this same period. While initial forays into this field were often framed as a dramatic challenge to conventional economic processes, the perspective was subsequently appropriated and rearticulated into arrangements that conformed with the growing hegemony of neoliberal thinking (Nelson 2014). Perspectives such as Buzz Holling's (1973) "resilience" theory, for instance, thus

> took something that began as a critique of existing capitalist ecologies . . . and redeployed its critical energies as a new mode of capitalist management, rejecting the kind of knowledge-based planning that characterized Keynesian economics, and replacing it with modes of governance that did not require "a precise capacity to predict the future, but only a qualitative capacity to design systems that can absorb and accommodate future events in whatever unexpected form they may take." (Braun 2015: 9; see also Reid 2013; Nelson 2014)

Finally, during this same period, private sector firms were reacting to the rise in environmental legislation in the late 1960s and early 1970s in several high-income societies by organizing to promote an alternative approach to self-regulation through "corporate social responsibility" (see, e.g., Beder 1998, 2001). This led to formation, in 1990, of the Business Council for

Sustainable Development (BCSD) headed by Swiss industrialist Stephan Schmidheiny (see Schmidheiny 1992). This growing campaign was supported by a collection of conservative think tanks, including the Heritage Foundation in the United States and the Institute of Economic Affairs in the United Kingdom, which sought to "provide corporations and private firms with an alternative to restrictive legislation and the rhetoric to make the argument against that legislation in terms that are not obviously self-interested" (Beder 2001: 130–131).

All of this culminated in the foundational 1992 Rio Earth Summit, at which these different interests groups converged to chart a global program for pursuit of the sustainable development called for by the Bruntland Commission. This Summit, chaired by Canadian oil magnate Maurice Strong (who had also headed the UN's previous Conference on the Human Environment in 1972), erected the main pillars of the global environmental governance architecture that remains dominant to this day, including the Convention on Biological Diversity (CBD), the United Nations Framework Convention on Climate Change (UNFCCC), and Agenda 21. In the same year, the IUCN's first WCC endorsed essentially the same agenda. Following the Summit, additionally, Strong came together with Schmidheiny to expand the BCSD into the World Business Council for Sustainable Development (WBCSD) in 1995.

SUSTAINABLE DEVELOPMENT 2.0

The years following the Rio Summit, however, witnessed growing difficulty in actually achieving its stated aim to successfully reconcile environment and development goals. By the ten-year follow up to the original Rio conference, held in Johannesburg, South Africa, in 2002 (the UN Conference on Sustainable Development, or Rio +10), the slow progress made thus far on the original Rio program had already inspired substantial frustration and critique (Mowforth and Munt 2003). This only grew in subsequent years, leading Park and colleagues to conclude, in the introduction to their 2008 volume *The Crisis of Global Environmental Governance*, that

> few can claim seriously that the period since the Rio meeting has been one of great accomplishment on global environmental governance, human development, or the chimerical notion of "sustainability." . . . Governments of the North have shown little interest in investing in Agenda 21, the laundry list of

responses crafted for endorsement at the Earth Summit. . . . Governments of the South have shown little ability or inclination to stand in the way of the globalization of consumerism. International environmental diplomacy has stalled on issues ranging from climate change to the world's forests to toxic hazards. (Park et al. 2008: 14–15)

Such dissatisfaction was merely exacerbated by the global economic crisis beginning in this same year, which further eroded faith in the capacity of the prevailing development paradigm to deliver on either its economic or environmental promises (United Nations Environment Program [UNEP] 2009).

All of this spurred elaboration of a renovated approach to sustainable development in the leadup to the next UN reunion held again in Rio in 2012 (again called the UN Conference on Environment and Development, or Rio +20). Central to promotion of this new perspective was UNEP, which labeled it pursuit of a "Green Economy," a concept that the organization and others championed as a central platform of both the Rio+20 Summit and the renewed global sustainable development program slated to follow from the Summit (UNEP 2011b). As UNEP's then executive director Achim Steiner explained at the time, the Green Economy was intended not as a "replacement for sustainable development" but merely "a way of realizing that development at the national, regional and global levels and in ways that resonate with and amplify the implementation of Agenda 21" (Steiner 2011: v). How exactly this approach differed from the sustainable development it intended to complement was never clearly explained. UNEP's own definition of the Green Economy was always quite vague, describing it merely as an economy "that results in *improved human well-being and social equity, while significantly reducing environmental risks and ecological scarcities*" (UNEP 2011b: 2, emphasis in original)—goals that could of course be equally attributed to most approaches to sustainable development already in discussion. Steiner gave assurance that a "green economy does not favour one political perspective over another. It is relevant to all economies, be they state or more market-led" (Steiner 2011: v), but this did little to clarify the matter.

Yet a closer reading of UNEP's Green Economy report and a set of related documents published in the same period reveals that what most exemplifies this renovated approach to sustainable development championed by the organization as part of a growing global consortium is its central assertion that "ecosystems—environments of interacting plants, animals, and microbes, from coastal tide pools to Loire Valley vineyards to expanses of Amazonian rain forest—can be seen as capital assets, supplying human beings with a stream of services that sustain and enhance our lives" (Daily and Ellison 2002: 5). From this perspective, in other words, sustainable development should now center on the economic valuation of the "ecosystem services" provided by "natural capital" as the basis of income generated not merely through balancing environment and development concerns, as the original Rio agenda intended, but by making pursuit of environmental sustainability *the basis of economic growth itself.*

Despite an energetic campaign by UNEP and collaborators to establish the Green Economy at the center of the new global agenda, the concept received strong criticism from civil society groups during Rio+20 (see Brand 2012; Wanner 2015) and subsequently receded from the prominent place in public discussion it had commanded prior.[7] Yet core elements of the perspective it championed have remained central to elaboration of the post-2015 global Sustainable Development Agenda that grew out of the Summit by a growing group of actors and organizations. Hence, it can be considered a key component of a reinvigorated—and even more neoliberalized—*sustainable development 2.0.*

NEOLIBERAL CONSERVATION: A GENEALOGY

Conservation has come to occupy an increasingly central place within this renovated sustainability agenda. While catalyzed at Rio+20, this emphasis on conservation as a central pillar of sustainable development had been in formation for some time prior, beginning in the years directly following the original Rio Summit. A watershed moment in its institutionalization was 1997 with the convergence of three significant events. First, the Kyoto Protocol of the UNFCCC codified "flexible mechanisms" centered on carbon markets as central to the global climate change governance regime (Bumpus and Liverman 2008). Second, Stanford University's Gretchen Daily spearheaded an edited volume—called *Nature's Services*—that asserted the importance of understanding nature as an ecosystem service provider (Daily 1997). Simultaneously, foundational ecological economist Costanza (also a contributor to *Nature's Services*) and colleagues published their seminal effort to monetarily value the world's aggregate ecosystem services (Costanza et al. 1997).

All of this placed discussion of conservation as a central sustainable development strategy squarely on the public stage, sparking its growing elaboration into the twenty-first century. Thus, in 2001 the Millennium

Ecosystem Assessment (MEA) was initiated, explicitly building on these 1997 efforts to assess the state of the world's ecosystem services and hence place this concept at the center of global discussions. Publication of the MEA in 2005 is widely seen as another catalytic movement in the establishment of the new approach. Daily and colleagues relate: "The Millennium Ecosystem Assessment took a giant step forward in developing a widely shared vision, a conceptual framework, and a synthesis of existing knowledge. It spawned a suite of further efforts, including an Intergovernmental Science-Policy Platform for Biodiversity and Ecosystem Services. . . . By almost any measure—scientific papers published, media mentions, Google search trends—awareness of natural capital and efforts to sustain it have skyrocketed since the Millennium Assessment" (Daily et al. 2011: 3). Tallis and Polaski add, "Within a year of its completion, findings from the M[E]A were incorporated into the Convention on Biological Diversity, the RAMSAR Convention on Wetlands, and the Convention to Combat Desertification" (2011: 35)

Also in 2001, the architecture for the global carbon markets defining Kyoto's flexible mechanisms was codified within UNFCCC meetings, while the Protocol itself was finally ratified and its carbon markets established in 2005, when the MEA appeared as well. In that same year, IUCN, having developed its Global Business and Biodiversity Program in 2003, entered into formal partnership with the WBCSD, which by that time had grown to encompass some two hundred of the world's largest and most prominent transnational corporations, including BP as well as Shell, Rio Tinto, Holcim, Coca-Cola, and Toyota (MacDonald 2010a). At the IUCN's fourth WCC held in Barcelona, Spain, in 2008, the WBCSD partnership was front and center and business promotion rampant, leading one reporter, indeed, to describe the meeting as essentially an argument that "conservation has failed because it has not embraced the fundamental tenets of business management" (Kantner, cited in MacDonald 2010a: 256). As previously noted, this business promotion increased such that at the 2012 WCC the WBCSD was even more centrally showcased, and promotion of natural capital valuation and accounting was pervasive (Fletcher 2014a). Meanwhile, in 2010 the WBCSD had released its own *Vision 2050* report charting a business-led course for a future in which "9 billion people live well, and within the limits of the planet" (WBCSD 2010: 6).

Back in 2006, the famous *Stern Review* had already introduced economic valuation into the realm of climate change governance (Stern et al. 2006), while in the same year Daily teamed up with TNC and WWF (and subsequently also the University of Minnesota) to initiate the Natural Capital Project to develop detailed metrics for natural capital accounting. Building on the MEA and Stern Review, subsequently, in 2007 UNEP began its initiative called The Economics of Ecosystems and Biodiversity (TEEB) to quantify the global ecosystem services that the MEA had defined, releasing its first results in 2008 (TEEB 2008). These were then incorporated into UNEP's commentary on the 2008 crisis (UNEP 2009) and Green Economy campaign, while also inspiring similar efforts elsewhere. Promotion of TEEB, for instance, became a central element of the 2010 CBD Conference of the Parties in Nagoya, Japan (MacDonald and Corson 2012), where the World Bank launched a new initiative (Wealth Accounting and Valuation of Ecosystem Services, or WAVES), explicitly modeled on TEEB, to develop national-level mechanisms for natural capital valuation throughout the world. TEEB was then strongly promoted as part of UNEP's Green Economy campaign at Rio+20 as well and helped to inspire the Intergovernmental Science-Policy Platform for Biodiversity and Ecosystem Services (IPBES) established that same year under UNEP's leadership. It also inspired formation of a TEEB for Business Coalition in 2012 that renamed itself the Natural Capital Coalition (NCC) two years later. In 2020, the NCC was subsequently absorbed into an overarching Capitals Coalition also comprising Social and Human Capital Coalitions and boasting more than 370 member organizations.

While UNEP's overarching Green Economy platform receded from prominent public discussion following the resistance it faced at Rio+20, the Summit instead resulted in publication of a Natural Capital Declaration by private-sector representatives working closely with the WBCSD, which is claimed to have "developed based on an extensive consultation process with the financial community over the course of 2010 and 2011, including meetings in London, Nagoya, Hong Kong, Munich, Washington D.C. and São Paulo" (United Nations Environment Programme Finance Initiative [UNEPFI] 2012). This and the fifth WCC occurring later that year inspired establishment of a series of World Forums on Natural Capital (WFNCs) held in 2013, 2015, and 2017 in Edinburgh, Scotland. Meanwhile, the Natural Capital Project had published its first collection of results in 2011 (see Kareiva et al. 2011), while in 2014 Costanza and colleagues updated their 1997 assessment of total global ecosystem service value based on refined methodology (Costanza et al. 2014). TNC partnered with JPMorgan Chase to launch the NatureVest initiative in 2014 as well. Building on all of this, in 2016 the Natural Capital Coalition published its Natural Capital Protocol to "harmonize existing best practice and produce a standardized, generally-accepted, global approach" (Gough 2016: 1) to natural capital accounting.

Consequent to all of this, Mooney contends, "Throughout the world ecosystem service concepts are now being incorporated into development and strategic planning. The concept that ecosystem services benefit society has resonated with an extraordinary breadth of constituencies" (Mooney 2011: xv). Daily and colleagues (2011: xvii) add that "thousands of scientists and policy makers around the world are striving to incorporate nature's value into their work. There are hundreds of stories that reveal personal and institutional discoveries surrounding nature's benefits."

A TRANSNATIONAL CONSERVATION CLASS?

In the development and dissemination of this new neoliberal approach to conservation-as-development (West 2006), the previous convergence of forces in the formation of neoliberal environmentalism has become even more pronounced as novel alliances and expanded collaborations develop among an increasingly interconnected group of organizations and actors from around the world. Daily's work, for instance, influenced Mark Tercek to develop an environmental program within the prominent investment firm Goldman Sachs, where he served as managing director, resulting in a partnership with the Wildlife Conservation Society to develop a project in Chilean Patagonia. Tercek subsequently left Goldman Sachs in 2008 to become CEO and president of TNC, whose chief scientist at the time, Peter Kareiva, had two years prior initiated the Natural Capital Project with Daily and WWF (see Mooney 2011). Daily subsequently became a member of TNC's board of directors too (see Tercek and Adams 2013). In 2019, Tercek resigned from TNC and was replaced as interim CEO by Sally Jewel, formerly secretary of the interior under Obama and a key founding member of the Coalition for Private Investment in Conservation initiative spearheaded by IUCN during the 2016 WCC, as related in the introduction. Jewel was subsequently replaced the next year by Jennifer Morris, former chief operating officer then president of CI, where she led that organization's Center for Environmental Leadership and Business. Lynn Scarlett, mentioned in the introduction, also subsequently moved on from CI to become TNC's chief external affairs officer.

Meanwhile, Steiner had served as executive director of IUCN from 2001 to 2006, during which time the organization's partnership with WBCSD and its business agenda began, before moving on to become UNEP executive director from 2006 to 2016, when he spearheaded both the TEEB and Green Economy initiatives and continued to participate actively in IUCN (Fletcher 2014b). After a brief stint at Oxford University, Steiner then became administrator of UNDP from where he also leads the United Nations Sustainable Development Group. Directly leading UNEP's TEEB initiative, meanwhile, was Pavan Sukhdev, previously a global manager of Deutche Bank. Joshua Bishop also participated in the TEEB initiative while serving as IUCN chief economist and leading the campaign for business engagement within that organization (see MacDonald 2010a; TEEB 2010) before moving on to WWF to serve as national manager of the organization's Australian Markets, Sustainability and Business Partnerships. WWF has also partnered with Credit Suisse and McKinsey business consultants to produce a series of reports (Credit Suisse et al. 2014; Credit Suisse and McKinsey 2016), endorsed by IUCN, to "establish conservation finance in mainstream investment markets" (Credit Suisse and McKinsey 2016: 5). IUCN's president from 2009 to 2012, Ashok Khosla, served as cochair of UNEP's International Resources Panel (IRP) during this period as well, helping to produce a series of reports on "decoupling" (UNEP 2011a, 2014) that fed into the Green Economy campaign (more on this below). Inger Anderson, meanwhile, left the World Bank to become IUCN director general from 2015 to 2019 before again moving on to head UNEP.

And this is merely the beginning. Russ Mittermeier was president of CI from its founding in 1989 until 2014, during which time he was also active in IUCN, serving as a vice president of the organization from 2009 to 2012. The series of WFNCs has been organized by Jonathan Hughes, CEO of the Scottish Wildlife Trust and a global councilor of IUCN, in collaboration with IUCN as well as UNEP, the WBCSD, and the TEEB for Business/Natural Capital Coalition. Central to this growing alliance have also been several prominent charitable organizations, particularly the Moore and Rockefeller Foundations, which have supported the reports produced by Credit Suisse and collaborators as well as numerous related initiatives. TNC works closely with BP and Dow Chemical, among others, CI with Chevron and Monsanto, and the IUCN with Royal Dutch Shell as part of its overarching partnership with the WBCSD. The Capitals Coalition brings together most of the organizations in this growing network, including IUCN, CI, TNC, WWF, UNEP, the WBCSD, the World Bank, The Natural Capital Project, Credit Suisse, The Moore Foundation, and World Resource Institute, among many others. This Coalition has also now spawned the previously mentioned spinoff Coalition for Private Investment in Conservation, which includes many of the preceding as well as the Global Environment Facility (GEF), WCS, Rainforest Alliance, Fauna and Flora International, and the Scottish Wildlife Trust.

The latest group of players to join this ever-expanding network comprises big-tech firms emanating from Silicon Valley and elsewhere. These firms are mostly focused on integrating "smart technologies" relying on artificial intelligence (AI) and other digital infrastructure into ongoing conservation efforts. Much of this work is focused on increasing capacity for effective surveillance and monitoring of perceived biodiversity threats but includes efforts to expand market-based initiatives too. Toward this latter end, for instance, Apple Inc. has partnered with Conservation International (CI) and Goldman Sachs to launch a $200 million "Restore Fund" aiming to "remove at least 1 million metric tons of carbon dioxide annually from the atmosphere" (Apple 2021). Similar partnerships have also formed among Google, CI, WWF, Wildlife Conservation Society (WCS) and others (Google 2021), between Intel and WWF (Kaihao 2018), between Microsoft and TNC (Spelhaug 2018), and between Huawei and IUCN (Hauwei 2021).

Through all of these initiatives, then, neoliberal conservation is championed via a growing merger among environmental, intergovernmental, commercial, and financial organizations worldwide. From a broad birds-eye view this can be interpreted, indeed, as a wholesale colonization of the global conservation movement by the forces of a uniquely *transnational* capitalism that gained ascendance within the global economy in the neoliberal era (Robinson 2014). In this way, analysts assert, members of a "transnational capitalist class" have sought to create a "sustainable development historic bloc" in order to manage the capitalist world-system's environmental impacts in the interests of ensuring the system's long-term sustainability (Sklair 2001; Igoe et al. 2010). From this perspective, researchers have describe the rise of a "transnational conservation elite"[8] comprising an interconnected network of the leaders of prominent environmental organizations, international financial institutions, multinational corporations, philanthropic foundations and transnational policy groups—as well as, increasingly, popular media celebrities (Brockington 2009)—its coherence and agenda cemented through participation in periodic meetings during which policies are negotiated and synchronized (MacDonald 2010a; Fletcher 2014b). The preceding discussion strongly supports this conclusion.

CONJURING NATURAL CAPITAL

As previously noted, the central focus of the neoliberal conservation project championed by this ever-expanding transnational network entails promotion of economic valuation in order to properly price natural resources and thereby incentivize their internalization within decision-making processes on the part of both governments and private-sector firms. Foundational to this endeavor is thus the reconceptualization of natural resources as "natural capital." The concept of "natural resources," as numerous critics have pointed out, had already embodied an instrumental approach emphasizing those elements of the biophysical environment that could be productively utilized by humans (Escobar 1995). Yet "natural capital" takes this instrumentalism to an entirely new level. Despite the concept's centrality to the neoliberal conservation vision, however, what exactly "natural capital" denotes remains subject to dispute. The term itself has a long history, having been invoked in different ways by environmental and ecological economists for several decades (Sullivan 2018). In the understanding advanced by ecological economists, the concept referred merely to measurement of "stocks" or "flows" of natural resources. Thus Daly explains that "the word 'capital' in its original non-monetary sense means 'a stock or fund that yields a flow of useful goods or services into the future'" (Daly 2014).

Yet in the concept's uptake and proliferation within neoliberal conservation discourse its meaning has changed significantly to increasingly emphasize the monetary value of natural resources specifically. Natural capital, in this sense, is not merely ecological stocks and flows but the conversion (or potential for conversion) of this into forms of monetary wealth. While some proponents claim this is not the case, many are actually quite explicit about this. Sukhdev, for instance, explains, "Wealth comes in many forms, and its financial measure is called capital" (2012: 198). The Natural Capital Declaration (UNEPFI 2012) elaborates, "The term 'capital' has been borrowed from the financial sector to describe the value of the resources and ability of ecosystems to provide flows of goods and services such as water, medicines and food." Juniper relates, "The ecosystems that naturally renew themselves, and which supply us with the huge range of commercially valuable services and benefits, are sometimes seen as analogous to financial capital, and are increasingly referred to as 'natural capital'" (2013: 268). Bakker makes this equation even more explicit, explaining, "You have financial capital, you have social capital, and now you have natural capital. And so if you're a modern business leader, of course you manage for natural capital just as you would manage your financial capital" (in Fletcher 2014b: 335). Sukhdev, in sum, asserts that the idea of natural capital promotes "a new definition of capital" as "anything that facilitates the production of income" and thus recognizes that "human capital, social capital, and natural capital are just as able to produce income as is financial capital" (2012: 198, 200).

But what, precisely, constitutes the specifically "natural" dimension of this formulation? Some seem to understand natural capital as almost a shorthand for the whole of "nature" itself. Thus UNEP describes, "Natural assets such as forests, lakes, wetlands and river basins are essential components of natural capital at an ecosystem level" (2011b: 8). Yet as this definition makes clear, it is only those natural elements that constitute assets to humans that count in this understanding. And this is only to the extent that they are relatively untransformed by human thought and labor. Helm explains, "Capital is an input into production, which in turn produces a flow of goods and services for the ultimate benefit of humans. What makes it *natural* is that it is not itself produced by humankind" (2015: 2, emphasis in original).

In this framing, of course, a long-standing conceptual distinction between opposing realms of "nature" and "society" is invoked (see Castree 2013; Descola 2013). Countering the contention that everything humans produce can be considered natural capital in some sense, since it all ultimately derives from natural resources at some point, Helm responds, "Treating everything as natural capital gets us nowhere in trying to identify *which* particular assets the next generation should inherit" (2015: 62). Hence, he advises limiting the concept to designate only those products and services that experience relatively little human alteration. In considering a building, for instance, "The tarmac and the bricks are all derived from nature. They use non-renewable natural capital and are sustained by renewable natural capital. The builders need food, and are ultimately natural products themselves. The designs, concepts and know-how are a bit different. While the brain is biological, science and technology may be best thought of as distinct" (Helm 2015: 61).

Hence, while the raw materials, food (and even the laborers?) used to construct the building can be considered natural capital, even if they are subject to some human elaboration, the building itself should be considered a distinct form of *built* or *physical* capital. This is because "once man-made capital has been created, it has a life of its own, whatever it is ultimately made from" (Helm 2015: 62).

Complementing promotion of natural capital is frequently an insistence that the concept is not a recent invention but in fact what (sustainable) development has always been—at least implicitly—concerned with. Thus Sukhdev claims that the idea of natural capital "is not a new thought. It goes right back to Adam Smith's concepts of 'land, labour and capital'" (Sukhdev 2011). Helm asserts, "When welfare states were being established in Europe after the Second World War, natural capital was part of the framework, albeit under a different name" (2015: 60). And the Natural Capital Declaration (UNEPFI 2012) begins by stating, "Twenty years ago the first Earth Summit in Rio de Janeiro focused on the importance of the natural environment and the services it provides (collectively, Earth's 'Natural Capital') in sustaining human existence."

Ecosystem services is the label given to the actual benefits provided by natural capital. As UNEP explains, "the present value of these ecosystem services is a fundamental part of 'natural capital'" (2011b: 8). As opposed to ecosystemic processes writ large, however, ecosystem *services* are, like natural capital, restricted to only those processes that benefit humans in particular. Costanza et al. thus define *ecosystem services* as "the relative contribution of natural capital to human well-being" (2014: 153), and TEEB defines them as "flows of value to human societies as a result of the state and quantity of natural capital" (TEEB 2010: 7). Tallis and Polaski explain, "Until there is some person somewhere benefiting from an ecological process, it is only a process and not an ecosystem service" (2011: 38). The Natural Capital Protocol thus describes the relationship between natural capital and ecosystem services as follows: "*Natural capital* is another term for the *stock* of renewable and non-renewable natural resources on earth (e.g., plants, animals, air, water, soils, minerals) that combine to yield a *flow* of benefits or 'services' to people" (Natural Capital Coalition [NCC] 2016: 12, emphasis in original).

As with natural capital, advocates often frame ecosystem services not as a concept or metaphor recently created by analysts but entities that have always existed in the world, independent of how we understand them, that we are now merely labeling in this way. Frequently this view is supported by claims that previous observers have long (at least implicitly) described ecosystem services as well (Kareiva et al. 2011; Helm 2015). Thus Myers and Reichert claim, "A cognizance of ecosystem services, expressed in terms of their loss, dates back at least to Plato and probably much earlier" (1997: 5).

A GLOBAL VISION

In promoting a neoliberal conservation project centered on these key concepts, TEEB thus envisions "the development of a new economy: one in which the values of natural capital, and the ecosystem services which this capital supplies, are fully reflected in the mainstream of public and private decision-making" (2010: 4). Central to this latter aim is the creation of an "enabling environment" establishing appropriate incentives to motivate private firms to be able to profit from and therefore invest in sustainable resource use. As the Natural Capital Declaration (UNEPFI 2012) advises, "governments must act to create a framework regulating and incentivizing the private sector—including the financial sector—to operate responsibly regarding its sustainable use." This aim has been accompanied by a reconfiguration of the classic three-pillar model of sustainable development as encompassing environmental, social, and economic dimensions into the idea of a "triple-bottom line" in which business accounting will consider not merely economic returns but also environmental and social performance. In this way, sustainable development's three pillars are translated into support for "people, planet, and profit" simultaneously (see Figure 3). In contrast to the previous understanding of sustainable development as pursuing a balance between environmental and development objectives, therefore, this new vision imagines a much more intimate relationship in which development results primarily from the sustainable use of natural resources themselves (see Figure 4). This, Sukhdev claims, constitutes a "three-dimensional capitalism" that encompasses capital "in all its dimensions—physical capital (financial assets and other man-made assets), human capital (education, health, relationships, law and order, communal harmony, etc.) and natural capital (freshwater, forests, biodiversity, etc.)" (Sukhdev 2011).

Within this vision, environmental degradation is understood to result chiefly from a "gross misallocation of capital," as UNEP (e.g., 2009, 2011b) had repeatedly asserted, provoked by the fact that natural resources are not generally appropriately priced within conventional markets sufficient to

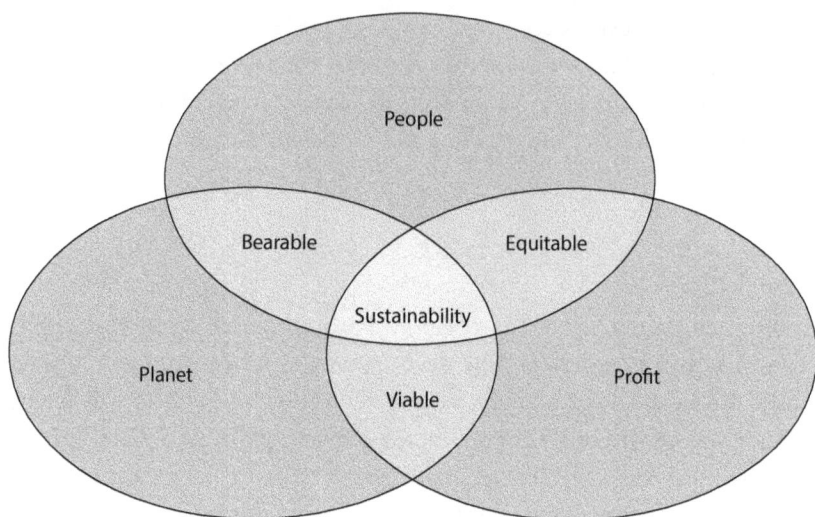

FIGURE 3. The triple bottom line: SOURCE: Grand Rapids Institute for Information Democracy, https://griid.files.wordpress.com/2010/03/sustainablitychart.jpg.

motivate their sustainable use. This situation, proponents commonly claim, can thus be understood as "market failure," and it therefore follows that the solution is to reform markets to "internalize" resources that have formerly been excluded—externalized—such that their price will now reflect their full value and thus allow the forces of supply and demand to optimize efficient—sustainable—allocation.

A variety of rationales are commonly offered to establish the importance of this neoliberal conservation vision. First and foremost is the contention that environmental resources are being degraded and depleted at alarming rates and thus that urgent action is needed. Virtually every tract in this genre begins by citing the litany of environmental abuses humans have wrought upon the planet over the last century in particular. This situation, pundits then commonly assert, demonstrates that previous conservation strategies have not been working and hence that a dramatic reorientation is demanded. Indeed, within this frame it is environmental degradation itself that has made this new perspective so imperative, since the value of ecosystem services is most apparent precisely when they are in the process of disappearing.

A second, closely related rationale starts with the assertion that environmental degradation is exacerbated by the fact that a broad public is not sufficiently motivated by conventional campaigns grounded in aesthetic,

FIGURE 4. The new economics of nature. SOURCE: 123RF.com.

moral, and/or spiritual concerns to consider conservation important. This argument is sometimes supported by the assertion that human nature compels self-interest, grounded in a rational actor perspective in which humans are assumed to be concerned first and foremost to maximize their material utility. From this perspective, it is argued that for conservation to gain more widespread appeal it must speak directly to this self-interest rather than asking people to transcend their base concerns in pursuit of some elusive common good. As Daily and Ellison explain:

> We still think of conservation basically as something to do for moral or aesthetic reasons—not for survival and certainly not for profit. Nevertheless, the record clearly shows that conservation can't succeed by charity alone. It has a fighting chance, however, with well-designed appeals to self-interest. The challenge now is to change the rules of the game so as to produce new incentives for environmental protection, geared to both society's long-term well-being and individuals' self-interest. (2002: 12)

Or as Helm phrases it more bluntly, "Let's start with human nature and what we actually do" (2015: 42). It is in assertions such as this that the particularly neoliberal biopolitics informing the neoliberal conservation project is most readily apparent.

A third rationale claims that to properly value natural resources we must develop a common, universal language and set of measures, and since the majority of relevant stakeholders think primarily in economic terms, this language and set of measures must also be monetary in nature. Thus WRI's Hanson contends, "The more we can value nature in terms everyone understands—that would be economics—the more we can get everyone on board" (in Fletcher 2014a: 335). Myers and Reichert explain that "economic markets play a dominant role in patterns of human behavior, and the expression of value—even if imperfect—in a common currency helps to inform the decision-making process" (1997: 10), while Tallis and Polaski assert that "many decision-makers are conditioned to analyzing policy alternatives in terms of the net benefits measured in monetary terms" (2011: 36).

This rationale is reinforced by decision-makers themselves. As Bakker explains, "The language of biodiversity and ecosystems and service provision—all these words—it's incredibly difficult. Now I used to be a simple businessperson. Now I'm here. But there's a new language which is emerging, which is called "natural capital." For a businessperson that is much easier to understand (in Fletcher 2014b: 335).

A final common rationale concerns the relationship between environment and development aims. Proponents commonly point out that the environmental problems they highlight will likely be dramatically exacerbated in the future due to the combined effects of population growth and poverty alleviation, which will augment consumption by an expanding and increasingly affluent humanity. In relation to this, advocates frequently asserted that substantial economic growth will be needed to deliver development to this expanding population, but that this growth will need to be increasingly resource efficient if it is not to drive global ecosystems to collapse. The only way to accomplish this is by making resource conservation itself the source of growth, necessitating economic valuation and creation of markets for trade in the resources in question. In this vision, moreover, properly valuing natural capital is seen as a key means of addressing poverty itself. This is because the poor tend to be those most directly reliant on the natural resources emphasized in this perspective. Sukhdev articulates a common position when he states that "the poor . . . rely disproportionately on the world's natural and social capital, and so would benefit disproportionately from its valuation and increase" (2012: 231).

The vision thus justified in these ways is commonly framed as "radical," requiring a transformative "revolution" in business thinking and policy making (see Brockington 2012; Fletcher 2014b). Daily and Ellison, for instance, state that realizing it will "require a revolution more sweeping than any humanity has yet experienced" (2002: 232) while Bakker asserts similarly, "We need a revolution, we need radical transformation, and we need to start it now" (in Fletcher 2014b: 338).

This "radical" proposal is, first and foremost, a vision of a world in which individuals work to accumulate various forms of capital that they can invest and trade to maximize the value of their holdings. For policy makers, then, the challenge is to intervene in such a way that individuals' decisions are not directly dictated but rather that the valuation process on which these decisions are made is brought into alignment with the collective good, defined as an economy that grows at a steady rate so as to be able to include more and more people without degrading the natural environment in the process. To do this requires revealing the full value of the different forms of capital among which individuals decide and then designing appropriate mechanisms to bring this value into the spaces within which they interact. The outcomes of this intervention can then be observed, on the basis of which the mechanisms can be recalibrated in increasingly refined ways so as to narrow, over time, the gap between individual motivation and the collective good.

MAKING THE MARKET

Central to this neoliberal biopolitical vision is a very particular understanding of the nature of economic markets. While markets for exchange in goods and services have existed in various forms throughout the world for millennia (Polanyi 1944; Graeber 2011), "The Market" is conceptualized quite specifically within neoliberal discourse. *Classic* liberals, epitomized by Adam Smith, envisioned economic markets as merely a special realm that demanded a degree of autonomy to flourish within societies then nearly wholly dominated by autocratic sovereigns (Foucault 2008). In this way, "the economy" would increasingly be understood as a distinct, separate sphere of human activity with its own rules and logic rather than an integral element of a holistic lifeworld, as livelihood activities had previously been understood in most societies (Polanyi 1944; Foucault 2008). For Smith and other liberals, the state's main role in this newly autonomous economy would be to intervene after the fact, in the market's *effects*, to ensure free and fair transactions (by, for instance, punishing unscrupulous businesspeople).

*Neo*liberals tend to envision the market quite differently. When foundational neoliberal theorists looked out at the world in the immediate post-WWII period, they saw not the entrenched autocratic societies of the mercantilist era but rather new regimes in the process of resurrection following wartime devastation. Rather than merely intervening in the market's effects, therefore, neoliberals asserted that states must intervene from the outset to "make the market possible" (Foucault 2008: 146). Having been intentionally constructed, moreover, these markets then demanded constant state oversight to function effectively. Hence, Foucault insists that neoliberalism, in contrast to classic liberalism, "should not be identified with laissez-faire, but rather with permanent vigilance, activity and intervention" (132).

However, for neoliberals this intervention should occur in a very particular way. As Foucault describes, states should intervene not in actual market "mechanisms" but only in the market's "conditions"—not in the game itself but merely in defining the "rules of the game" (2008: 174). In explaining this distinction, Foucault distinguishes between "regulatory" and "organizing" actions, contending that while neoliberals commonly seek to minimize the former, which require state agents to intervene directly in markets to allocate and distribute resources, they actually promote the latter, which focus on establishing the institutional conditions (the legal and educational systems, the state of technology, etc.) that make the market possible.[9] Hence, Foucault describes neoliberalism as prescribing "a minimum of economic interventionism, and maximum legal interventionism" (167). This intervention, however, should not be planning; Foucault in fact calls it the "opposite of a plan" (172). In other words, the state does not actively direct the market's outcome (this should be left to market forces themselves, which can ostensibly allocate resources much more efficiently than a monolithic state) but merely to create and maintain the proper structures enabling the market to operate smoothly and efficiently.

In this understanding, then, the state need not refrain from engagement in the market but should do so only in very specific ways. It is this emphasis on the proper form of action in relation to the markets that most distinguishes neoliberalism from the classic liberalism with which it is commonly but incorrectly conflated.

Yet for neoliberals, "The Market" is of even greater significance. Rather than merely designating a separate sphere in which a certain mode of behavior—Smith's famous propensity to "truck, barter and exchange"— should be given free reign, neoliberals go further to envision market transactions as the model for social behavior in general (Foucault 2008; Brown 2015; Birch and Siemiatycki 2016). In this way, neoliberalism seeks to extend the type of behavior operating within markets into other realms (e.g., politics and social relations). All of these realms become envisioned as spaces, like the market, in which rational actors compete to maximize their control of scarce resources, and thus governance in all of these areas—including by and within state institutions themselves—should seek to construct appropriate incentive structures to direct actors' behavior in appropriate ways. For neoliberals, therefore, marketization can be understood as what Carrier and colleagues (Carrier and Miller 1998; Carrier and West 2009) term "virtualism," a project that seeks to reshape the world in conformance with its predetermined vision while claiming to merely reflect the reality it seeks to transform. Thus, Lemke (2001: 203) describes neoliberalism as a "political project that endeavours to create a social reality that it suggests already exists." Marketization, from this perspective, is understood as merely realizing the potential already contained within all arenas of human endeavor by virtue of rational actors' ostensibly natural propensity to engage the world as "entrepreneurs of themselves" (Foucault 2008).

Within this vision, as Foucault describes, "the market is no longer a principle of government's self-limitation," as in classical liberalism; "it is a principle turned against" the state itself (2008: 247). As a result, neoliberalism commonly prescribes "marketization" for a wide range of processes, up to and including government administration (Birch and Siemiatycki 2016). Even in arenas where neoliberals view continued state involvement as essential, consequently, it is often a particular, neoliberalized form of governance that they envision.

In the face of such pervasive marketization, as Thrift (2005: 4) observes, it becomes "increasingly difficult to conceive of the world in any terms except those of a calculus of supply and demand." Within neoliberal conservation discourse, therefore, the entire world becomes envisioned as one enormous market (or set of interconnected markets), in terms of which "nature" is consequently understood as a factory or business providing services to "clients"—that is, to the humans who occupy and depend upon this world for survival. Hence, IUCN asserts, "It's time to recognize that nature is the largest company on Earth working for the benefit of 100 percent of humankind—and it's doing it for free" (in Sullivan 2013a: 205). Ecosystem services, from this perspective, "can be seen as the 'dividend' that society receives from natural capital" (TEEB 2010: 7). Conceiving nature as a business,

Strong can thus assert that "in addressing the challenge of achieving global sustainability, we must apply the basic principles of business. This means running 'Earth Incorporated' with a depreciation, amortization and maintenance account" (in Sullivan 2013a: 206). And this in turn entails clearly defining the consumers of these services and distinguishing them from providers. In this way, ecosystem services can be freely bought and sold within capitalist markets in much the same way as more conventional commodities. Consequently, TEEB explains, "successful environmental protection needs to be grounded in sound economics, including explicit recognition, efficient allocation, and fair distribution of the costs and benefits of conservation and sustainable use of natural resources" (2010: 3).

VALUING THE INVISIBLE

This foundational understanding of the world as market shapes neoliberal conservation's central preoccupation with "value." The root cause of environmental degradation, from this world-as-market perspective, is that to date most of nature's "services" have been provided for free, and thus recipients—clients—have not valued these to the same degree as if a use fee were charged. What is needed, therefore, is something to compel consumers to pay these services' full price and hence to value them in proper proportion. After all, within this neoliberal vision it is natural resources' "economic invisibility" that is considered to be "a major cause of their undervaluation, mismanagement and ultimately resulting loss" (UNEP 2011b: 8). As TEEB elaborates, "The invisibility of biodiversity values has often encouraged inefficient use or even destruction of the natural capital that is the foundation of our economies" (2010: 3).

To correct for this oversight, a value must be ascribed to natural resources sufficient to incentivize their sustainable management. The WBCSD thus envisions an economy in which "true values, including externalities such as environmental impact and the benefit of ecosystem services, are built into the marketplace for all competitors. Reward systems recognize sustainable behavior and as a result business can deliver solutions that are both sustainable and competitive. Consumers can choose sustainable products not just because they are sustainable but because they deliver better value" (TEEB 2010: 3).

To render the invisible visible and thus calculable within decision-making processes necessitates appropriate measurement and accounting procedures—hence Turnhout et al.'s (2014) assertion that "measurementality" stands at the heart of neoliberal governance. Sukhdev (e.g., 2012) is fond of quoting the classic management mantra "You can't manage what you can't measure" in support of this position. As Polaski et al. (2011) explain, ecosystem services can be measured in either of two ways—in *biophysical units* or in *monetary values*—and commentators commonly assert that the latter is only one of many ways in which value can be measured. TEEB, for instance, explicitly "acknowledges the plurality of values which people hold for nature, as well as the multitude of techniques available for their assessment' (2010: 3). The Natural Capital Protocol thus includes the potential for wholly qualitative value measurement too. Yet, to be incorporated into decision-making, many go on to assert, measurement in economic terms must be privileged: "To make rational choices among alternative uses of a given natural environment, it is important to know both what ecosystem services are provided by that environment and what those services are worth. The first item lies in the realm of fact; the second, the realm of value" (Goulder and Kennedy 1997: 23). From this perspective, "Valuation is seen not as a panacea, but rather as a tool to help recalibrate the faulty economic compass" dominating conventional decision-making (TEEB 2010: 3). This valuation serves to send the proper "price signals" concerning ecosystem services' full costs.

Hence, various proponents claim that "economic valuation does not replace or undermine the intrinsic value of nature, nor the moral imperative to conserve it. . . . Instead, valuing ecosystem services and natural capital complements these moral concerns, broadening our understanding of the roles nature plays in our lives and the reasons for conserving it. If we can add how nature contributes to human well-being to the arguments for conservation, why wouldn't we?" (Daily et al. 2011: 4). Such assertions clearly reflect, once again, the neoliberal biopolitics underpinning this discourse.

Proponents also commonly justify economic valuation by claiming that this is in fact inevitable, since valuation is already happening regardless of whether we explicitly acknowledge it. TEEB asserts, "Natural resources are economic assets, whether or not they enter the marketplace" (2010: 26). Consequently, "Societies cannot escape the value issue: whenever societies choose among alternative uses of nature, they indicate (at least implicitly) which alternative is deemed to be worth more" (Goulder and Kennedy 1997: 23). Costanza et al. thus contend that "valuation is unavoidable. We already value ecosystems and their services every time we make a decision involving trade-offs concerning them" (2014: 154). Helm, finally, states: "Benefits require valuation, and the units are explicitly or implicitly money. Hence a price has to be put on nature" (2015: 116). After all, "If nature is priceless then there is no obvious way of sorting out which assets matter most, where the efforts of conservationists should be concentrated, and which projects offer the greatest extra benefits" (4)

Economic valuation is considered particularly important if the significance of ecosystem services is to gain widespread policy purchase: "Mainstreaming ecosystem services into everyday decisions requires a systematic method for characterizing their value," claim Daily et al. (2011: 4). Helm explains: "Once nature is viewed as a set of assets it can be valued in economic calculations. Valued assets are worth looking after" (2015: 6). Even more emphatically: "Ecosystem services that lack market prices are often not considered in project evaluations, enabling other interests to determine decisions. Economic valuation of non-marketed ecosystem services makes their values clear in monetary terms, enabling comparison of all costs and benefits of proposed projects" (McKenzie et al. 2011: 341). Economic valuation also allows different concepts and elements to be considered together: "Because results are reported in a single metric (i.e., dollars), managers can compare apples with apples rather than with oranges" (Polaski et al. 2011: 260). What this valuation actually signifies remains a matter of contention. While some caution that "there exists no absolute value of ecosystem services waiting to be discovered and revealed to the world" (Myers and Reichert 1997: 7), others claim, to the contrary, that the aim of valuation is to reveal nature's "true" value. Thus the WBCSD explains, "The aim is to ensure we can discover true value, true costs and thus true profits" (2010: 30).

Ecological economists have developed a variety of methods to assess ecosystem services' value; the most commonly referenced include "direct pricing," "revealed preferences," "benefit transfer," and "contingent valuation."[10] Despite their differences, however, almost all of these eventually boil down to a measure of people's "willingness to pay" for the services themselves: "Nearly every empirical approach assumes that the value of a given natural amenity is revealed by the amount that people would be willing to pay or sacrifice in order to enjoy it. Willingness to pay is thus the measure of satisfaction" (Goulder and Kennedy 2011: 20). Hence, discovering ecosystem services' "true" value is ultimately about understanding how a particular group of people subjectively value these services at a specific point in space and time.

The overarching goal of valuation is to incorporate this into benefit-cost analysis, which, according to Goulder and Kennedy, "offers a rather convenient way of measuring the overall social values of alternative policies. Thus it provides a basis for making difficult policy decisions" (2011: 16). After all, "perhaps the most important basis for supporting a policy that would protect otherwise threatened ecosystem services is evidence that society gains more value from such protections than it gives up. This requires an assessment of the values that human beings place on such services—values that often are not expressed in markets" (31–32).

Helm insists that benefit-cost assessment is necessary because in a world of limited financial resources not all natural capital can—or even should—be preserved and thus hard choices must be made based on the relative total benefit of different outcomes. Consequently, he suggests that assessment should focus on "two classes of renewable natural capital—those that are at risk of no longer delivering their benefits, and those that have the greatest benefits" (Helm 2015: 97).

Benefit-cost analysis can then be incorporated into comprehensive accounting procedures assessed at various scales, from individual firms to particular sectors and beyond, with the aim that "ideally, changes in stocks of natural capital would be evaluated in monetary terms and incorporated into the national accounts" (UNEP 2011b: 5). Such national-level assessments could then be further aggregated to create a comprehensive global assessment of natural capital stocks, with the ultimate goal of following what Helm (2015) calls the "aggregate natural capital rule," whereby the total value of natural capital worldwide is sustained or even increased over time.[11]

CONCLUSION

The preceding discussion has helped to flesh out the particular biopolitical perspective underpinning the neoliberal conservation project. In terms of this perspective, nature can only be protected if its value is sufficiently demonstrated to incentivize its preservation over alternative forms of economic activity entailing more ecological impact within markets wherein limited resources must be allocated among competing potential users and uses so as to maximize utility. To allow preserved resources to successfully outcompete other forms of capital that necessitate their extraction and conversion into mobile commodities requires resources' reconceptualization as "natural capital" so that their equivalency with other forms of capital can be established and assessed.[12]

It is from this perspective that the singular importance of economic valuation to the neoliberal conservation project can be understood. To be able to make informed decisions concerning the proper disposition of different entities requires accurate assessment of their relative value (whether or not this value is considered "true"). Otherwise, authorities cannot—and cannot be expected to—take these entities into account in decision-making. Consequently, decisions concerning what should be made to live and what must be left to die given limited resources cannot accommodate those entities whose value remains uncalculated and hence invisible within a neoliberal governance framework.

But demonstrating a given entity's value is one thing; actually realizing this value such that it can contribute to an individual's or organization's bottom-line and hence influence future decision-making is quite another. And if it is difficult, as we have seen, to agree on what constitutes an accurate, universal measure of value, an even bigger challenge is to establish the markets needed for this value to be introduced into such calculation. It is this particular challenge upon which the next chapter focuses.

_____

THREE

Imagining the Market

The continuing disappearance of Earth's last healthy ecosystems is sadly no longer news. What is news is that saving these ecosystems is not only affordable, but profitable.

TIDJANE THIAM, former CEO, Credit Suisse (2016: 3)

The last chapter outlined the core pillars of the particular biopolitical vision underpinning the neoliberal conservation project. This chapter now explores how the project aims to operationalize this vision within conservation policy and practice via a set of mechanisms intended to bring the value of natural capital and ecosystem services into economic and political decision-making in order to demonstrate the importance of "nature's" sustainable maintenance. A variety of such mechanisms are proposed within the literature, among which four are most commonly highlighted: "direct regulation," "subsidies" (including elimination of "perverse" subsidies), "taxation," and "market-based instruments" (MBIs). While proponents of neoliberal conservation commonly insist that a comprehensive policy must utilize all available tools and include all relevant actors and institutions, from governments to private firms to ordinary citizens, it is clearly the private sector and market mechanisms that most see as the primary policy focus. The overwhelming emphasis of the neoliberal project is therefore to create mechanisms that price natural resources at their full value such that forces of supply and demand will facilitate resources' optimal allocation within private capital markets. As Bakker explains this approach: "A capitalist is somebody who optimizes returns from capital. The mistake we've made in our economic model is that capitalists only optimize returns from financial capital.... What we need to do, is we need two more elements of capital—natural capital and social capital—and tell the capitalists to go and optimize that" (in Fletcher 2014b: 336).

The importance of this approach is justified in a number of ways. As described in chapter 2, from the perspective of neoliberal conservation, environmental degradation is commonly described as primarily a function of "market failure." As Stern phrases it, "Many or most of our problems lie in combinations of market failure and irresponsible and short-term behaviour" (2012: i). If this is the case, then reforming markets must of course be central to solving these problems too.

This claim is frequently reinforced by the assertion that a majority of global economic activity is controlled by private sector firms and hence that their activities must be a principle focus of attention. Sukhdev thus explains that "the corporation today is the most important and pervasive institution in political economy. The private sector delivers nearly 60 percent of GDP worldwide, employs 70 percent of workers, and corporate taxes comprise a significant slice of government revenues" (2012: 10). In addition, "Large businesses control huge amounts of natural resources, often more than governments" (Tercek and Adams 2013: xvi). Indeed, it is precisely large corporations' size that makes them a key focus in this strategy:

> Changing the behavior of thousands of farmers or potentially millions of consumers will be difficult if not impossible. But there may be a better way. The idea, laid out forcefully by Jason Clay of the World Wildlife Fund (WWF), is to work not with either of those large groups but with a much smaller but hugely influential group of companies that sits in between the producers and the consumers. Clay has pointed out that a relatively small number of commodities companies control the majority of the markets for those commodities. If conservationists can influence these companies by demonstrating the effectiveness of conservation on their own bottom lines, the companies can have a major impact on how sustainably commodities are produced. (Tercek and Adams 2013: 94–95)

Consequently, "The bigger the company's footprint, the bigger the opportunity for the company to reduce its impact on the environment by changing its behavior" (Tercek and Adams 2013: 165).

This focus is further reinforced by frequent reference to the fact that as a result of this economic dominance, corporations also control the vast majority of financial resources. Particularly in the post-2008 economy, proponents assert, most states and NGOs lack resources to adequately fund environmental initiatives and thus must appeal to the private sector for finance. As the abstract for a "high-level dialogue" at the 2016 WCC explained: "If the planet is to sustain humanity in a climate-challenged world, we have to invest in nature. Public money will not be sufficient; an order of magnitude more investment will be needed if nature is to continue supporting our agriculture and economies, and that investment will have to come from the private sector."

From the side of the private sector, demand for investment opportunities in sustainability initiatives is asserted to be on the rise as well. Credit Suisse and McKinsey thus claim, "More and more investors . . . seek new opportunities to invest their capital in a way that generates both a market-rate financial return and a nonfinancial impact (i.e., environmental and/or social)" (2016: 8). This dynamic has been reinforced by the lingering effects of the 2008 global economic crisis, as a result of which "the current low-interest environment is likely here to stay, at least in the medium term. Investors—in particular, institutional investors—are searching for a positive yield at this point. They welcome any new opportunities with reasonable risk-return profiles and no or little correlation to traditional equity markets" (12).

Consequently, neoliberal conservationists increasingly assert that engaging private-sector firms is in fact now the single most important strategy in the current quest for sustainability. Participants in a roundtable discussion at the 2016 WCC's Opening Ceremony, for instance, all agreed that increasing sustainability in the private sector was *the* most important focus for the global conservation movement going forward. Even Sally Jewell, then representing the US government as secretary of the interior, emphasized the need to make "a very clear business case and incent[ivize] business to do the right thing, because until we do that we will not have change."

Much of the thrust of the neoliberal conservation agenda has therefore been aimed at making this "business case" that incorporating environmental concerns into economic decision-making make sense within strict accounting terms. As Sukhdev explains, "If a particular change is profitable, and if it does not absorb corporate managerial bandwidth at the cost of other equally profitable changes, then chances are that particular change will indeed happen" (2013: 209–210). Tercek states: "The testable hypothesis is that, once businesses can quantify a broad range of services they depend on from nature, they will see a bottom-line payoff from investing in the natural assets that generate those services. If proven right, a straightforward business calculation will cause them to change their practices to favor nature" (Tercek and Adams 2013: 180).

Neoliberal conservation's market-centric perspective is exemplified by Inflection Point Capital Management (IPCM), a financial firm that describes itself as "the world's first multistrategy asset management boutique offering exclusively sustainability-enhanced investment products across a broad range of asset classes" (in Sullivan 2013a: 203). In offering such "products," IPCM claims, "we aspire to mobilize and leverage the enormous power of the financial markets, and help redirect their investment flows to promote—rather than undermine—the necessary global transition to a more environmentally and socially sustainable economy" (Inflection Point n.d.). The "fundamental logic" informing this strategy is "deceptively simple": IPCM explains that "major multinational companies arguably have greater environmental and social impacts than any other institution in contemporary society." Yet these "corporations' priorities and behaviour are heavily influenced by the expectations and requirements of their major institutional investors." "Change the priorities of the investors," therefore, "and one inevitably changes the priorities—and behaviour—of the companies themselves." Consequently, "If sustainability factors could be systematically—and credibly—injected into investment analysis, major corporations would be forced to improve their performance on environmental, social, and strategic governance (ESG) issues dramatically."

IPCM is the brainchild of Matthew Kiernan, former president of the WBCSD and author of *Investing in a Sustainable World: Why Green Is the New Color of Money on Wall Street* (Kiernan 2009). In his book, published the same year as IPCM's foundation, Kiernan situates his firm's strategy within a broader vision of a "Sustainable Investment Revolution," arguing:

> Any serious attempt to make a systematic impact on global environmental and social problems will absolutely require the fundamental reengineering of the very "DNA" of the capital markets. . . . Those issues must be brought from the periphery of the investment decision-making making process-at best-into its very center. Nothing less comprehensive could possibly suffice. . . . All of the key actors in the investment "food chain" will need to be convinced of the potential materiality of ES [environmental and social] factors to companies' financial performances. (2009: xiv)

MOVING THE MARKET

The key lever for the change considered necessary within this approach entails establishing the "enabling conditions" that allow sustainability to become more profitable than resource depletion. A central question is thus: "How might government create incentives for companies to invest in and protect nature rather than degrade it?" (Tercek and Adams 2013: 166). Natural capital accounting is considered useful here in endeavoring to demonstrate that the aggregate benefits of sustainable resource management are greater than its costs. Hence, "The challenge now is to provide data and tools that companies can use as factors in decision-making alongside more traditional business costs and benefits" (Tercek and Adams 2013: 183). This, advocates hope, will lead to "the breakthrough insight . . . when companies recognize that the services they rely on from nature but heretofore took for granted and got for free, such as clean water and flood protection, will be neither guaranteed nor free in the coming years" (167). In this way, "businesses that sustainably manage land or water resources may increase efficiency, differentiate their brand, reduce costs, and even generate new sources of revenue through markets for ecosystem services" (McKenzie et al. 2011: 342).

To achieve this requires demonstrating that there are both risks in not accounting for natural capital and opportunities in doing so, such that comparison between the two produces a positive benefit-cost ratio sufficient to motivate action. As the Natural Capital Coalition (NCC) explains, "The business case for undertaking a natural capital assessment is based on identifying the risks and opportunities that arise from impacts and/or dependencies on natural capital that might be invisible, overlooked, misunderstood, or under-valued. Once you have identified these and can start to measure and ultimately value them, you can consider how best to integrate them into your business decisions" (NCC 2016: 18).

The aim of this effort is thus to: "Determine the *total value of natural capital* linked to your business activities or *assess net impact* to determine whether a business activity creates net positive or net negative impacts on natural capital" (NCC 2016: 36, emphasis in original). The end goal should be, minimally, to achieve "no net loss" and ideally move beyond this to follow mining giant Rio Tinto's leadership in promoting "net positive impact" as an even more desirable outcome (International Union for the Conservation of Nature [IUCN] 2015; see also Robertson 2000).

All of this is encapsulated in the idea of assessing a business's triple bottom line transcending conventional economic accounting to include measures of environmental and social performance as well and hence the "net value addition of corporations for society" (Sukhdev 2012: 199). Yet the case to consider these latter two dynamics commonly refers back to the first, based in the assertion that not including social and environmental issues may negatively impact one's economic performance too. Consequently, rather than promoting an expansion of business thinking to genuinely adopt environmental and social concerns on their own terms, this perspective often conversely emphasizes merely including these within standard financial considerations. The Natural Capital Protocol thus makes the case for assessing the wider "social impacts" of one's business model by suggesting that not doing so may ultimately threaten future revenue streams, by, for instance, jeopardizing one's "social license to operate" through antagonizing local stakeholders or raising "the risk that some environmental externalities may be 'internalized' through new regulations or environmental markets" (NCC 2016: 33).

This last point is particularly revealing, highlighting a key component of the particular "business case" being made within this discourse. Consistent with one of the main pillars of neoliberal conservation evident since its origins (see Beder 2001), the implication here is that if businesses do not embrace this approach and find ways to effectively self-regulate to address the environmental and social consequences of their practice, they may eventually face even greater threats to profitability in the form of newfound state-imposed restrictions. Hence, self-regulation in the present can proactively address this threat and thereby enhance financial performance down the line.

In addition to documenting and addressing negative social and environmental impacts commonly externalized within conventional business models, natural capital accounting is also, as briefly noted before, intended to capture the value of "positive" externalities. This refers to the ways that one's current business practices may actually generate social and environmental value, rather than merely costs, that should also be included in a comprehensive account. In relation to the social realm, for instance, Sukhdev claims: "Corporations offer skills training that builds earnings potential or 'human capital' for employees. This enables the creation of new relationships and new communities that build 'social capital' among employees, suppliers, and customers. One company, Infosys, creates valuable job skills for hundreds of thousands of young Indians. Another, Natura, builds greater economic security and improved family and social status for the million housewives who are its sales agents in Latin America" (2013: 5). Such positive value generation can then be incorporated into capital accounting to balance out negative costs. In this way a case for net positive impact at the conclusion of such balancing can potentially be made.

Given the importance of private business in this scenario, it is considered imperative that advisers and decision-makers have or acquire strong business skills and savvy, capacities seen as commonly lacking within conventional conservation organizations: "Few government agencies or financial institutions make the effort to link the benefits of natural infrastructure with financing these projects. Changing this situation requires creative financing expertise—expertise too rarely used on environmental projects" (Tercek and Adams 2013: 162–163). Hence the need to recruit managers from the private sector where such expertise is prevalent. In this way, as previously noted, Tercek was recruited from Goldman Sachs to run TNC while former Holcim executive Gerard Bos moved on to head IUCN's Business and Biodiversity program—complementing investment banker Sukhdev's role in directing the TEEB initiative. The inclusion of JPMorgan Chase and Credit Suisse within recent conservation finance development is justified in similar terms.

To realize the overarching vision guiding the neoliberal conservation project, the WBCSD imagines an economy in which "the bases of profit and loss, progress, and value creation are redefined to consider longer term environmental impacts and personal and social well-being. Prices reflect all externalities: costs and benefits. New rules for financing and innovative financial products stimulate widespread entrepreneurship and participation in an inclusive and innovative global economy" (World Business Council for Sustainable Development [WBCSD] 2010: 17).

All of this taken together, Sukhdev asserts, should work to incentivize

a new species of corporation. Corporations, like biological species in a dynamic environment, respond to external stimuli which, in their case, include policies and prices. They adapt and evolve, with the strongest and fittest surviving over time. Changing external conditions such that the input costs of natural and social resources converge with their true value to society would enable a Darwinian process by which corporations most able to adapt in this efficient environment would survive and facilitate the creation of more such businesses. In the long run, therefore, the social benefits and social costs of corporations' activities would be reflected in their accounts as much as possible, thus realigning the corporations' profits with society's gains. (2012: 12–13)

Whether or not realizing this vision requires creating actual markets for sale and purchase of "natural assets" remains contested. Various commentators insist, for instance, that economic valuation does not necessitate either privatization or commodification. TEEB claims that "valuation does not imply that all ecosystem services must necessarily be privatized and traded in the market" (TEEB 2010: 12), while Costanza and colleagues assert that "expressing the value of ecosystem services in monetary units does not mean that they should be treated as private commodities that can be traded in private markets" (2014: 157). Likewise, former Credit Suisse CEO Thiam asserts that the aim of valuation is not to turn nature "into a commodity, but rather into an asset treasured by the mainstream investment market" (2016: 3).

Yet privatization is commonly considered a particularly effective means of governing ecosystem services. Daily and Ellison explain that

> when ownership rights to Nature's goods and services are assigned, the new owners—be they private citizens, communities, corporations, interest groups, or governments—face unshared risk of those rights diminishing in value. Thus, as explained by economist and Nobel laureate Ronald Coase, they are motivated to fight for the asset's protection. In other words, establishing ownership of natural capital and services allows bargaining between those affected by an externality and those causing it. (2002: 13)

Neoliberal conservation markets are typically envisioned in relation to the common neoliberal conception of human beings as rational actors who function as "entrepreneurs of themselves," bent on maximizing their material utility relative to others, and who can therefore be influenced by manipulating the costs versus benefits of alternative courses of action (Foucault 2008; Fletcher 2010a). This can be clearly observed within promotion of payment for environmental services (PES), for instance, which, McAfee and Shapiro (2010: 595) contend, commonly "constructs human behavior as determined by individual, material self-interest." The World Bank states quite explicitly, in fact, "Market-driven PES programs are more likely to be sustainable because they depend on the self-interest of the affected parties rather than on taxes, tariffs, philanthropy, or the whims of donors" (quoted in McAfee and Shapiro 2010: 593).

In paradigmatic neoliberal fashion, however, advocates of course also emphasize the need for government intervention to establish the effective operating conditions for conservation markets: "Governments and individuals should encourage and welcome voluntary environmental initiatives by business. But to scale such initiatives up in a meaningful way, governments will need to enact strong and effective policies" (Tercek and Adams 2013: xvii). This is because "while individuals and companies can value nature, sometimes the only investor capable of making a significant difference will be the government. Only governments can establish laws that allow markets to flourish" (114). Hence, Sukhdev asserts, "Only by creating a regulatory framework that clearly allocates rights to resources can governments avoid the 'tragedy of the commons'" (2013: 228). Or as Henry Paulson (formerly of Goldman Sachs then US treasury secretary under Obama) explains: "Philanthropy is a way to distribute profits. Investing is a way that private sector generates profit. Deliberately investing at a loss isn't a realistic business model. That is why, to realize the potential of private sector investment in nature protection and conservation, governments must put in place policy measures—such as tax breaks, de-risking guarantees, and regulatory requirements—that induce the private sector to invest" (in Deutz et al. 2021: 3).

ACCUMULATION BY CONSERVATION

But there is another important reason why neoliberal conservation so centrally emphasizes creation of markets for trade in the ecosystem services provided by natural capital to realize its vision rather than alternative (i.e., direct) governance mechanisms. This is because establishing the enabling conditions for resource preservation and sustainable use is only one face of the project. The project's overarching aspirations are far grander than this: rather, as asserted in the introduction, it can be understood as an ambitious effort to render the capitalist system as a whole sustainable in the face of increasing skepticism concerning this possibility as well as mounting obstacles to continued accumulation posed by global natural resource depletion and associated pollution buildup including climate change producing greenhouse gas emissions. This is a dynamic that elsewhere Bram Büscher and I have termed "accumulation by conservation" (AbC), that is, the endeavor to make resource conservation itself "an integral component of capital accumulation on a global scale" (Büscher and Fletcher 2015: 274). In other words, AbC aims to initiate a new cycle of accumulation able to transform natural resource limits from an obstacle to a source of accumulation itself (see Büscher and Fletcher 2015). In this way, as previously noted, neoliberal conservation shifts the emphasis of neoliberal environmentalism from seeking merely to render conventional development less ecologically damaging to instead harnessing resource conservation *itself* as the basis of development.

On the one hand, this AbC strategy entails an often quite explicit re-framing of conservation in capitalist terms. Thus, Bakker states baldly of his then newfound involvement in conservation policy making, "I'm from business. That means—and I apologize—I'm a capitalist" (in Fletcher 2014b: 336). Sukhdev (2011) relates similarly, "I am often asked how I reconcile my capitalist background with my commitments to nature and the environment. I give my stock reply 'I don't reconcile them—I am a total capitalist'" Kareiva and colleagues concur, asserting:

> Conservation should seek to support and inform the right kind of development—development by design, done with the importance of nature to thriving economies foremost in mind. And it will utilize the right kinds of technology to enhance the health and well-being of both human and nonhuman natures. Instead of scolding capitalism, conservationists should partner with corporations in a science-based effort to integrate the value of nature's benefits into their operations and cultures. (Kareiva et al. 2011)

The flip side of this is that prominent corporate executives have increasingly voiced the importance of including environmental considerations in their business planning, as the preceding discussion has made readily apparent. Thus, the WBCSD explains of its *Vision 2050*:

> There will be a new agenda for business leaders. Political and business constituencies will shift from thinking of climate change and resource constraints as environmental problems to economic ones related to the sharing of opportunity and costs. A model of growth and progress will be sought that is based on a balanced use of renewable resources and recycling those that are not. This will spur a green race, with countries and business working together as well as competing to get ahead. Business leaders will benefit from this change by thinking about local and global challenges as more than just costs and things to be worried about, and instead using them as an impetus for investments that open up the search for solutions and the realization of opportunities. (WBCSD 2010: ii)

In a further example, the founder of Avoided Deforestation Partners—a self-styled "international network dedicated to advancing US and international climate and energy policies along with business solutions that include robust incentives to protect tropical forests"—explains:

> In recent years, a group of visionary corporate leaders have been quietly teaming up with a growing number of environmental groups to take a hard look at what's left of our planet's natural resources. Together, they agree: we are

past the point where our land and oceans can meet the food, energy and commodity demands of our planet's seven billion inhabitants. More sobering still, they estimate that by 2050, at our current rates of consumption, it will require three planet earths to meet the needs of our expected population of nine billion people. The take-away message for businesses that rely on finite resources such as water and forests is that "sustainability" is no longer a matter of choice, but a matter of economic survival. (in Büscher and Fletcher 2015: 279)

Via AbC, capitalism effectively pursues what Castree (2008) terms a series of "environmental fixes" in quest of new avenues for accumulation, and thereby seeks to overcome what James O'Connor (1988) famously identified as capitalism's "second contradiction" in which scarcity (in this case growing scarcity of opportunities for profiting from natural resources caused by mounting environmental regulation forcing internalization of environmental conditions within the production process) leads to falling rates of profit until new founts of capital can be secured. And this strategy, of course, requires the creation of markets in which natural capital's value can be realized and appropriated as the basis of accumulation.

MARKETIZING CONSERVATION

As the preceding discussion makes clear, the ultimate prize in neoliberal conservation is thus the creation of markets in which natural resources can be bought and sold in ways that both sustain these and generate significant financial return to investors—to make sustainability, as Thiam explains in this chapter's epigraph, "not only affordable, but profitable" (2016: 3). Hence, "The challenge for conservationists is not to abandon the market, which works well in many other respects, but how to tweak such a sophisticated tool to ensure environmental benefits are valued appropriately" (Tercek and Adams 2013: 10–11). After all, "Businesses and communities tend to resist new regulations, seeing them, rightly or wrongly, as burdensome. Far better, then, to engage these businesses and communities as providers of a valuable service to a willing market" (25–26). What is needed, from this perspective, is "truly sustainable market growth that also delivers measurable conservation benefits" (Credit Suisse and McKinsey 2016: 7).

Efforts to achieve this have in fact already been in development throughout the world for several decades (see Table 1 for an overview). UNEP asserts that "tried and tested economic mechanisms and markets exist, which can be

TABLE 1. Environmental market-based instruments (MBIs)

Instrument	Type (from Pirard 2012)	Market	Capital
Sustainable agriculture (certified)	Direct market/ (voluntary price signals)	Extractive	Fixed
Sustainable Forestry (Certified)	Direct market/ (voluntary price signals)	Extractive	Fixed
Non-Timber Forest Products (NTFPs) (certified/fair trade)	Direct market/ (voluntary price signals)	Extractive	Fixed
Bioprospecting (certified/ fair trade)	Direct market/ (voluntary price signals)	Extractive	Fixed
Ecotourism (Certified)	Direct market/ (voluntary price signals)	Nonconsumptive	Fixed
Payment for Environmental Services (PES)	Coasean-type agreements/ regulatory price signals (when state directed)	Nonconsumptive	Fixed
Reduced emissions through avoided deforestation and land degradation (REDD+)	Coasean-type agreements	Nonconsumptive	Fixed
Species banking	Tradeable permits	Nonconsumptive	Fixed
Wetlands banking	Tradeable permits	Nonconsumptive	Fixed
Carbon markets	Tradeable permits	Nonconsumptive	Fluid
Green financial products	Mixed	Mixed	Fluid

Author's own elaboration based on Pirard 2012; Büscher 2013; Deutz et al. 2020.

replicated and scaled up, including from certified timber schemes, certification for rainforest products, payments for ecosystem services, benefit-sharing schemes and community-based partnerships" (2011b: 9). Credit Suisse and McKinsey, likewise, highlight "proven project types and business models," particularly in "sustainable forestry, sustainable agriculture, and ecotourism" (2016: 10). Building on all of the above, the grand aim is to extend natural accounting beyond these existing markets to enhance sustainability in other sectors as well, including oil and gas, mining, and more conventional logging and agriculture industries. In this way, neoliberal conservationists envision a world in which the principles of natural capital accounting collated in the Natural Capital Protocol are eventually applied throughout the global economy (see especially Deutz et al. 2021).

Pirard (2012) distinguishes six main categories of environmental MBIs: (1) *direct markets* (e.g., ecotourism); (2) *tradable permits* (e.g., cap-and-trade systems); (3) *reverse auctions* (in which landowners bid for specific land use rights); (4) *Coasean-type agreements* (in which price, supply, and demand are negotiated through market engagement); (5) *regulatory price signals* (e.g., ecological taxation schemes); and (6) *voluntary price signals* (e.g., fair trade certification). Existing MBIs can be further distinguished between those focused on resource extraction and conversion into commodities, on the one hand, and those focused on "non-consumptive" resource use, on the other—that is, between markets focused on *extraction* and *conservation*, respectively. While these are distinct strategies of accumulation, AbC effectively conjoins them in that each fundamentally relies on the other for both legitimization and sustenance within a neoliberal governance framework (Le Billon 2021).

The essential link between extraction and conservation is of course the concept of *offsetting* (Robertson 2000, 2004; Brockington et al. 2008). Under neoliberalism, in other words, extractive enterprise depends for its justification as an environmentally benign—even potentially beneficial—practice on the fact that its damage can be offset by protection—conservation—elsewhere. By the same token, neoliberal conservation receives the bulk of its funding from resource extraction, which justifies this expense precisely because of its function as an offset for environmental damage. In this way, the two seemingly opposite processes are in fact mutually reinforcing and symbiotic, comprising two sides of the same neoliberal coin—what Le Billon (2021), building on Büscher and Davidov (2013), calls a "conservation-extraction nexus."

Offsetting is commonly framed as only one of a number of different ways to mitigate extractive impacts—most frequently as a last resort when no other option remains. The so-called mitigation hierarchy developed by Rio Tinto in pursuit of its agenda of "net positive impact" and widely employed in neoliberal conservation planning, for instance, frames offsetting as the final strategy for mitigation after potential for all others ("Enhance," "Avoid," "Minimize," "Restore," and "Compensate," in order of descending priority) have been exhausted (see Sullivan 2013b; Business and Biodiversity Offsets Programme [BBOP] 2018) (see Figure 5). Yet, for impacts that cannot be mitigated in any other way, offsetting becomes an essential strategy to pursue the "no net loss" that the extractive industries commonly strive for under neoliberal conservation scenarios.

In terms of the examples outlined earlier, extractive commodity markets include sustainable agriculture and forestry and sale of non-timber rainforest products (NTFPs), while ecotourism and PES are the main examples of

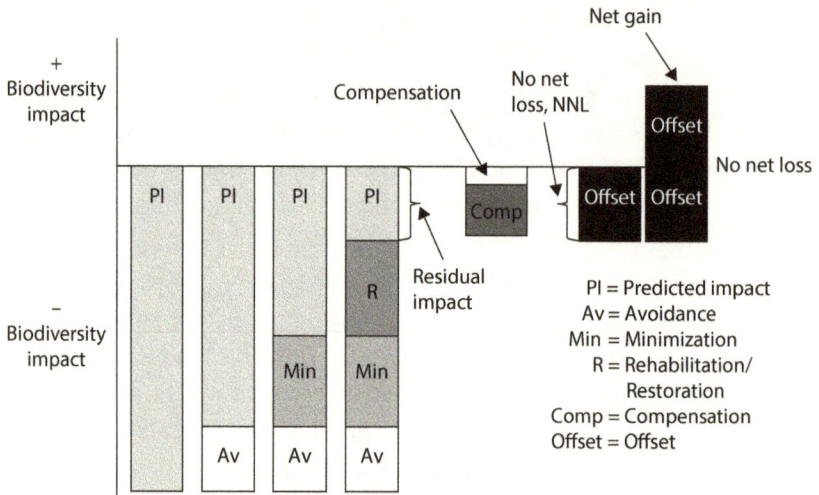

FIGURE 5. The mitigation hierarchy. SOURCE: BBOP (2018), adapted from Rio Tinto and Government of Australia.

markets in resource nonconsumption (i.e., conservation). There is a particular logic to this latter strategy that clearly distinguishes it from the former, namely its aim to generate economic value by leaving natural resources intact rather than transforming them into transportable commodities as extraction most commonly does. This strategy is thus essentially the pursuit of what Harvey (1989) labels "fictitious capitalism" through trade in what Polanyi (1944) calls "fictitious commodities": resources that cannot actually be transformed into commodities in a conventional way (i.e., through material separation from the surrounding environment and physical circulation; see Castree 2003) and are instead treated as if they were commodities through attribution of an abstract exchange value that can circulate globally even while their biophysical basis remains in situ (Büscher 2013). This has indeed been the overarching trend in development of neoliberal conservation markets: a progressive abstraction over time of the value of conservation "products" from the particular places where conservation governance ostensibly occurs in order to reduce the "transaction costs" of this value generation and hence maximize potential for profit. As we have previously described:

> Fortress-style protected areas . . . require substantial investment in fixed capital, as does agriculture, forestry, bioprospecting, cultivation of non-timber forest products and other forms of ostensibly sustainable resource use. Even ecotourism, requiring the movement of consumers to tourism destination,

fixes value to particular locations. PES, on the other hand, begins the process of value abstraction, allowing buyers in one place to connect remotely with services in another. (Büscher and Fletcher 2015: 287)[1]

In PES programs, owners of biodiversity-rich land are paid to keep this land intact rather than converting it to other uses, usually as an offset for destructive development elsewhere (Dempsey and Robertson 2012). PES is thus often tied up with carbon trading, by means of which greenhouse gas emissions can be offset via investment in forest protection among other activities (Fletcher 2012b). PES is commonly considered *the* archetypal conservation market within this vision, frequently pointed to as the main model for the "scaling up" of such activity in the future.[2] This is because PES is able to divorce generation of economic value from actual resource use to a much greater degree than the other markets previously described (even ecotourism requires significant material inputs—food, labor, airplane and ground vehicle fuel, etc.—to operate). There are currently more than 550 PES projects in operation around the world generating annual payments totaling more than thirty-six billion dollars, from nationwide programs like Mexico's and Costa Rica's (see chapter 4) to smaller-scale initiatives functioning at regional or community levels (Salzman et al. 2018).

These PES programs are considered the main model, moreover, for the REDD+ (Reduced Emissions through avoided Deforestation and forest Degradation) mechanism, an ambitious global effort to link campaigns to halt deforestation, conserve biodiversity and mitigate climate change in one coherent package and one of the conservation MBIs widely considered to have the most future potential. Since its origins in UNFCCC negotiations more than a decade ago, the mechanism has been enthusiastically promoted by most organizations central to neoliberal conservation who have helped to initiate more than 500 REDD+ pilot projects worldwide (International Institute for Environment and Development [IIED] 2015; Sunderlin et al. 2015). While a minority of these receive some payment through the voluntary carbon market (VCM), the majority are funded by multilateral and bilateral donors including the World Bank, the UN REDD initiative, and the Norwegian government. Most of this donor funding is intended for "REDD+ Readiness": to develop the governing capacity necessary to manage REDD+ funding properly, including implementing "cobenefit" arrangements and "social safeguards" for local stakeholders. At some point, this seed money is intended to be replaced by payments linked directly to the conservation outcomes pursued with financing secured through offset trading on a reinvigorated carbon market. In this vision, then, REDD+ is conceptualized as a quintessential MBI in its aim to incentivize forest conservation by correcting "market failure" in sustainable forest management through ascribing monetary values to standing forest that would cover the opportunity costs of alternative land use and so make conservation more profitable than destruction.

Yet within PES and its REDD+ offshoot "value is still fixed to the particular resources ostensibly providing these services" to be traded (Büscher and Fletcher 2015: 287). Hence, they require direct investment in concrete material space in order to develop the physical infrastructure needed to realize their particular "products." They are therefore limited in their capacity to generate significant liquid capital that can be grown directly through investment within financial markets. Consequently, neoliberal conservation seeks to move from concrete markets in goods and services to engagement in global financial markets—what Büscher (2013) calls the pursuit of "liquid nature" (see also Sullivan 2013a). This entails abstracting value from investment in specific projects so that it can become fungible and hence convertible across a greater range of instruments.

At present, however, very little such investment actually exists (Credit Suisse and McKinsey 2016; Dempsey 2016; Dempsey and Suarez 2016), and commentators identify a number of significant obstacles to its future expansion. These include: low reward-to-risk ratios and high transaction costs; the relatively small size of most natural resource preservation projects; and a lack of examples of successful "scalable" projects that can serve as models for new ones. All of these obstacles, then, are highlighted as challenges to now be addressed in the effort to develop a new "asset class" of environmental financial products. The aim is then to combine different income streams into a composite instrument, since "few conservation projects today are big enough to be structured as marketable standalone investment products. Thus, aggregating distinct but complementary projects with potentially different structures is required. These aggregators need to be able to bundle a diverse set of cash flows . . . and mold them into a single investment product. (Credit Suisse and McKinsey 2016: 13)

Such developments have spurred the rise of financial investment firms specifically devoted to consolidating and rendering interchangeable environmental "investment products across a broad range of asset classes," as IPCM describes its mission (in Sullivan 2013a: 203). Likewise, EKO Asset

Management Partners declares itself in the business of "discovering and monetizing unrealized or unrecognized environmental assets" for exchange within and across multiple "environmental markets," including those for carbon, water, and biodiversity (203).

Markets are also being developed in such novelties as "weather risk management," extending "beyond carbon trading to include a whole new spectrum of novel financial instruments designed to price and manage the risks associated with extreme weather events, natural catastrophes and unexpected temperature fluctuations" (Cooper 2010: 170). These novel markets include "catastrophe bonds, securities that manage the risks of improbable but catastrophic natural events, and environmental derivatives, financial instruments that respond to unpredictable fluctuation in the weather" (175).

A further set of financial instruments gaining increasing attention are "green bonds." Bonds can be considered "green" in two main ways: "either the proceeds of the bond are (supposed to) be ring-fenced for environmentally beneficial projects—called 'use of proceeds' bonds; and/or the issuers themselves badge them as 'green' with an accompanying narrative—called 'self-labelled' bonds" (Bracking 2016: 76). An additional modality, "project bonds," are "dedicated to a classified green activity, such a solar power" (76). One innovative form of green bonds is called "index-linked," in which returns are connected to environmental performance (see Sullivan 2013a). In a proposed index-linked carbon bond, for instance, "interest payments are linked to the actual greenhouse gas emissions of the issuing country against published targets. An investor in this bond receives an excess return if the issuing country's emissions are above the government's published target" (Z/Yen n.d.)

Once viable financial instruments have been established, the aim is then to roll these out as standardized models that can be replicated and scaled up to achieve a substantial volume of total investment. Proponents commonly assert that there is tremendous potential for such initiatives to develop into an enormously lucrative global market: "Like a business that doesn't implement efficiency measures that would produce financial gains (to say nothing of welfare improvements), it seems that we are collectively walking by piles of cash, choosing not to pick them up" (Sukhdev 2012: 228–229). In terms of hard numbers, Credit Suisse and McKinsey earlier suggested "a total investment potential of USD 200–400 billion in the conservation market between now and 2020" (2016: 10), while hedge fund manager Stanley Fink envisions even more grandly "a vast $18 trillion business opportunity" in rainforest conservation alone (cited in Brockington and Duffy, 2010: 469). All in all, Tercek tells us, "The good news: investing in nature is a great deal. Even if you set aside the benefits to nature and take a steely-eyed look at the bottom line, the opportunities are too good to pass up" (Tercek and Adams 2013: 197).

GREENING GROWTH

At the heart of this campaign to develop neoliberal conservation markets stands the age-old question of whether there are indeed fundamental limits posed by the biophysical environment to sustained economic growth. This was indeed one of the central questions prompting neoliberal conservation's rise, as noted in chapter 2, following the issue's first popular framing in the Club of Rome's famous *Limits to Growth* report published at the dawn of the neoliberal era (Meadows et al. 1972). While this seminal discussion, controversially, identified *population* rather than *economic* growth per se as the main challenge to environmental limits, similar questions have been posed time and again in subsequent years, particularly by ecological Marxists who assert, in various ways, that a demand for continual growth—what Sandler (1994) caricatures as the "GOD" (Grow Or Die) principle—is intrinsic to capitalism itself, precipitating O'Connor's second contradiction and thus rendering the system essentially unsustainable. While critics contend that capitalism as a whole demands incessant growth in this way, this imperative is seen as particularly pressing under neoliberalism, which seeks to minimize forms of wealth redistribution and must hence rely—much more so than Keynesianism, for instance—on economic growth to redress inequality. Foucault thus calls growth neoliberalism's "one true and fundamental social policy," in that "Economic growth and only economic growth should enable all individuals to achieve a level of income that will allow them the individual insurance, access to private property, and individual or familial capitalization with which to absorb risks" (2008: 144). For economic growth to be sustainable in purely financial terms, therefore, it must also be sustainable in social (in terms of redressing the inequality that might otherwise fuel such discontent as to threaten the system's future) as well as environmental dimensions. It is for this reason that economic growth is so central to the specifically neoliberal form of biopolitics shaping the neoliberal conservation project.

In response to the limits to growth discussion, consequently, neoliberal conservationists commonly insist that far from necessitating an end to economic growth, their project demonstrates how economic growth can be reconfigured so that long-term sustainability is actually enhanced rather than compromised—a dynamic now commonly termed "green growth" (see Anderson et al. 2016; Fletcher et al. 2019). A similar insistence has been apparent since the beginning of the sustainable development discussion, of course, as when the Bruntland Report asserted, "Far from requiring the cessation of economic growth, [sustainable development] recognizes that the problems of poverty and underdevelopment cannot be solved unless we have a new era of growth in which developing countries play a large role and reap large benefits" (WCED 1987: 40). Similarly, Helm contends, "Growth is not the problem. It is the sort of unsustainable growth that we have now which is the problem" (2015: 38). Yet, he asserts, "It is perfectly possible to achieve sustainable economic growth" (Helm 2015: vii). Such growth, proponents insist, is imperative for sustainable development to be able to address poverty alongside environmental degradation, for, as Steiner relates, "it is clear in a world of nearly seven billion people, climbing to around nine billion in 40 years' time, that growth is needed to lift people out of poverty and to generate employment for the soon to be two billion people either unemployed or underemployed" (2011: xiii).

Yet how exactly green growth can be achieved is rarely spelled out in significant detail. Helm offers very little guidance on this issue, merely insisting repeatedly on the possibility of sustainable growth without clearly defining what this would look like in practice. The few illustrative examples that he provides include the creation of sovereign wealth funds from the proceeds from nonrenewable resources, as Norway has done, or creating offset markets for the damage caused by economic development, such as already occurs via biodiversity and wetlands banking (see Dunlap and Sullivan 2020). In his recent manifesto promoting the Sustainable Development Goals (SDGs), celebrity economist Jeffrey Sachs (2015) is equally vague on this question. Sukhdev, meanwhile, suggests enigmatically that we must "shift away from growth via size and toward growth via complexity. We must go from an economy based on cutting, burning, and digging to one based on conservation, resource efficiency, and most important, innovation" (2012: 232). Yet what this actually means or how it might occur is not further explained.

There is one dimension of the green growth agenda that has been further elaborated, however. Assertions of the possibility of sustainable growth frequently invoke the need for "decoupling" (see Fletcher and Rammelt 2017). UNEP offers the most elaborate discussion of this concept in a series of reports prepared by its IRP as a key component of the Green Economy campaign, but the concept has also been much more widely endorsed within the global SDG agenda.[3] UNEP's first report, released in 2011, explains that "decoupling means using less [*sic*] resources per unit of economic output and reducing the environmental impact of any resources that are used or economic activities that are undertaken" (UNEP 2011a: xv). Steiner elaborates: "Decoupling at its simplest is reducing the amount of resources such as water or fossil fuels used to produce economic growth and delinking economic development from environmental deterioration" (2011: xiii).

The idea of decoupling is grounded in a series of key conceptual distinctions. The first is between "relative" and "absolute" decoupling, the former designating a reduction in "the rate of use of (primary) resources per unit of economic activity" such that "less material, energy, water and land resources" are needed to achieve "the same economic output" (2011a: xxiv). *Absolute* decoupling, by contrast, describes an overall decrease in resource use even as the total economy grows. UNEP likens this scenario to the (in)famous Environmental Kuznets Curve.[4]

The second key distinction is between "resource" (i.e., input) and "impact" (i.e., output) decoupling, where "resource decoupling could be referred to as increasing resource productivity, and impact decoupling as increasing ecoefficiency" (2011a: xxiv). Third, UNEP distinguishes "material" from "immaterial" resources, the former being those "whose value is characterized by the qualities that render it useful for certain applications" (xxi) and the latter those "whose use has no effect on the qualities that make them useful; nor can they easily be given an economic value" (xxi). The main material resources UNEP identifies are energy, materials, water, and land (xxii), while examples of immaterial resources include "the song of a bird inspiring a composer" and "the shine of a star used by a captain to find his way" (xxi). The key difference between these categories, of course, is that unlike material resources "using immaterial resources does not change the qualities that make them useful, or reduce the range of available applications" (xxi).

Finally, UNEP differentiates "economic" and "physical" growth, the former designating an increase in GDP or similar financial measures of economic value, the latter representing the material inputs and stockpiles providing the basis for this value.

Grounded in these distinctions, the main objective of decoupling is to promote "nonmaterial economic growth" that minimizes physical growth based in material resources, thereby increasing the gap between economic value, resource use, and environmental impact—a dynamic that UNEP terms "dematerialization." In this way, the organization claims, "it becomes conceptually possible for economic growth (defined now as money flow, or value) to be decoupled from physical growth of the economy (resource consumption) and associated environmental pressures" (UNEP 2011a: 34). This, UNEP, quoting Ekins (2000), goes on to assert, raises *the theoretical possibility of GNP growing indefinitely in a finite material world*" (in UNEP 2011b: 34, emphasis in original). Achieving this necessitates a "paradigm shift" in which "prosperity ceases to mean increasing consumption of material goods" and instead becomes geared toward the desire to "participate meaningfully and creatively in the life of society" (UNEP 2011a: 35). In the WBCSD's *Vision 2050*, likewise, "concepts of *success* and *progress* begin to be redefined in ways that create new markets" (2010: 18, emphasis in original). After all, as Gallopin (2003) explains, "While demographic growth and material economic growth must eventually stabilize, cultural, psychological, and spiritual growth is not constrained by physical limits" (in UNEP 2011a: 34).

It is precisely this possibility of decoupling, in short, that supports the potential for sustainable (green) growth within the neoliberal conservation vision. Peter Hennike, one of the IRP reports' main authors, indeed states quite baldly, "Staying within 'planetary boundaries' is impossible without decoupling" (2014: 1).

In endorsing the possibility of decoupling to facilitate green growth, various proponents point to the vital role of "innovation" in realizing this. The WBCSD insists, "A key basis for achieving success is unremitting innovation" (2010: 30); Sukhdev states that "it is only via substantial and sustained innovation that we will be able to meet the energy demands of a growing and rapidly developing world without pushing our natural resources to the brink" (2012: 233). UNEP asserts: "The key to decoupling in practice will be innovations that make it possible to increase resource productivity, thereby reducing metabolic rates.... Innovation for resource productivity, therefore, may well define the core challenge for sustainable resource management for the coming decades" (2011a: 38).

It is commonly cautioned, however, that this refers not merely to technological innovation—the proverbial "technofix"—but to other forms as well: "Innovation means more than developing new gizmos and gadgets"

(Sukhdev 2012: 233). Thus, UNEP (2011a) highlights both "institutional innovation" and "relational innovation" as well, while WBCSD explains: "Technological innovation will only be a piece of the puzzle. Social innovation, for example in the form of new business models, new customer behavior and action, and new ways of interacting between providers and users, will also be crucial to developing attractive, effective and accessible solutions" (2010: 52).

Beyond such abstract calls for innovation, however, proponents remain short on specifics concerning the economic strategies and instruments via which decoupling can be achieved. In a rare yet brief exception, the Sustainable Development Solutions Network (SDSN) led by Jeffrey Sachs to help guide the SDG agenda highlights as an example of ostensibly dematerialized value creation the "shift from vinyl albums to online music and from books to e-books" (in Fletcher and Rammelt 2016: 460).

While this is seldom explicitly acknowledged, however, dematerialized value is precisely what the neoliberal conservation markets previously outlined aim to create. The rise of neoliberal conservation can thus be viewed as a direct response to what Sukhdev (2011) calls a "three-dimensional" challenge to the sustainability of industrial capitalism on environmental, social, and economic terms simultaneously. This response asserts, first, that economic growth is necessary to alleviate poverty, since governments lack both capacity and perspective to achieve this through top-down redistribution (Milton Friedman [2008], after all, had famously pronounced as the welfare state's central fallacy the conviction that one could "do good with other people's money"). It then argues that there are no absolute limits to such growth—and hence nothing inherently deficient in capitalism either—as long as environmental inputs are managed efficiently. Decoupling is thus essential to operationalization of the neoliberal biopolitics outlined in previous chapters. And neoliberal conservation is fundamental to pursuit of this decoupling.

Neoliberal conservation can be understood, therefore, as essentially a campaign to make economic growth—and hence capitalism—itself "sustainable" by transforming it into "green growth." Via decoupling, such green growth could, in theory at least, be sustained indefinitely (see Fletcher and Rammelt 2017). It is this peculiar promise of infinite growth through dematerialized value creation as a potential redemption for the global capitalist economy (Büscher and Fletcher 2015) that the neoliberal conservation project most ambitiously aims to realize.

Having explored the rise and foundational vision of the neoliberal conservation project in the preceding two chapters, we are now in a position to better understand BP's curious claim to pursue carbon neutrality introduced in chapter 2. This neoliberal conservation vision, I have argued, forms the condition of possibility for BP's ambitious plan. Most centrally, it is the promise to be able to offset the environmental impacts of resource extraction through investment in conservation (as well as carbon capture and storage) that is essential to realization of this plan. While BP promises to reduce impacts across its various realms of production, fossil fuel extraction remains central to its plan moving forward; hence neutralizing the impacts of this extraction is only conceivable through investment in conservation. Without this potential for offsetting to achieve "no net loss," the plan would be nothing but a pipedream.

Similarly, the plan depends on the promise of *innovation* to develop the processes and technology to progressively minimize the "carbon intensity" of BP's production in other arenas, thereby pursuing "relative" decoupling through dematerialization. Via this combination of offsetting, dematerialization and carbon capture, BP claims, production across its operations can move toward carbon neutrality while continuing to maintain the profitability essential to retaining shareholders. Most essentially, then, BP's is a vision grounded in the promise of decoupling, in which accumulation can continue apace, thus satisfying shareholders' desire for returns, while the ecological impacts of this accumulation can be progressively minimized (thereby achieving relative decoupling) to the point that they disappear altogether and absolute decoupling is attained. Meanwhile, conservation organizations like BP's longstanding collaborator TNC seek to harness plans like this as the basis for the finance needed to expand their own neoliberal conservation programming. In this way, a growing symbiosis is envisioned as the effort to green extractive enterprise finances expanded conservation in the process.

These are the conditions of possibility that allow BP's plan to be understood as a credible potentiality rather than merely the corporate propaganda skeptics consider it—along with a suite of similar claims coming from a growing range of other prominent transnational firms. But what are the actual prospects for the plan's successful realization? It is to this question of neoliberal conservation's performance in past, present and future practice that the next two chapters turn. I begin by exploring how the project has played out thus far in Costa Rica, one of the most long-standing and important testing and development sites for neoliberal conservation ideas and mechanisms.

FOUR

The Neoliberal Ecolaboratory

Oh what irony! Judge for yourself, Costa Ricans. Yes, our environmental history is full of ironies.

ALEXANDER BONILLA, Costa Rican environmentalist
(in Evans 1999: 139)

In 1969, two young biologists, Mario Boza and Alvaro Ugalde, were placed
in charge of Costa Rica's fledgling National Park Service. They immediately
set to work identifying and expropriating representative parcels of forest
across the small country's diverse ecozones to place under state protection.
The first in a new generation of home-grown conservationists, Boza and
Ugalde had been inspired and trained by foreign biologists doing research in
the country who had drawn the two men's attention to both the spectacular
biodiversity and highly endangered status of their patrimonial landscapes.
Recognizing the urgency of their mission in the face of rapidly expanding
agricultural interests, Boza and Ugalde used any creative means at their dis-
posal to lay claim to the land they targeted. As Boza explained, "The idea
was to seize any favorable opportunities or circumstances that came up, even
unexpectedly, to invent a thousand and one tricks to get what we needed"
(in Evans 1999: 76). Similarly, in an interview Ugalde later recalled that "we
went park after park. Whether it started for turtles, or for historic reasons,
or whatever opportunity came, we could say . . . we need a piece as big as
possible for every ecosystem in the country. So if there was an opportunity,
take it. Because we don't have it in the system."

From the outset, however, Boza and Ugalde were divided in their vision
concerning how conservation should function in relation to the overarching
economy. Boza, who had modeled his own vision on the highly visitor-
oriented US National Park System, saw tourism revenue as an important
source of support for Costa Rica's own conservation areas. Hence, right
from the outset he had asserted, "Although from a commercial viewpoint
parks might seem an unnecessary investment, they could become one of the

major sources of revenue for the nation" (in Evans 1999: 216). But Ugalde, who replaced Boza as Park Service director in 1974 with a change in presidential administration, wanted a park system solely dedicated to biodiversity preservation. "I will not resort to tourism as a way to maintain parks," he told reporters in 1982. "Management of the ecosystem in parks in perpetuity is the Park Service's main goal" (in Evans 1999: 224).

TROUBLE IN PARADISE

A similar tension between the forces of conservation and development embodied in the divergent approaches of these two godfathers of Costa Rican conservation has been reflected in the nation's approach to natural resource management ever since. On the one hand, the country has come to occupy an almost mythical place in the global imaginary as a veritable ecotopia, leading Evans (1999) to label it "The Green Republic." Countless representations—from tourism advertisements to magazine articles to visitors' blogs to NGOs' reports—continually propagate this green image throughout the world. Terms such as "paradise," "green," "sustainable," "natural" and "eco" crop up constantly in association with the country (see Map 1).[1]

This formidable reputation is grounded in the disproportionate level of biodiversity the nation contains. Commonly cited figures claim 4–5 percent of the world's total, contained in only 0.035 percent of global land mass, with high rates of endemism (see Honey 2008: 160). This is considered the product of Costa Rica's location at the "transcontinental meeting point" between North and South America (Evans 1999: 3), bringing together the distinctive bounty of both landscapes and making it the "only place in the world that is 'both interoceanic and intercontinental'" (Hall 1984, cited in Evans 1999: 3).

Yet it is Costa Rica's apparent foresight and success in preserving this abundant biodiversity that has earned it such international acclaim. This is based primarily on four interrelated factors, namely the country's: development of an extensive system of national parks and other protected areas; promotion of ecotourism and PES as primary revenue streams for conservation; reliance on renewable sources (chiefly hydroelectric power) for most of its energy needs; and proactive programs to address anthropogenic climate change. The widespread perception of the country as an uncommonly peaceful place within such a historically conflict-ridden region—having famously abolished its formal military in 1948, seen the Nobel Peace Prize

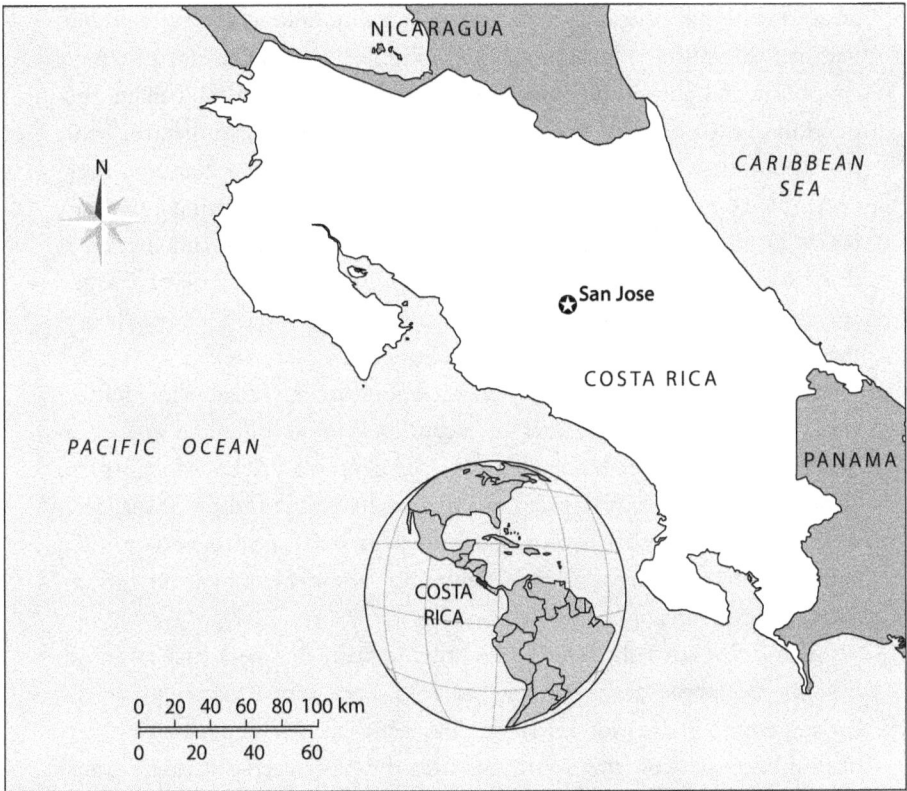

MAP 1. Map of Costa Rica. SOURCE: Nations Online Project, https://www.nationsonline .org/oneworld/map/costa-rica-map.htm.

conferred on former president Oscar Arias Sánchez in 1987, and been active in promoting human rights both domestically and internationally (Brysk 2009)—reinforces this reputation. In short, the US Department of State (2012) asserts, "Costa Rica's record on the environment, human rights, and advocacy for the peaceful settlement of disputes give it a weight in world affairs far beyond its size."

At the same time, however, Costa Rica has also been frequently criticized for actions in direct opposition to all of the above. Thus, Evans (1999: xii) highlights a "grand contradiction" represented by "Costa Rica's development of extraordinary national parks simultaneous to massive deforestation in un- protected areas." Responding to Boza's (1993) early lauding of the country's environmental achievements, in 1994 US biologist Robert Hunter published a scathing critique asking, "Is Costa Rica Truly Conservation-Minded?," and answering his own question by describing "an almost anticonservation trend" within the country (Hunter 1994: 595). Hunter went on to cite a litany of environmental abuses, including extensive forest clearing for banana production in the northeast Sarapiquí region, "dry season burning in the Santa Rosa National Park," and "gold mining in the Corcovado National Park" (595). He concluded by admonishing Costa Rica for "adopting a two-face policy on environmental and conservation matters . . . aided and abetted by those who seek personal advantage while hiding behind a mask of care and concern for nature" (595). Similar charges have been leveled repeatedly over the years (see, e.g., Vandermeer and Perfecto 2005; Isla 2015).

In the face of such critiques, and responding specifically to Hunter's (1994) bitter commentary, Boza and coauthors (1995) countered with an article titled "Costa Rica Is a Laboratory, Not Ecotopia." Acknowledging that "Robert Hunter is right to point out that we haven't found a panacea," they write, "Costa Rica is the world's laboratory for tropical conservation. . . . It is the proving ground for all the schemes that come under the rubric of sustainable development" (1995: 684).

In this chapter, I therefore follow this framing of Costa Rica as an important "ecolaboratory" (see Fletcher et al. 2020) for experimentation in cutting-edge conservation initiatives. In its enthusiastic embrace of a variety of quintessential conservation MBIs over the past several decades, Evans's (1999) green republic can also be considered a green neoliberal one. Isla, indeed, goes so far as to pronounce Costa Rica the world's "first green neoliberal project" (2015: 599). From this perspective, the country provides a useful test case to assess how the neoliberal conservation vision outlined in previous chapters is playing out in practice in one of its most advanced and celebrated testing sites. What such an assessment demonstrates, I will argue, is that the introduction of neoliberal conservation is in fact largely responsible for Costa Rica's contradictory image—as simultaneously environmental protector and destructor—previously described. Under pressure from neoliberalization, over the past several decades biodiversity conservation and other forms of environmental management have progressively shifted from state-centered to market-based approaches. This is consistent with changes in the overarching society, which has likewise undergone intensified neoliberalization over the past three decades under the influence of international forces (Edelman 1999). On the other hand, representatives of the Costa Rican government have long resisted some of the more extreme restructuring measures advocated by IFIs and hence the state retains a strong regulatory presence in a variety of sectors. In the environmental realm, this peculiar mix of market-based and state-led governance has produced a paradoxical situation wherein conventional extractive industry and fortress-style conservation management expand in concert. This situation, I believe, results less from the inept management or cultural idiosyncrasy on which it is often blamed by critics like Hunter than from the increasing reliance on neoliberal policies that lack the capacity to contain industrial expansion and thus provoke a heavy-handed state response to preserve resources threatened by this expansion. In this way, the rollout of neoliberal conservation in Costa Rica exemplifies the project's overarching function as an "anti-regulation machine" undermining its own efforts to minimize the state-centered regulation that it instead paradoxically extends.

THE NEOLIBERAL TURN

Costa Rica's neoliberalization began when the country was subject to widespread structural adjustment following its implication in the 1980s debt crisis. Prior to this time the nation had boasted a strong welfare state that developed incrementally over the previous century (Edelman 1999: 50). By the end of the 1970s, the Costa Rican state had indeed come to exercise a pervasive influence over all sectors of society, employing "one-fifth of the workforce" and controlling "nearly one-quarter of the gross domestic product" (74). As a result of the strong welfare policies implemented by this apparatus, "Costa Rica could boast social indicators far better than those of most Third World countries" (Molina and Palmer 2007: 119).

All of this changed dramatically during the next decade. The cost of the country's previous prosperity had been a dramatic increase in public debt, such that "between 1977 and 1981, Costa Rica's terms of trade fell by one-third and its debt service quadrupled" (Edelman 1999: 74). Such issues, combined with "a second oil shock, a sharp fall in coffee prices, and soaring interest rates" (Molina and Palmer 2007: 145), precipitated an economic collapse in 1980, which forced Costa Rica to default on its international loans the following year (the country was actually the first in Latin America to do so, preceding more notorious Mexico), having registered "one of the highest per capita debts in the world" (Edelman 1999: 74). Over the next decade and a half, the country underwent three successive rounds of structural adjustment under the direction of the World Bank and IMF as conditionality for new loan agreements (Edelman 1999; Borges-Méndez 2008). In addition to mandating substantial cutbacks in state spending as well as privatization of governing institutions in a variety of sectors, these reforms encouraged Costa Rica to relax the strong system of import tariffs erected during the Great Depression to insulate the domestic economy from foreign competition. SAPs also prescribed development of a number of so-called nontraditional exports, including textile production as well as pineapple and ornamental plant cultivation, to enhance international competitiveness, in addition to provision of tax breaks and other incentives (such as relaxation of legal barriers to external land ownership) to encourage foreign direct investment. Price supports for staple crops such as maize, rice, and beans were targeted for reduction or elimination. Such reforms explicitly "sought to redirect Costa Rican development from domestic and Central American markets to new international ones" (Edelman 1999: 79).

Neoliberal policies have of course always been implemented quite differently and to varying degrees within different societies (Brenner et al. 2010a, 2010b), and Costa Rica is no exception. Neoliberalization within the country as elsewhere has always been a complex and somewhat contradictory process. On the one hand, the state has been subject to strong pressure to liberalize policies and institutions from a variety of international actors, including IFIs as well as bilateral actors such as the US government, which through USAID (the United States Agency for International Development) in particular has been a strong champion of liberalization (Wilson 1994; Edelman 1999; Corson 2010; Isla 2015). While Costa Rican authorities for the most part bowed to such pressure in adopting a series of SAPs, at times they also resisted through a variety of foot dragging tactics, implementing some liberal reforms halfheartedly or on a much slower time frame than that demanded by international advisers (Edelman 1999).

This largely passive resistance was at times accompanied by overt popular protest over certain neoliberal reforms. "Shock therapy" introduced by the Fournier regime in accordance with the second SAP, for instance, was met by "139 strikes and stoppages between 1990 and 1993, of which 75 were led by public employees" (Molina and Palmer 2007: 154). Meanwhile, mass protest succeeded in blocking entirely a plan to privatize the national electricity commission along with several other government agencies in 2000.

In other instances, however, Costa Rican officials have actually championed neoliberalization in excess of that demanded by IFI-administered SAPs, using the excuse of international pressure to claim "that the institutional and economic transformation of Costa Rica they sought was really the result of a prior agreement they had no power to question" (Molina and Palmer 2007: 157). Wilson (1994) describes one instance in which members of the social democratic Partido Liberación Nacional (PLN), under the Monge administration in the early 1990s, pushed for denationalization of the banking system, long a highly contested issue within the country, even though this had not been mandated as part of structural adjustment. As one party member admitted,

> Some people within the administration, myself included, tried to use the multilaterals to fight within the PLN, to use the AID, to use the IMF, to use the World Bank. Sometimes we would try to sell them some ideas so that they would not be presented as my ideas, or XX's ideas, but would appear like the World Bank or AID was pushing an idea. Sometimes we were able to go through the back door to get our neoliberal ideas accepted. (in Wilson 1994: 175)

Another high-ranking official claimed, indeed, that "90 percent of the neoliberal policies implemented during the Monge regime would have been done without any international conditionality" (Wilson 1994: 156).

The upshot of all this is that Costa Rica has managed to retain, to varying degrees, many of the strong welfare state institutions previously pervading the country (Edelman 1999). As Edelman therefore argues, "Costa Rican neoliberalism has rarely been as liberal as it claims to be" (1999: 82). For instance, until recently the state maintained a virtual monopoly on such basic services as electricity production, telecommunications, and insurance provision, as well as a strong system of tariffs on foreign imports. Certain commodities, such as dairy production, also remain largely dominated by state-owned cooperatives. This persistent state interventionism, as described further below, also influences many aspects of environmental governance. It is, indeed, this legacy of ambivalent neoliberalization, I will show, that helps account for the frequently contradictory nature of domestic environmental policy and practice—simultaneously protective and destructive, extractivist and conservationist alike.

NEGOTIATING CONSERVATION AND DEVELOPMENT

Consistent with the strongly statist approach to governance in general prior to neoliberal restructuring, environmental management in Costa Rica initially assumed a strongly state-centered form. Throughout the nineteenth and twentieth centuries, Costa Rica's economy was grounded in primary resource extraction and processing for sale on the international market, first centered on coffee production, followed by banana cultivation, then periodically introducing such other problematic commodities as palm oil and cattle into the mix (Edelman 1999). This led to rapid forest clearing, exacerbated by introduction of the chainsaw in the 1950s, which allowed the agricultural frontier to expand much more quickly than prior (Cole-Christensen 1997; Evans 1999). All of this was encouraged by a national forestry policy decreeing that title to new land could be claimed only by "improving" (i.e., clearing) it. In the 1970s, deforestation accelerated further due to the growth of the global fast food industry, whose demand for beef compelled increased forest clearing for pastureland (Edelman 1995; Evans 1999). By the end of the 1980s, Costa Rica had thus become the foremost supplier of beef to the North American fast-food market while its deforestation rate was among the highest in the world (Evans 1999).

In the postwar period, however, the alarming pace and impacts of deforestation were increasingly recognized by the biologists, mostly Europeans and North Americans, who had begun to document Costa Rica's impressive biodiversity (Evans 1999; Chornook and Guindon 2008). They and others started to campaign for protection of the remaining rainforest in the face of agricultural expansion, appealing to private landholders as well as the national government. While initially facing "nearly total indifference to the problem of environmental protection" (Boza, in Steinberg 2001: 3), both efforts eventually found sympathetic audiences. Campaigning on the private front resulted in establishment, in 1973, of the famous Monteverde Cloud Forest Reserve, owned by an immigrant community of Quakers from the United States and managed by the Tropical Sciences Center, a research institute based in San José (Vivanco 2006). Meanwhile, political lobbying led to a new Forestry Law in 1969 that established the National Park Service to preserve remaining pockets of biodiversity from the very agricultural expansion that other organs of the Costa Rican state were supporting, through such mechanisms as price supports, import tariffs, and tax incentives, at the same time (Edelman 1999; Evans 1999). This aggressive fortress-style conservation was supported in substantial part (although certainly not entirely) by funding (as well as technical advice) from foreign donors. Indeed, Steinberg relates that "it is difficult to find a major conservation policy initiative of the past thirty-five years . . . that did not receive significant support from overseas" (2001: 12). TNC, for instance, began to support domestic national park management in the 1970s (Cuello et al. 1998), while the MacArthur Foundation provided substantial funding for state conservation efforts as well (Steinberg 2001).

As in most nations around the world, Costa Rica's government, under pressure from numerous international interests, has thus long endeavored to support both development and conservation simultaneously. Hunter, for instance, argued that the environmental abuses he identified were not haphazard but actively supported by state policies, such as "tax breaks and other incentives, including permission to deforest" (1994: 592) granted to the mostly foreign, multinational producers of bananas and other commodities (see also Vandermeer and Perfecto 2005). The consequence has been a long-standing frenetic contest of sorts between the forces of expansion and preservation, each encouraged by its own arm of the government, each striving to claim as much remaining available land as possible before the other could gain hold of it.

Ambivalence of this sort extends back to the 1969 Forestry Law itself. Steinberg relates that while "Costa Rican environmentalists consider this legislation to be a watershed that facilitated the creation of their now-famous park system . . . parks and wildlife were only minor considerations in the Forestry Law. The intent of the legislation was unmistakably conservationist, but it was of the reforestation genre, emphasizing plantations, harvesting techniques, cut permits and incentives for reforestation" (2001: 58–59). Thus, Costa Rica, like most places elsewhere in the tropics, came to be "characterized by a mosaic of large plantation-type agriculture (some of it intensive and some extensive, including pastures) interspersed with medium and small farms and forest fragments" (Perfecto and Vandermeer 2008: 175).

GREEN NEOLIBERALIZATION

As a consequence of SAPs encouraging expansion of agricultural exports to generate foreign exchange, initial neoliberal "roll-back" reforms resulted in a dramatic increase in environmental destruction countrywide, such that by the end of the 1980s forest cover had fallen by more than half its 1950 levels to less than 25 percent of the country's total area (Evans 1999). Exacerbating this problem, at the same time, state cutbacks meant that "the Park Service staff was reduced by a fifth and in real terms the equipment and maintenance budget fell by an estimated 80 percent or more between 1980 and 1990" (Steinberg 2001: 75).

This prompted recognition, by both Costa Rican state agents and their international advisors, of the need for new rollout strategies to combat this devastation consistent with the overarching neoliberal governance model in the process of formation. In the late 1980s, capitalizing on award of the Nobel Peace Prize to then president Arias in 1987, the country began to promote itself as a prime destination for ecotourism, a concept just then gaining international prominence, and quickly rose to become "ecotourism's poster child" (Honey 2008: 160). By 1993, tourism had thus become Costa Rica's largest economic sector, another nontraditional "export" of sorts generating approximately "20 to 22 percent of Costa Rican's foreign exchange earnings and 7 to 8 percent of its GDP" (2008: 163–164). At present, Costa Rica receives more than two million international visitors per year, and at least 60 percent of these claim to be "nature bound" (Honey 2008: 164). Ecolodges both large and small, low-key and luxurious, have arisen throughout the country, the owners of some becoming international consultants instructing others on how to achieve similar results elsewhere.

In 1989, meanwhile, the National Biodiversity Institute (INBio) was established as a semi-autonomous "parastatal" entity responsible for inventorying the country's natural resources (Evans 1999). From the outset, INBio embodied a paradigmatic neoliberal conservation approach, charged, as its mission statement explains, with "conservation of the country's wildland biodiversity through facilitating its use as a resource . . . under the assumption that a developing tropical society will succeed in conserving a major portion of its wildland biodiversity only if this area can generate enough intellectual and economic income to pay for its upkeep and also contribute to the national economy in rough proportion to its area" (cited in Hammond 2013).

A key component of this strategy was bioprospecting. In "one of the first and most widely publicized prospecting arrangements" in the world (Hayden 2003: 50), INBio signed an agreement in 1991 with the US-based pharmaceutical company Merck, Sharpe, and Dohme "for the two to jointly exploit Costa Rica's biodiversity to seek new drugs" in exchange for a payment of roughly $1 million per year (Hammond 2013). As Hammond (2013) describes, "Businesses and a number of large environmental organizations praised the deal, characterizing efforts to commercialize biodiversity and derive royalty income from patented products as the wave of the future in biodiversity conservation."

During this same period, liberalized foreign ownership regulation led to a wave of land grabbing by external actors, such that by the early 1990s approximately 80 percent of the country's beachfront property lay in foreign hands (Honey 2008: 164). This spurred development of an extensive network of private nature reserves, owned both by NGOs and discrete individuals, which began to take an active role in the country's conservation (Langholz 2003; Kull et al. 2007; Horton 2009). Although rigorous documentation is scarce, Langholz (2003) estimates that such reserves have come to number at least one thousand. Many of these new landowners invested in (eco)tourism development too.

In the midst of this reform, in 1986 a Ministry of Natural Resources, Energy, and Mines (MIRENEM) was proposed (and formally established in 1990), thus consolidating within one institution the long-standing tension represented by simultaneous state support of resource extraction and conservation. (One former minister described his experience of being treated as the enemy at whichever meetings—energy or environment—he attended.) In 1994, the centralized National Park Service was replaced by a decentralized National System of Protected Areas (SINAC), which organized the country into eleven dispersed "conservation areas" (Heindrichs 1997; Evans 1999) encompassing the numerous national parks and other protected areas previously administered by the NPS (Evans 1999). The new conservation strategy promoted by MIRENEM (subsequently renamed MINAE; the Ministry of Environment and Energy) under the SINAC system to replace the state-centered management dominant in the previous era embodied this same tension, dividing each conservation area into three distinct land-use categories: "*Core areas* subject to absolute protection"; "*Buffer zones*, or multiple use areas"; and "*Intensive extraction zones*" (Brandon 2004: 301).

Key to this green neoliberal restructuring has been intervention and funding by a range of international institutions and actors. By the mid-1990s, as Boza and colleagues described at the time, "dozens of governments, international nongovernmental organizations, and aid agencies have projects here" (1995: 684). Decreased state funding as a component of structural adjustment led to a "governance gap" of sorts increasingly filled by NGOs, both domestic and international, grown fat on funding from IFIs and private donors as an ostensibly more efficient and flexible alternative to unwieldy state institutions (Levine 2002). These NGOs became increasingly influential in conservation efforts in the face of the roll-back of the national government. TNC increased its long-standing support of protected-area maintenance while CI, having split from TNC in 1987, followed suit in the 1990s, focusing mainly on community development in protected area buffer zones in support of integrated-conservation-and-development projects (ICDPs) through a newfound partnership with McDonald's (Miller 2003). Other prominent international NGOs, including WWF and National Resources Defense Council as well as others less well known outside the country, have also been influential. This allowed these organizations to implement largely autonomous conservation policies espousing a variety of MBIs, including several of the first "debt-for-nature swaps" negotiated with the Costa Rican state (Edelman 1999; Isla 2015). This quickly developed into a de facto division of labor of sorts between outside interests and the Costa Rican government, with the state providing predominantly command-and-control style protection within its national parks and international NGOs taking responsibility for most of the community-based development work to support this protection in surrounding areas.

The World Bank has been a particularly strong influence in Costa Rica's neoliberal restructuring, expanding from its role in overseeing structural adjustment generally to prescribing reform in the realm of environmental governance specifically, in line with its own green reorientation during the same period (Goldman 2005). Another key player in this process was USAID (Isla 2015), which in 1991 provided a $7.5 million grant to create an incentive structure to address deforestation in the particularly impacted Sarapiquí province in the northeast of the country (Borges-Méndéz 2008). Out of this initiative grew the NGO FUNDECOR (Fundación para el Desarrollo de la Cordillera Volcánica Central) to manage the program, titled Forest Resources for a Stable Environment (FORESTA), which became the pilot project for an innovative PES program.

GOVERNING PES

Of all the conservation MBIs Costa Rica has implemented over the years, its PES program is probably the best known and most widely discussed. Daniels and colleagues indeed, claim that it "pioneered the nation-wide PES scheme in the developing world" (2010, 2116) and hence frequently serves as a model for other programs elsewhere as well as an exemplar of the mechanism's potential more generally (see, e.g., Pagiola 2008; Blackman and

Woodward 2010). Titled Pago por Servicios Ambimentales (PSA), Costa Rica's program was officially established in 1997 by a renovated forestry law (Ley Forestal No. 7575) enacted the previous year to replace outdated 1969 legislation. PSA recognizes four distinct ecosystem services that forests are seen to provide carbon-sequestration, clean water, biodiversity conservation, and scenic beauty. The program functions by providing direct payments to the owners of forest parcels for the services their land provides. The program has proven quite popular over its lifetime, such that by 2008 a total of 668,369 hectares had been officially enrolled (Daniels et al. 2010: 2118), and administrators continue to receive at least five times the number of applications that they are able to fund (Sierra and Russman 2006).

In line with PES development generally, at its inception PSA was explicitly designed as a quintessentially neoliberal MBI (see Heindrichs 1997; Pagiola 2002, 2008; Sierra and Russman 2006). Both the program and law that founded it were in fact instituted as part of the conditionality attendant to a third SAP, to which receipt of the nation's third major World Bank loan was attached (Daniels et al. 2010). In forest management, the 1996 law proclaimed that "the current promotional (subsidy-based) system must be replaced by new, creative mechanisms to revive the forestry sector" (quoted in Heindrichs 1997: 28). These previous forest subsidies, established by the 1969 law but not implemented until 1979, took a number of forms, the most common being a reduction in net worth taxation for reforestation efforts (Heindrichs 1997: 28; see also Brockett and Gottfried 2002). Under the 1996 law (which also turned MIRENEM into MINAE and reinforced SINAC), program administration was assigned to the Fondo Nacional de Financiamiento Forestal (National Forestry Financing Fund, or FONAFIFO), another "parastatal" agency that had existed since 1990 to manage aspects of the preexisting forest policy (based largely in the provision of subsidies for reforestation efforts noted above).

PSA payments are intended to cover the opportunity costs of refraining from timber extraction or other alternate land uses. Amounts depend on the specific aspect of the program in which a given parcel is enrolled. Initially, PSA financed three different forms of forest management: conservation of standing forests, reforestation, and sustainable forestry. As Sánchez-Azofeifa and colleagues describe each of these,

> Forest conservation contracts required land owners to protect existing (primary or secondary) forest for 5 years, with no land-cover change allowed.

Reforestation contracts bound owners to plant trees on agricultural or other abandoned land and to maintain that plantation for 15 years. Sustainable forest management contracts (eliminated briefly in 2000) compensated landowners who prepared a "sustainable logging plan" to conduct low-intensity logging while keeping forest services intact. Just as in the reforestation contracts, obligations for sustainable forest management contracts were for 15 years, although payments arrived during the first 5 years. (2007: 1167)

Due to the difficulty of defining and enforcing "sustainable" forestry practices (such as depicted in Figure 6), this last strategy has been the most controversial, briefly discontinued then reintroduced with more stringent requirements for regulation and monitoring. Two additional mechanisms— natural forest regeneration and agroforestry—were subsequently added too (agroforestry in 2003 and natural regeneration in 2005), although these remain a small percentage of the overall program (Daniels et al. 2010). Compensation for each strategy ranges from approximately $64/hectare paid over five years for preservation to $816/hectare paid in decreasing installments over several years for reforestation, yielding average annual returns of between $22 and $42 per hectare per year before maintenance costs (Sánchez-Azofeifa et al. 2007; Daniels et al. 2010).

The neoliberal vision informing PSA development is clearly illustrated by a comprehensive assessment of the program by the German Agency for Technical Cooperation (Deutsche Gesellschaft für Technische Zusammenarbeit GmbH [GTZ]) on behalf of the Costa Rican government soon after its introduction (Heindrichs 1997). This document of course presents a particular vision not necessarily shared by all program planners (as discussed further below). It does, however, represent something of an ideal model for implementation promoted by influential members of the international community involved in PSA design.

First and foremost, the GTZ report states, PSA was intended to promote direct transfers from consumers to producers of environmental services, based on the market-oriented "user pays" principle endorsed at the 1992 Rio Summit. In so doing, the program sought to explicitly "attach noticeably greater monetary value to these environmental services, which have hitherto been largely ignored" (Heindrichs 1997: 33) and to harness market forces to determine payment amounts by "making payments for services at market rates" instead of providing price supports via subsidies (23). In sum, PSA was designed to encourage Costa Rican forest policy to move "away from deficit-plagued, subsidized operations that are only able to survive with the aid of

FIGURE 6. Teak plantation enrolled in Costa Rica's PSA program. SOURCE: Robert Fletcher.

state 'alms' and toward a form of profitable, competitive land use based on sound business principles" (23).

PSA was also explicitly designed to shift the locus of resource control and financing from the state toward nonstate actors—particularly the "private forestry sector"—in order to "put into practice ideas such as administrative decentralization" and "mixed public and private financing" (Heindrichs 1997: 11). The structure of FONAFIFO reflects this neoliberal emphasis. In a self-conscious strategy to achieve "maximum decentralization" (43), FONAFIFO receives its funding directly from the payments it brokers and is largely autonomous in its design and administration of PSA funding. In addition, the organization was established as a "parastatal" institution, partly under the auspices of MINAE but with two of its five managing directors drawn from the private sector (Heindrichs 1997). Finally, the organization is funded through internalizing 5 percent of the funds it generates for service payment to provide managers with "a vital interest in identifying and developing new sources of funding" (43).

Neoliberalization within the PSA program is most clearly exemplified, perhaps, by the example of FUNDECOR, the domestic NGO charged with administering it in the Sarapiquí province. Having been originally created jointly by the Costa Rican state and USAID in 1991 to manage the FORESTA grant previously mentioned, the organization subsequently expanded its operations by capitalizing on its cut of the environmental services it sold, its own financial investments, and further grants received from various multilateral agencies. When the 1996 Forestry Law officially recognized PSA, FUNDECOR was incorporated into this system as the liaison between FONAFIFO and landholders in Sarapiquí. This further solidified its financial base, along with an expansion of the original USAID grant through "market capitalization of its financial assets and other fund-raising" (Borges-Méndez 2008: 373).

In addition to its status as a largely independent NGO ostensibly more responsive to local realities than the unwieldy central government, FUNDECOR's neoliberal orientation is illustrated in its approach to working with landowners. Defying the conventional wisdom within policy circles at the time, FUNDECOR largely dispensed with attempts to build community among its target stakeholders and instead sought to negotiate with private landholders on an individual basis (Borges-Méndez 2008). The organization's main strategy has been from the outset self-consciously market-based. As Borges-Méndez describes, "The international sale of carbon offsets . . . have been at the heart of FUNDECOR's anti-deforestation activity" (373). FUNDECOR has recently increased promotion of direct transfer of payments between private Costa Rican businesses that benefit from environmental services (e.g., clean water for beer brewing) and forest owners providing these services as well. The organization's motivational strategy is also self-consciously neoliberal, explicitly intended to provide sufficient incentives for landholders to choose to preserve their forests in situ (Borges-Méndez 2008).

PSA IN PRACTICE

Despite the neoliberal vision explicitly informing its design, however, PSA's actual execution thus far has deviated substantially from this framing. As with Costa Rica's ambivalent neoliberalization more generally, this situation results in part from the particular micropolitics surrounding the program's formation. Brockett and Gottfried (2002: 21) relate that PSA's actual design was the outcome of a compromise between two competing factions within the Costa Rican government, broadly glossed as a "market-oriented coalition" and a more state-centered "interventionist reform coalition." The authors thus characterize PSA as a "hybrid forestry regime" combining "market-oriented and interventionist approaches" (2002: 21, 7). In addition, as several administrators emphasized in interviews, many PSA personnel charged with implementing the program on the ground care little about the particular philosophy informing it, seeking merely to find the most cost-effective solutions to combat deforestation and poverty by whatever means available, whether market-based or otherwise, in the midst of myriad competing demands on land both domestic and international.

Even assessed in terms of a hybrid market-state governance model, however, there are important questions concerning the extent to which PSA is in fact grounded in market mechanisms at all. While the program, as noted above, is in general explicitly framed not as a subsidy but rather as providing a payment for services rendered, in reality the self-sustaining market the initiative was expected to stimulate has largely failed to develop. As Sierra and Russman (2006: 133) describe, "PES programs are expected to be an intermediary stage in the formation of true markets for environmental services." In other words, government supports contrary to free market principles were intended to be temporary measures to be replaced over time by self-regulating markets in which the state merely facilitates voluntary exchanges between producers and consumers of ecosystem services.

In order to provide initial support, the 1996 law established a 15 percent consumer fossil fuel tax, one-third of which was intended to go to FONAFIFO to finance service payments (Rojas and Aylward 2003). In reality, however, these funds were rarely delivered by the Ministry of Finance, which collected the tax (Sánchez-Azofeifa et al., 2007). Hence, in 2001 a new law amended this arrangement to provide 3.5 percent of the fuel tax directly to FONAFIFO. Revenue generated by this tax was intended to be quickly superseded by development of an international carbon market allowing FONAFIFO to finance its payments through the sale of emissions reduction credits. Yet by 2007, as Sánchez-Azofeifa et al. reported, "no significant market for carbon abatement has emerged. The only sale has been to Norway, which consisted of $2 million in 1997 for 200 million tons of carbon sequestration" (2007: 1167; see also Daniels et al. 2010).

In addition, PSA was envisioned to stimulate an internal market for "user financing," that is, direct voluntary (i.e., not tax-based) payments by domestic consumers of ecosystem services to the owners of land producing these services (Sánchez-Azofeifa et al. 2007; Blackman and Woodward 2010). One of the main components of this was to be the sale of watershed protection to private hydroelectricity producers. While the vast majority of hydroelectricity generation in the country is controlled by the national government, a small portion (about twenty-four small run-of the-river plants) is privately owned (Blackman and Woodward 2010). Of these, five plants had collectively contributed just under $1 million to FONAFIFO for watershed services as of 2009, and in total, "direct user financing from all sources has funded less than 3% of the area enrolled in the PSA program" (Blackman and Woodward 2010: 1627).

Hence, revenue from the fossil fuel tax (supplemented since 2006 by a 25 percent share of the national water-use tariff imposed on consumers of the public water supply) remains one of the primary sources of PSA revenue (Sánchez-Azofeifa et al. 2007; Blackman and Woodward 2010), averaging $6.4 million/year as of 2003 (Pagiola 2002) and comprising, according to a 2010 assessment, 41 percent of total funding (Blackman and Woodward 2010). While this tax has long been construed as an expression of the "user pays" principle, since it targets one of the main user groups—automobile drivers generating greenhouse gas emissions—of carbon sequestration services (Heindrichs 1997), it still departs from orthodox neoliberal policy in that it functions through direct state intervention in the market to reallocate resources according to a predetermined plan rather than allowing market players to determine appropriate resource distribution. It is, in other words, precisely the sort of intervention the PSA program was explicitly designed to replace. In addition, the tax fails to charge users of the other ecosystem services encompassed by the program, calling into question its conformance to the "user pays" principle.[2]

In addition to the fuel and water taxes, an even greater share (about 45 percent) of total PSA financing is provided by IFIs, including both loans and grants from the World Bank (to be repaid through future fuel tax revenue) and grants from GEF (Blackman and Woodward 2010). These funds were initially provided, in direct recognition of the program's failure to develop self-sustaining sources of financing via carbon markets, to support current service payments as well as to extend contracts to areas of importance for the Mesoamerican Biological Corridor project (see Finley-Brook 2007) and to support capacity building within FONAFIFO itself (Sánchez-Azofeifa et al. 2007). Another 10 percent is financed by a donation from the German Development Bank (Kreditanstalt für Wiederaufbau) to support reforestation in the north of the country (Blackman and Woodward 2010).[3] While these sources of funding were intended to provide temporary support for the current payment system while simultaneously encouraging the future development of self-regulating markets (the World Bank/GEF assistance, for instance, comes under a so-called "Ecomercados" [ecomarkets] program), at present they merely perpetuate the program's current state-centered structure in that they are collected and redistributed by the very government organs the PSA market was intended to circumvent.

In sum, while PSA's state-centered structure is intended to eventually give way to a self-regulated economic market, in the interim it functions "through the creation of quasimarkets . . . based on subsidies provided by conservation agencies, multilateral organizations and governments" (Sierra and Russman 2006: 133). Consequently, in actual implementation PSA thus far has deviated substantially from the market-oriented model promoted by many of its designers both domestic and international, signaling a significant gap between vision and execution in the program's administration in at least four essential aspects: financing, governance, motivation, and outcomes. Thus, while the program is often framed as a quintessential market mechanism, it could equally be described as a subsidy in disguise (Fletcher and Breitling 2012): a means of supporting forest conservation through provision of funds generated primarily through government borrowing and redistribution of tax revenue to forest owners as a form of compensation, not so much for the opportunity costs of alternate land use voluntarily forgone as for the state-mandated prohibition on their right to clear their land. While the program claims to rely substantially on market mechanisms, therefore, in reality its administration employs strategies strikingly similar to the welfare-state institutions neoliberalization has ostensibly sought to dismantle and replace with self-regulating markets.

This dynamic appears less intentional than forced on the program by its inability to achieve intended aims. First, the program's failure to tap and/or create significant markets for trade in ecosystem services, either domestic or international, has compelled its continued reliance on the domestic fuel tax that was initially intended merely to jumpstart the program. Yet even this has been insufficient to fund either the program's current scope or its intended expansion, and hence administrators have had to appeal to international lenders to compensate for their funding shortfall. This is hardly a long-term solution, however, as in the case of the World Bank loans at least, repayments must come from the very tax revenue insufficient to fund the program in the first place, and thus these loans also provide merely a temporary fix aimed, as with the fuel tax, to support the eventual creation of free-standing markets. Such markets remain largely unrealized, however, and thus the government has been increasingly compelled to turn to domestic sources of revenue generated not through markets but through further taxation, as exemplified by the newer water-use tariff for PSA funding mentioned earlier.

CHASING THE MARKET

Notwithstanding this reality, program administrators continue to pursue the elusive markets envisioned since the program's inception—under pressure, as in Mexico's PES program (McAfee and Shapiro 2010), from international advisors from the World Bank and elsewhere to make PSA more conventionally neoliberal (Brockett and Gottfried 2002). For instance, Costa Rican negotiators attended the December 2009 UNFCCC negotiations in Copenhagen with the explicit intention to locate trading partners to bankroll a dramatic expansion of PSA to encompass the many eager applicants the program currently lacks resources to include. As with many other less developed societies, this aim was stymied by the meeting's (as well as subsequent UNFCCC COPs') failure to produce a binding agreement to succeed the Kyoto Protocol. Moreover, Costa Rica's ability to attract international funds for emissions offsets is hampered by its small size and total forest relative to more attention-grabbing nations such as Indonesia and Brazil, as well as the fact that Costa Rica has already achieved relatively substantial forest protection.

In the domestic realm, FONAFIFO continues to actively solicit new participants in PSA's currently marginal user-financed component (Blackman and Woodward 2010). In this effort, two novel sources of domestic fundraising have also been introduced (Soto 2010). The first entails an arrangement with Costa Rica's national bank (Banco Nacional) whereby customers can select an optional "eco" debit card that designates a portion of one's transaction fees for contribution to PSA. In the second, automobile owners may choose to offset their total emissions (rather than only the portion covered by the current fuel tax) by voluntarily selecting a more costly "ecological" version of their annual registration fee (Marchamo Ecológico). The funds generated by both of these mechanisms are matched by GEF grants, doubling PSA's total benefit, under a second "Ecomercados II" program (again encouraged by the World Bank).

Matulis (2013) identifies several additional ways that intensified neoliberalization within PSA has been pursued. First, he contends that the newer water *tariff* is more market-oriented than the longstanding fuel *tax* since the former is designed to be specific to particular watersheds, transferring payments from downstream users to upstream providers, and is therefore more faithful to the "user pays" principle than the latter, which simply charges all domestic carbon emitters willy-nilly. Second, he identifies neoliberalization in the fact that responsibility for creation and implementation of PSA management plans is contracted to private operators rather than state employees. Finally, Matulis observes that the program has recently sought to encourage individual over collective contracts to more accurately assess compliance, a move that "effectively constitutes individualization of participation in the PSA . . . consistent with the ideological preferences of neoliberalism" (2013: 258).

Yet such measures have still largely failed to establish the substantial voluntary markets PSA envisions. To date, consequently, PSA has been facing a contradiction of sorts between ends and means. In order to try to make the program function in its capacity as a neoliberal institution providing incentives to motivate behavior change in support of conservation, the government has been forced to intervene in ways contrary to the neoliberal principles underlying this very aim.

This is certainly not to imply that *all* government intervention is inherently opposed to neoliberalism, as chapter 2 makes clear. Even given a nuanced Foucauldian understanding of the role of the neoliberal state, however, it is clear that many of the forms of government intervention involved in PSA thus far are contrary to neoliberal principles, for they are the very "regulatory" rather than "organizing" actions that, in Foucault's (2008) analysis, neoliberalism seeks to minimize. Despite such violation of specific neoliberal dictates, on the other hand, the program remains faithful to an overarching neoliberal approach to governance in its continued emphasis on motivating proper stakeholder behavior through providing external incentives—even if, as previously described, this effort has itself often failed to perform as intended.

WAITING FOR REDD+

As in much of the rest of the (particularly lower-income) world, stakeholders throughout Costa Rica are placing much of their hope to further capitalize on conservation in the future of the REDD+ mechanism. Costa Rica was, in fact, one of the original architects of this initiative, having first proposed (with Papua New Guinea) a simpler RED plan focused only on avoiding emissions from deforestation at the 2005 UNFCCC COP-11 in Montreal (Papua New Guinea and Costa Rica 2005). This proposal urged the UNFCCC "to take note of present rates of deforestation within developing nations, acknowledge the resulting carbon emissions, and consequently open dialogue to develop scientific, technical, policy and capacity responses to address such emissions resulting from tropical deforestation" (Papua New Guinea and Costa Rica 2005: 2). It concluded by highlighting "the climatic importance of deforestation and facilitat[ing] meaningful discussion by suggesting some possible approaches. Parties must effectively address the significant emissions resulting from deforestation and the associated implications relative to lasting climatic stability. Time is of the essence" (Papua New Guinea and Costa Rica 2005: 10).

In subsequent meetings this proposal was expanded to include issues of land degradation (the second D) as well as conservation and enhancement of existing forest stocks (the +) and was thus eventually promoted as an expanded REDD+ initiative, endorsed by the UNFCCC in 2007 at COP-13 in Bali and finally adopted as policy at COP-16 in Cancun.

Since that time, Costa Rica, along with many other lower-income nations around the world, has been working to tap this new source of funds for its future climate initiatives. Costa Rica was among a number of countries awarded early seed funding (initially $3.4 million) through the World Bank Forest Carbon Partnership Facility's (FCPF) "REDD Readiness" initiative to develop the rigorous measuring, reporting, and verification (MRV) procedures requisite to program implementation. Daniels et al. (2010: 2124) observe that REDD+ "will undoubtedly include using PES as a mechanism to address deforestation," and this is particularly true for Costa Rica, whose Readiness Plan states quite explicitly that the PSA program "will act as a basis of Costa Rica's REDD+ Strategy" (Government of Costa Rica 2010: 9). Hence, the majority of REDD+ funds, should they materialize in the future, will likely be managed by FONAFIFO, which hopes to use this money to address the perennial excess demand by landowners for inclusion in PSA. And indeed, the FCPF recently committed a further $64 to purchase future emissions offsets once the Costa Rica's National REDD+ Strategy is approved, which would build on the World Bank's previous support of PSA via the Ecomercados I and II programs (Ramírez Cover 2017). Meanwhile, FUNDECOR has also sought to access REDD+ funds for its PSA projects in Sarapiquí through an agreement with another NGO called

Pax Natura to broker avoided deforestation credits on the voluntary carbon offset market (see Bumpus and Liverman 2008).[4]

As Phelps and colleagues (2010) observe, the emphasis on national-level accounting in most REDD+ discussions may have important ramifications for the future of environmental governance generally, possibly functioning to reverse the dominant neoliberal trend toward decentralization, noted above, increasingly promoted over the past several decades by recentralizing forest governance in the hands of the state institutions responsible for MRV implementation. This, indeed, seems likely to occur in Costa Rica, where, as noted above, REDD+ policy is intended to be directed primarily by the national government via FONAFIFO. Still, most authorities continue to envision REDD+ as an intensification of neoliberal policies. As the Costa Rican REDD Readiness Plan states, while some stakeholders, including indigenous groups and civil society representatives, demand that REDD policy "would not exclusively target global carbon markets for the reward of avoided deforestation and enhancement in forest carbon stocks," the majority of stakeholders apparently "agree that the compensation for the reduction of emissions or improvement of stocks in privately owned forests is more viable through local and global market mechanisms" (Government of Costa Rica 2010: 9).

NEW WAVES

Costa Rica was also among the first five "core implementing countries" included within the World Bank's WAVES pilot program in 2012. As briefly noted in chapter 2, WAVES was formally launched during the CBD COP-10 in Japan in 2010 "to promote sustainable development by ensuring that natural resources are mainstreamed in development planning and national economic accounts" (Wealth Accounting and Valuation of Ecosystem Services [WAVES] n.d.a). A self-proclaimed "global partnership," it "brings together a broad coalition of UN agencies, governments, international institutes, nongovernmental organizations and academics to implement Natural Capital Accounting (NCA) where there are internationally agreed standards, and develop approaches for other ecosystem service accounts" (WAVES n.d.a). More specifically, the World Bank explains, "By working with central banks and ministries of planning and finance across the world to integrate natural resources into development planning through NCA, we hope to enable more informed decision making that can ensure genuine green growth and long-term advances in wealth and human well-being" (WAVES n.d.a).

At present WAVES is being piloted in several core implementing countries as a precursor to global rollout.[5] In each of these sites it has "established national steering committees, carried out stakeholder consultations, identified policy priorities and designed work plans that are now being implemented" (WAVES n.d.a). Results from these pilot studies will then feed back into the overarching WAVES strategy, which will be used to guide implementation in other countries as well. Via this initiative, the World Bank thus seeks to operationalize its vision of

> a world where measuring and valuing the environment leads to better decisions for development. . . . Natural capital accounts can provide detailed statistics for better management of the economy, like accounts for the sectoral inputs of water and energy, and outputs of pollution that are needed to model green growth scenarios. Land and water accounts can help countries interested in increasing hydro-power capacity to assess the value of competing land uses and the optimal way to meet this goal. Natural capital accounts can help countries rich in biodiversity design a management strategy that maximizes the contribution to economic growth while balancing tradeoffs among ecotourism, agriculture, subsistence livelihoods and other ecosystem services like flood protection and groundwater recharge. (WAVES n.d.b)

Costa Rica was, as mentioned, one of the five countries selected for the initial piloting of WAVES. As the World Bank explains, "With support from WAVES, Costa Rica is developing two natural asset accounts to address key questions and inform policy decisions. A national water account will integrate hydrological, economic, and social data in a coherent and consistent framework, while a forest account will incorporate physical and monetary values of services provided by forests and estimate the economy-wide impact of an expanding forest cover" (WAVES n.d.c).

Preliminary results of these assessments presented at the Central Bank of Costa Rica in May of 2016 revealed that

> forests contribute more to Costa Rica's Gross Domestic Product (GDP) than previously thought: around 2 percent, including returns from timber, other forest products, and economic activities that make use of forest products. This is in sharp contrast to industry figures from national accounts that only consider timber extraction, which alone added just 0.2 percent to GDP in 2011, and just half of that amount in 2013. Since Costa Rica's forests are more

valuable than expected, it will be crucial for forestry policies to be adjusted to effectively protect and build these resources. (World Bank 2016).

Suggested measures to realize this aim include, unsurprisingly, tapping further into REDD+, "securing the integrity of Costa Rica's protected areas and strengthening its Payment for Environmental Services program" (World Bank 2016). Building on all this, Costa Rica is now also "working on accounts for ecosystem services, to truly capture the value of benefits like water filtration and biodiversity protection" and in so doing "gain an even deeper understanding of forests' 'hidden' contributions" (World Bank 2016).

CONCLUSION

What this chapter's discussion demonstrates, most strikingly, is that in the face of growing efforts to integrate conservation and development under the auspices of green neoliberalization, the long-standing strain between extraction and preservation within Costa Rica has, paradoxically, intensified. Expansion of cattle ranching and other forms of commodity production to augment foreign exchange first exacerbated the deforestation already rampant throughout the country (Evans 1999). Subsequently, rapid growth in MBIs like ecotourism and PSA was encouraged by IFIs, the national state, NGOs, and private actors alike as a support for conservation efforts. A similar tension played out within the growing tourism industry itself: state support (primarily via tax incentives) for tourism development privileges large conventional enterprises to the detriment of many of the small-scale ecotourism operations in the country,[6] while at the same time the state actively promotes Costa Rica internationally as a destination for both ecotourism and mass resort-style travel.

It was in this context that Hunter and others voiced their concerns regarding the worsening environmental impacts of this precarious situation. Such dynamics continue at present in myriad ways throughout the country, from confrontation over water use for golf course development in the northwest Guanacaste province to criticism of the watershed contamination and deforestation wrought by pineapple cultivation in the northeast and southwest, gold mining in the north, upgrading of an oil refinery on the Caribbean coast, and turtle poaching and shark finning in the Caribbean Sea (see Fletcher et al. 2020). Despite such ongoing issues, however, recent assessments suggest that Costa Rica's forests have now largely recovered to 1950s levels (official records claimed 52.38 percent total cover in 2011; see Fondo Nacional de Financiamiento Forestal [FONAFIFO] 2012).

Within Costa Rica, therefore, the conservation-extraction nexus displays something of a Janus face, with both processes encouraged by the same set of policies and practices, championed by the Costa Rican state as well as a variety of other interested parties both domestic and international. All of this, I have shown, is rooted in the successive waves of neoliberalization to which the country in general has been subject over the last several decades. This neoliberalization, while partial and unevenly implemented, has in fact encouraged foreign direct investment in the form of both extractive industry and conservation simultaneously. The contradictory processes by which these two forces create value, however, along with the divergent actors advocating them, commonly bring them into conflict, paradoxically compelling state intervention contrary to the neoliberal principles supporting both forces in order to adjudicate the dispute in support of one side or the other. Hence, far from the aggressively antagonistic adversaries they are commonly considered, extraction and conservation can be understood as two sides of the same neoliberal coin in this context. This dynamic, as I have shown, plays out at multiple scales, involving articulation and negotiation among international governance regimes, national policy formation, and the local place-based politics that actively appropriate and reshape overarching structures in the course of their ground-level implementation.

As we will see, however, such paradoxical dynamics are far from unique to this neoliberal ecolaboratory but are in fact pervasive throughout the many contexts and forms in which neoliberal conservation has been operationalized. The next chapter thus pulls back to the global level again to explore neoliberal conservation's function as an "anti-regulation machine" more generally.

FIVE

The Anti-regulation Machine

> If there is an enduring logic to neoliberalization, it does not follow the pristine path of rolling market liberalization and competitive convergence; it is one of repeated, prosaic, and often botched efforts to *fix* markets, to build quasi-markets, and to repair market failure.
>
> JAMIE PECK, *Constructions of Neoliberal Reason* (2010: xiii)

This chapter draws back from the Costa Rican case study developed in the last chapter to highlight that study's overarching lessons and situate them within an assessment of the neoliberal conservation project more broadly. Most generally, I suggest, the previous chapter's analysis demonstrated a significant gap between the idealized vision promoted within neoliberal conservation policy formation and how this translates into actual practice, both locally and nationally. In the roll-out of Costa Rica's PSA program, for instance, what was initially promoted as a quintessentially neoliberal conservation strategy has become impressively variegated in complex and somewhat contradictory ways in the course of its implementation over the last several decades. But why exactly has this occurred? Rather than adapting to the local landscape as it has done in practice, after all, PSA was instead intended to transform this landscape to conform to the idealized neoliberal vision it promoted. Yet after more than two decades of development, the program has still largely failed in this effort and has instead come to function quite like the command-and-control mechanisms it was intended to supplant. It might be tempting to simply chalk this up to the common process via which hybridization with local institutions produces variegated neoliberalization (Brenner et al. 2010a, 2010b) and leave it at that. But this would fail to explain why a specific form of variegation has occurred in this particular way. Notwithstanding resistance on the part of some program formulators, after all, it was not for want of trying that PSA failed to develop stronger market mechanisms. Rather, it was the fact that there has been very little market demand for the services it aims to sell.

There are several factors that help to explain this outcome. The first concerns the level of payments the program makes, which were established by state fiat based on estimation of the opportunity cost of the main competing land use (at that time logging) rather than left to forces of supply and demand. Consequently, payments have not actually been sufficient to outperform activities such as palm oil and pineapple production that are in fact far more profitable. But this is a consequence not merely of inaccurate calculation on the part of state agents but of a basic disjuncture between where funding is supposed to come from and what it aims to achieve. While the envisioned global offset market assumes that "buyers" will pay only for the pollution they cause, to achieve conservation in pure market terms, these funds must cover the entire costs that "sellers" incur in foregoing other forms of production. Hence, there will always be a need to supplement market payments with other forms of nonmarket finance no matter how extensive the market actually becomes.

A similar dynamic, I have suggested, explains the overarching pattern of hybrid neoliberal-sovereign governance evident throughout Costa Rica's environmental management regime. Despite small-scale success in particular initiatives, overarching promotion of neoliberal conservation via bioprospecting, ecotourism, PSA, and other ostensive MBIs has, I have shown, largely failed to achieve its intended incentivization of biodiversity preservation relative to environmentally destructive forms of land use. On the contrary, neoliberalization has on the whole actually accomplished the opposite in loosening restrictions on extractive industry and, hence, instead perversely incentivizing the latter's expansion. Conservation finance is generally unable to counter this expansion in direct market terms, and consequently, in the face of the expansion it itself has facilitated, the national state is forced to extend its sovereign intervention to accomplish what MBIs cannot (Vandermeer and Perfecto 2005). The result is growing disjuncture between the overarching vision governing intervention and the reality of this intervention in practice.

What this analysis points to, in short, is that state-centered command-and-control style policies are in fact responsible for much of the environmental achievements for which Costa Rica has been widely celebrated, and for which more recent neoliberal reforms are often mistakenly credited. This is true, as we have seen, of the PSA program as well as other forms of biodiversity conservation throughout the country (Fletcher 2012a). Yet the influence of continued state-centered support for environmental governance can be seen to extend beyond this. It could be argued, additionally, that the Costa Rican state's general funding of social development domestically has in fact served as an indirect subsidy for environmental protection: widespread provision of public education, socialized health care, social security benefits, and other such services paid for by a (relatively) progressive income tax, which have persisted despite the liberalization promoted in many sectors, have meant that poverty in the country—and thus pressure on protected natural resources from local residents needing sustenance—has been far less than it would likely have been otherwise.

Edelman (1999: 73) makes a similar case with respect to Costa Rican development more generally, contending that much of "the apparent 'success' of free-market policies since the 1980s resulted not only from the application of neoliberal measures, but from the legacies of the earlier, 'statist' social democratic model." As Edelman shows, the national government's substantial investments in education and related social services, infrastructure development, energy generation, and other initiatives contributed significantly to the renewed economic growth the country experienced following the neoliberal reform to which proponents commonly attribute this prosperity. He summarizes:

> Traditional neoliberal tools—lowered tariffs on imports, interest rate liberalization, privatization, and cuts in public spending—have been less important in bringing stability and fueling the export boom than a variety of non-market factors: the massive US aid in the 1980s, the result of Costa Rica's strategic geopolitical position between Nicaragua and Panama; the new exporters' profiting from CAT subsidies, a program established under Figueres in the unabashedly statist 1970s; the expansion of US quotas for key products under the Caribbean Basin initiative; the constant currency devaluations demanded by the international lending institutions and pro-export lobbies in Costa Rica; the decision of many foreign investors to locate in Costa Rica because of its well-developed infrastructure and its highly educated, healthy labor force, both legacies of the social democratic model, not of neoliberalism. (Edelman 1999: 83–84)[1]

This continued state support of both conservation and development despite neoliberal reform can be seen, in part, as a classic Polanyian double movement (Polanyi 1944). As previously noted, the common inability of market-based strategies to achieve their goals provokes a heavy-handed response by the state in order to correct for this ostensible "market failure."

Meanwhile, persistent welfare-state support in the face of neoliberalization continues to partly combat the poverty that market mechanisms not only fail to alleviate but often also exacerbate. Again, Edelman highlights this same dynamic with respect to the overarching political economy: "Both the state and the lending and aid agencies have attempted to blunt the negative social impacts of structural adjustment policies. As Costa Rica's public sector shrank and social safety net unraveled, foreign aid agencies, NGOs, and even the multilateral lenders began to provide 'social compensation' funds to ease the crisis caused by large-scale dismissals of public-sector employees, declining real wages, and cut-backs in state services" (1999: 85).

THE (PERVERSE) USES OF NEOLIBERALISM

There is, however, one important sense in which neoliberal restructuring has, ironically, provided an important, if unintended, support for environmental protection in Costa Rica. Several researchers observe that SAPs in the 1980s and 1990s, entailing progressive elimination of the price and other supports that had made agricultural production viable for many small producers, resulted in their widespread abandonment of such production in many parts of the country (a process called *decampesinamiento*, roughly translated as "de-peasantization"), often provoking the sale of land and migration to urban centers in search of wage labor. This process has been documented both in the country as a whole (Edelman 1999) and within specific regions (van den Hombergh 2004). Thus, van den Hombergh observes, "Structural adjustment measures, even more than the availability of arable land, became the major obstacles to agricultural production in the Southern zone" (2004: 73). This has produced the paradoxical effect of supporting to a degree reforestation efforts. One World Bank study, for instance, found that between 1987 and 1997—that is, before PSA was implemented—secondary forest growth had increased thirteen thousand hectares per year across the country (cited in Sierra and Russman 2006: 132). Similarly, another study found that by the time PSA was introduced to the country's southwestern province in the late 1990s, much agricultural land was already returning to forest (Rosero et al. 2002), leading Sierra and Russman (2006: 139) to conclude that "a similar land cover outcome could probably be achieved in the medium to long run without payments."[2] Yet, while this abandonment of agriculture in some cases decreased pressure on forests in certain places, it also exacerbated poverty, resulting in substantial outmigration, unemployment, and increased pressure on marginal land (van den Hombergh 2004)—a consequence that may in fact offset any net environmental benefit via increasing resource pressure elsewhere.

Simultaneously, dictated by the same neoliberal policies, large industrial interests, many of them foreign owned, were frequently offered very favorable economic circumstances as an inducement for their relocation to Costa Rica to stimulate foreign direct investment (Edelman 1999). For instance, a US-based conglomerate, Ston Forestal, was granted duty-free imports of equipment and fertilizer and exemption from land and income taxes for its Gmelina plantations in the southwest region (van den Hombergh 2004). These contradictory dynamics—neoliberal policies disadvantaging the poor and favoring the wealthy—resulted in many cases in increased inequality, the progressive transfer of resources up the economic ladder (Edelman 1999), consistent with Harvey's (2005) depiction of neoliberalism in general as a strategy of accumulation by dispossession. In the southwest, van den Hombergh (2004) describes numerous small farmers indebted by SAPs abandoning rice production and leasing their lands to Ston Forestal at rock-bottom prices.

In other words, paradoxically, a *lack* of market-based economic opportunities for poorer residents (rather than the increased opportunities pursued via MBIs) appears to have been a significant factor in increased environmental protection throughout Costa Rica. This dynamic was in fact documented by a different study on the central Pacific Coast, which recorded a significant increase in forest cover to multiple factors including "labor out-migration, growing tourism and expatriate land acquisition" (Kull et al. 2007: 724). The environmental consequences of all this activity beyond the valley itself, however, such as the impacts of out-migrants' activities in their new homes or their compulsion to colonize marginal land for survival there, were not taken into account. Neither were the social impacts of these processes, as the authors themselves observe: "Rapid and unmitigated neo-liberal reform has impoverished many. . . . Migrant workers trading places with wealthy expatriates has a cruel irony that is not lost on those involved" (2007: 734).

On the other hand, as noted above, it is in fact the market opportunities available to large producers, facilitated by neoliberal policies, that have increased pressure on natural resources in other respects. Meanwhile, the growing concentration of resources in fewer hands displaces resource pressure elsewhere, as the dispossessed colonize increasingly marginal land, and exacerbates poverty as well. Thus, while neoliberalization may diminish resource pressure in one respect, it increases it twofold in another.

THE JANUS FACE OF THE
CONSERVATION-EXTRACTION NEXUS

All of this helps to explain Costa Rica's Janus-faced reputation as simultaneously environmental savior and destructor: the curious mixture of neoliberal and sovereign governance embodied in environmental policy (and elsewhere) encourages forces of conservation and extraction at the same time and in multiple combinations. Neoliberal efforts to capitalize on natural resources promote both extraction and (market-based) conservation as profitable forms of resource exploitation, supported by tax breaks, the promise of "non-consumptive" income-generation activities, and other financial incentives. At the same time, command-and-control strategies continue to subsidize both extraction and conservation (fortress-style as well as surreptitious approaches like PSA) through, for instance, the production of pallets for agricultural exports from PSA-funded tree plantations (Lansing 2013) and direct use of state tax revenues for PSA financing and protected area management. Meanwhile, other environmental issues, such as freshwater pollution and fossil fuel emissions, continue to be externalized from conservation efforts due to the latter's failure thus far to attract market finance or to receive sufficient regulatory attention by a progressively resource-starved and rolled-back state.

My research demonstrates that this dynamic is not merely the product of an idiosyncratic Costa Rican governance structure but is in fact directly inscribed in the very nature of the neoliberal conservation approach increasingly central to environmental governance in the country. Reliance on incentive-based MBIs to achieve environmental protection means that policy makers lack recourse to robust regulatory measures to enact policy and must therefore depend on market forces to generate sufficient revenue to offset the opportunity costs of alternate (extractive) land use. The main difficulty with this strategy, of course, is that many extractive industries are in fact quite lucrative, hence their opportunity costs are far beyond the limited resources that MBIs are able to marshal. This is particularly the case in a neoliberal policy climate that has systematically dismantled states' capacity to exercise a strong direct regulatory presence and in which, consequently, producers can easily externalize much of the social and environmental costs of production in pursuit of higher profit.

In Costa Rica, this has led to the contradictory situation in which the failure of MBIs to effectively achieve substantial conservation or development in the face of the unchecked (and indeed uncheckable, within a neoliberal framework) expansion of extractive industry necessitates intervention on the part of the national state in order to preserve through command-and-control measures the conservation outcomes that market mechanisms have proven unable to achieve. As a result, notwithstanding their ostensive opposition as contrary approaches to natural resource use, resource extraction and conservation are intrinsically linked by the very policy mechanisms through which they are, in theory, divided. While it is true that in the previous era extraction and conservation were often pursued simultaneously through self-conscious state policy, in the contemporary period, my analysis shows, this Janus-faced strategy is in fact *necessitated* by neoliberalism's characteristic negation of state-centered mechanisms of resource redistribution and regulation.

Consequently, as noted earlier, the state finds itself compelled to subvert its own neoliberal policies by intervening directly to allocate resource use when the incentive structures created to strike a delicate balance between conservation and development interests fail to perform in this respect. This is the essential paradox of neoliberal governance (see Kiely 2018, 2021) that functions as what I call the "anti-regulation machine." Within this dynamic, the Janus face of the conservation-extraction nexus thus becomes threefold: not only does the state encourage both market-based conservation and extractive industry at once, but it also acts directly to preserve natural resources from the forces of extraction when MBIs fail to accomplish this aim, employing both neoliberal and command-and-control mechanisms to do so. In this process, in sum, the state supports market-based mechanisms, industrial extraction, and fortress conservation simultaneously.

SCALING UP

Similar dynamics are apparent within neoliberal conservation more generally. For instance, a growing body of research has documented how, in practice, most PES programs worldwide seem to be structured quite similarly to Costa Rica's: as ostensible MBIs that in fact contain few if any direct market transactions and are instead based largely on state-based appropriation and redistribution of finances.[3] Following the initial euphoria concerning promotion of PES as a quintessential MBI, increasing empirical scrutiny quickly demonstrated that in practice few "actually existing" programs neatly conformed to the idealized market model (Wunder 2007). More detailed empirical case studies subsequently demonstrated that a number of prominent PES programs in addition to Costa Rica's, including in Cambodia (Milne and Adams 2012), Mexico (McAfee and Shapiro 2010; Shapiro-Garza 2013), and Vietnam (McElwee 2012), also contained little if any actual market exchange, instead relying almost entirely on state appropriation and redistribution of revenues and hence functioning more like the command-and-control subsidies they were usually explicitly intended to replace. Studies also showed how this dynamic commonly resulted, in part, from how programs are often "adapted and used for multiple purposes, and how they are attributed alternative meanings" by local actors in the course of implementation (Van Hecken et al. 2015a: 122).[4]

Induction from these and other cases has confirmed a more general pattern.[5] Wunder thus concludes "that PES are only exceptionally being realized through markets" (2015: 240). As Vatn summarizes: "A very large fraction of transactions between public intermediaries and 'providers' does not take the form of trade, but are better characterized as subsidies. Combining this with the Milder et al. (2010) data, we can therefore conclude that a substantial part of PES is non-market. Where markets exist, they are mainly of the incomplete kind" (2015: 229). What is most significant in this pattern is the common disjuncture between the overarching neoliberal effort to incentivize conservation by mobilizing resources to make standing forests worth more than alternate land uses, on the one hand, and the reality of mostly state-based forms of finance and governance, on the other. In the case of Costa Rica, as I have shown, this has resulted from the fact that the direct market transactions intended to finance incentivization have largely failed to materialize, compelling continued reliance on state-based taxation and other forms of non-market funding to generate the resources needed to run the program. Yet even with this extra-market funding, resources are insufficient to directly compete with the very lucrative forms of extraction that potential participants may also choose, hence recourse to the Forestry Law to prohibit land use change anyway, for which PSA then constitutes something of "a *quid pro quo* for legal restrictions on clearing" (Pagiola 2008: 9).

Considering this analysis, a key question becomes whether, given alternative forms of policy and practice, a PES program such as PSA could actually have or still become the more genuine MBI it was intended to be? My research suggests that it could not. Even given a larger market for trade in offsets internationally, to be a true "Coasean-type" MBI (Pirard 2012) the program would still need to generate more resources for payments than the profits derivable from other forms of land use such as palm oil or pineapple production. Yet given that this market funding would need to come, via offsetting, from the profits of productive activities elsewhere, this would require at least a substantial portion of these profits to be able to achieve the necessary payment levels. In cases where transactions are based in the same type of extractive industry that PSA is intended to counter, this would paradoxically require *mobilizing even more funds than the entire profits from this extractive activity* (since this would be what potential program participants would have to expect to earn from engaging in extraction themselves for it to be an attractive proposition).[6] Yet even the relatively low number of producers who do participate in this and other offset trading schemes expect only to pay to compensate for the specific quantity of emissions or other environmental damage they produce. Consequently, there seems to be a basic disjuncture between the source of payments and what these payments are intended to accomplish. This, as previously explained, appears to be not merely a consequence of the idiosyncratic implementation of PSA, nor of subversion by "the actions of local actors" (Van Hecken et al. 2018), but is rather an essential structural feature of the basic PES mechanism. After all, it is not only Costa Rica's program that exhibits this disjuncture but the global mechanism more generally, which has transformed in similar ways in diverse contexts irrespective of their local particularities.

But the reality of PES programming is even more daunting than this. As a paradigmatic neoliberal conservation mechanism, PES aims to internalize the sort of social and environmental problems commonly externalized in conventional production. To achieve this would require mobilizing even more funding to counter not only the base profits of alternative land use but also the social and environmental costs excluded from these calculations. For many Costa Rican *campesinos*, for instance, palm oil production is more lucrative than other forms of employment but still does not provide more than a base subsistence living (Beggs and Moore 2013). Hence, it also requires reliance on cheap food and other products that carry their own social and environmental costs. For PSA to not only outcompete palm oil profits but also support an adequate standard of healthful living (United Nations 2014) would require generating even more funding to cover these costs. In this sense, as McAfee (2012a) points out, rather than working to alleviate global poverty and inequality, neoliberal conservation actually *depends on it*. To stay directly competitive with alternate land uses, on the other hand, would require PSA to itself externalize social and environmental costs that must be borne elsewhere for the program to survive.[7] Thus it would contradict the basic aims of the neoliberal conservation project (Lohmann 2011). In cases where revenue comes from the profits of conventional production itself—even relatively benign activities like beverage manufacturing—this revenue is itself partially generated through externalization of social and environmental impacts, only some of which are addressed in the offset payments per se.

Similar dynamics are evident in the REDD+ mechanism, which, as previously noted, is usually explicitly modeled on PES. As with PES, REDD+ was envisioned as a neoliberal conservation mechanism relying on global carbon markets to mobilize funding for payments to incentivize local forest conservation. Like Costa Rica's PSA, seed money to put projects in place has been provided by IFIs including the World Bank and UN-REDD program, as well as national governments like Norway. Yet after more than a decade of development, the international market for REDD+ payments is still quite small, operating mostly in the voluntary offset market, and hence like PES the mechanism has progressively shifted from an MBI to just the sort of non-market strategy for centralized appropriation and redistribution of resources as PES (IIED 2015; Angelsen 2017). The Centre for International Forestry (CIFOR) thus concludes, "While the scheme was initially conceived as a market-based instrument that would be funded by a massive global carbon market, that vision no longer fits reality. In the absence of that market, REDD+ has since evolved into a form of results-based aid, with various kinds of financing from governments, civil society, and the private sector" (Evans 2017).

Yet even this alternative funding is far less than needed to support all of the programs currently in development worldwide, let alone the multitude planned for the future, and hence in reality the majority of projects are faltering, while some have collapsed altogether (Sunderlin et al. 2015). Moreover, even in projects that do survive, major problems are commonly encountered in terms of displacement and other abuses of local people as well as difficulty in ensuring adequate preservation of targeted resources and combating leakage of environmental damage to other places beyond the project site (Cavanagh et al. 2015; Asiyanbi 2016).

In short, very similar dynamics to those in PES development seem to be replicated in the evolution of REDD+. While proponents commonly attribute this reality to the fact that a global offset market for REDD+ payments has not yet developed due to the stalling of UNFCCC negotiations (Sunderlin et al. 2015; Angelsen 2017), my analysis suggests that such a market, however extensive and robust, could never fully finance a market-based mechanism anyway. The progressive shift from MBI to nonmarket finance in REDD+ rollout, I therefore conclude, is due not only to lack of political will or technical deficiencies in implementation but more fundamentally to an inherent contradiction in the mechanism's basic design (Fletcher et al. 2016; Fletcher and Büscher 2017).

A similar disjuncture between vision and execution has been widely documented with respect to other MBIs elsewhere.[8] Büscher and Dressler (2007) thus describe a common gap between "reality" and "rhetoric" in neoliberal conservation policies while Carrier and West (2009) identify a similar disjuncture between vision and execution in neoliberal environmental governance more broadly. Based on all of this, McAfee (2012a, 2012b) concludes that few ostensible MBIs anywhere in the world really function as markets in any meaningful sense at all.

THE LIMITS OF NEOLIBERAL CONSERVATION

What does all of this mean for the future of a neoliberal conservation project that explicitly aims to build upon such MBIs as the basis of its global promotion of natural capital and ecosystem service valuation? I believe that what my analysis points to, more generally, is the essential impossibility of achieving equitable, environmentally-sustainable development within the context of a neoliberal capitalist system that in fact directly militates against this. Neoliberalism, after all, seeks to individuate and disaggregate risk, initiating a frontal assault on welfare-state institutions that seek to aggregate and collectivize risk and responsibility through mechanisms of centralized resource collection and redistribution (Baker and Simon 2002). Consequently, as previously described, to address poverty and other social concerns neoliberal governance strategies must necessarily promote economic growth. This growth, however, inevitably places greater pressure on the natural resources upon which it is based, thus frequently forcing into opposition the very social and environmental concerns neoliberal policies ostensibly seek to reconcile. At the same time, lacking effective mechanisms for resource redistribution on a substantial scale, free-market policies characteristically increase inequality as well, thus exacerbating the poverty they purportedly seek to alleviate (McAfee 2012a, 2012b). As a result, neoliberal policies not only fail to effectively address but paradoxically augment both the environmental degradation and poverty they claim to reconcile and resolve.

Supporting this analysis in relation to Costa Rica, Matulis (2013: 258) contends that recent innovations, described in chapter 4, intended to make the PSA program *more* neoliberal actually make the program less effective, in that "in each case where neoliberalization has occurred, the result is uneven development, consolidation of control over resources, and accumulation of benefits among wealthier, larger landowners." Indeed, the share of PSA revenue captured by private firms, as opposed to the individual landholders envisioned as the ideal payment recipients, "has increased steadily since the beginning of the programme, rising from about 30 per cent of all contracts (and 20 per cent of annual funds distributed) in 1997 to almost 50 per cent of contracts and funding by 2008" (Porras 2010: 13). Meanwhile, complementing both this and earlier discussion of the conservation-extraction nexus, Lansing (2013) demonstrates that PSA's controversial reforestation (via tree plantation) modality compounds the program's general tendency to subsidize conservation by providing an indirect subsidy to Costa Rican industrial agriculture interests, given that most of the wood produced is turned into pallets for use in agricultural export. Conversely, most of the newer measures intended to correct the PSA program's general tendency to concentrate revenue and make it function more effectively as an instrument of poverty reduction (e.g., specifically targeting areas with a lower Social Development Index, limiting the number of contracts a participant can possess), actually entail increased state intervention to counter the tendency toward monopoly of a less-regulated mechanism (Porras 2010).

VICTORY IN DEFEAT

With respect to neoliberal conservation, my analysis shows, problems arise whether or not sufficient revenue is in fact generated from conserved resources to make them profitable. If revenue is not sufficient, projects will be unable to compete with alternative forms of land use (agriculture, logging, cattle raising, etc.), the opportunity costs of which they are intended to counter. If projects are able to generate significant profit, on the other hand, then a new problem arises. Žižek (2007: 12) asserts that "a true victory is a victory in defeat," wherein advocacy of one's position becomes so successful that it is adopted by one's adversaries and championed as their own. Such a dynamic seems to occur with neoliberal conservation. This is because efforts to harness the economic value of conserved resources become subject to the same capitalist dynamics as other, more conventional industries. Hence, if profits are available, elites are incentivized to capture these profits by whatever means available—and the greater this potential profit, the greater the incentive. As West asserts of the campaign for "ethical" consumption in general, if "products are found to have enough value to make their extraction really a possibility for bringing significant cash income or development—the state, or other powerful actors, would create and manage new markets at the expense of the people who live where these products naturally occur" (2006: 214).

This is precisely what is happening in the spread of neoliberal conservation in Costa Rica, with revenue from the PSA program and ecotourism, for instance, becoming concentrated in fewer hands over time (Porras 2010; Fletcher 2012a). Lohmann observes a similar logic in the rise of the global carbon markets, explaining that

> once carbon pollution rights become an asset, a stubbornly fossil fuel-dependent industrial sector becomes as enthusiastic about securing maximum free allocations from governments as it ever was in urging lower taxes or curbs on conventional regulation. The distinction between the design of a market mechanism and the profit-seeking activities that it enables quickly goes by the board. With it goes any pretense of governments being able to set emissions caps according to scientific criteria. (2011: 96)

As a result, he concludes, "offset finance is being captured by corporate bad hats and large landowners rather than ordinary people" (97). It is clear that such dynamics—what Fairhead et al. (2012) call "green grabbing"—are only likely to accelerate in the future if reliance on relatively unregulated capitalist markets is the dominant approach to enacting conservation.

Indeed, it is hard to imagine how this dynamic can be countered without the kind of heavy-handed intervention by the state or some other entity to appropriate and redistribute resources to prevent excessive accumulation that is occurring in Costa Rica. This is, of course, a commonly acknowledged problem within neoliberal economics in general, when, for instance, ecological economist William Rees observes, "if we were serious about having a true market economy, mergers and acquisitions and other means of concentrating power would be disallowed" (in Fletcher 2013b: 805). Such action would, of course, run contrary to the fundamental principles of neoliberalism, requiring not only organizing but also regulating actions on the part of the state, and thus it reinforces the conclusion that such an economy is in fact characterized by an essential contradiction, rendering it incapable of effectively redressing either social inequality or environmental degradation on a global scale.

This conclusion resonates with Graeber's (2015) invocation of an "iron law of liberalism" positing that "any market reform, any government initiative intended to reduce red tape and promote market forces will have the ultimate effect of increasing the total number of regulations, the total amount of paperwork, and the total number of bureaucrats the government employs" (9). Or as Gray, channeling Polanyi (1944), phrases it, "*Laissez-faire* must be centrally planned; regulated markets just happen" (1998: 17). This certainly seems to have been the case with respect to the trajectory of neoliberal conservation interventions thus far, which, far from reducing state regulation, have, as I have shown, more commonly merely intensified it in myriad ways over time.[9] Indeed, Graeber goes so far as to argue that global discussion of "'free trade' and the 'free market' [has] really entailed the self-conscious completion of the world's first effective planetary-scale administrative bureaucratic system" (2015: 30). From this perspective, "'free trade' and 'the free market' actually meant the creation of global administrative structures mainly aimed at ensuring the extraction of profits for investors" (31).

This understanding of neoliberal conservation as a paradoxical anti-regulation machine extending state regulation under the pretense of reducing it helps to resolve ongoing debate concerning how neoliberal conservation MBIs actually are in practice. In discussions of PES, for instance, acknowledgment of the common gap between vision and execution in program implementation has led some commentators to conclude that if actually existing PES programs are not very market-based or entail significant direct commodification, they should therefore not necessarily be characterized as expressions of neoliberalization at all.[10] McElwee et al., for instance, assert that "seemingly neoliberal policies like PES are actually a mix of both market economic incentives and regulatory approaches, and thus should not be labelled solely 'neoliberal' per se" (2014: 423) They thus call for "moving away from overly simplistic analysis of 'neoliberal natures'" (2014: 436) in characterizing PES programs and instead devoting "more attention to their particularities and outcomes rather than broadly characterizing them as 'neoliberal'" (2014: 435). This call for analysis of particularity in actual PES implementation has been echoed by numerous others.[11]

Yet conceptualizing neoliberal conservation as an anti-regulation machine suggests a more nuanced view, in terms of which PES's characteristically contradictory manifestation can be understood as precisely how neoliberal governance tends to function in practice. Even when it fails to conform to an idealized model of neoliberal governance by embracing non-market mechanisms, consequently, PES can still be seen to embody an essentially neoliberal overarching vision in its widespread conceptualization "as a transfer of resources between social actors, which aims to create incentives to align individual and/or collective land use decisions with the social interest in the management of natural resources" (Muradian et al. 2010: 1205). As Jan Breitling and I have argued previously, Costa Rica's PSA program continues to promote a strongly neoliberal approach in its continued aim to incentivize conservation via service-oriented payments even if its actual policies and practices exemplify a more state-centered mode of governance (Fletcher and Breitling 2012).

A second issue of victory in defeat concerns challenges posed to neoliberal conservation by its very success. Concerning Costa Rica's environmental track record, for instance, Steinberg (2001: 30) asks, "Why should donors provide financial incentives to countries that already consider environmental protection a priority?"—particularly when there are so many other countries that clearly do not, as evidenced by the very environmental degradation requiring attention within their borders. Hence, perversely, in allocating scarce resources within a competitive market, a poor environmental track record (as well as rampant poverty decreasing production costs) can attract funding, while a strong track record (and higher standard of living) can discourage it. This is one of the principal concerns with REDD+ as well: that it may actually encourage nations to increase their deforestation initially in order to attract attention and funding, while countries like Costa Rica that have already succeeded in reducing forest loss to some extent may be bypassed by the mechanism, given that the country's remaining forests are already relatively well preserved by its PA system, thus calling into question the additionality of future offset payments. By the same token, Costa Rica's status as a middle-income country due to its past development achievements means that conservation has become increasingly more expensive there relative to other lower-income societies, challenging the venerable logic of pursuing conservation where it can be accomplished most cheaply on the principles of economic efficiency underlying early PA creation as well as contemporary carbon emissions offsetting, ecotourism, and similar neoliberal mechanisms.

AN ENDLESS ALGEBRA

This leads to a further contradiction in neoliberal conservation logic alluded to earlier. As Lohmann (2011) observes, the attempt to internalize externalities (both environmental and social) central to neoliberal conservation commonly results merely in the creation of new externalities obfuscated in the benefit-cost calculus of supposed rewards—what he labels performance of an "endless algebra." Lohmann contends, for instance, that complexities of the "performative equations" involved in calculating equivalencies between carbon emitted and sequestered via carbon markets means "that, with respect to the climate crisis in particular, internalizing externalities through commodity formation, however profitable the result, constantly gives rise to fresh externalities that are so overwhelming that, from an environmental point of view, they invalidate the project" (2014: 178). Elsewhere I have described similar dynamics in the development of carbon control policies in Costa Rica (Fletcher 2016), showing how efforts to mitigate climate change end up creating environmental externalities in terms of the other ecological issues marginalized and/or intensified by these policies, while at the same time obscuring aspects of the projects themselves that detract from their overall ecological benefit (e.g., unaccounted greenhouse gas emissions from hydroelectricity production). In addition, I have demonstrated a parallel process with respect to social externalities: efforts to employ market-based carbon action as a mechanism for income generation and thereby internalize the social problems (e.g., income inequities and forms of marginalization) brought on by conventional capitalist production create new forms of inequality due to the same drive to consolidate profit that these mechanisms are intended to combat.

This is partly due to the fact that, just as the potential profit deriving from market mechanisms creates incentives to capture this profit, it also creates powerful incentives to externalize both ecological and social costs of production in the interest of maximizing profit. More fundamentally, however, this externalization also follows from the reality that were the total environmental and social costs of production internalized, capitalist markets would likely collapse altogether. Ultimately, all new economic value—and hence profit—derives from appropriating the surplus value of productive labor, externalizing environmental costs of production, and/or transferring value between groups of holders (the process Marx called primitive accumulation and Harvey updates as accumulation by dispossession). As feminist Marxists in particular have long argued, far from commodifying everything in their path, capitalist markets thus actually depend fundamentally on not commodifying substantial quantities of both human and nonhuman labor so that these can be exploited without actually paying for them as the basis for increased profit (Isla 2015; Collard and Dempsey 2016; Bhattacharya 2017). Consequently, "To fully commodify the reproduction of labor-power would do away with the unpaid work that allows accumulation to proceed at acceptable rates of profit" (Moore 2014: 292).

To the extent that producers seek to redress either of these dynamics by internalizing social and/or environmental expenses, overall production costs must therefore rise, which means either raising prices as well or accepting reduced rates of profit. In the former case, aggregate profit must still also fall, as higher prices reduce overall demand, unless of course a premium is charged for including social and environmental benefits (as with organic and fair trade products), in which case the higher production costs are passed on to consumers. Yet even in such cases a viable market requires that some costs remain externalized, otherwise prices would rise to impossible levels—as evidenced, for instance, by growing criticism of the social and environmental problems remaining in many current organic and fair trade production schemes (see e.g., Moberg and Lyon 2010). Patel (2010), for instance, suggests that the average fast food hamburger would cost on the order of $200 if all social and environmental implications of its production were included in its purchase price. Fully internalizing the costs of both production and consumption in the way neoliberal conservation promises, in short, would make it so expensive that most conventional commodity markets could no longer function.

All in all, available evidence demonstrates that neoliberal conservation's central promise to effectively redress poverty and environmental degradation simultaneously appears largely unsubstantiated anywhere in the world. This is particularly apparent with respect to bioprospecting. While the strategy was widely championed in the 1990s (Hayden 2003; Neimark 2012), it quickly became apparent "that drug discovery from nature is extremely difficult, especially in the highly competitive market of global pharmaceuticals. On the production side alone, firms (mainly located in the US, Europe and Japan) must access biodiversity in distant tropical locations, which are difficult to traverse, while also contending with a host of political barriers (such as regulations and property rights) as well as sporadic local resistance to collecting material" (Neimark 2012: 424).

This is reflected in Costa Rica, where in 2013 INBio announced its decision to "surrender" its facilities and extensive sample collection to the Costa Rican state (Hammond 2013). The Merck deal struck in the 1990s never resulted in a commercially viable product, and INBio struggled unsuccessfully to develop other forms of market engagement ever since. As a result, the organization remained dependent on foreign aid, which "peaked at US $4 million in 1999, only to fall to a mere $79,000 by 2007" (Hammond 2013). The decision to divest its assets thus provoked acknowledgment of "the irony of INBio seeking a government bailout after it fought for years to strip government institutions of responsibility for biodiversity" (Hammond 2013). Overall, the global benefits of bioprospecting have followed this pattern, falling far short of initial expectations (Hayden 2003; Neimark 2012).

Likewise, despite their initial exponential growth (see Fletcher 2012b), global carbon markets have largely stagnated. Similar to ecotourism, moreover, the capacity of carbon markets to address anthropogenic climate change has been increasingly questioned of late (see Böhm and Dabhi 2009; Lohmann 2009), while a full accounting of the costs and benefits of these markets would likewise require greater attention to the actual outcomes of carbon trades (Lohmann 2011). Bond, for instance, asserts that "the limits of the market for solving climate crises via carbon trading are now clearly evident, as demonstrated by the 2011 collapse of the European Emissions Trading Scheme through hacking and credit-theft in January and a general lack of confidence in subsequent months and the 2010 demise of Chicago's carbon exchange" (2011: 17). This was compounded by the European Union's landmark decision not to reduce bloated emissions allocations in its Emissions Trading Scheme (ETS), driving the carbon price to an all-time low and effectively crippling the global market (Monbiot 2013).

A similar situation, as noted earlier, is apparent with REDD+. At the 2014 World Parks Congress in Sydney, project coordinators uniformly lamented the difficulty of securing sustained funding for projects they had invested considerable time and energy in developing, working hard to overcome resistance by local community members increasingly suspicious of outsiders arriving with promises of future benefits. A recent empirical analysis of a cross-section of pilot projects found that the majority were stagnating due to lack of funding while several had been abandoned altogether (Sunderlin et al. 2015). Pledges from Norway, Germany, and the United Kingdom to continue to directly fund REDD+ projects to the tune of around $5 billion are drastically insufficient to support all projects currently in development. While the Paris Agreement codified at COP-21 still includes REDD+ as a component of a larger multidimensional landscape-level forest conservation strategy, the mechanism's original promise to generate a global market in carbon credits is already effectively finished.

In point of fact, the only MBI to achieve demonstrable success in genuinely harnessing in situ resources as a source of economic growth via direct market transaction on a substantial scale thus far has been ecotourism, which the UN World Tourism Organization (UNWTO 1998) claims to have been expanding approximately 30 percent per year throughout the world.[12] Ecotourism, however, remains a small portion of the overall global tourism industry (Honey 2008). Moreover, for a complete accounting of ecotourism's benefits one must take into account the activity's full range of costs and benefits and how these are distributed (Carrier and Macleod 2005; Neves 2010). While ecotourism can be an effective force for biodiversity conservation, a growing criticism, as climate change increasingly replaces biodiversity as the fulcrum of global environmental efforts (see Fletcher 2016), concerns the industry's contribution to global warming due to its dependence on long-haul air transport (Carrier and Macleod 2005). Thus, the costs of such transport to remote corners of Costa Rica, for example, should be included in calculations of ecotourism's net environmental benefit, which in the numerous studies assessing ecotourism environmental benefit is almost never done (cf. Driscoll et al. 2011). In addition, to be most effective, ecotourism, by definition, must remain a small-scale enterprise (Honey 2008), and as

Stem and colleagues (2003) point out, small-scale efforts can only ever have small-scale effects.

This general assessment is supported by Dempsey and Suarez (2016) in their meta-review of the neoliberal conservation literature. In line with the latest wave of PES research outlined earlier, their analysis concludes that despite widespread promotion of neoliberal measures to incentivize conservation of in situ resources around the world over the past several decades, in reality very little actual market exchange has taken place thus far and the majority of trade that does occur has been directed by states. Hence, they describe genuine "free" market transactions among private parties as merely "slivers of slivers of slivers" of the activities actually occurring (Dempsey and Suarez 2016: 5).

THE ILLUSION OF DECOUPLING

Faith in the future promise of decoupling is unlikely to improve this situation. UNEP and other organizations assert that some relative decoupling has been occurring in certain places and industries (see, e.g., UNEP 2011a; NCE 2014, 2015) and that all of this can be scaled up in the future to move from this to the absolute decoupling ultimately needed to sustain green growth in the long run. Yet all of these findings are contested by others as part of a growing body of research calling into question the possibility of significant decoupling altogether.[13] On a global scale, Ward et al. (2016) indeed conclude that absolute decoupling is in fact impossible.

Even UNEP's own analysis, while ostensibly supporting the potential of decoupling, actually demonstrates the opposite, revealing a reality quite at odds with its optimistic proclamations. In terms of both conceptual and empirical substantiation, UNEP's 2011 report admits, the decoupling concept remains largely vacuous: "The conceptual framework for decoupling and understanding of the instrumentalities for achieving it are still in an infant stage" (Von Weizsäcker and Khosla 2011: xi). Empirically, meanwhile, decoupling is quite difficult to measure, a difficulty compounded in the case of impact decoupling:

> Socio-technical changes that have reduced negative environmental impacts in the past may have resulted in the decoupling of economic growth from certain specific impacts, while other impacts remained unchanged or even accelerated. Therefore, it can be problematic to consider impact decoupling

in general without acknowledging that specific interventions can have unintended consequences or else ignore some impacts. It follows that it may be difficult to design a system-wide set of interventions capable of decoupling resource use from all negative environmental impacts simultaneously. (UNEP 2011a: xxvi)

In short, "Across those scale levels, impact decoupling is not easy to assess" (2011a: 19). Burton (2016b), for example, highlights the serious methodological uncertainties behind recent data from WRI and others pointing to absolute decoupling in carbon emissions.

The limited evidence for decoupling that does exist generally refers to relative decoupling, since "absolute reductions in resource use are rare" (UNEP 2011a: xxv). And even in places where some relative decoupling seems to have occurred, UNEP acknowledges that this may be offset by "a shifting of the material and environmental burden into developing countries" (2011a: 16) through offshoring production. For example:

> Even in the two countries which arguably have made the most explicit efforts towards decoupling, Japan and Germany, and where at first glance domestic resource consumption shows stabilization or even a modest decline, deeper analysis shows that many goods contain parts that have been produced abroad using major amounts of energy, water and minerals. Thus some of the advanced countries are managing the problem of high resource intensity by "exporting" it elsewhere. The Report observes that trade—not surprisingly—is generally enhancing energy use and resource flows and thus, overall, impeding rather than promoting decoupling. (2011a: xi)

In addition, UNEP recognizes that apparent decoupling may be further offset by a "rebound effect," also termed the Jevons Paradox, in which "efficiency gains in resource use may paradoxically lead to greater resource use" (2011a: xvi) (see Figure 7). In sum, the 2014 report admits, "breaking the link between human well-being and resource consumption is necessary and possible but in reality is hardly happening" (2014: xii).

Despite the preceding admissions of methodological complexities, however, UNEP elsewhere claims evidence for some modest relative resource decoupling on a global scale: "Annual global resource extraction and use increased from about 7 billion tons (7 Gt) in 1900 to about 55 billion tons (55 Gt) in 2000, with the main shift being from renewable biotic resources to non-renewable mineral ones. Even in the existing economic environment of continuously declining resource prices, some decoupling of resource use

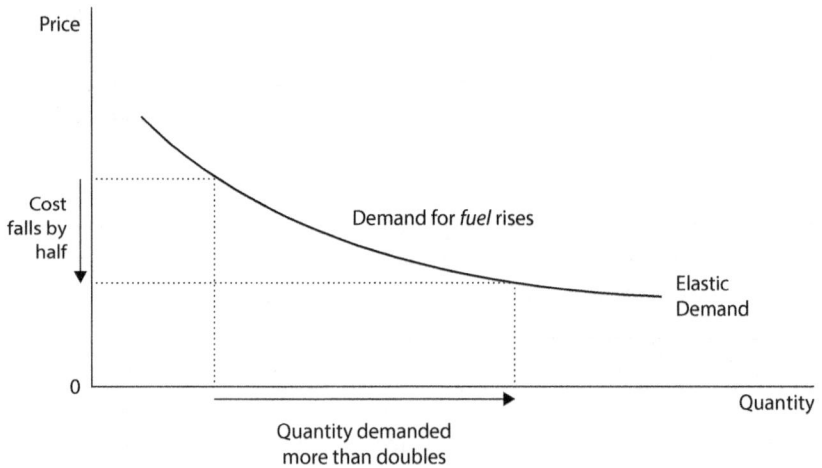

FIGURE 7. Classic illustration of the Jevons Paradox. SOURCE: Lawrence Khoo.

from economic activity has taken place: *the world economy has been dematerializing*" (2011a: 17, emphasis added). Here, incredibly, a massive global increase in resource use is reframed as evidence of decoupling instead!

Subsequently, however, the report changes tone once again, as much as admitting that the sustainable decoupling it advocates is impossible to achieve. UNEP outlines three hypothetical scenarios for future resource use: (1) the ubiquitous "business-as-usual"; (2) a modest contraction and convergence "requiring industrialized countries to reduce their per capita resource consumption by half the rate for the year 2000" (2011a: xvii); and (3) a "tough contraction and convergence [that] would keep global resource consumption at its 2000 level, but redistribute the resources so all countries achieve roughly the same per capita metabolic rate" (73). Of these, UNEP admits that only the third scenario is both "consistent with the IPCC assessments of what would be required to prevent global warming" and "compatible with the existing (if unknown) limits to the Earth's resource base" (32). Yet even this "scenario would not lead to an actual global [absolute] reduction in resource use" (73). Moreover, notwithstanding its insufficiency, it "would be unlikely to be politically acceptable" (73) anyway, for "most politicians are likely to regard this scenario as too restrictive in terms of developmental goals such as reducing poverty and providing for the material comfort of a rapidly expanding middle class" (32). Hence, the proposal would need to be "supported by a clear case as to why poverty reduction in a resource scarce world will depend more on innovations for decoupling than if investments continue to prioritize BAU production and consumption technologies and systems" (32). In sum, despite acknowledging that only this last scenario comes close to offering a vision of a sustainable future, UNEP admits that it "can hardly be addressed as a possible strategic goal" (32).

While asserting the necessity of dramatic decoupling for any hope of genuine green growth, in short, UNEP simultaneously admits that there is virtually no evidence that (absolute) decoupling works; that the conceptual basis for even imagining its possibility is weak; and that even if it were possible, it would be politically infeasible. Such rhetorical gymnastics are necessary because decoupling (in an absolute form at a global scale) is in fact impossible (Hickel and Kallis 2020). As Ward et al. (2016) demonstrate, a growth-based economy will always demand growing resource inputs. Even so-called "non-material" economic activity has material consequences in terms of both inputs and outputs. Hence, UNEP acknowledges, for instance: "Although some assumed that computerization would lead to a dematerialized "knowledge economy," material extraction also increased from about 35 billion tons (35 Gt) in 1980 to nearly 60 billion tons (60 Gt) in 2005, with substantial increases in particular in the extraction and use of construction minerals and ores (reflecting the twin impacts of accelerated urbanization and population growth on resource requirements)" (2011b: 64). Other ostensibly nonmaterial processes invoked to support the possibility of decoupling display similar dynamics. The "shift from vinyl albums to online music and from books to e-books," for instance, still requires, among other inputs, material production of computers and e-readers in addition to energy to transport these items (Arboleda 2020), as well as to power all of the equipment through which these digital media are delivered, to say nothing of the manifold resources used by consumers to generate funds to purchase these "nonmaterial" products.

Yet even if decoupling were possible in a strictly biophysical sense, it would remain unviable in purely financial terms. In a "mature" global economy sustaining growth over time becomes increasingly more difficult as the size of the economy grows. Harvey (2014) emphasizes this point, demonstrating that the nature of compound interest necessitates that, over time, the same rate of growth requires ever greater expansion in economic activity. Hence, he describes: "To keep to a satisfactory growth rate right now would mean finding profitable investment opportunities for an extra nearly $2 trillion compared to the 'mere' $6 billion that was needed in

1970. By the time 2030 rolls around, when estimates suggest the global economy should be more than $96 trillion, profitable investment opportunities of close to $3 trillion will be needed. Thereafter the numbers become astronomical" (228).

It is unclear, moreover, what exactly would replace current sectors of the economy that must be curtailed for decoupling to proceed. Fossil fuel extraction is currently the largest industry in the world, generating an estimated US $4 trillion in 2014 and accounting for between 4.6 and 6.5 percent of global GDP (IBISWorld 2015), while the second leading sector is tourism, which is fundamentally grounded in fossil fuel use too (United Nations World Tourism Organization [UNWTO] 2018). Countless spillover industries also depend either directly or indirectly on oil production and consumption. It is generally agreed that the world will need to move away from a fossil-fuel-based economy for decoupling to occur (see especially Sachs 2015), yet despite the environmental gains such a transition would potentially achieve, it is unclear what if anything could replace the economic value that would be lost in this transition to not only make up the enormous shortfall but actually sustain still further growth in the future. As Ferguson (2015) points out, drawing on Žižek (2010), oil has seemingly magical properties, defying the labor theory of value in its capacity to generate tremendous profit relative to the investment in (conventional forms of) its extraction (as long as environmental costs are externalized, of course).

Malm goes further, contending that global capitalist expansion since the industrial revolution has in fact been fundamentally predicated in intensified fossil fuel use: "At a certain stage in the historical development of capital, fossil fuels became a necessary material substratum for the production of surplus-value. But they are not merely necessary as leather for boots, raw cotton or iron ore for machines: they are utilized *across the spectrum of commodity production* as the material that sets it in physical motion" (2016: 288, emphasis in original).

When social issues are taken into account these essential dilemmas in the decoupling agenda become more pronounced still. Curiously, despite its emphasis on the importance of poverty reduction as motivation for the continued economic growth necessitating decoupling, UNEP spends no time at all discussing how decoupling relates to poverty rates. GDP is the only development indicator used in the report (and not even in per capita terms, let alone in relation to international or national distribution). UNEP states that throughout the twentieth century "growth rates of CO_2 emissions . . .

are smaller than the respective growth rates of GDP, so a relative decoupling has occurred" (2011a: 19).

Yet during this same period, global inequality has also increased dramatically (Milanovic 2011; Piketty 2014). Hence, whatever decoupling has occurred has not necessarily been concomitantly matched by one of the central aims of the initiative and an explicit rationale for the need for sustained growth, namely poverty alleviation (notwithstanding limited gains in extreme poverty reduction over the past several decades focused mostly on China; see Sachs 2015).[14] Without strong policy measures to redistribute revenue, even if decoupling were to be achieved, it would not necessarily lead to poverty reduction, but would, on the contrary, likely exacerbate inequality still further.

Yet the problem is more fundamental than even this, for the limited "dematerialization" that UNEP identifies is in fact *dependent on* cheap labor, since this allows more value to be realized from the same "metabolic rate" of resource throughput—a dynamic that, paradoxically, decoupling requires to reconcile poverty alleviation with continued economic growth (Hennike 2014). In order to compensate for this gain in labor efficiency even more growth is required, which of course must further exploit either labor itself or extract natural resources to also sustain a significant rate of profit. Consequently, environmental protection must inevitably come into conflict with social equity in the quest for "green growth."

FICTITIOUS GROWTH

It is here, finally, that the rapidly growing emphasis on financialization within the neoliberal conservation project highlighted in chapter 3 becomes so significant. The only way to appear to avoid the dilemmas previously outlined and so create the illusion of decoupling is to encourage the creation of "fictitious" value deriving from no real material source whatsoever. In promoting a "dematerialized economy," therefore, what UNEP seems to be advocating, essentially, is increased reliance on "fictitious capitalism" via financialization (Harvey 1989). The "dematerialization" that decoupling promotes, in other words, appears to be precisely the transition from the standard M-C-M' route to capital accumulation to an M-M' strategy in which money multiplies directly upon itself without recourse to initial conversion into commodities.

What this amounts to, bluntly stated, is creation of the illusion of economic growth through an increase in debt (Bjerg 2014). As Satyajit Das explains, "Debt is the oxygen of financialization" in the sense that "trading in financial markets is to a large extent carried out with borrowed money" (in Bjerg 2014: 194).[15] And since this growth is largely imaginary—numbers on a computer screen—it can proceed without evident environmental impact. During the same period in which UNEP identifies relative decoupling in the global economy, after all, the majority of economic value has been financed primarily through the creation of massive quantities of debt due the introduction of "post-credit" money and financial derivative markets enabling value to multiply seemingly ad infinitum—a process facilitated by deregulation of banks and financial markets via neoliberal reforms (Bjerg 2014; Harvey 2014). The decoupling that UNEP advocates, therefore, is really the decoupling of the global monetary system from the material world it is intended to accurately value within a natural capital accounting framework!

Yet this can hardly be a sustainable long-term strategy since this type of "casino capitalism" is in fact a major destabilizing force in the global economy (Harvey 1989), a dynamic largely responsible for the 2008 economic meltdown as well as many previous crises including the 1929 stock market crash and subsequent global depression. As Gray points out, "Financial markets do not tend to equilibrium. Overshoot is their normal condition. The volatility at the core of deregulated financial institutions makes a world economy that is organized as a system of free markets a very unstable place" (1998: 197).

Arrighi (2009), in fact, considers this shift from investment in the material economy to pure financialization as the basis of accumulation a "signal crisis" of the imminent exhaustion of a given regime of accumulation. In this dynamic, falling returns on material investment provoke investors to abandon "the 'general circuit of capital'—that is, the long and tedious process of leasing factory space, buying machinery and raw materials, renting land, finding the right kind of labor power, organizing and implementing production, and marketing commodities" and instead pursue "speculative ventures of all kinds" (O'Connor 1994: 80). In this way,

> Money capital, based on the expansion of credit, or money that cannot find outlets in real goods and services, jumps over society, so to speak, and seeks to expand the easy way—in the land, in stocks and bond markets, and in other financial markets. Hence the present economic anomaly: the value of

claims on the surplus or profits grows at the same moment that the real value of fixed and circulating capital stagnates or declines. (O'Connor 1994: 8)

Arrighi agrees that "financial expansions are taken to be symptomatic of a situation in which the investment of money in the expansion of trade and production no longer serves the purpose of increasing the cash flow to the capitalist stratum as effectively as pure financial deals can" (2009: 8). James O'Connor contends, however, that this strategy "is as simple as it is economically self-destructive," for it "tends to make a bad economic situation worse" by causing "growing indebtedness and the danger of financial implosion" (1994: 8).

This appears to be precisely what is occurring within the neoliberal conservation project at present. From this perspective, the growing focus on financialization can be seen as something of a last, desperate attempt to finally successfully harness the long-promised capacity of conserved nature to pay for itself and deliver a profit that heretofore it has failed to achieve on a significant scale. Until now, as previously noted, in its function as an anti-regulation machine, global conservation has functioned mostly as a (global) subsidy system, redistributing resources to support conservation under the recurring assurance that this is merely a short-term support for the effort to generate self-sustaining markets, to eventually be withdrawn once such markets finally materialize (see, e.g., Fletcher and Breitling 2012). When these global markets fail to develop—as they have until now—the system turns to financialization instead to try to realize the promised potential than other mechanisms have proven unable to deliver.

ACCUMULATION WITHOUT COMMODIFICATION

This is certainly not to imply that all of the neoliberal conservation activity described in this book does not have concrete implications, however. Despite their contention that efforts to stimulate conservation finance have produced very little concrete investment thus far, Dempsey and Suarez caution that this promotion may still have important ideological effects, functioning "to re-affirm narrowed, antipolitical explanations of biodiversity loss, to reinforce neoliberal political rationalities among conservationists, and to foreclose alternative and progressive possibilities" (2016: 655). Even as it fails to actually establish markets, in other words, neoliberal conservation still seeks to promote its philosophy for adoption by stakeholders ranging from BINGO executives to local project participants. In their exploration of the potential to develop an asset class in conservation finance, for instance, Credit Suisse and McKinsey (2016) essentially imply that in order to achieve this the global conservation community will need to fundamentally restructure itself to start thinking and acting like the investors it wishes to attract. Shaw (2016), founder of the tech firm Internet of Elephants, goes further in explicitly asserting, "To achieve large-scale, long-term success, wildlife conservationists need to think like the private sector and invest in business innovation. . . . As conservationists, we want people to support nature for the same reasons we do. But we must look at things through the eyes of our "customers"—those who we are looking to engage. This is something that successful businesses would never fail to do." Meanwhile, on-the-ground implementation of neoliberal conservation projects in many places encourages local people to conceptualize their relationship with the surrounding environment in terms of monetary valuation and benefit-cost calculation in anticipation of promised benefits (see Fletcher et al. 2019).

Such ideological effects are compounded by significant material impacts. Despite the widespread failure of neoliberal conservation to establish functional markets for trade in natural capital thus far, quite a lot of money has still been circulated and accumulated by diverse intermediaries involved in the process of endeavoring to develop these markets, from state officials to carbon market brokers to countless consultants of every variety to local recipients of project funds (Lund et al. 2017; Asiyanbi and Lund 2020). We might term this a paradoxical process of "accumulation without commodification," wherein efforts to actually profit from natural resources largely fail, yet the process of *trying* to commodify them still facilitates the flow of funding and allows for substantial wealth to be amassed by some actors for as long as this seed money flows. The European Commission (2018), for instance, reports that between 2008 and 2015 €17.2 billion in direct public funding was invested in REDD+ worldwide, the vast majority of which has been siphoned off by implementing states and their intermediaries rather than reaching the local stakeholders whose conservation efforts it was intended to support. Via dynamics such as this, not merely despite but actually *through* its overarching failure, neoliberal conservation still has important (if unintended and paradoxical) effects in both ideological and material registers.

CONCLUSION

What the analysis in this chapter suggests, most fundamentally, is that there are in fact essential tensions within a neoliberal capitalist economy between the concerns for poverty alleviation, environmental protection, and profit generation that neoliberal conservation insists are reconcilable. Biophysical growth—no matter how "dematerialized"—remains finite, while growth of the global economy continues to demand ever-increasing natural resource use (UNEP 2011a; Malm 2016; Arboleda 2020). Meanwhile, even sustaining economic growth on its own terms, irrespective of its environmental impacts, is increasingly difficult as the global economy grows in absolute terms. At the same time, moreover, economic growth in and of itself will do nothing for poverty alleviation without strong redistribution policies contrary to strict market logic.

Considered together, these problems raise serious questions concerning the viability of the decoupling that must occur for neoliberal conservation to succeed. And if this is the case, why does the project nonetheless continue to charge forward with such seemingly unbridled momentum? The next chapter addresses this fundamental conundrum.

SIX

How to Fail Forward

It doesn't matter whether your objectives are in the area of art, business, ministry, sports, or relationships. The only way you can get ahead is to fail early, fail often, and fail forward.

JOHN C. MAXWELL, *Failing Forward: Turning Mistakes into Stepping Stones for Success* (2000:12)

How do so many intelligent people involved in development and promotion of neoliberal conservation not conclude what I believe the analysis developed in this book makes obvious: that the project is inherently contradictory and hence destined to fail? This is the key question I take up in this chapter, drawing on the psychoanalytically inspired understanding of power developed in chapter 1. I begin by describing how the neoliberal conservation project can indeed be understood to have "failed forward" through the years as part of the persistence of a "zombie" neoliberal program more generally.

THE BEATINGS WILL CONTINUE

In the immediate aftermath of the 2008 financial meltdown, a variety of pundits quickly pronounced this the death of neoliberalism (Peters 2008; Wilson 2014a). As former World Bank chief economist Joseph Stiglitz proclaimed at the time: "Neo-liberal market fundamentalism was always a political doctrine serving certain interests. It was never supported by economic theory. Nor, it should now be clear, is it supported by historical experience. Learning this lesson may be the silver lining in the cloud now hanging over the global economy" (Stiglitz 2008).

Yet less than a year later, following the infamous bailout packages implemented in a number of high-income countries, such voices had largely fallen silent or even reversed their positions (Wilson 2014a). Thus, the IMF stated in its 2009 Annual Report: "The seeds of the global crisis were sown during the years of high growth and low interest rates that bred excessive optimism and risk taking and spawned a broad range of failures—in *market discipline, financial regulation, macroeconomic policies, and global oversight*" (International Monetary Fund [IMF] 2009:9, emphasis added). The last three of these "failures" refer to errors in state governance, while the first concerns the "irrational exuberance" of market players themselves.[1] Similarly, an open letter signed by more than two hundred economists published in the *New York Times* in January 2009 asserted, "Lower tax rates and a reduction in the burden of government are the best ways of using fiscal policy to boost growth" (cited in Peck 2010a: 270).

Reflecting on what Crouch (2011) subsequently termed this "strange non-death of neoliberalism," Peck (2010b) diagnosed the resurrection of the neoliberal program in an undead "zombie" form—while Hendrikse and Sidaway (2010) pronounced it the rise of "neoliberalism 3.0."[2] As Peck described, in this brave new era, neoliberalism has "entered its zombie phase. The brain has apparently long since stopped functioning, but the limbs are still moving. . . . The living dead of the free-market revolution continue to walk the earth, though with each resurrection their decidedly uncoordinated gait becomes even more erratic" (2010b: 109).

In the realm of conservation, Christine MacDonald (2009) documented this zombie-like movement during the IUCN's 2008 WCC, writing:

> By early October, when the world's conservation elites gathered in Barcelona for their biggest meeting of the year, markets were crashing around the world, spreading panic and doubt about the wisdom of unbridled free market economics. But the conservationists, corporate CEOs, billionaire philanthropists, and heads of state and royal houses don't seem to have heard the news. In Barcelona's conference rooms and banquet halls, the conversation centered on how environmental groups must become even more like corporations.

Ken MacDonald (2010a, 2010b) also observed an intensified emphasis on market mechanisms at the 2008 WCC, depicting this as the moment when a corporate agenda previously contested among the IUCN membership became institutionalized within the organization. As I have shown in earlier chapters, this neoliberal emphasis only increased in the IUCN as well as numerous other conservation organizations in subsequent years. At the 2021 WCC, as well as in post-congress reflections (e.g., Timmermans et al. 2021), exponents still offered little clarity concerning exactly how natural capital valuation would lead to establishing markets for trade in ecosystem services sufficient to finance the dramatic expansion in conservation acknowledged as needed to counter global biodiversity loss, yet they continued to insist that this remains absolutely essential going forward.

Neoliberal conservation's undead forward lurching is particularly evident with respect to the REDD+ mechanism. Notwithstanding mounting evidence of the mechanism's failure to either generate market funding or translate this into effective forest protection, proponents continue to offer ambivalent endorsement of REDD+ in the face of its ongoing practical challenges. At a CIFOR-sponsored Global Landscapes Forum Investments Case Symposium held in Washington, D.C., in May 2018 (entitled "REDD+ Money for Green Results: What REDD+ Needs to Succeed"), for instance: "Christopher Martius, CIFOR's Climate Change team leader and panel moderator, set the stage for a discussion that would be both productive and critical as some delegates debated its efficacy and future potential. . . . Panelists acknowledged the extent of the challenges facing the voluntary climate change mitigation approach program, but also came forward with a range of useful propositions for helping achieve the emission reduction results so urgently needed" (Evans 2018). In the face of critiques such as Rainforest Foundation UK's (2017) contention that REDD+ "has not yet prevented a single gram of forest carbon from entering the atmosphere," Gabriel Labbate, regional coordinator of the Latin American and the Caribbean region for the Poverty-Environment Initiative (PEI) and the UN REDD program, claimed that REDD+ was indeed progressing by asserting that in fact "about 6 gigatons of carbon emissions have already been avoided as a result of the program. 'I think it is remarkable that in this environment we still get these types of results,' he concluded" (Evans 2018). Building on this positive spin, Dharsono Hartono, president director of PT Rimba Makmur Utama ("an Indonesian based company developing a 108,255 hectare peatland forest REDD+ project in Central Kalimantan"), affirmed that he "remained hopeful that the best for REDD+ is yet to come. 'The tipping point is almost here,' he said. 'People understand carbon much more now than ten years ago; we are in a very exciting time'" (Evans 2018). Firmly cementing REDD+'s zombie-like trajectory, finally, World Bank Lead Carbon Finance Specialist Ellysar Baroudy declared, "I don't give up. . . . I am totally an optimist in this space. I think it behoves on us all to really push the barriers and keep going, and to me there's just no other option than to make it happen" (Evans 2018).

Notwithstanding the essential contradictions in formulation and consistent failure in practice highlighted in the last chapter, in short, neoliberal conservation, like neoliberalism more broadly, displays a remarkable resilience, an uncanny capacity to explain away its own deficiency and roll out one new and more ambitious initiative after the next even as the previous begins to collapse. Elsewhere I have labeled this a "beatings will continue until morale improves" strategy (see Fletcher 2103b), in which neoliberal failure is answered merely by calls to intensify neoliberalization still further. Others have identified similar dynamics in other domains of neoliberal policy (Hendrikse and Sidaway 2010; Wilson 2014a).

THE ARTS OF RESISTANCE

This is certainly not to suggest that the advance of neoliberal conservation has proceeded unproblematically. On the contrary, as with the neoliberalization more generally (see McNally 2006; Cahill 2014), the project's promotion has long been met with a steady stream of criticism and pushback. From the outset of its global roll-out, for instance, REDD+ has encountered strong resistance by local community groups around the world as well as larger coalitions claiming to represent them (e.g., Newswire 2011). Bioprospecting and carbon markets have experienced similar questioning and opposition. On the ground, PES has been contested in some places by local groups calling for its reorientation toward locally defined meanings and priorities.[3] Thus, Asiyanbi and Lund (2020) describe "policy persistence" in REDD+ as the outcome of the interaction between opposing forces of "stabilization" and "contestation." The same could be said of many other neoliberal conservation mechanisms.

Meanwhile, promotion of MBIs for biodiversity conservation more generally has been contested from the outset by prominent conservation biologists themselves. As early as 1988, Ehrenfeld, reacting to the newly coined biodiversity concept, cautioned, "In the long run, basing our conservation strategy on the economic value of diversity will only make things worse, because it keeps us from coping with the root cause of the loss of diversity" (1988: 214). Shortly following the 1992 Rio Summit, Willers reinforced this critique by asserting that harnessing conservation to economic development movement "guarantees the continued deterioration of ecosystems and the loss of biodiversity" (1994: 1147). In the next decade, in an influential commentary in the prestigious journal *Nature*, McCauley asserted that "market-based mechanisms for conservation are not a panacea for our current conservation ills. If we mean to make significant and long-lasting gains in conservation, we must strongly assert the primacy of ethics and aesthetics in conservation" (2006: 27). The rest of the decade saw similarly critical assessment of MBIs published by other prominent mainstream voices in core conservation discussion venues.[4] Such skepticism has more recently inspired a new wave of commentary. Thus, McCauley (2015: 36) reaffirmed his earlier critique in even more explicit terms, asserting that "market-based mechanisms for conservation are not, unfortunately, the panacea that they have been made out to be." Others decry "justifying biodiversity protection based on narrowly conceived human well-being (essentially cost-benefit analysis)" (Johns 2014: 33); "decision-making dominated by the desires to optimize for efficiency and maximize short-term gains" (Mackey 2014: 132); and "exploiting nature for the exclusive purpose of human gain" (Locke 2014: 147).

More broadly, Sandbrook and colleagues (2013) describe an attitude of "cautious pragmatism" among rank-and-file members of many prominent conservation organizations, skeptical about the capacity of market mechanisms to deliver conservation benefits yet unsure how else to proceed in a world where funding from sources other than the market or corporate partners grows increasingly scarce. The authors find their small sample of skeptics divided roughly into two broad camps: one displaying "outcome focused enthusiasm" concerning the potential for markets to deliver substantial gains; the other evincing more "ideological skepticism" concerning the market-based approach as a whole. Consequently, Sandbrook et al. highlight "a likely dissonance between the values held by individual employees of large conservation organisations and the official positions adopted by the organisations themselves" (2013: 238). A follow-up study found similar dynamics among a larger cross-section of respondents (Holmes et al. 2017). Even professed proponents of MBIs are themselves often conflicted concerning the approach's viability (Dempsey 2016; Watt 2021).

Yet within overarching public discussion, such "critical messages are often ignored by mainstream organizations and media, and if they are acknowledged, often denied or twisted to suit particular neoliberal objectives" (Büscher et al. 2012: 22). In the face of such internal dissent, consequently, the leadership of organizations including IUCN, TNC, CI, and WWF have solidified their endorsement of neoliberal conservation and entrenchment within a growing global network pushing its promotion. Seemingly unfazed by such critiques, advocates of natural capital valuation have merely set their sights still higher, "scaling up" their ambitions to adopt an abstract "landscape-level" approach that shifts focus from concrete investment in particular on-the-ground projects toward courting investment bankers to develop financial instruments capable of generating market funding on an order of magnitude greater. In this way, the messy realities of practical implementation can be ignored in adopting a distanced, bird's-eye view from which the world far below assumes a well-ordered smoothness and coherence.

Amid all of this commotion, therefore, neoliberal conservation seems to develop not merely in the face of but precisely *through* its widespread failure in practice. Neoliberal visions are developed in the conference rooms of BINGOs and IFIs and propagated in global policy meetings, after which they are disseminated through the capillaries of the global network for implementation in diverse local contexts worldwide. This implementation sometimes moves through national governments in the contexts in question, while in other cases it flows directly to the ground through local branches of the transnational organizations within the network itself or via partnership with (or merely distribution of financing to) domestic NGOs and community groups. Evidence of complexity in practice is then filtered back through these domestic agents as it flows upward through the network to be scrutinized and discussed in further policy discussions, both within the headquarters of particular organizations and in the larger meeting spaces through which these organizations connect. Based on this deliberation, the intervention is either modified to correct for deficiencies or retired and replaced with another championed as able to do the job better via internalization of lessons learned from previous failure (Li 2007; Chambers et al. 2022). Redford et al. thus describe the history of global conservation as a progressive rollout of a series of "fads" that "are embraced enthusiastically and then abandoned" in favor of the next innovative promise (2013: 437). In this way, conservationists chase the latest new fad from bioprospecting to ecotourism to PES and REDD+, financial derivatives, green bonds, environmental hedge funds, then on to blockchain and NFTs.[5] In the overarching international landscape, similarly, Agenda 21 is replaced by the MDGs, then the SDGs, "sustainable development" with the "green economy," "green growth," "decoupling" and so forth. In this process, as Li relates, "failures invite new interventions to correct newly identified—or newly created—deficiencies. The limits of each governmental intervention shape its successor" (2007: 19). In all this frantic movement forward, meanwhile, evidence of previous failure gets brushed under the rug in the scramble for the next silver bullet.

Policy thus develops in an iterative cycle, a back-and-forth movement between abstract discussion and concrete implementation, each of which informs the next manifestation of the other. This complicates the common depiction of policy as a one-way linear movement from formulation to implementation, supporting much more a "mobilities" perspective in which polices are seen to circulate in non-linear fashion, "mutating" and undergoing reinterpretation at multiple scales as they do so (see especially Peck and Theodore 2015). This perspective, then, can appreciate the agency of local actors and processes in terms of pushing back against, resisting, or appropriating influences originating externally or promoted from outside as well as extending this influence back to the centers of origin in the course of further policy mutation.

Yet this should not be viewed as a horizontal process in which all actors have equal power in shaping outcomes, as some more extreme actor-oriented approaches assert (see especially Long 2003; Van Hecken et al. 2018). In the neoliberal conservation network examined within this book, actors positioned at the major political centers clearly have much more power to shape policy than most local resource users (who of course are also not uniform but also have differential levels of power and influence)—not least because the former tend to control most of the funding for which local-level actors usually have to compete and thus conform to guidelines not of their own making. By the same token, these elite actors are much more easily able to access the spaces occupied by the local stakeholders with whom they work than vice versa. High-level global meetings like the WCCs, UNFCCC and CBD COPs, and UN Summits, for instance, all contain "VIP" spaces to which only those with the proper certification are permitted access and from which the majority of participants, even those who have paid full fare, are wholly excluded. And of course these meetings are themselves highly exclusive spaces, often prohibitively expensive for individuals without organizational affiliation and funding.

KEEPING THE FAITH

Like neoliberalism in general, via this iterative process neoliberal conservation keeps failing forward from one botched experiment to another, their "repeated manifest inadequacies" giving rise not to a fundamental questioning of the basic approach but rather "further rounds of neoliberal intervention," as (Peck 2010a: 6) describes. Dempsey thus characterizes neoliberal conservation as "clunky and plodding, something more like a jalopy puttering along with flat tires and occasional backfires (but with a professional pit crew working furiously on a project of constant reassembly)" (2016: 256).

This of course raises the key question of how the project is able to accomplish this. How can its proponents simply explain away the failure of one initiative after another without considering the possibility that this might compromise the essential efficacy of the overarching approach? In their analysis of conservation "fads," Redford et al. assert that "we must take such fads more seriously . . . and study where new ideas come from . . . why they are adopted, why they are dropped, and what residual learning remains" (2013: 438). This is my aim in the remainder of this chapter.

There are a number of different ways to approach such thorny questions. Here we can revisit the theoretical synthesis grounding this book's analysis, as each of the perspectives comprising this synthesis has something to contribute to a holistic understanding of the dynamics in question.

For Marxists, of course, there is actually quite little to explain here. If, from this perspective, neoliberal ideology is not primarily intended to accurately account for reality at all, but merely to obfuscate the class project it seeks to legitimate, then ostensible "failure" is not really failure at all as long as accumulation proceeds apace. In this way, neoliberal conservation's promise to "green" capitalism may function merely to deflect critique by directing it toward discussion of how problems in current practice will be redressed via future action. For many captains of global industry benefitting from the status quo, therefore, in endorsing neoliberal conservation, "they also know that more fundamental questions about the logic of our economy and who benefits from it are not asked. And hence they do not have to provide any answers" (Büscher and Fletcher 2016). Thus, regarding the growing promises to implement "sustainable mining," Kirsch asserts:

> From the recognition that the mining industry is inherently unsustainable, leaving behind scarred and ruined environments, the industry now promotes itself as practicing sustainable mining. . . . The discursive shift also covers up the fact that there have been no significant reforms in how mining is practiced, or overall reduction of its harmful impacts, which the term sustainable might seem to imply. The promotion of mining as a form of sustainable development also makes it more difficult for critics of the mining

industry to increase recognition of its true social and environmental costs. The deployment of corporate oxymorons like sustainable mining is one of the key strategies corporations use to conceal harm and neutralize critique. (2010: 92)

While this approach is undoubtedly true for some corporate actors and others, it cannot explain the situation entirely, for there are clearly many advocates of neoliberal conservation, including conservationists and ecological economists as well as those fighting an uphill battle to promote sustainability within prominent MNCs themselves, who are clearly earnest in their intention to promote the approach on its own merits and who seem quite convinced of its efficacy despite all evidence to the contrary. Hence, my analysis supports Dempsey's assertion that "many advocates emphatically deny that ES [ecosystem services] opens up a new site for accumulation, often understanding their science as an attempt to intervene in and regulate status quo economic development" (2016: 103).

Also taking such convictions at face value, Büscher et al. thus ask "why the neoliberalizing of environmental conservation is so opaque and seductive to those involved with conservation work" (2012: 24). In answering their own question the authors highlight three main strategies via which proponents of neoliberal conservation obfuscate fundamental contradictions in its deployment: (1) use of "win-win" rhetoric asserting that these contradictions can be resolved through the very processes that stimulate them; (2) media spectacle creating "the *appearance* of general consensus with the ideological assumptions of neoliberal capitalism" (Büscher et al. 2012: 18, emphasis in original); and (3) the aggressive disciplining of dissenting voices that question these representations. All of this, they contend, produces "closed loop" thinking, "whereby in failing to take into account the wider processes of which it is part, the self-corrective actions of an ill-functioning system perpetuate illness-causing conditions, while providing temporary illusion of improvement" (Büscher et al. 2012: 14). Dempsey (2016) complements this analysis by outlining a number of challenges commonly cited by advocates as obstacles to realizing conservation markets, including a lack of convincing language, lack of defined standard of measurement, combined ecological-economic data, lack of a solid track record, and lack of supporting state regulation.

Yet while there is undoubtedly truth in this analysis too, it implies a logical coherence within neoliberal conservation discourse that the discussion in previous chapters suggests may not really be present in many cases. On the contrary, conservationists' own endorsement of the project often displays widespread gaps, inconsistencies, skepticism, and ambivalence belying any such pretense of coherence. Büscher et al. themselves in fact note that in promotion of neoliberal conservation "alternative viewpoints do not always need to be actively suppressed in order to be disciplined. Indeed, they can perversely be stimulated as some kind of catharsis, without impacting on the broader hegemonic system" (2012: 22). This is essentially the dynamic Bell (1992) labels "redemptive hegemony." While highlighting this dynamic within the neoliberal conservation project, however, the authors' discursive analysis cannot explain why and how it occurs.

WHAT COMES AFTER FARCE?

Moreover, the discussion in preceding chapters has demonstrated that there is so little conceptual and empirical support for the neoliberal conservation project's efficacy, and in fact so much accumulating evidence to refute this, that to wager potential future collapse of the global ecosystem on such a flimsy premise—as proponents are effectively doing—is tantamount to collective suicide.[6] In the following I introduce two interrelated examples that exemplify the gravity of the issues at stake here.

The first concerns global climate negotiations organized by the UNFCCC, within which MBIs like PES and REDD+ to facilitate carbon offset trading have become increasingly central over the past several decades (Bumpus and Liverman 2008; Fletcher 2012b). In UNFCCC discussions, it is now widely accepted that raising global atmospheric temperatures more than 1.5 degrees Celsius above preindustrial levels creates the potential for impacts that may spiral out of control due to feedback processes such as the melting of polar ice caps and arctic tundra, spontaneous rainforest combustion, and so forth. Likely consequences of this change include massive human displacement due to sea level rise, increased intensity and unpredictability of weather events, and loss of agricultural capacity in many food-vulnerable areas (Intergovernmental Panel on Climate Change [IPCC] 2021).

Acknowledging such issues, the UNFCCC has met in a COP every year since 1995, three years after the Convention's enactment at the 1992 Rio Summit.[7] Despite more than two decades of such meetings to date, however, the UNFCCC has failed entirely to achieve its intended aim to reduce

GHG emissions a mere collective 5 percent over 1990 levels. On the contrary, global emissions have risen substantially throughout the period during which they were intended to diminish (IPCC 2021).

There is disagreement concerning how much carbon dioxide the atmosphere can accommodate before exceeding this 1.5 degree rise, but common estimates range between 350–550 PPM. In 2014 the planet exceeded 400 PPM for the first time in recorded history, and we continue to release CO^2 at ever-increasing rates. Hence, many commentators are beginning to acknowledge that our failure to achieve meaningful mitigation over the past two decades of UNFCCC negotiation means that remaining within the 1.5 degree window is increasingly less likely. Accomplishing this would require immediate and drastic action to dramatically reduce GHG emissions in industrialized societies around the world. Conservative estimates suggest that global emissions would need to peak by 2025 then drop to half of current levels by 2050 (IPCC 2021). Less restrained assessments assert that global emissions must in fact have already peaked by 2017 and quickly reduce to 90 percent of current levels thereafter (Klein 2014). But critics warn that even this may allow for a global temperature increase of 3–4 degrees or even greater due to climate effects already set in motion by past action (Jordan et al., 2013).

Yet the degree of socioeconomic transformation necessary to achieve even more conservative reductions in GHG emissions is staggering to consider. To put the issue into perspective, consider this assessment of the UK's 2008 Climate Change Act envisioning a relatively modest emissions reduction of at least 34 percent over 1990 levels by 2020: "Assuming a GDP growth of 2% p.a., a year-on-year annual rate of decarbonization of 5.3% is required to reach the Act's target; whereas there is no record of any economy having achieved greater than 2.0%, and then only for short spells. In sum, this Act requires the UK to achieve the impossible" (Prins et al., 2009: 9). Extrapolate this to other industrialized nations, and for the more stringent targets that are really needed to adequately address global warming, and one begins to appreciate the enormity of the challenge. Bluntly stated, truly reversing current climate trajectories would require dramatic transformation in political, economic, and social structures at every level and throughout the world. As Klein (2014) asserts, it would require changing virtually everything about our way of life within contemporary capitalist society.

The Paris Agreement enacted at the UNFCCC's COP-21 in December 2015 may correct for this to some degree, offering a new global compact in which nearly every nation in the world has promised (albeit in a non-binding framework) to substantially reduce emissions according to Nationally De-termined Contributions. Yet analyses of these commitments concur that if fully realized in their current form they are likely to result at best in a 2.7- to 3-degree temperature increase (see, e.g., Goldenberg et al. 2015), thus poten-tially allowing for many of the fearsome feedback effects the IPCC predicts. And as with the UK Climate Act noted earlier, achieving even the inadequate goals codified in the Paris Agreement would require dramatic socioeconomic change in most societies. Hence, in all likelihood, the sobering truth is that we remain firmly on a path toward climate catastrophe in the not-so-distant future. Yet the UNFCCC continues to meet year after year, as it has for the last twenty-five, asserting (in public at least) that the agreement needed to effectively address this catastrophe is always almost within reach, despite the fact that the dramatic structural transformation required for this never even enters the discussion. In this way, UNFCCC negotiations perfectly exem-plify Fredric Jameson's famous observation, quoted by Taussig (1998b) in one of his essays on public secrecy, that "it is easier to imagine the end of the world than it is to imagine the end of capitalism" (2003: 76).

Meanwhile, among the growing chorus of corporate players who claim to acknowledge the daunting implications of climate change is ExxonMobil, one of the largest oil companies in the world and one of the most profitable MNCs generally. Copious evidence now demonstrates that ExxonMobil, along with other fossil fuel producers such as the infamous Koch brothers, has in fact been aware of the climatic implications of fossil fuel emissions for decades yet has spent many millions to suppress and/or distort public discussion of these issue (see, e.g., Greenpeace 2013). More recently, how-ever, as evidence for climate change becomes increasingly pervasive and incontrovertible, the company's position has become more complicated. In one report, for instance, ExxonMobil (2014) explicitly acknowledged the decisive findings of the latest IPCC assessment released the very same day (IPCC 2014) yet stated that these findings would be unlikely to provoke a significant regulatory response by most governments and hence that the company's primary obligation to its shareholders required that it continue to extract and sell all available oil despite the admittedly apocalyptic im-plications of so doing (see ExxonMobil 2014).[8] As a satirical news headline subsequently lampooned this decision, ExxonMobile effectively told the world to "drop dead" (Turnbull 2014).

In this way, ExxonMobile's report represents an acknowledgment of climate change on a superficial level, while still not accepting the serious implications of the phenomenon in terms of the dramatic impacts that should force any reasonable person to end actions contributing to the problem if it were fully acknowledged. Far from coherent or rational ideological positions, therefore, perspectives such as that espoused by ExxonMobile and the UNFCCC in their perpetual deferment of the effective climate action all agree is essential appear much more to evidence a particular form of disavowal that Žižek describes as asserting, "The situation is catastrophic but not yet serious" (1992: 27). Adapting his general formula for disavowal, Žižek explains this perspective as maintaining, "I know very well (that the situation is catastrophic), but . . . (I don't believe it and will go on acting as though it were not serious)" (1992: 27). In terms of such disavowal, as Žižek paraphrases Sloterdijk's (1988) account of cynical reason, actors seem to "know very well what they are doing, but still, they are doing it" (Žižek 1989: 26).

Disavowals of this sort appear widespread within neoliberal conservation discourse. It is evident, for instance, in UNEP's discussion of decoupling, wherein the possibility of decoupling is repeatedly affirmed even as the analysis itself largely discredits this (see Fletcher and Rammelt 2017). Consider, as well, ecological economist Rees's statement cited in chapter 5 that "if we were serious about having a true market economy, mergers and acquisitions and other means of concentrating power would be disallowed." For free markets to exist, Rees seems to be saying, they must be regulated in ways diametrically opposed to the essential neoliberal principle dictating that the state should not intervene directly in the market to regulate players' resource allocation decisions. *I know free markets are impossible*, Rees thus admits, *nevertheless I believe that they can function*.

In a further paradigmatic example, Farley and Costanza assert, in response to certain critics, that PES schemes "do not require commodification" (2010: 2060) but may include services involving the "capacity of ecosystem structure to reproduce itself" rather than merely instrumental services such as "food, fiber, fuel, and water" (2010: 2062). Likewise, such services can be "based on reciprocity rather than conditional monetary incentives" (2010: 2063). Similarly, the authors claim that PES "can *propertize* ecosystems and their services without privatizing them," since property may be held collectively rather than individually (2010: 2061, emphasis in original).

Yet inconsistency in their argument is rampant. While PES may encompass intrinsic values and work through reciprocity, as the authors claim, it must still commodify resources if it is to provide the monetary compensation that stands as its most essential feature (and even Farley and Costanza's main example of a "reciprocal transaction"—providing up-front extension payments—involves such compensation). Likewise, property collectively held is still privatized if others are denied access and payments are delivered only to the owners. Despite its claim to transcend the reduction of complex socioecological systems to base economic valuation, in other words, this logic ends up advocating precisely this while obfuscating the process by which it does so.[9] Thiam (2016) does something similar when he claims, as quoted in chapter 4, that financialization can turn nature into an "asset" without commodifying it. Apologies such as these facilitate disavowal through the use of esoteric language that renders its reasoning difficult to understand, and thus critique, thereby obscuring logical inconsistencies in their presentation.

Inspired by Marx's famous statement (itself inspired by Hegel) that significant historical events tend to occur twice, "the first time as tragedy, the second time as farce," Žižek (2009b) uses this same sequence to connect 9/11 to the 2008 economic crisis as twin consequences of a destructive capitalist system. Increasing promotion of neoliberal conservation as an antidote to this same destructive tendency might be seen to constitute a third stage in this succession,[10] wherein farce is replaced by something more tragic still: an impossible fantasy of capitalist redemption in the face of mounting ecological crises that capitalist production itself continues to intensify in its headlong rush for profit.

STRATEGIES OF DISSIMULATION

Accounting for contradictory dynamics of the sort outlined above calls, I believe, for analysis in terms beyond those offered by either Marxist or post-structuralist positions. Following Žižek, I suggest that psychoanalysis offers the analytical framework appropriate to explain the paradoxical discourse that underpins neoliberal conservation and sustains its incessant failing forward. In the rest of the chapter, I therefore draw on the psychoanalytic understanding of power developed in chapter 1 to outline the dynamics that I believe help to facilitate this zombie-like progression.

A Libidinal Economy of Expectations

Most centrally, neoliberal conservation's failing forward is sustained by the project's functioning as what Borup et al. (2006) call an "economy of expectations," which attains support through the promise of concrete benefits that are perpetually deferred into the future. In this sense, Dempsey contends that neoliberal conservation "is best conceptualized as promissory, a socioecological-economic utopia whose realization is always *just around the corner*" (2016: 3, emphasis in original). Evidence of deficiency can thus be quickly dismissed as a product of the fact that, despite more than two decades of formulation, these are still "early days" in the project's development and hence that errors can be corrected through future planning and innovation. In 2002, Daily and Ellison already described a number of forerunners frustrated by their inability to develop initiatives that successfully combined conservation and profit. Yet, a decade later, Daily and other members of the Natural Capital Project (NCP) were still asserting that "there need to be examples of projects or enterprises that—as a result of properly valuing ecosystem services and natural capital—end up with improved decisions, institutions, and human well-being" (Daily et al. 2011: 768–769). Yet they remained "convinced" that these were "within striking distance. The environmental movement has a much bigger and more diverse and powerful community behind it now than ever before. . . . Science is beginning to provide tools and methods that will reduce the transaction costs. And there are enough policy experiments underway that compelling examples of natural capital stewardship enhancing human well-being should be forthcoming" (768–769). Nearly a decade on from this, Credit Suisse and McKinsey (2016) were still forecasting potential for a substantial conservation finance market while lamenting the difficulty of establishing this in practice or even identifying significant examples of its potential.

A similar economy of expectations is certainly present in promotion of decoupling. Notwithstanding its tacit admission that significant decoupling is not yet happening and is unlikely to be possible in any meaningful sense, UNEP, along with a growing body of collaborators, nonetheless continues to assert that it can and will happen in the future. Rather than actually explaining how this will occur, however, UNEP merely assures us that "the IRP intends to seek answers to such questions in its future work" (2011a: 75). The Sustainable Development Solutions Network led by Jeffrey Sachs, meanwhile, defends its own faith in decoupling by arguing:

> There are many pessimists regarding decoupling who feel that the only way to limit resource use is to limit overall economic growth. We disagree. Decoupling has not yet been tried as a serious global strategy, and we believe that advances in areas such as information and communications technologies,

energy technologies, materials science, advanced manufacturing processes, and agriculture will permit continued economic growth combined with a massive reduction in the use and waste of key primary commodities, a sharp drop in greenhouse gas emissions and other forms of pollution. (in Fletcher and Rammelt 2017: 463)

In such framing, advocacy of decoupling does not require evidence or even coherent conceptualization, but merely faith in its potential—faith that cannot be contested until the project has been rolled out in a coherent global program and its consequences assessed. This faith is sustained through further blind faith in the potential of "innovation" to resolve not only technical but also political obstacles in the face of actualizing the agenda. Since decoupling has in fact never happened on a significant scale, this reasoning is essentially unassailable. Yet it is also entirely circular, for if decoupling is impossible, then it can never be achieved, and hence one can never prove that it is unachievable. *The solution to sustainable development is decoupling*, this perspective asserts; *hence, if sustainable development is not achieved, it is because decoupling has failed.* The solution, consequently, is of course more decoupling.

All of this is reinforced by the meta-fantasy at the heart of neoliberal governance, generally, which Dean (2008), drawing on Žižek, calls the "fantasy of free trade." As Dean describes,

> The fantasy of free trade covers over persistent market failure, structural inequalities, the violence of privatization, and the redistribution of wealth to the "have mores." Free trade sustains at the level of fantasy what it seeks to avoid at the level of reality—namely actually free trade among equal players, that is equal participants with equal opportunities to establish the rules of the game, access information, distribution, and financial networks, etc. (2008: 55)

Via recourse to this fantasy, any shortcomings of neoliberal policies can be explained away in terms of the logic that these problems are due not to policies themselves but merely to failure to implement them properly and to a sufficient degree. From this perspective, failure is never failure of market logic but merely "market failure," a technocratic rather than political problem (Li 2007; Büscher 2010) remedied by redoubled efforts to "get the market right." Hence, the fantasy of free trade dictates that no matter how greatly neoliberal policies fail in practice, the fiction can be sustained that this failure is due not to any fundamental errors or contradictions in these policies' internal logic but rather to the fact that they have been implemented incompletely, and thus that if only neoliberalism could function with less inhibition, less state regulation, it would actually perform as intended. As Žižek observes, this fantasy asserts that (neoliberal) capitalism fails because it is not pure *enough*, reinforcing his observation that "ideology really succeeds when even the facts which at first sight contradict it start to function as arguments in its favour" (1989: 50). In this way, critique of neoliberal logic itself is effectively neutralized. As in Taussig's analysis of shamanism, within neoliberal conservation's economy of expectations, failure in practice merely reinforces the fantasy of future success, evoking the constantly "receding shadow of the real in all its perfection" (1998: 247).

As with any ideology, psychoanalysis suggests that sustaining neoliberal conservation's economy of expectations is the promise of *jouissance*, rendering this economy a libidinal as well as monetary one (see Lyotard 1993; Sioh 2014). For the intended recipients of neoliberal conservation interventions, such *jouissance* of course inheres in the benefits (primarily economic revenues and the goods/services this can buy) commonly promised to enlist their participation (see, e.g., West 2006; Massarella et al. 2018; Fletcher et al. 2019). For those championing neoliberal conservation, on the other hand, the promise of *jouissance* encouraging attachment to the project can come from several sources. First is the particular emotional reward commonly accompanying one's sense of "doing good" via philanthropic work, which Bishop and Green indeed describe as a "dopamine-mediated euphoria often associated with sex, money, food, and drugs" (2008: 39). Second is the affective charge of flying around the world to participate in seemingly important discussions at major international events that are specifically staged to maximize their sense of drama and significance. As I have previously described of the 2012 World Conservation Congress (Figure 8) during which neoliberal conservation was a central topic of promotion, for instance:

> Much of the Congress was pure spectacle.... The opening ceremony was particularly dramatic. Presided over by a professional Master of Ceremonies, it presented, as one component, a classic drama of fall and redemption in which dancers dressed like butterflies fled as the auditorium darkened and enormous drill bits bored outward through the screens, ushering in a postapocalyptic world of industrial decay.... Likewise, at the end of the closing session triumphant music filled the air, while the screens strobed neon, and cannons arrayed along the auditorium's edges spewed paper butterflies over the crowd. Exiting, participants passed through a gauntlet of young ushers clapping and cheering wildly. (Fletcher 2014b: 332–333)

FIGURE 8. Opening ceremony at the 2012 World Conservation Congress, Jeju Island, South Korea. SOURCE: Robert Fletcher.

This sense of import is enhanced by the attribution of VIP status to select participants, entailing receipt of distinctive name tags signaling this status and access to excusive backstage spaces as well as organization personnel assigned to personally chaperone VIPs throughout the event.

The increasing enrollment of well-known celebrities in the neoliberal conservation project adds a third source of *jouissance*, allowing conservationists to rub shoulders with cultural elites in the course of carrying out their work (Brockington 2009; Fletcher 2015). Which celebrities will be present at a given event indeed becomes a frequent topic of discussion among meeting participants. Neoliberal conservation thus increasingly entails the public staging of encounters among an array of powerful actors across public, private, intergovernmental, and cultural sectors that rank-and-file conservationists can also witness and hence vicariously participate in as well.

Other dynamics could be mentioned; the point is that, in various ways, provision and promise of *jouissance* compels affiliation with the project and its expectations of future fulfilment regardless of present realities, on the part of both proponents and recipients of the envisioned interventions. In this way, neoliberal conservation can generate an "irrational exuberance" in excess of the conclusions a dispassionate assessment of the project's prospects might otherwise provoke.

In addition to redemptive hegemony, Büscher and colleagues' observation that critique of the neoliberal conservation project "can perversely be stimulated . . . without impacting on the broader hegemonic system" (2012: 22) calls to mind Taussig's discussion of public secrecy introduced in chapter 1. In his analysis, Taussig asserts that public secrecy "not only thrives on a corrosive scepticism" but in fact "scepticism and belief actively cannibalize one another" (1999: 235). Hence, the success of public secrecy lies not in "skilled concealment but in the skilled revelation of skilled concealment" (222).

While Büscher and colleagues assert that an ideology "needs to be believed in; its central tenets should not be questioned" (2012: 15), the occurrence of public secrecy suggests that critical questioning may at times actually reinforce the ideology in question (as the authors themselves also note but do not explain). Within neoliberal conservation, consequently, skepticism on the part of conservationists, ecological economists, critical analysts, and others concerning the efficacy of the approach, such as that previously documented, may in fact function to support the disavowal sustaining the ideology seemingly problematized in this way (see also Watt 2021).

Even more essentially, however, the central public secret at the heart of the neoliberal conservation project may in fact be the inherent unsustainability of the capitalist system itself. There is, after all, no shortage of critical analysis widely available in the public sphere asserting precisely this.[11] Moreover, the prospect that capitalism may entail inevitable negative ecological consequences is in fact commonly introduced into critical discussion of neoliberal conservation itself.[12] Despite the prevalence of this critique, however, it is rarely included within conservation policy discussions that do, by contrast, quite explicitly and earnestly raise the prospect of global ecosystemic collapse if urgent, drastic action is not taken to prevent this.[13] Echoing both Jameson and Taussig, Žižek observes of such discussion that "it seems easier to imagine the 'end of the world' than a far more modest change in the mode of production, as if global capitalism is the 'real' that will somehow survive even under conditions of a global ecological catastrophe" (Žižek 1994: 1). Elsewhere, Žižek (2000) reiterates this suggestion that capitalism indeed seems to increasingly occupy the space of the Real in being considered immutable and hence impossible to transcend, thereby setting "a limit on resignification" and consequently also on potential critique. In this way, acknowledgment that capitalism essentially constitutes "a destructive force operating beyond the limits of human control" (Wilson 2014a: 309) is excluded from explicit discussion and instead looms as a public secret within official policy discourse.

Overpopulation and Other Scapegoats

Capitalism's retreat into the space of public secrecy with neoliberal conservation discourse may be facilitated by other dynamics too. One of the main supports to ideology highlighted by Žižek is the common practice of invoking a "scapegoat," an "external element" or "foreign body" ostensibly "introducing corruption into the sound social fabric" (1989: 142) and thereby subverting the fulfillment that would otherwise supposedly be achieved. In this manner, "what is excluded from the Symbolic . . . returns in the real as a paranoid construction of" (1989: 143) that which is repressed. Consequently, Žižek explains, "one of the ideological strategies is to fully admit the threatening character of a dysfunction, and to treat it as an external intrusion, not a necessary result of the system's inner dynamic" (2008: 389).

Neoliberals' central scapegoat is of course the opposite of free trade, namely socialism—or rather, the "paranoid construction" of a caricatured and stereotyped socialism ostensibly corrupting the capitalist system. Thus, Peck observes, "Even after decades of neoliberal reconstruction, it is remarkable how many present-day policy failures are still being tagged to intransigent unions, to invasive regulation, to inept bureaucrats, and to scaremongering advocacy groups" (2010a: 7–8). This perennial specter of socialism is used to silence criticism and reaffirm neoliberalism, as ideologues from Thatcher to Fukuyama have insisted, as the sole tenable social order (resulting in the common opposition between capitalism and socialism framed as diametrically distinct—and the only conceivable—options).

Another common scapegoat within discussions of neoliberal conservation specifically, along with other forms of environmentalism, is the venerable specter of "overpopulation."[14] Within neoliberal conservation discourse, such scapegoating is most clearly evident in the *Dasgupta Review*, one of the latest and greatest (at more than six hundred pages) contributions to the growing cannon (Dasgupta 2021). Commissioned by the UK Treasury, directed by Oxford economist Partha Dasgupta, and released to much fanfare in February 2021, the *Review* begins by rehearsing the familiar case for natural capital valuation outlined in previous chapters. In explaining why global biodiversity has become so depleted over time, subsequently, the Review returns time and again to the impact of human population growth. Yet its treatment of this issue is characterized by a persistent disavowal. On the one hand, the *Review* is at pains to distance itself from a troublesome Malthusian legacy. "There is a risk," Dasgupta admits, "that *any* study of the overshoot in the global demand for the biosphere's goods and services that includes population as a factor is read as a Malthusian tract. But that would be to misread the Review entirely" (2021: 33, emphasis in original).

Despite this disclaimer, however, the *Review* then repeatedly invokes overpopulation as a main root cause of biodiversity loss. In countering a Malthusian reading of his text, for instance, Dasgupta defines his aim as instead "to explain how individual and group actions over the years have led globally to" our current environmental predicament (2021: 33). To develop this explanation, the *Review* begins by outlining humans' emergence as a distinct species. "As our human numbers grew," it explains, "our impact on the planet increased with them" (2021: 22). As human population and resource use increased in concert over time, it continues, this reached a point where "the excess of impact (I) over the biosphere's regenerative rate (G)" became evident (2021: 32). Echoing the ubiquitous I = PAT equation,[15] the *Review* describes this outcome as one of "Impact Inequality," in terms of which "*I* is in turn decomposed into three factors: human population numbers, global GDP per person, and the efficiency with which we convert the biosphere's goods and services into GDP" (2021: 32–33). (Here again, ambiguously, the *Review* acknowledges and warns against the potential "that the Impact Inequality and the decomposition of the impact we have chosen to work with will be read as a piece of Malthusian arithmetic" [2021: 33]).

In subsequently focusing on family planning as a potential instrument for effective environmental management, Dasgupta reemphasizes that "expanding human numbers have had significant implications on our global footprint, and the global population is only expected to continue to rise" (2021: 491). Notwithstanding this reality, however, "the SDGs are reticent about family planning, and yet it is hard to imagine that they can be met without addressing the subject" (2021: 237). Likewise, the *Review* points out that researchers "have sketched scenarios of lower global population growth that lead to reductions in greenhouse gas emissions by 16–29%. And yet, the Paris Agreement of December 2015 on climate change made no mention of population" (2021: 238, note #283).

All in all, then, the *Review* asserts:

We should therefore ask whether the biosphere could support on a sustainable basis a global population of between 9.4 and 12.7 billion, which is the error bar round the UN Population Division's population median projection of 10.9 billion for year 2100 (UNPD, 2019b) at the material standard of living we are encouraged to seek. In effect we are asked in contemporary growth and development economics and the economics of climate change to imagine that the population numbers being projected today will be able to enjoy, at the very least, the current global living standard, even while making smaller demands on the biosphere than we do currently. (2021: 32)

Our present situation, Dasgupta consequently claims, is "analogous to each of a crowd of people trying to keep balance on a hanging bridge, with a risk of bringing it crashing down" (33).

Invoking the overpopulation scapegoat in this way to explain why policies have failed to alleviate either poverty or environmental degradation obfuscates the role of the capitalist economy in exacerbating both (Baker-Médard and Sasser 2020), hence preserving fantasies of such policies' future potential. Essentially, diagnoses of the conjoined problems of poverty and environmental degradation boil down to either of two causal factors: overpopulation or structural inequality produced by global capitalism. A focus on overpopulation, in this sense, displaces focus from this second potential cause, blaming individuals themselves for their predicament rather than the overarching political economy in which they are embedded (Baker-Médard and Sasser 2020). Or as Hartmann (1998: 115) phrases it, "The grossly unequal division of wealth in a society of resource abundance and waste demands the ethic of social scarcity to explain poverty." In this way, the overpopulation scapegoat functions as Žižek describes: blaming failure on an ostensibly external, corrupting element rather than on capitalism's intrinsic deficiencies. This focus on overpopulation may therefore help capitalism to occupy the space of the Real, as Žižek contends, setting a limit on what can be realistically imagined and, consequently, imagined otherwise.

What is striking about how overpopulation is invoked within environmental discourse is its common framing as an issue that has in fact been widely suppressed or excluded from public discussion thus far.[16] Yet concerns about "overpopulation" have in fact been consistently raised for more than a century now by innumerable actors and institutions, from academics to politicians, from UN agencies to the Gates Foundation (see Fletcher et al. 2014). Such concerns, however, are usually framed in precisely the terms of public secrecy: as something that no one else wants to talk about but that must now be confronted, nonetheless. Overpopulation is thus, as Foucault famously depicts Western European discussion of sexuality, an issue that "speaks verbosely of its own silences" and "takes great pains to relate in detail the things it does not say" (1978: 8). Framing in these terms helps, I suspect, to explain the issue's persistent recurrence within environmental discourse despite a long history of solid research and analysis demonstrating why this is in fact the wrong way to think about the problems it confronts.[17]

Those concerned with population growth commonly acknowledge that it is the combination of such growth *and* increased consumption that is responsible for environmental degradation. Yet in so doing, they frequently shift quite quickly from a brief nod to the latter to sustained focus on the former, contending that while of course overconsumption in a few wealthy countries is the principal source of environmental degradation *currently*, imagine how much worse the problem would be if all of the world's poor end up consuming at similar rates *as well*. Weld (2016) is paradigmatic in writing: "Those who deny that overpopulation is a problem say the poor don't consume much. Yet the poor want nothing more than to consume more, as proved by India and China. Who can blame them? And a burgeoning number of desperately poor people does have a major impact: they cut down forests to grow food, drain rivers, deplete aquifers, and overfish and over-hunt in their local area." In this way, the emphasis quickly shifts from addressing real issues in the here and now to a hypothetical future scenario that becomes the principal focus of attention. Such a stance clearly points once again to the presence of disavowal. Within such discourse, moreover, inequality itself is actually defended as in the interest of sustainability.

In a further twist of their project's essential biopolitical approach, finally, some neoliberal conservationists actually endeavor to address the "overpopulation problem" through further neoliberal programming. Building on the logic of offsetting unpinning PES, REDD+, and other neoliberal MBIs, conservationists thus increasingly promote population control programs as an offset mechanism, grounded in the rationale that reducing population growth will reduce future emissions relative to BAU scenarios (Baker-Médard and Sasser 2020).[18]

Fetishizing Failure

When all else fails to obfuscate failure, one can instead switch to fully acknowledging this failure yet framing it in a particular manner—as merely a stage on the road toward eventual success. In this way, failure is increasingly praised and celebrated by contemporary business and management consultants not as a problem to be avoided but, on the contrary, as an inevitable and valuable learning experience. In a previous book with the same title as this one, leadership guru John Maxwell (also quoted in this chapter's epigraph) thus claims, "Failure is simply a price we pay to achieve success. If we learn to embrace that new definition of failure, then we are free to start moving ahead—and failing forward" (2000: 343). He elaborates, "If you can change the way you see failure, you gain the strength to keep running the race. Get a new definition of *failure*. Regard it as the price you pay for progress. If you can do that, you will put yourself in a much better position to fail forward" (2000: 391, emphasis in original). Indeed, Maxwell goes so far as to claim, "If you're not failing, you're probably not really moving forward" (2000: 171). His book is filled with similar quotations from other gurus offering quite similar advice.

Or consider Fail Forward, a Toronto-based firm that defines itself as "the world's first failure consultancy" and its mission as "support[ing] people and organizations to allow, acknowledge, and adapt to failure in pursuit of innovation" (in Chambers et al. 2022: 105723). The firm explains, "Not many would call themselves Failure Experts with a sense of pride and purpose . . . but we do. Since 2011, we're proud to say that we have helped diverse businesses, governments, funders and non-profits harness their failure to learn, innovate, and build resilience" (105723). Through the trainings, coaching sessions, event design workshops, and other activities they offer, Fail Forward thus promises to teach participants how to "reframe failures as opportunities" (105723).

Such framing is increasingly prevalent within international development circles, where, Best (2014: 3) observes, "Over the past two decades, the main organizations involved in financing international development have become preoccupied with the problem of failure" (see also Mascarenhas 2017). This preoccupation is reflected, among other initiatives, in the proliferation of "Failure Reports" (e.g., EWB Canada 2017) and "Fail Festivals," the latter advocating "celebration of failure as a mark of leadership, innovation, and risk-taking in pushing the boundaries of what is possible in scaling ideas from pilots to global programs" (in Chambers et al. 2022: 105723). As Mascarenhas describes, "Fail Festivals have become all the rage in the media seeking forerunners of the humanitarian assemblage. The World Bank alone hosted three Fail Faire events in fifteen months. UNICEF has also hosted several themed Fail Faire events, including 'Fail to Scale'" (2017: 114).

Within the realm of conservation specifically, fetishization of failure has recently grown in popularity too (Chambers et al. 2022), as exemplified by two newfound initiatives. The first, a project called "Embracing Failure in Conservation," was launched by the Cambridge Conservation Initiative (CCI) in 2018. Acknowledging widespread failure of conservation interventions in the past, the project asserts that such failure is primarily due to lack of "objective, rigorous evidence" and "standardization in the way that conservation failures are reported." This, CCI claims, limits "the ability of practitioners to gather, analyze and summarize information from multiple cases and mainstream learning into the hands of those who would find it useful" (Dickson n.d: 1). In order to address these deficiencies, the project proposes a "taxonomy of root causes of failure in conservation" to guide future efforts to discuss and learn from project failure.

A second project, the Wildlife Conservation Society's (WCS) "Failure Factors Initiative" (FFI), began the following year in 2019. This initiative explains its aim as to "create a safe space for sharing information and experience to allow us to harvest the lessons offered by failure more easily" (Wilderness Conservation Society [WCS] 2020). WCS points out that "the military, aviation and engineering sectors have long embraced failure to learn and adapt, and the tech sector is increasingly pushing for a similar cultural change." However, "the development and conservation sectors have been slower to adopt" (Wilkie et al. 2019: 1). The FFI is thus intended to create a space for conservationists to anonymously share and discuss "things that did not work out as expected, even within otherwise successful projects," with the aim to assist "teams and organizations to learn faster and avoid the same pitfalls in the future" (2019: 1).

Consequent to fetishization of this sort, failure—even when explicitly acknowledged as such—need not be seen as signaling a fundamental problem with one's strategy but, quite to the contrary, as a sign that one is actually on the path to success after all.

CONCLUSION

The various dynamics explored in the preceding discussion, I believe, contribute to the peculiar configuration of neoliberal conservation discourse, in which contradictions are concealed and faith sustained through fantasies of future fulfilment. Yet even fetishists like Maxwell (2000) acknowledge that constructive or "intelligent" failure must be distinguished from "continual failure." As he explains, "Particularly stubborn people sometimes try to leave their troubles behind by working harder and faster, but without changing their direction. They're like the person trying to get the square peg in the round hole who first tries to place the peg in the hole, then tries to shove it in, then takes a hammer and tries to pound it in. They're working hard but getting nowhere" (392). For cases like this, Maxwell advises,

> There's really only one solution to the gridlock on the failure freeway, and that's to wake up and find the exit. To leave the road of continual failure, a person must first utter the three most difficult words to say: "I was wrong." He has to open his eyes, admit his mistakes, and accept complete responsibility for his current wrong actions and attitudes. Every failure you experience is a fork in the road. It's an opportunity to take the right action, learn from your mistakes, and begin again. (2000: 393)

This book's analysis suggests that the neoliberal conservation project has reached such a fork. In the final two chapters, I therefore turn to the pressing question of where to go from here in effectively addressing the daunting social and environmental challenges remaining before us. First, however, I describe a newfound challenge to neoliberal conservation and other forms of environmentalism that has exploded onto the world stage in recent years, namely the rise of right-wing authoritarianism and the flat-out war it has declared against environmental protection of any sort.

SEVEN

Neoliberal Conservation in Ruins?

The connection between free markets and "law and order" policies has never been inadvertent. As intermediary social institutions and the informal social controls of community life are
weakened by market-driven economic change the disciplinary
functions of the state are strengthened. The endpoint of this
development comes when the sanctions of the criminal law
become the principle remaining support of social order.

JOHN GRAY, *False Dawn* (1998: 32)

In the face of neoliberal conservation's widespread failure to implement genuine market-based instruments to achieve effective environmental protection, we have witnessed instead the rise of a variety of alternative approaches
to addressing these issues as part of a more general effort to confront deficiencies with the overarching neoliberal economic program. This chapter
explores these responses, among the most worrying of which is a recent resurgence of right-wing populism in a number of societies worldwide. In the
face of this disturbing development, one might be forgiven for pining for
a seemingly simpler time in which, momentarily, the frontiers of capitalist
accumulation seemed to focus on figuring out how to capitalize on conservation rather than returning to the rampant resource grab we are currently
witnessing. Yet it is within this moment of increasing peril that I believe it
remains most important to stay with the trouble, as Haraway (2016) advises,
because I am convinced that there remains much to learn from neoliberal
conservation's rise and fall that might help us understand how to confront
these dark new forces currently undermining the project too.

Indeed, one could argue that this right-wing backlash is itself in large
part a response to the failure of neoliberal mechanisms, in conservation
as elsewhere, to achieve their envisioned aims (Brown 2019). The inability of
conservation to establish itself as a viable foundation for sustainable capital
accumulation on a global scale (Büscher and Fletcher 2015), in other words,
may have provoked a return to intensified resource extraction—what Arsel

et al. (2016a) call an "extractive imperative"—to restore this accumulation in the wake of the 2008 economic crisis, as well as necessitating coercive suppression of resistance to this activity on the part of environmental defenders of the type we are currently witnessing in many places (Global Witness 2019).

The rest of the chapter develops this analysis and explores its implications for the future of global conservation efforts. I begin by charting the emergence and demise of an erstwhile challenge to neoliberal orthodoxy recently posed by so-called "post-neoliberalism."

THE POST-NEOLIBERAL IMPASSE
AND THE EXTRACTIVE IMPERATIVE

The rise of a number of political regimes promoting a renovated form of state-led developmentalism after the turn of the century (see especially Grugel and Riggirozzi 2012; Yates and Bakker 2014)—particularly in the Andean region of South America, beginning with Venezuela under Hugo Chavez then soon followed by Morales in Bolivia, Correa in Ecuador, and others—prompted their description as a novel "post-neoliberalism."[1] Such regimes were commonly divided into two broad camps: a more radical one comprising Chavez's Venezuela, Morales's Bolivia, and arguably, Correa's Ecuador, on the one hand, and another encompassing more mainstream regimes such as the Kirchners' Argentina, Lula's Brazil, Bachelet's Chile, Ortega's Nicaragua, and Tambo's Peru, on the other (see especially Yates and Bakker 2014). Despite their many differences, these various regimes generally all advocated a return to direct state management of the economy, including re-nationalization of important industries, as the basis of robust new redistributive social programs, a move sometimes framed in explicit challenge to a conventional neoliberal development model (see Rival 2010; Arsel 2012).

Many of these regimes achieved quite impressive gains in social protection, particularly with respect to marginalized populations suffering under the austerity imposed by previous neoliberal reforms. Yet in order to fund expanded social programs, most of them were forced to intensify raw material extraction as their main income-generation strategy, exacerbating natural resource exploitation and thereby augmenting pressures on conservation. This dynamic points to a more widespread tension between conservation and extractive industry throughout Latin America, whose place in the global economy, despite decades of efforts to generate domestic industry via import substitution policies, remains primarily as an exporter of raw materials for processing elsewhere (Miller 2007). Following widespread neoliberalization via SAPs during the 1980s and 1990s, during which the previously dominant import substitution development model was largely abandoned in favor of export-led growth, such extraction expanded dramatically, placing increasing pressure on natural resources at the same time as they were gaining mounting attention from international conservationists, not least as potential offsets for destructive activity elsewhere (Robinson 2008). Such pressures have intensified greatly in recent decades due in large part to a dramatic increase in foreign direct investment in resource extraction in the region by representatives of East Asian countries and others in quest of raw materials to fuel their own economic expansion (Arsel et al. 2016a; Arboleda 2020). As Escobar (2010: 47) thus observes, for instance, despite Bolivia's impressive social gains under the Morales regime, "Overall the development model is such that it continues to wreak havoc on the natural environment due to its dependence on accumulation fuelled by the exploitation of natural resources (e.g., hydrocarbons, soy, sugar cane, African oil palm)" (see also Anthias 2018). Arsel et al. (2016a) document the widespread occurrence of this "extractive imperative" throughout the region.

Ecuador under former President Rafael Correa offers a telling illustration of this general dilemma. In 2006, Correa was elected on a platform including an explicit critique of neoliberalism, which he claimed to reject in pursuit of a novel model of development situated "between Marx and markets" (Arsel 2012; see also Rival 2010; Shade 2015). To enact this transformation, Correa instituted a variety of reforms, including near-total nationalization of the oil and gas industries and enshrinement of the "Rights of Nature" within a renovated constitution. In its actual operationalization, however, the Ecuadorian economy remained heavily dependent upon extraction of raw natural resources, particularly fossil fuel drilling and mineral mining, for sale on the global market (Shade 2015; Arsel et al. 2016b). Moreover, even anti-neoliberal reforms remained strongly state centered and hence criticized by NGOs and indigenous groups for their lack of democratic participation. Hence, the regime's "post-neoliberal" content appeared more as a return to elements of the pre-neoliberal statist development model—reintroduction of a classically sovereign mode of governance in the form of "neo-structuralism" (see Wilson and Bayón 2017)—than any genuine movement forward toward the type of "twenty-first century socialism" that Correa, as a nominal member of the more radical wing of the post-neoliberal turn, claimed to pursue. Consequently, the project could be more properly seen as what Brenner et al. (2010a) call "orchestrated counter-neoliberalization" than *post*-neoliberalism per se. Yet even this counter-neoliberalization remained thoroughly capitalist, albeit in a strongly statist form, bent on ceaseless accumulation to generate the surplus needed to fund social programs (Arsel et al. 2016b; Wilson 2021).

In this way, most problematically, the regime remained thoroughly reliant on sustained economic growth to achieve its social development aims. Hence, it encountered further difficulties when conservation was also considered. Correa's rhetoric included strong language decrying commodification of natural resources and instead promoting nature's intrinsic value and inherent right to exist (Rival 2010). Meanwhile, certain of his advisers took this further to advocate "bio-socialism" as an explicitly anti-capitalist mode of accumulation (see Wilson and Bayón 2017). Yet the regime's environmental practices were decidedly at odds with this rhetoric. Essentially, Ecuador, like Costa Rica, sought to pursue both sides of the conservation-extraction nexus simultaneously, expanding raw material exploitation while also pursuing market-based conservation finance (Wilson and Bayón 2017). In theory, at least, this process was intended to progressively shift the emphasis from extraction to conservation over time by using revenue from the former to fund development of effective mechanisms for the latter (Shade 2016; Wilson and Bayón 2017). Yet in practice, as throughout the world, market-based conservation initiatives largely failed to develop. Consequently, the regime encountered great difficulties in supporting conservation, and was forced instead to increase reliance on extractive expansion to meet development objectives.

This is exemplified by the rise and demise of the infamous Yasuní-ITT initiative (see Figure 9). Originally proposed by environmental NGOs within the country, the initiative was subsequently taken up by the Correa administration to establish a mechanism whereby previously planned oil extraction in a small portion (called the Ishpingo-Tambococha-Tiputini, or ITT, sector) of the massive Yasuní National Park, an important biodiversity hotspot, would be forgone in exchange for the voluntary mobilization of funds by the international community to cover the opportunity costs of this decision. When this funding proved elusive, the initiative was repackaged as a more specific carbon sequestration mechanism whereby refundable CO_2 offset certificates would be provided in proportion with payments received,

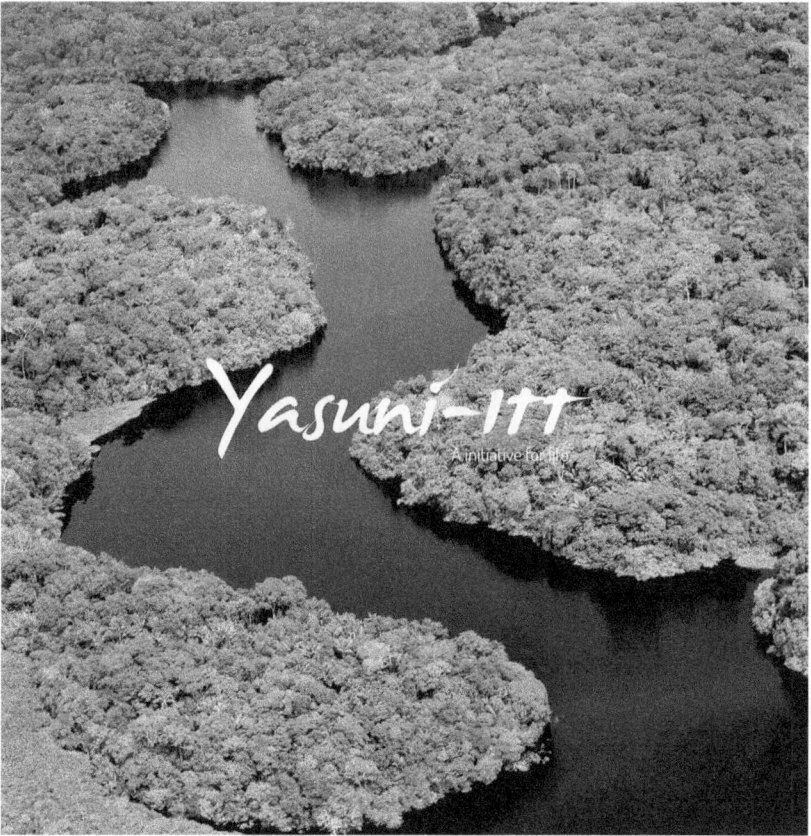

FIGURE 9. The Yasuní-ITT initiative. SOURCE: Jorge Proaño, https://www.hidden-node
-problem.com/archive/yasuni-itt.

thereby individualizing the financing from the originally envisioned collective international effort (Rival 2010). Yet even this revamped initiative
proved largely unappealing to potential investors, with only a small fraction of the requested funds committed and even less actually delivered, and
hence the initiative was subsequently abandoned and oil drilling in the ITT
sector begun (Monbiot 2014).

The Yasuní-ITT scheme proposed a particularly idiosyncratic form of
governance. Firstly, the land in question was fully state-owned and hence
ostensibly already protected via fortress conservation mechanisms. In addition, the funding ultimately requested (around $3.5 billion) was calculated
as merely half of the total profits projected from the forgone oil extraction.

Rather than a direct incentive for conservation, therefore, the requested funds were framed more as a "compensation" for the state's decision to forgo oil extraction (in addition to a covert incentive via the underlying subtext that if funds were not provided, extraction would be necessary)—a common framing of PES (as well as REDD+) in "alternative" perspectives too.[2] Like actually existing PES, moreover, from the outset the initiative was presented as a strongly state-centered program, with revenue collected and redistributed as the basis for social development projects by the national government.

It would be difficult, therefore, to consider Yasuní-ITT a conventional MBI, even the type of "regulatory price signal" mechanism that most PES programs exemplify in practice (Pirard 2012). In reality it was something quite unique, drawing on the example and rhetoric of other more paradigmatic MBIs yet proposing a quasi-market lacking either prices determined by forces of supply and demand or direct transactions between market players. Couched in anti-neoliberal and -capitalist rhetoric, moreover, it was nonetheless promoted as an individuated, voluntary offset for conventional capitalist industry. Hence, it was neither a market for trade in ecosystem services nor a command-and-control form of environmental governance (unlike the national park in which it was situated, for instance), offering a convincing proposition for neither advocates of fortress nor neoliberal conservation. In this sense, it was as contradictory and convoluted as Ecuador's post-neoliberal project in general.

The Yasuní-ITT initiative's failure, grounded in a fundamental disjuncture between the envisioned source of funding and what this funding was intended to accomplish, reinforces the analysis developed in previous chapters. Structurally, there was no way to finance even the half-market the initiative proposed, as this would have required diversion of a substantial portion of the surplus value generated by other (predominantly) extractive activities elsewhere in the world. Moreover, continued growth in a global economy still—indeed, increasingly—dependent on fossil energy necessitates increased reliance on oil supplies such as Ecuador's (Arsel et al. 2016b). Consequently, to whatever extent the professed intention to move toward post-neoliberal environmental governance was genuine, Ecuador was forced to remain in its historical position as a supplier of raw materials for the global market, as this is the only significant source of domestic value this market desired (Arsel et al. 2016b; Wilson and Bayón 2017). Wilson and Bayón (2017) offer a similar analysis of Ecuador's efforts to develop conservation-based finance mechanisms generally, which in seeking to shift from exploitation of finite primary resources to harnessing the ostensibly "infinite resources" of in situ biodiversity, as well as indigenous knowledge thereof, has been forced instead to increase reliance on the former, as the latter are unable to generate the value needed to support either conservation or development, let alone their integration. Hence, in Correa's Ecuador and other post-neoliberal regimes, conservation and extraction were frequently driven into opposition by the same (post-)neoliberal mechanisms intended to unite them.

Wilson and Bayón (2017) suggest that Ecuador's experience illustrates a fundamental contradiction at the heart of the post-neoliberal project generally, which indeed has now largely collapsed throughout Latin America (while still leaving important remnants in the form of persistent social programs erected during that period) (Wilson 2021). In essence, the post-neoliberal agenda appears to have succumbed to the same fantasy that continued economic growth could be reconciled with environmental sustainability that animates the neoliberal conservation project. In this sense the agenda remained very much within the boundaries of a growth-based capitalist political economy writ large even in its transcendence, in both rhetoric and to a lesser degree actual practice, of some particular neoliberal tenets.

THE RISE OF AUTHORITARIAN NEOLIBERALISM

Collapse of the post-neoliberal project has instead opened space for the ascent of authoritarian right-wing regimes and (male)[3] heads of state in a number of societies—including some previously considered post-neoliberal—over the last decade in particular (see, e.g., Brown 2019). This includes Trump in the United States, Bolsonaro in Brazil, Xi in China, Duterte (and now Marcos Jr.) in the Philippines, Putin in Russia, Erdoğan in Turkey, Modi in India, and Orbán in Hungary, among others. While some view this as a novel political-economic force bolstered by popular backlash against the ravages of austerity policies previously imposed as part of neoliberal reforms that seeks to transcend neoliberalism altogether (e.g., Jacques 2016; West 2016; Peters 2018), others characterize it as the rise of an "authoritarian neoliberalism" entailing the "the intertwinement of authoritarian statisms and neoliberal reforms" (Bruff and Tansel, 2019: 233; see also Arsel et al. 2021). As McCarthy describes this trend:

Although the specific trajectories and genealogies of these political formations are always unique at some level, they also share many general features:
nationalism articulated and justified in the name of frighteningly exclusive
and often racialized iterations of "the people"; the demonization of alleged
enemies internal and external; support for and selection of authoritarian
leaders who rise to power by exciting such fears and promising simple, direct,
often brutal action to protect and strengthen the nation; and contempt for
and direct assaults on democratic norms and institutions. (2019: 302)

As McCarthy (2019) further observes, of the many disturbing "reforms"
promoted by authoritarian neoliberal regimes, some of the most virulent
have been the widespread dismantling of mechanisms for environmental
protections enacted previously. Among such measures, McCarthy highlights
these regimes' tendency to

assert "blood and soil" claims of indissoluble links between the nation and
the biological and physical environment; deploy resurgent tropes of ter-
ritorialized bodies politic, contagion, and disease; exploit national natural
resources to buy political support and underwrite their political agenda;
attack environmental protections and activists to give extractive capital free
reign; eliminate or attack environmental data and science in a "posttruth"
era; and [initiate] dysfunctional political responses to the security threats,
fears, and divisions associated with climate change. (2019: 302)

How does this authoritarian neoliberal anti-environmentalism relate to
neoliberal conservation specifically? There are several ways one might approach this question. The first, and seemingly most straightforward, would
be to argue that whatever positive potential neoliberal conservation mechanisms held was aborted and reversed by this anti-environmental backlash.
This would be in line with Dempsey's (2016) assertion that neoliberal conservation fails because it "is still in many ways too radical and too challenging to the status quo to become mainstream," and hence is "in part foiled by
economic self-interest and by contemporary concentrations of wealth and
political power" (2016: 236).

Yet, an alternative explanation, supported by this book's analysis, suggests
that there may be something in the basic nature of conservation MBIs themselves that is causing forces of capital accumulation that previously rallied
around them to now abandon them in favor of intensified resource extraction. After all, the fundamental aim of neoliberal conservation was to demonstrate that by creating the right sort of markets for trade in natural capital,

resources left intact could be more lucrative than those extracted and transformed into mobile commodities. This, my analysis suggests, was always an impossible fantasy, since for market conservation to work, it must pay more than an alternate form of resource extraction carried out on the same land. But the money to pay for this conservation must come predominantly from extraction itself in the form of offsets. In order to succeed in pure market terms, therefore, conservation would need to be able to mobilize all of the revenue from the extraction it offsets, plus a premium to make it even more lucrative, plus a further premium if it is to be truly sustainable and hence internalize the various environmental and social externalities that allow extraction to be so profitable in the first place. There is, my analysis demonstrates, no conceivable way to generate this level of finance in strict market terms and hence neoliberal conservation becomes an impossible pipedream.

What *does* pay is extraction, and especially in a post-2008 economy desperate for new founts of growth, capitalism has hence turned back to extraction with a vengeance in order to jumpstart accumulation through a whole new series of time-space fixes following a brief period of over-productive stagnation precipitated by the global financial collapse. To make this intensified extraction work in the face of the growing range of rather obvious environmental and social problems it precipitates as it pushes into ever more distant frontiers, however, requires increasingly aggressive suppression of the inevitable double (social) movements such problems provoke. In the face of the failure of conservation to function as a viable new accumulation strategy, in other words, capitalism must become increasingly authoritarian in order to keep doing the same unsustainable things it has always relied upon since its inception as its main source of growth. From this perspective, therefore, neoliberal conservation and authoritarian neoliberalism are neither disconnected nor antithetical; rather, failure of the former can be viewed as an important factor stimulating the latter's current ascendance.

In this sense, neoliberal conservation might be understood as the peculiar product of a particular era—one in which relatively moderate forces on the political left and right in a number of societies converged around promotion of a "progressive neoliberalism" (Fraser 2017) as part of a "Third Way" political program more generally consolidated around the so-called Washington (and Post-Washington) Consensus (Corson 2010). As Fraser describes, "Progressive neoliberalism is an alliance of mainstream currents of new social movements (feminism, anti-racism, multiculturalism, and LGBTQ rights), on the one side, and high-end 'symbolic' and service-based business sectors (Wall Street, Silicon Valley, and Hollywood), on the other. In this alliance, progressive forces are effectively joined with the forces of cognitive capitalism, especially financialization" (2017: 131). In this way, progressive neoliberalism "mixed together truncated ideals of emancipation and lethal forms of financialization" (2017: 132). Neoliberal conservation can be understood as the quintessential expression of this "progressive" consensus in the realm of environmental governance. From this perspective, it, like progressive neoliberalism more generally, appears as "an increasingly desperate struggle to hold reality together, against the traumatic incursions of the Real of Capital" (Wilson 2014a: 315) in the form of mounting environmental destruction and social inequality.

Yet this progressive neoliberalism ultimately proved incapable of staving off these incursions and establishing conditions for sufficient continued accumulation to stabilize the capitalist system, leading to the 2008 recession and the wave of Occupy-style protests that arose in its wake. In the face of these as well as concurrent protests contesting the environmental implications of the intensified extraction employed to restimulate growth as a resolution for the global recession, progressive neoliberalism has in many places now been superseded by authoritarian neoliberalism as the only force capable of restoring conditions for continued accumulation. Disturbingly, it does so precisely by suppressing protests while simultaneously removing remaining environmental regulations impeding access to natural resources on which expanded extractive accumulation depends.

VIOLENT NEOLIBERALISM

In their unholy fusion of neoliberal and authoritarian forms of governance, "many contemporary authoritarian regimes are pursuing and deepening long-standing neoliberal goals with respect to the environment, removing restrictions on capitalist production by withdrawing from constraining international agreements and standards, rolling back domestic environmental protections, and appointing heads of polluting corporations to head the very agencies that are supposed to regulate those corporations" (McCarthy 2019: 306). Yet these regimes commonly combine such neoliberal reforms with "authoritarian statisms" entailing, among other measures, direct state intervention to appropriate valued natural resources (or facilitate their appropriation by private firms) for purposes of extraction. Among the consequences of such measures is authoritarian regimes' tendency to "present themselves as being, and often truly are, willing and even eager to use violence against opponents internal and external" (McCarthy 2019: 303). Graeber, indeed, goes so far as to identify as "the essence of right-wing thought" its propensity to allow "violence to define the very parameters of social existence and common sense" (2015: 87–88). With respect to environmental issues, this dynamic manifests in the fact that "state violence, and state-sanctioned private violence are increasingly evident in efforts to keep fossil fuels flowing" (McCarthy 2019: 306). Particularly in Latin America and Southeast Asia, recent years have witnessed an exponential increase in violence directed against those opposing development projects, particularly extractive enterprises, on environmental grounds (Arsel et al. 2016a; Global Witness 2019; Middeldorp and Le Billon 2019). Neoliberal authoritarian regimes, particularly Brazil and the Philippines, are the foremost hosts (as well as perpetrators) of such violence (Global Witness 2019; Middeldorp and Le Billon 2019). Tactics employed in this campaign include cultivation "of impunity for perpetrators associated with the lack of independent and effective judiciary and media reporting; tight and unaccountable networks between political, economic, and military elites; and social habituation to homicides on the part of authorities—including as a result of recent wars and state-tolerated or -encouraged vigilante activity" (Middeldorp and Le Billon 2019: 327).

During this same period, meanwhile, a different form of environment-related violence has risen in other spaces: what Büscher and Ramutsindela call "green violence," defined as "the deployment of violent instruments and tactics towards the protection of nature" (2016: 2).[4] In this respect, Southern and Eastern Africa in particular have witnessed a surge of "green militarization" (Lunstrum 2014) whereby increased poaching of endangered megafauna such as elephants and rhinos has been met with a resurgence of state-sponsored, often lethal violence to reinforce protected areas (see also Fletcher and Büscher 2018). This has included the use of military tactics, weaponry, and even personnel to defend protected areas against incursion by those wishing to extract wildlife and other resources. Such exercise of physical violence has been accompanied by violent rhetoric advocating often extreme forms of punishment for the perpetrators of these incursions (Büscher and Ramutsindela 2016; Lunstrum 2017). We have also witnessed incorporation of such dynamics within overarching efforts to address "terrorism" and other issues of global geopolitics by conventional military forces (Duffy 2016).

While seemingly quite different—even diametrically opposed—it may be possible to account for violence both in support of and against environmental protection in terms of the analysis developed in this chapter. That is, a common failure of neoliberal mechanisms to achieve both conservation and development appears to have forced recourse to intensified forms of fortress protection, in the case of Sub-Saharan Africa, while in Latin America and Southeast Asia this has provoked aggressive suppression of resistance to expansion of the raw material extraction that was intended to be replaced by global market integration grounded in higher-tech production (Arsel et al. 2016a).

It is tempting to extrapolate from these dynamics to suggest a more general historical pattern in the relationship between neoliberalism and violence. Introduction of neoliberalism in the initial roll-back period, after all, was frequently accompanied by violence needed to force through unpopular reforms and quell protest against these (McNally 2006; Springer 2016). This was most pronounced in Chile under Pinochet but occurred in many other places too. In the transition from roll-back to rollout phases (Peck and Tickell 2002), this violence was intended to give way to creation of new neoliberal institutions and instruments able to deliver both development and conservation benefits sufficient to compel voluntary acceptance of the process—that is, to institute a form of properly neoliberal (bio)power. Following widespread failure of these efforts, augmented by the 2008 economic crisis, it seems that a more general recourse to intensified forms of violence has sought to force through what neoliberal rollout reforms could not. In this way, one of the main characteristics of the authoritarian neoliberalism proliferating since the 2008 crisis may in fact be its mobilization of unprecedented forms of violence to achieve its ends, a resurgence of sovereign governance with a vengeance to keep a zombie political-economic program staggering forward. This dynamic exemplifies the essential dialectic between power and violence outlined in chapter 1: when compliance can no longer be achieved through obtaining subjects' ideological buy-in, or at least by convincing them that resistance is futile, authorities turn instead to exercise of direct violence to maintain the capitalist social order.

While seemingly opposed to neoliberal conservation, consequently, green violence may in fact be more intimately connected to the former than commonly presumed. Dunlap and Fairhead (2014: 938), for instance, contend that "militarisation and marketisation of nature" are actually two sides of the same coin, in that "new global 'green' markets . . . remain dependent on resource intensive structures and a military-industrial complex to police them." Gray foreshadowed this same argument some time ago in this chapter's epigraph. Graeber (2015: 31) agrees, warning more bluntly, "Whenever someone starts talking about the 'free market,' it's a good idea to look around for the man with the gun." Keucheyan goes even further to argue more generally that "financialization and militarization are the system's two reactions to" periodic crisis. He explains,

> Throughout capitalism's existence, faced with crisis situations and the aggravated inequalities that they engender, it has resorted to the two solutions of financialization and war. In generating "fictitious" capital, finance allows for the deferral and thus the temporary attenuation of the contradictions inherent to capitalist production (as its subprime lending mechanism recently once again demonstrated). War is the fruit of the inevitable conflicts that these contradictions periodically generate. The shrinking of profit opportunities and the need to guarantee control over the extraction and circulation of resources—but also the growing opposition to the system—tend to make political conflictuality increasingly acute. (2016: 47)

THE DRIVE FOR GROWTH

Far from "dematerializing," as in the decoupling fantasy, consequently, since 2008 the global economy seems to have instead been dramatically *rematerializing* by intensifying reliance on raw material extraction as the main source of continued growth (Hickel and Kallis 2020). The World Bank, indeed, concludes just this in acknowledging that "Currently, the world economy is . . . on a path of re-materialization and far away from any—even relative—decoupling" (cited in Hickel and Kallis 2020: 472). This book's analysis suggests that this is partly due to the fact that the neoliberal conservation intended to facilitate decoupling is inherently incapable of generating the quantity of finance needed to both outcompete extractive industry and to support requisite levels of accumulation within the global economy more generally. In the face of this failed promise of economic dematerialization through resource non-use, consequently, capitalism has returned to intensified extraction to recapture the economic growth that accumulation by conservation has been unable to deliver.

This relentless quest for accumulation in the face of mounting social unrest and environmental devastation can thus be understood as a manifestation of the capitalist *drive* dynamic outlined in chapter 1. As explained there, drive describes a self-destructive compulsion to continue to pursue an object even when its achievement is impossible and its continued pursuit presents an existential threat to the pursuer. Žižek thus describes drive as a "blind insistence that follows its course with utter disregard for the requirements of our concrete life-world" (2001: 98). This is precisely where capitalism appears to be headed at present under the direction of authoritarian neoliberalism. A flat-out war on the foundation of life itself, this drive exemplifies a biopolitics turned inward, as in Dean's (2010) description, cannibalizing itself in a Lacanian death spiral the sheer excess and audacity of which is breathtaking.

This drive for growth is clearly evident in ExxonMobile's decision, discussed in the previous chapter, to continue to extract oil to the fullest extent possible despite explicit recognition that doing so will accelerate the acknowledged disastrous climate impacts of GHG emissions to which fossil fuels contribute. It is evident in the Trump administration's insistence during the initial phase of the global COVID-19 pandemic that the US economy be reopened as quickly as possible despite the greater loss of life this move would admittedly cause (Milman 2020). It is evident in UNFCCC negotiations' continual repetition of a failure to achieve effective climate mitigation while industrial civilization as a whole thus continues its half-conscious journey toward self-destruction. In such positions, Jameson's dictum that capitalist expansion is championed even at the expense of the planetary life that sustains this is readily apparent.

THE SPECTER OF CAPITAL

Within neoliberal conservation, consequently, capital becomes the "the spectral and traumatic presence that the neoliberal social fantasy operates to disavow" (Wilson 2014a: 305). Taking the form of disavowal rather than outright denial, capitalism's ecological impacts do at times actually enter into the discussion but are then dismissed via neoliberal conservation's assertion that such impacts are not inherent to capitalism per se but can in fact be redressed by harnessing capitalist mechanisms themselves in this effort—thus asserting, like neoliberalism more generally, that "the solution to the pathologies of global capitalism is to be found in capitalism itself" (Wilson 2014a: 316). From this perspective, neoliberal conservation discourse can be understood as "explaining away the symptoms of the Real of Capital in such a way that the contours of the neoliberal fantasy can be retained" (2014a: 307).

Thus, in the final analysis, one could argue that neoliberal conservation fails, most centrally, precisely because of this refusal to fully acknowledge capitalism's essential unsustainability and hence the need to transcend it entirely for conservation to have any hope of success in the long run. In this way, capital becomes the central specter haunting the neoliberal conservation project, the public secret always present yet unable to be addressed openly and productively within the bounds of the project's discourse. It is in this sense—the inability to include discussion of capitalism's essentially destructive nature within the symbolic order of neoliberal policy making—that capital can be understood as occupying the place of the Real within this project. As Žižek explains, the *"real (the part of reality that remains non-symbolized) returns in the guise of spectral apparitions"* (2006: 241, emphasis in original). With respect to capitalism, therefore, "'reality' is the social reality of the actual people involved in the productive process, while the Real is the inexorable 'spectral' logic of Capital which determines what goes on in social reality" (Žižek 1999: 331). In terms of neoliberalism specifically, Wilson asserts,

> As a system of norms, individuals and institutions, capitalism is incorporated into neoliberal ideology. But the Real of Capital is excluded from this symbolic order. The source of profit in exploitation is concealed by the understanding of economic value as an expression of subjective preferences, rather than a measure of socially necessary labour time. The inherent tendency for capitalism to generate vast economic crises is papered over by the assumption that efficient markets operate under conditions of "perfectly competitive equilibrium." And the power of capital as an abstract form of domination is represented as the benign operation of the invisible hand of the market. For the neoliberal subject, market economics is, therefore, not a policy framework that can be easily discarded, but is a structuring principle of social reality, which protects the subject from the traumatic Real of Capital. (Wilson 2016: 582)

What a focus on neoliberal *conservation* adds to this analysis is the way that capitalism's environmental impacts become part of what is disavowed in this manner.

Failing to fully acknowledge and confront the main cause of the ecological problems it addresses, consequently, neoliberal conservation becomes akin to Wilson's reference to "the private investigator Harry Angel in Alan

Parker's gothic thriller *Angel Heart*, who fruitlessly pursues a serial killer through numerous false leads, only to make the final horrific discovery that he himself is the murderer" (Wilson 2016: 585–586). In a similar manner, Wilson argues, neoliberalism "compels its agents to engage with the symptoms of capitalism, but in a disavowed form that prevents them from identifying themselves as those responsible for the exacerbation of the very symptoms that they are attempting to address" (2014a: 315).

This inability to address the root causes of the issues it confronts due to its own implication within these same causes compels neoliberal conservation to continually miss the target it pursues, namely effective conservation, propelling the shift from desire to drive within which the object becomes instead a perpetual repetition of this very failure. It is in this sense, Wilson asserts, that "the death drive of zombie neoliberalism is the Real of Capital itself" (2014a: 316).[5] Animated by this drive, neoliberal conservation becomes characterized "by all kinds of frantic activity . . . precisely in order that nothing Real should happen" (Daly 2009: 294). Or as Swyngedouw phrases it, the project insists that "we have to change radically, but within the contours of the existing state of the situation . . . so that nothing really has to change" (2010: 219).

NEOLIBERAL CONSERVATION'S SUBLIME OBJECT

Central to ideology, in the Lacanian sense, stands relentless pursuit of a "sublime object" (Žižek 1989), Lacan's *objet petit a* to which desire becomes attached. An "object that both obscures and embodies the void of the Real," a "sublime object provides stability to the symbolic structure by concealing the traumatic Real within it, yet at the same time, the Real 'shines through' this object, illuminating it with an uncanny presence that is both terrifying and compelling" (Wilson 2014a: 312).

The sublime object of neoliberal conservation is of course the ever-elusive *natural capital*. It is an object that is simultaneously present (at the center of neoliberal conservation policy discussions) and absent (incapable of being precisely defined such that all can agree upon this definition and therefore make it the basis for policy making); simultaneously material (the "stocks and flows" of natural resources forming the basis of human livelihoods) and imaginary (the ostensive "value" of these stocks and flows that circulates globally via capital's function as "value in motion"). An object of fictional, ephemeral value, its "true" worth can only ever be measured in its absence, that is, by accounting for what has been lost in and through "nature's" conversion into financial capital whose value can in fact be concretely measured. Within this sublime object, meanwhile, the Real of Capital "shines through," illuminating the specter of traumatic destruction that this reframing of capital as mere stocks and flows seeks to obfuscate.

In the shift from desire to drive, then, neoliberal conservation's aim becomes not valuation and preservation of natural capital so much as failure to achieve this, that is, failure to accurately value natural capital and create effective frameworks for its maintenance. In this way, the sublime object constantly hovers on the horizon, always just on the brink of becoming the basis for effective policy making as at the same time it diminishes faster than conservationists can calculate its vanishing value.

THE DIALECTIC OF FREEDOM AND SECURITY

Capitalism's insatiable drive for growth forming the basis of the neoliberal biopolitics via which authorities aim to exercise governance in the contemporary era, finally, helps to further explain neoliberal conservation's common tendency to expand the very state regulation it claims to supersede. In this way, Dean suggests, "Psychoanalysis (or, more specifically, some of the insights developed in recent psychoanalytic theory) allows us to draw out and make explicit a logic implicit in Foucault's account of a liberal governmentality that ends up doing what it most seeks to avoid" (2010: 3). As Dean explains, "Liberalism cannot be reduced either to the provision of freedom or the maintenance of security. Its dynamic oscillation between the two, its compulsive circulation from the one to the other, indicates that extra dimension of enjoyment necessary for any political-ideological formation. Biopolitics is one of the arrangements of this circuit of freedom and security" (2010: 9).

In the imperative to regulate markets in the interest of biopolitics—or further, under neoliberalism, to use market forces themselves to achieve biopolitical ends—the state must continually intervene to increasingly restrict the very freedom that liberal markets are intended to embody and preserve. In this way, "stimulation of danger incites the extension of procedures of surveillance and control. . . . Instead of producing freedom," the mechanisms of (neo)liberalism "produce—or risk producing—a wide, dispersed, field of control" (Dean 2010: 9). Consequently, Dean asserts,

Liberalism ends up doing the opposite of what it intends, in effect proving that its suspicions were justified all along: government does bring with it the risks of its own over-reaching. For Foucault, liberalism's inability to move heaven, that is to say, its recognition of the market as a site of spontaneous truths that must be obeyed and natural mechanisms that must be allowed—even made—to function opens up a new kind of hell. (2010: 3)

Of neoliberalism specifically, Wilson contends, "It is this continual struggle, advancing through multiple processes of repression and disavowal, which has driven the neoliberal project towards ever more intensive forms of social engineering, resulting in the social production of the supposedly natural order of a market society" (2014a: 315). Consequently, the biopolitical imperative to maintain security ends up cannibalizing the very freedom in whose name security is pursued, in the process exercising increasingly intense forms of violence over the people as well as environments supposedly intended to be protected.

CONCLUSION

There is, I believe, a simple lesson in this chapter's analysis. However much we might pine for the days when it seemed that market mechanisms might actually deliver on their promise, this promise was illusory. On the contrary, the turn toward market mechanisms helped, in and through their failure, to usher in the brave new authoritarianism we are currently confronting. There will, of course, always be small spaces of hope wherein certain groups of people in particular places may find ways to turn capitalist forces to their own advantage, at least for a time, as examples of actually existing PES that have deviated substantially from market logic among others show. But these spaces must inevitably become smaller and further between as capitalist extraction continues its relentless advance.

There is no going back; there is only going forward. What does the future of progressive political praxis in the realm of conservation therefore look like? Chapter 8 turns to this essential question.

EIGHT

There Is No Alternative to Degrowth

> What counts today, the question which is looming on the horizon, is the need for a redistribution of wealth. Humanity must reply to this question, or be shaken to pieces by it.
>
> FRANTZ FANON, *The Wretched of the Earth* (1963: 69)

In an exclusive neighborhood of the Indian megalopolis Mumbai, billionaire businessman Mukesh Ambani has constructed a singularly luxurious home for his family of four (AD Insider 2019). Twenty-seven stories high, with roughly four hundred thousand square feet of floor space, the building includes a full six floors of residential space along with six more devoted to parking for 168 cars as well as "a mega-temple, a host of guest suites, a salon, an ice-cream parlour and a private movie theatre to accommodate 50 people" (AD Insider 2019) The entire project is estimated to have cost somewhere between one and two billion dollars.

Meanwhile, in their bestselling book *Poor Economics*, Nobel Prize-winning economists Abhijit Banerjee and Esther Duflo address the age-old question of why poverty persists within a world of such plenty (Banerjee and Duflo 2011). Of the many studies discussed in the book, one explored this question via research conducted among poor women in another Indian city, Hyderabad. This study's findings point to the fact that, rather than saving the scant surplus income these women derive from their participation in various informal economic activities, they instead choose to spend some of this money to drink a daily cup of tea. The reason for this, the authors conclude, and hence for the women's inability to convert this money into the capital needed to instead lift themselves out of poverty, is a lack of *self-control*. As the authors explain, "To be able to save every week or every month, they have to surmount self-control problems over and over again. The problem is that self-control is like a muscle: It gets tired as we use it, and therefore it would not be a surprise if the poor find it harder to save" (200).

The extent of the inequality that the juxtaposition of these two examples illustrates—and of the astounding intellectual obfuscation necessary to avoid recognizing the obvious connection between them—is quite simply obscene. There is no other term that does justice to the perversity of this reality. At the center of this book's analysis thus stands the fundamental question of inequality and how to resolve it. It is by now well-established that the rise of neoliberalism has precipitated an enormous increase in socioeconomic inequality both within and among societies throughout the world. As Gray concludes of a comparative analysis of neoliberalization within Mexico, New Zealand, and the United Kingdom, "In each country the free market acted as a vice within which the middle classes were squeezed. It enriched a small minority and increased the size of the excluded class" (1998: 53). Edelman (1999) paints a similar portrait of Costa Rica, while Wilkinson and Pickett (2010) point to a much more widespread pattern.

But as my analysis has also shown, inequality in access to natural resources also exacerbates environmental degradation on the part of both haves and have-nots. Silva reaches this same conclusion with respect to Costa Rica, writing,

> The majority of unorganized poor smallholders and peasants are left to their fate in the market. The entrepreneurial among them may individually attempt microenterprises, only to find that they cannot succeed, as has occurred in ecotourism. The eligibility requirements, paperwork, and bureaucratic rules for meager per hectare conservation benefits discourage individual participation in the conservation certificate or reforestation program. From the smallholding, poor peasants' point of view, the market encourages selling or abandoning their holdings, migrating to cities, or becoming day laborers on banana plantations. (2003: 114)

Rappel and Thomas observe a similar dynamic on a global scale, contending that

> biodiversity loss in the Third World is largely the result of the exploitation of marginal areas by both big landowners and impoverished farmers, who have either been dispossessed or otherwise experienced the systematic erosion of their economic security. Numerous studies have shown that these processes have been accelerated by the opportunities for the commercial exploitation of land generated by the structural adjustment policies enforced by the

World Bank and the IMF, operating in the context of highly inequitable systems of land tenure. (1998: 100)

Meta-analysis of conservation across a number of societies, moreover, demonstrates a strong correlation between domestic economic inequity and biodiversity loss generally (Mikkelson et al. 2007; Holland et al. 2009; Hicks et al. 2016).

The necessity of attending directly to inequality applies at the international level too. Most ecosystems are capable of sustainably supporting a domestic population, even a fairly substantial and dense one, as long as resource access is relatively equally distributed. It is when this same ecosystem is called upon to also support a foreign population via export for trade that sustainable production becomes much more difficult. As Galeano (1997) demonstrates, the main cause of environmental degradation throughout Latin America, for instance, has always been agricultural production and resource extraction for export, whereby from the time of Spanish conquest a majority of the region has been transformed from forest to monoculture plantations while entire mountains have been leveled in pursuit of gold, silver, copper, and other minerals (see also Miller 2007; Arboleda 2020). Meanwhile, increasing evidence suggests that, notwithstanding venerable theories holding that tropical rainforests are incapable of substantial populations due to their ecological fragility, the Amazon Basin, at least, may have boasted a population density exceeding that of Europe at the time of colonial conquest, comprising complex societies based in intensive agriculture that, in many cases, actually increased the productivity and biodiversity of the region's fragile landscapes (see, e.g., Mann 2005; Erickson 2008).

Today, when the entire world has become intricately enmeshed within a globally encompassing economy, overexploitation of certain environments via international trade to facilitate extravagant lifestyles in others has intensified, producing conditions of unsustainability in most locations. The scope and impact of this is far from trivial. Weinzettel and colleagues calculate that "the land footprint displaced through international trade was significant on a global level, corresponding to 1.8 billion gha or 24% of the global land footprint in 2004. The net displacement through trade from high-income countries (defined here as OECD member states as of 2011) to lower-income countries (non-OECD members) corresponded to 6% of total global land footprint or 25% of the total footprint associated with internationally traded products" (2013: 3). One perverse result of this is that, on a global scale, not only is industrial manufacturing in high-income societies increasingly offset by conservation in low-income ones (a dynamic upon which the REDD+ initiative among others seeks to build), but the reverse is also true: conservation in high-income countries is facilitated by outsourcing primary sector extraction and production (agriculture, cattle ranching, logging, and related activities) to their low-income counterparts. Thus, Weinzettel et al. (2013: 3) document a "net displacement of land use from high-income to low-income countries [that] amounted to 6% of the global land demand, even though high-income countries had more land available per capita than low-income countries"—as a consequence of which, ironically, the former could "spare more land for nature."

IN DEFENSE OF DEGROWTH

What this book's analysis demonstrates, most essentially, is that to continue to believe that it is possible to redress both inequality and environmental degradation while sustaining economic growth is a dangerous delusion. Contra Thatcher, we must therefore assert that for a progressive future to truly transcend the inherent limitations of neoliberalism there is in fact no alternative to *degrowth* in the long run (see Figure 10).

Degrowth describes a process of "planned economic contraction" (Alexander 2012) leading eventually to the type of steady-state economy at a sustainable level of aggregate throughput long advocated by Herman Daly and others (e.g., Daly 2008; Dietz et al. 2013).[1] The idea has developed through social activism since the turn of the twenty-first century, been elaborated through a series of international conferences since 2008 (D'Alisa et al. 2013), and is promoted through a great profusion of recent literature.[2] Within this diverse discussion, degrowth is understood in different ways, from a narrow economic transformation to a far broader cultural paradigmatic shift. Central to most strands of degrowth discourse, however, is the aim "to understand critically and undo the phenomenon of growth—a material, ecological, historical, discursive and institutional phenomenon that is at the heart of the Western imaginary and its colonial dominance—and to propose alternatives to it" (Kallis 2018: 9). This project comprises both macro- and micro-level initiatives. At the macroeconomic level, "degrowth refers to a trajectory where the 'throughput' (energy, materials and waste flows) of an economy decreases while welfare, or well-being, improves" (Kallis 2018: 9).

FIGURE 10.   Degrowth. Warsaw, Poland. SOURCE: Paul Sableman.

Specific policy proposals for implementing degrowth include: "resource and CO2 caps; extraction limits; new social security guarantees and work-sharing (reduced work hours); basic income and income caps; consumption and resource taxes with affordability safeguards; support of innovative models of 'local living'; commercial and commerce free zones; new forms of money; high reserve requirements for banks; ethical banking; green investments; cooperative property and cooperative firms" (Kallis et al. 2012a: 175).

But degrowth also comprises a substantial strain of grassroots activism, entailing organization and mobilization by community groups promoting a diversity of grounded initiatives including "cycling, car-sharing, reuse, vegetarianism or veganism, co-housing, agro-ecology, eco-villages, solidarity economy, consumer cooperatives, alternative (so-called ethical) banks or credit cooperatives as well as decentralized renewable energy cooperatives" (D'Alisa et al. 2013: 218). Links among such initiatives have facilitated their scaling up into national and transnational networks. D'Alisa and colleagues summarize: "Explicit degrowth networks have also emerged nationally and regionally since 2000 in France, Italy, and Spain, with also an informal international academic network consolidating around degrowth conferences. The movement is now spreading to Belgium, Switzerland, Finland, Poland, Greece, Germany, Portugal, Norway, Denmark, Czech Republic, Mexico,

Brazil, Puerto Rico, and Canada; more than 50 groups from around the world organized simultaneous 'picnics' for Degrowth in 2010 and 2011" (2013: 217).

An important question concerns the extent to which degrowth is compatible with a capitalist economy and society (Foster 2011; Liodakis 2018; Feola 2019; Schmelzer et al. 2022). As Kallis and coauthors point out, degrowth advocacy often "fails to explain how a capitalist economy would work without a positive profit rate, a positive interest rate or discounting" (2012a: 177). Raising this issue some time ago, Foster indeed pronounced degrowth within capitalism an "impossibility theorem," arguing, "The ecological struggle . . . must aim not merely for degrowth in the abstract but more concretely for *deaccumulation*—a transition away from a system geared to the accumulation of capital without end" (2011: 33, emphasis in original). Responding to this challenge, Kallis and coauthors indeed acknowledge that "capitalist economies can . . . either grow or collapse: they can never degrow voluntarily" (2012b: 177). Kallis thus admits that implementing degrowth would require "such a radical change in the basic institutions of property, work, credit and allocation, that the system that will result will no longer be identifiable as capitalism" (2011: 875). Revisiting this discussion more recently, he adds, "Growth is part and parcel of capitalism: abandoning the pursuit of growth requires a transition beyond capitalism" (Kallis 2018: 163). As an explicitly *post-capitalist* program, therefore, degrowth would need to pursue forms of production not based on private appropriation of surplus value and forms of exchange not aimed at capital accumulation. These would need to fully internalize the environmental and social costs of production in a manner that does not promote commodification and that are grounded in common property regimes.[3]

SHARING THE WEALTH

Making degrowth "socially sustainable" (Martinez-Alier 2009) would necessitate robust forms of redistribution to redress inequality. As Daly (2008: 12) asserts, "Without aggregate growth, poverty reduction requires redistribution." Hence, serious degrowth ultimately demands a dramatic redistribution in control of land and resources (Kallis 2019b)—an imperative, even more urgent now than in Fanon's day, to more equitably share the abundant wealth of the world.

Such redistribution must emphasize the appropriation of surplus production for collective use. After all, an economic system is defined most fundamentally by how it "organizes the production, appropriation and distribution of surplus" (Resnick and Wolff 2002: xi). And central to this must of course be a focus on rebuilding the commons—"commoning"—which have been one of the main casualties of neoliberal capitalist policies (Hardt and Negri 2009; Singh 2017). In opposition to Garret Hardin's classic "tragedy of the commons" thesis, which asserts that common pool resources will be inevitably degraded if left to their own devices and thus require "either socialism or the privatism of free enterprise" (1968: 682) to be sustainably managed, research has documented numerous situations in which stakeholders, under certain specified conditions, may work collectively to manage resources as common property regimes (CPRs) for the long-term benefit of the group.[4]

This essential need for expanded redistribution is increasingly acknowledged even within mainstream development circles. As Oxfam UK senior advisor Duncan Green, author of the popular book *From Poverty to Power* (2012), explains, "We can even talk about redistribution these days without apologizing like we used to" (Green 2013). Even the IMF, intriguingly, has recently admitted that "the benefits of some policies that are an important part of the neoliberal agenda appear to have been somewhat overplayed" and hence that "evidence of the economic damage from inequality suggests that policymakers should be more open to redistribution than they are" (Ostry et al. 2015: 40, 41). The exponential expansion of cash transfer programs (CTPs) as an important new form of international development assistance over the past three decades, now encompassing some 720 million people in more than 130 countries (World Bank 2015), can indeed be understood as something of a de facto acknowledgment of this need.

Yet this remains only a tiny drop in the immense bucket of what is truly needed to effectively redress inequality worldwide. And as Saad-Filho (2016) points out, CTPs' transformative potential is constrained precisely by the overarching neoliberal political economy in which they operate. The same is true of common property regimes (Berkes 2007; Ostrom and Cox 2011), as well as post-neoliberal experiments and PES, all of which remain constrained in their transformative potential by their inability to significantly alter the overarching structural conditions shaping them.

Ultimately, given the extent of uneven development throughout the world grounded in primitive accumulation and other processes of violent expropriation (Dunlap and Sullivan 2020), a truly transformative program seeking to redress inequality at its roots would need to move beyond mere wealth redistribution to pursue reappropriation of physical space for collective use—what Shaw and Waterstone (2019: 104) term pursuit of "geographic justice." As these authors argue, "Without the appropriation of space, we can only tinker with capitalism's circuits" (Shaw and Waterstone 2019: 99). Tuck and Yang also consider redistribution of space essential for decolonial politics more broadly, asserting that "decolonization brings about the repatriation of Indigenous land and life" (2012: 1).

One such potential strategy in this regard is of course land reform—what Akram-Lodhi (2013) calls "pro-poor gender-responsive redistributive agrarian reform"—to correct for current inequities. Yet there are few more contentious issues. As Pellegrini and Dasgupta phrase it, "Genuine land reforms remain intense political acts due to their redistributive element" (2011: 275). In Latin America, in particular, calls for land reform have frequently inspired violent reaction, resulting, for instance, in the overthrow of President Arbens in Guatemala (Schlesinger 1999) and President Allende in Chile (Guardiola-Rivera 2013) in 1954 and 1973, respectively. Moreover, historical experience of land reform has produced mixed results; while programs have succeeded in dramatically reducing inequality in certain cases, most notably Taiwan and South Korea (Kay 2002), in others they have been far less effective (De Janvry and Ground 1978).

DECOLONIZING DEGROWTH

An important and growing critique of degrowth discussions concerns the extent to which they are applicable beyond the wealthy Global Northern societies in which they originated. Escobar thus highlights a widespread perception "that degrowth is 'ok for the North' but that the South needs rapid growth, whether to catch up with rich countries, satisfy the needs of the poor, or reduce inequalities" (Escobar 2015: 6). He describes degrowth as one among a number of "transition discourses"—proposals calling "for a significant paradigmatic or civilizational transformation"—that have proliferated particularly since the turn of the century, "emerging from a multiplicity of sites, principally social movements and some NGOs, and from intellectuals with significant connections to environmental and cultural struggles" (Escobar 2015: 2).[5] Among such diverse proposals, Escobar focuses particularly on comparing and contrasting *degrowth* and *postdevelopment*. The latter is a perspective that Escobar was himself influential in helping to establish, the aim of which is to question and develop alternatives to conventional economic development in concrete practice.[6] Postdevelopment proposals commonly promote direct democratic decision-making, collective resource management, local autonomy, and cultivation of traditional ecological knowledge (TEK). While they do not all necessarily claim the explicit label, examples of postdevelopment in practice are often seen to include, among others, the global food sovereignty movement promoted by La Vía Campesina (Borras 2008), promotion of a "Buen Vivir" philosophy by various indigenous groups (Gudynas 2011), the Zapatista movement in Chiapas (Esteva 2012), and the COMPAS endogenous development network (see COMPAS 2007).

While discussions of degrowth and postdevelopment developed largely independently (although postdevelopment has certainly influenced degrowth to some degree), Escobar highlights a number of points of convergence between them, noting that they "share closely connected imaginaries, goals, and predicaments, chiefly, a radical questioning of the core assumption of growth and economism, a vision of alternative worlds based on ecological integrity and social justice, and the ever present risk of cooptation" (2015: 1). "In both cases," he claims, "the common denominator is the pressures exerted by neo-liberal globalization" (2015: 1). Yet Escobar also highlights a number of significant (though certainly not absolute) differences between the two positions. First, while postdevelopment has predominantly emerged out of social movements in the Global South, degrowth proposals have mostly arisen from societies in the Global North. Second, degrowth tends to focus more on environmental and postdevelopment more on development concerns. By the same token, degrowth tends to be more grounded in anthropocentric, economic thinking while postdevelopment includes more non-Western, biocentric, and explicitly spiritual modes of understanding (see especially Kothari et al. 2019). Notwithstanding such differences, Escobar envisions the possibility of bringing the two perspectives into closer conversation, in this way uniting micro- and macropolitical strategies, locally grounded initiatives and platforms for large-scale structural change, while at the same time contributing to "dissolution of the constructs of 'Global North' and 'Global South'" as well (2015: 2). Others advance similar calls for greater integration of the two approaches.[7]

Key to thinking through the transformative potential of transition discourses is of course an honest assessment of the extent to which they are, indeed, transformative. The difficult task in this is to "distinguish between simple transformations, which operate within a given structure, and real change, revolution if you will, in which the structure itself is transformed" (Ortner 1984: 136). Wright (2010) thus distinguishes between *symbiotic* transformations, which seek to effect change within existing systems of power, and *ruptural* transformations that seek to reconfigure these overarching systems themselves.

Additionally, Wright (2010) describes a third category of *interstitial* transformations aiming to develop localized alternative practices within niches or margins of existing social formations. Recently, we have witnessed a resurgence of attention to such interstitial transformations: a growing focus on the ways that small scale efforts seek to carve out alternative lifeworlds on the margins of the capitalist system—what Tsing (2015) labels forms of "pericapitalism"—or on possibilities of developing new forms of governance that manage resources differently within the boundaries of the current political economic order.

In his exploration of the rise of CTPs in South Africa, for instance, Ferguson (2015), highlights the presence of substantial, relatively permanent "surplus populations" (Li 2010) worldwide that have few possibilities of ever finding productive employment. Hence, he points to CTPs as the potential seeds of a "new politics of redistribution" inspired by failure of the neoliberal development model to effectively alleviate significant poverty. In *Just Give Money to the Poor*, Hanlon and coauthors (2010) go further to describe the global rise of CTPs in general as a "quiet revolution" in development thinking originating from the Global South. In his own analysis, Ferguson explicitly turns away from a conventional Marxist focus on transforming property relations and ownership of the means of production as the basis of social action and instead simply accepts these as given, focusing instead on ways to distribute the fruits of this production to those who will always remain excluded from participation directly within it. Others, such as Tsing (2015), and arguably Escobar (2008) as well, point to the diverse ways that people may forge alternative lives on the margins of these same exclusionary structures. Recent actor-oriented PES research does something similar in advocating a turn away from analysis of the macroeconomic structures influencing program design to instead search within actually existing projects for "clues on how to forge ahead with *alternatives* to the tendency towards neoliberal natures" (Van Hecken et al. 2018: 317, emphasis in original). Crouch, most extremely perhaps, self-consciously turns away from structural considerations entirely in claiming to write to help people "cope as best they can with the world they find" and have little power to change (2011: i).

What none of these perspectives do, in other words, is place emphasis on large-scale ruptural transformation as the basis for progressive politics. Hence, such approaches have been criticized for advocating merely a palliative that does little to redress overarching conditions of structural inequality and violence that constrain the potential of progressive action (e.g., Hornborg 2017; Kapoor 2017; Nilsen 2021). The CTPs that Ferguson sees as the seeds of a transformative politics, for instance, have been critiqued for merely reinforcing the status quo. Thus, Saad-Filho contends that *conditional* cash transfer programs (CCTs) are "the social policies naturally associated ('best fit') with neoliberalism" (2016: 76).[8] He explains that "even though they can assist the target groups at the margin, they are, by design, insufficient to transform the economic, social and political structures perpetuating poverty. CCTs also introduce commercial mediations and arbitrary limitations to the rights of citizens, manage poverty only within narrow limits, and provide subsidies to capital that, ultimately, reproduce poverty rather than supporting its elimination."

This more normative framing of CTPs is supported by pointing out that they have been pursued equally by regimes on both the right and left of the political spectrum (Pena 2014). And indeed, CTPs are commonly described in quintessential neoliberal terms: as an "investment in human capital" intended to combat the chronic dependency created by extreme poverty (the so-called "poverty trap"). Likewise, they are often framed as a counter to the "nanny" state, not a "safety net" but a "springboard" to self-sufficiency designed to avoid cumbersome state bureaucracies and decentralize governance by harnessing the power of individual choice and responsibility (Ferguson 2010).

Even *unconditional* CTPs, which, unlike conditional programs, Peck and Theodore consider "anathema to neoliberal policy-makers" (2015: xxi), can be seen as compatible with neoliberal governance if implemented in a certain form. Of one such form, the proposal for "universal basic income" (UBI) gaining increasing traction in a number of societies worldwide (including

Canada, Finland, and others where pilot programs have already been implemented),[9] Clarke (2017a) cautions: "The hope of a social policy solution to the problems created by neoliberalism and the attacks associated with it is profoundly dangerous because that very 'solution' can so readily assume a form that furthers the very agenda that left BI advocates hope to escape. The institutions of global capitalism are taking an interest in Basic Income and the Davos crowd are even considering it."

As Clarke and others point out, even Milton Friedman (2002) endorsed a version of UBI in the form of a "negative income tax" as a replacement for welfare-state institutions he viewed as merely exacerbating poverty. More recently, Bowman, executive director of the neoliberal Adam Smith Institute, asserts similarly, "The ideal welfare system is a basic income, replacing the existing anti-poverty programs the government carries out" (O'Hagan 2017). In this way, UBI proposals may be merely "intended to provide political cover for the elimination of social programs and the privatization of social services" (Kleiner 2016). Clarke (2017b) again claims:

> If austerity driven governments and institutions of global capitalism are today looking favourably at basic income, it's not because they want to move towards greater equality, reverse the neoliberal impact and enhance workers' bargaining power. They realize that a regressive model of basic income can be put in place that provides an inadequate, means tested payment to the poorest people outside of the workforce but that is primarily directed to the lowest paid workers.

And this perspective does, indeed, resonate with views such as those of Jeffrey Sachs (2006), who has stated in relation to his own approach to poverty alleviation: "What a deal the poor world is offering the rich world! The poorest of the poor are saying 'We buy into your system. You can keep your wealth. We don't call for revolution. We just want a little help to stay alive.'... That is all the poor are asking for in this world."

Notwithstanding these significant concerns, in their actual practice, CTPs—even more ardently neoliberal conditional ones—are still essentially a form of redistribution, usually managed by national states via taxation (Hanlon et al. 2010) in a manner quite similar to how PES, despite its similarly neoliberal framing, tends to also function. Hence, while Ferguson (2010) considers (unconditional) CTPs a creative use of neoliberalism for progressive ends, they could equally be viewed, like most PES programs, as instead a subsidy in disguise. This does not mean that such de facto subsidies are necessarily directed in a progressive direction, however; as the Ontario Coalition Against Poverty explains, the type of UBI initiative endorsed by Bowman and others might become "in effect, a subsidy to employers, paid for out of the tax revenues" (Clarke 2017b). Yet Wright claims that, regardless of the intentions of the actors endorsing it, if implemented UBI effectively "reunites workers with the means of subsistence, even though they remain separated from the means of production; it thus directly modifies the basic class relations of capitalism" (2019: 109).

BETWEEN REFORM AND RADICAL

Just because a given proposal is not in itself deeply transformative does not mean it has no progressive merit. One of the main thorns in the side of progressive politics is in fact the long-standing divide between "reform" and "radical" positions, in terms of which adherents of each camp are often demonized by the other, the former for not being "realistic" and the latter for (inadvertently) reinforcing the status quo. What I would like to suggest here is that rather than seeing these different strategies as innately antagonistic, a more expansive perspective might view them as in some instances complementary in pursuit of broader, more long-term objectives.

In general, the evolution of the global conservation movement to increasingly embrace neoliberalism charted in this book can be seen as partly a consequence of the fact that most of its influential actors have been pursuing practical compromise with the forces of industrial capitalism they view as the main problem to address. As organizations grow larger, wealthier, and more influential in and through this process, many become incrementally more conservative. Hence, even BINGOs like Greenpeace have become less radical in their confrontational politics in the course of their growth and expansion. Meanwhile, others, like CI and TNC, have become even more centrist in their accumulation of resources to rival prominent transnational corporations. In decades past, other more radical organizations, such as EarthFirst! and the Earth Liberation Front, have worked to counter-balance this centripetal movement to some degree in their explicit promotion of anti-capitalist platforms for environmental action (see Fletcher 2018b). Rather than undermining the actions of mainstream environmental organizations, as they have usually been perceived, from a broader perspective, these more radical groups might be seen to actually support such actions:

while radicals work to hold a line in the sand and keep the overarching environmental movement from collapsing toward the middle, reformists work to move the mainstream further than would likely be possible without this additional pressure. This dynamic—what Haines (1995) calls a "radical flank effect"—was in fact explicitly acknowledged by EarthFirst!-er Hellenbach, who claimed that

> the actions of monkeywrenchers invariably enhance the status and bargaining position of more "reasonable" opponents. Industry considers main-line environmentalists to be radical until they get a taste of real radical activism. Suddenly the soft-sell of the Sierra Club and other whiteshirt-and-tie eco-bureaucrats becomes much more attractive and worthy of serious negotiation. These moderate environmentalists must condemn monkeywrenching so as to preserve their own image, but they should take full advantage of the credence it lends to their approach. (1993: 30)

More generally, Burgmann asserts:

> The history of social movement activity suggests that reforms are more likely to be achieved when activists behave in extremist, even confrontational ways. Social movements rarely achieve all they want, but they secure important partial victories by demanding considerably more and matching radical rhetoric with radical action. . . . By carving out political space for themselves, extremists manoeuvre moderate proponents of the same progressive viewpoint into an advantageous political position within the wider society. The moderates emerge as the voice of compromise and reason, because the extremists have influenced the spectrum of political debate, shifting it to a point where less radical versions of the challenging viewpoint seem reasonable—so reforms are conceded. (2018: 10–11)

Yet EarthFirst! and other radical organizations' support of private property destruction, leading to their widespread branding as "eco-terrorists," has forced them to largely recede from public view in recent decades (Fletcher 2018b). Hence there are few prominent environmental voices demanding truly radical change these days, allowing the movement as a whole to slip further toward the center (Malm 2021).

What is needed now, this analysis suggests, is thus more radical voices calling for alternative worlds to counter the current neoliberal inertia with conservation and other environmental policy circles. The critique of neoliberal conservation offered herein and elsewhere may therefore be constructive in this effort. All of this thus points toward a twofold strategy for progressive environmental politics going forward. The first element is to support and nurture the development and radicalization of alternate lifeworlds already in formation in interstitial spaces. The second is to further develop a coherent vision of a radically different world that we can use to make seemingly impossible demands of the current social order (more on this in the conclusion). The aim would then be to work to progressively diminish the distance between these two strategies, holding an uncompromisingly radical line in the face of reformist pressure while simultaneously pursuing incremental, practical improvements in the here and now (Büscher and Fletcher 2020).

ACTUALLY EXISTING REDISTRIBUTION

In this present, after all, there remain many millions of people around the world who cannot simply sit back and wait for some dramatic change to be able to allow them to live non-wasted lives (Bauman 2004; Li 2010). Hence, as suggested above, while we continue to advance radical demands for a better world, we can simultaneously support more immediate if less transformative reform in this one.

If capitalism is understood as a monolithic global system, then pursuing post-capitalism necessarily entails overturning this system entirely. But if we view capitalism as, instead, a multilayered patchwork of different processes that embody capitalist modes of production and exchange to varying degrees, options for challenging capitalist hegemony in less dramatic ways become more feasible (Wright 2019). Such a perspective draws substantial inspiration from the influential "diverse economies" framework pioneered by feminist geographers J. K. Gibson-Graham (see especially 1996, 2006), which Barca and colleagues, indeed, claim "could function as the basic platform from which to build a political economy of degrowth" more generally (2019: 3).[10] Challenging the common depiction of capitalism as an all-encompassing monolithic system, Gibson-Graham instead envision a "landscape of radical heterogeneity populated by an array of capitalist and non-capitalist enterprises; market, non-market, and altermarket transactions; paid, unpaid, and alternatively compensated labor; and various forms of finance and property—a diverse economy in place" (2011: 2). They thus describe capitalist relations as merely the tip of an economic iceberg concealing a wealth of alternative arrangements illuminated by microanalysis of the multidimensional "community economy" operating beneath the visible surface. Similarly, Graeber (2014) asserts that all societies, even capitalist ones, are founded on a certain "baseline communism" in which people produce and exchange in common beyond formal market transactions.

Diverse practices of this sort, according to Gibson-Graham, "have been relatively 'invisible' because the concepts and discourses that could make them 'visible' have themselves been marginalised and suppressed" (1996: xi). They understand such marginalization to result, in large part, from what they call "capitalo-centric" thinking: ascribing what they consider a false homogeneity to a given situation such that "other forms of economy (not to mention noneconomic aspects of social life) are often understood primarily with reference to capitalism: as being fundamentally the same as (or modeled upon) capitalism, or as being deficient or substandard imitations" (1996: 6).

This diverse economies perspective is sometimes taken to untenable extremes to assert that the ostensive global domination of the capitalist system described by Marxists is largely a fiction created by such theorists themselves who inadvertently imbue the system with an exaggerated power and coherence. Yet there remains a tremendous amount of exploitative wage labor as well as financial flows aimed at continual accumulation in the world. Hence, we must still insist with Dean that "in a world where one bond trader can bring down a bank in a matter of minutes . . . the dominance of capitalism, the capitalist *system*, is material" (2012: 4, emphasis in original). Even so, a diverse economies perspective may still allow us to identify a wide variety of de facto mechanisms for wealth distribution operating in the shadows of a neoliberal capitalist economy ostensibly directed wholly toward pursuit of growth. In the following, then, I offer a preliminary typology of such "actually existing" redistribution mechanisms as the basis for future research and praxis.[11]

Failed Growth

The first category comprises initiatives directed toward growth that have failed to achieve this end and consequently function as de facto redistribution mechanisms in that injected capital remains in the hands of those to whom it was given as the basis for the failed growth-based programming. In conservation policy, a common practice in this vein, as we have seen, has been to inject "seed money" into communities to develop MBIs that are intended thereafter to become self-financing on the basis of market transactions. Essentially, this

was the rationale for the integrated-conservation-and-development projects widely deployed in the 1990s, in which community-based conservation
was intended to be supported by generation of revenue for local livelihoods
through engagement in ecotourism, bioprospecting, and other mechanisms
to harness the value of in situ resources as the basis of income generation. As
has been widely documented by now, the vast majority of ICDPs have failed
to achieve their aim of jump-starting self-financing initiatives in the long run
(West 2006; McShane et al. 2011; Fletcher 2012a). In the short term, however,
the seed money given by conservation organizations is often used for community development, hence, in practice, functioning as precisely the subsidy for
rural livelihoods that neoliberal conservation was intended to dismantle and
replace (Simpson 2004).

A similar dynamic is occurring right now in evolution of the REDD+
mechanism. As noted in chapters 4 and 5, to develop the infrastructure and
capacity necessary to administer REDD+ effectively, many governments in
low-income societies, including Costa Rica, have received "REDD Readiness" funding from the World Bank and UN. There are, as I have shown,
growing concerns that REDD+ may fail to ever become the global market
mechanism it was intended to be. In the meantime, however, to the extent
that they are invested in community-level development projects, REDD+
funding redistributes finance, to some degree at least, from international
donors to local resources users.

Other mechanisms can be seen to function in similar fashion. In its eu-
phoric promotion as a magic bullet for poverty reduction globally, for instance, microfinance has morphed from a form of low-interest development
lending to the poorest of the poor to an attempt, as Roy (2010) and Aitken
(2013) describe, to financialize even the meager resources the impoverished
possess and thus further draw them into the domain of global capital. In
the process, of course, default rates have grown dramatically in many places,
raising concerns about the long-term viability of this erstwhile posterchild
of international development policy (Roy 2010). While investors may not
recover their investment on defaulted loans, however, to the extent that
funds remain in the hands of recipients (i.e., they are not forced to repay it
or do not commit suicide as many have done), microfinance can be seen to
function as a de facto redistribution mechanism much like the ICDP seed
money previously discussed.

It is intriguing to consider the extent to which this analysis might be extended to development finance as a whole. The more than $2.3 trillion in

development aid deployed globally over the past six decades has of course produced astronomical debt in societies around the world (Easterly 2006). Yet to the extent that this aid is not repaid through SAPs or siphoned off by self-aggrandizing elites and actually results in community-level development projects, it might also be viewed as a de facto form of redistribution. The scale of this dynamic, if conceptualized in these terms, could potentially be quite staggering.

Covert Redistribution

A second category comprises initiatives that claim to function as market mechanisms yet actually entail self-conscious means for redistributing resources. My main examples of this are of course PES and CTPs, both of which, as I have described, are commonly couched in neoliberal rhetoric yet in reality usually rely on forms of state-centered collection and redistribution of revenue more characteristic of welfare-state institutions. Again, it is intriguing to ponder the extent to which this analysis might also be extended, considering the way that so many ostensive markets worldwide are in fact essentially supported by state-based appropriation and distribution of resources. From state subsidies for oil and agricultural production to public investment in higher education, research, and publishing to the legion of spin-off industries supported by all of this, how much of the global economy might actually be understood as merely an immense subsidy system if viewed through this de facto redistributive lens?

Ad Hoc Redistribution

A third category includes forms of redistribution that are not organized or administered as such by particular organizations or agencies. My main example of this is the global rise of remittance flows, which have grown to become by far the largest source of foreign exchange for many low-income societies throughout the world and the most significant source of development financing globally, comprising a conservatively estimated five hundred billion dollars in 2011 (Robinson 2014). As Robinson (2008: 65) describes, "Worldwide, remittance flows dwarf most other sectors in the global economy, with the possible exception of oil/energy, and apart from the global financial system itself," with at least one out of six people on the planet now receiving some share of this funding. While Robinson is correct in pointing out that "remittances redistribute income worldwide in a literal or geographic sense but not in the actual sense of *redistribution*, meaning a transfer of some added portion of the surplus from capital to labor, since it constitutes not additional earnings but the separation of the site where wages are earned from the site of wage-generated consumption" (2003: 204, emphasis in original), this mechanism still moves money from high-income to low-income societies on a significant global scale. What other processes might also be conceptualized as examples of ad hoc distribution of this sort?

Intentional Redistribution

A fourth category comprises initiatives that are explicitly intended to redistribute resources as a corrective for current inequities. Foremost among such initiatives, and likely the most controversial, is of course land reform, as previously mentioned. A prominent example in recent decades has been Bolivia, where a second major wave of land reform initiated in 1996 has thus far succeeded in officially surveying and titling at least 157 million acres of land on behalf of more than one million people and redistributing another 3.5 million acres of state-held land to landless peasants and indigenous people (Achtenberg 2013). The majority of this occurred in the years after Evo Morales assumed office in 2006, promoting land reform as one of his central policy platforms: 85 percent (134 million acres) of newly titled land and almost all of the redistributed state land. During his tenure, Morales also appropriated approximately 25 million acres of unutilized land from private owners throughout the country (Achtenberg 2013). The Vía Campesina network has of course been active in promoting land reform both within Bolivia and globally too (Borras 2008).

A second form of intentional redistribution can be found in the rise of worker self-directed enterprises (WSDEs), in which workers "collectively become the directors deciding what, where, and how to produce and how to distribute the appropriated surplus" (Wolff 2012: 18). WSDEs have expanded dramatically in recent years in many places, especially in the wake of the 2008 crisis. As a mode of production in which surplus value is redistributed to those producing the labor value of accumulated capital, the widespread adoption of WSDEs would, as Wolff (2012: 21) states simply, "effectively end capitalism." A third form of intentional redistribution (in its progressive forms at least) is of course UBI, which has indeed become a cornerstone of current degrowth proposals too (Kallis et al. 2020). How the mounting global discussion of UBI, and the various pilot projects currently testing its efficacy as the potential basis for more widespread roll-out, develop in the future is thus another intriguing focus of inquiry from this perspective.

Anti-capitalism

A final category comprises efforts to promote not merely explicit redistribution but an openly anti- or post-capitalist agenda. This includes more radical strains of the degrowth movement. Other explicitly anti-capitalist platforms have been advanced from other quarters, for instance, by the Zapatistas (Esteva 2012), certain strands of the alterglobalization movement (McNally 2006), and by elements of the Occupy protests (Žižek 2012b).

CONCLUSION: DECOUPLING OR DEGROWTH?

In the final analysis, it seems that we have indeed reached a pivotal fork in the road in which two clear and quite different paths confront us: pursuit of decoupling, on the one hand, and of degrowth, on the other. If we cling to a growth-dependent economic model, then to remain ecologically sustainable there is no choice but to pursue decoupling. Yet if, as increasing evidence demonstrates and I have argued herein, decoupling is an illusory fantasy, then the only viable alternative is a serious movement in support of (post-capitalist) degrowth.[12] The sole remaining questions, then, are what this will look like and how do we get there?

In our recent book *The Conservation Revolution*, Bram Büscher and I draw on examples both theoretical and operational from around the world to outline the pillars of a comprehensive program for post-capitalist transformation in global conservation policy and practice that we call "convivial conservation" (Büscher and Fletcher 2020).[13] In this present book's conclusion, I want to add to this proposal by addressing an important prerequisite to the "unmaking" of the existing social order needed to realize this and other degrowth-oriented projects (see Feola 2019) that psychoanalysis helps to illuminate, namely, the need to confront and break libidinal attachment to the capitalist economy and the seductive *jouissance* it promises.

Conclusion

TRAVERSING THE NEOLIBERAL FANTASY

This is a paradox we have to accept: the extreme violence of
liberation, that you must be forced to be free. If you trust your
spontaneous sense of well-being you will never get free. Freedom
hurts.

SLAVOJ ŽIŽEK, *The Pervert's Guide to Ideology* (2012a)

This conclusion responds to a growing call within the social sciences for researchers to move beyond merely critiquing "things that they do not like"
(Igoe and Brockington 2007: 445) and instead also contribute to formulating
practical proposals for positive future directions. In the process, it also helps
to advance discussion of the more intimate (both intra- and interpersonal)
aspects of the transformation needed for degrowth to become possible. Thus
far, growing discussions of the potential for degrowth have largely neglected
in-depth attention to how this potential resonates at the level of (inter)
personal subjectivity, notwithstanding notable exceptions pointing in this
direction.[1] Yet psychological perspectives, most prominently psychoanalysis,
have long explored how a demand for infinite growth can be seen to inhere
at both personal (Žižek 1989) and societal levels (Kapoor 2015; Bjerg 2016).
The following discussion builds on these insights to explore how they might
also help chart a path toward embrace of a post-capitalist transformation in
pursuit of degrowth as well.

THE CRITIQUE OF CRITIQUE

Calls for critical researchers to move beyond mere critique are of course not
wholly novel. Foucault, for instance, was himself frequently criticized for
merely deconstructing dominant discourse rather than providing alternative
proposals for progressive collective action. In responding to such criticism,

he claimed that this strategy was intentional, asserting: "I am not looking for an alternative; you can't find the solution of a problem in the solution of another problem raised at another moment by other people. You see, what I want to do is not the history of solutions, and that's the reason why I don't accept the word 'alternative'" (1984b: 343).[2]

The point of critical analysis, Foucault maintained, was to highlight the relations of power with respect to which alternatives must be organized. As he explained: "And if I don't ever say what must be done, it isn't because I believe that there's nothing to be done; on the contrary, it is because I think that there are a thousand things to do, to invent, to forge, on the part of those who, recognizing the relations of power in which they're implicated, have decided to resist or escape them" (Foucault 1991b: 174). From this perspective, Foucault claimed that his intention was not to pronounce "that everything is bad, but that everything is dangerous, which is not exactly the same as bad. If everything is dangerous, then we always have something to do. So my position leads not to apathy but to a hyper- and pessimistic activism" (Foucault 1984b: 343).

Yet many social theorists, even those working in the Foucauldian tradition, have become increasingly uncomfortable with this stance. Bruno Latour (2004), for instance, became self-critical of his own role as one of the most trenchant and incisive critics of Western science, observing that rather than providing an opening for progressive social movements, his work may have been most influential in actually providing support for the "post-truth" politics of the reactionary right. Hence, he worried "that a certain form of critical spirit has sent us down the wrong path, encouraging us to fight the wrong enemies and, worst of all, to be considered as friends by the wrong sort of allies" (Latour 2004: 231).

Such critique of critique has only multiplied in recent years in the face of the increasingly daunting range of social and environmental problems confronting us.[3] Yet one must also remain careful not to move too quickly down the path from defining and analyzing problems to prescribing solutions. Despite his expressed opposition to this latter position, even Foucault could not resist the temptation at times, as exemplified by his curious if fleeting celebration of the progressive possibilities of the 1979 Iranian Revolution (e.g., Foucault 1999). With hindsight, it is easy to understand the seduction of this stance. At that historical moment, standing on the brink of the neoliberal onslaught he himself so presciently foretold (Foucault 2008), having witnessed the bitter failure of previous efforts to cast the Soviet Union in a progressive light as well as dissipation of the '68 euphoria, it must have appeared, as it did to Horkheimer and Adorno (1998: xi) some three decades earlier in the midst of World War II, that humankind "instead of entering into a truly human condition, [was] sinking into a new kind of barbarism" once more. At that point, it would have been difficult not to succumb to the siren song of any movement that might offer a ray of hope in the gathering darkness. Similarly misplaced optimism has afflicted otherwise even-keeled critical analysts time and again, from disavowal of Soviet atrocities by Cold War communist sympathizers to Žižek's (2008) praise of Chavez's Venezuela despite growing evidence of that regime's mounting totalitarian impulses.

Dynamics like these warn us to be wary in our eagerness to start celebrating ostensive alternatives too quickly. Pushing back against this growing trend, Konings, for instance, echoes Foucault in asserting:

> A major factor luring progressive intellectuals into the game of making policy proposals is the tyranny of "what is your alternative?"—that is, the notion that public intellectuals only behave responsibly if they do not only offer criticism but also put forward alternative policy proposals. However, in situations where we find ourselves at many removes from the levers of public authority, to prescribe policy alternatives is bound to be either presumptuous and pointless (because the political actors that we would like to carry our programs are nowhere to be found) or conservative in its political implications (because after many radical calls in the desert we learn to ratchet our ambitions down to a level where they can easily be taken up by existing agencies). Once we buy into the game of making policy proposals we can only sound ridiculous and irrelevant or end up participating in the legitimation of prevailing relations of power. We may be able to find a trade-off between these two extremes, but we will have structurally hobbled our capacity for the production of critical knowledge. (2009: 355)

Rather than succumb to this lure, Konings follows Hegel via Žižek (1993) in advising us to "tarry with the negative," suggesting that, "For the time being, the most productive role that progressive intellectuals can play is to . . . trace and publicize the inconsistencies between prevailing practices of power and their idealized representation in the official institutions, narratives and symbols of our polity" (2009: 356).

I agree that this type of critical analysis has utility in its own right, and that to be effective it must be followed through to the point that one is certain one has fully understood the contours of the problem at hand—what Haraway (2016), as previously noted, calls "staying with the trouble." But

I also agree with Haraway that we need not stop at that point; we can instead attempt to tread the "fine line between acknowledging the extent and seriousness of the troubles and succumbing to abstract futurism and its affects of sublime despair and its politics of sublime indifference" (2016: 4). While avoiding Konings' twin pitfalls of either vacuous utopian fantasizing or outlining politically pragmatic proposals—or alternately pursuing a diluted "trade-off between these two extremes"—we can, I believe, still continue to point toward the type of more radical change that would get us closer to the sort of world we truly want to inhabit.

In the passage (quoted in full in note 6 of chapter 2) made famous by Klein's (2007) analysis of his perspective as a "shock doctrine," Milton Friedman claimed that the "basic function" of his cohort of neoliberal ideologues was "to develop alternatives to existing policies, to keep them alive and available until the politically impossible becomes the politically inevitable" (Friedman 2002: xiv). In pointing to this function, Friedman highlighted the interrelationship between ideational and material dimensions of social change, asserting, "Only a crisis—actual or perceived—produces real change. When that crisis occurs, the actions that are taken depend on the ideas that are lying around" (2002: xiv). It is astounding how prescient this prognosis now appears, looking back upon the neoliberal ascendance Friedman himself helped to orchestrate: how the 1973 accumulation crisis indeed created the space for Friedman and colleagues to promote the ideas they had been nurturing for decades prior as the basis of the new world order, and in this way transforming a philosophy that had indeed seemed "politically impossible" only a short time before into what has now been able to assert itself as the inevitable outcome of a teleological development.

In a parallel yet opposite strategy, therefore, we might follow Friedman's lead in our own promotion of "vital alternatives" (Dressler et al. 2014) to neoliberal conservation.[4] For the reality, as outlined in chapter 8, is that there is already a wealth of alternative "transition discourses" in development throughout the world, via both on-the-ground practice and more abstract conceptualization. The main current impediment to fully realizing these is that, from the perspective of a persistent neoliberal hegemony, they do appear politically infeasible at present. Yet as Friedman among others has taught us, such perceptions can be subject to dramatic transformation over time (see also Yurchak 2013). After all, one of the main functions of hegemony, noted in chapter 1, is precisely to "define . . . what is realistic and what is not realistic, and to drive certain aspirations and grievances into the realm of the impossible, of idle dreams" (Scott 1990: 73). A main strategy of both socialist and anarchist politics has thus been to make "impossible demands" of the current social order so as to challenge this hegemony and sustain the idea that, as the World Social Forum asserts, another world is possible beyond the impoverished horizons of neoliberal capitalism.

In addition to highlighting already existing alternative practices and proposals and helping to flesh out the contours of the alternative world(s) to which they point—the focus of the previous chapter—another productive role for critical scholarship beyond critique may be to explore the conditions of possibility that would allow such alternatives to become first imaginable and then realistic. This is my aim in the following.

WHAT IS CRITIQUE TODAY?

To the extent that critique remains useful in its own right, however, a Lacanian perspective reminds us that it must be approached in a particular way. Acknowledging the implications of the public secrecy dynamic discussed in previous chapters, Žižek echoes Taussig in cautioning that "we must avoid the simple metaphors of demasking, of throwing away the veils which are supposed to hide the naked reality. We can see why Lacan, in his seminar on *The Ethic of Psychoanalysis*, distances himself from the liberating gesture of saying finally that 'the emperor has no clothes'" (1989: 25). Rather, Žižek suggests, the aim of critique must be "to detect, in a given ideological edifice, the element which represents within it its own impossibility" (1989: 143), to undertake a "symptomal reading" that seeks to "to discern the unavowed bias of the official text via its ruptures, blanks, and slips" (1997: 10). Or as Kapoor (2005: 1205) paraphrases, "this means tracking and identifying ideology's Real—its slips, disavowals, contradictions, ambiguities."

In other words, this Lacanian stance challenges the conventional approach to critique often termed the "education model of social change," entailing a conviction that provision of more facts concerning the realities of a situation will lead to greater awareness of the problem and, in turn, more effective action (cf. Weintrobe, 2013a). Yet a growing body of research in behavioral economics, social psychology, and related fields demonstrates what psychoanalysts have long asserted, namely that human behavior deviates substantially from this ideal and hence that rather than developing greater awareness and commitment to action, subjects often react to new information by becoming more firmly entrenched in their existing perspective (see Lakoff 2009). For psychoanalysts, this is explained by the fact that attachment to the status quo is commonly cemented by the promise of *jouissance* that it offers. While this *jouissance*, as previously noted, is rarely unequivocally pleasurable, rather offering pleasure and pain in equal measure, the fleeting pleasure it does provide reinforces commitment via the fantasy that the pain can be overcome and pure pleasure eventually attained.

Breaking attachment to ideology, therefore, requires loss of both this fantasy of total fulfilment and the limited *jouissance* actually experienced. Facing this loss requires a process of mourning, entailing acceptance of both the pain of separation and deprivation of pleasure. To avoid this pain, subjects tend to retain attachment at all costs, or when forced to endure loss, to turn away from and repress the suffering, in which case mourning is replaced by *melancholia*, a state of low-level depression precipitated by the inability to mourn and therefore dissipate the negative affect (Freud 1925). Melancholia is characterized by the movement from desire to drive in that one continually relives failure to attain the object in question. It is supported by a variety of defense mechanisms, one of the most significant of which is disavowal, allowing subjects to half-acknowledge their pain while simultaneously denying its full significance. Manifest as "perversion," this entails, paradoxically, a (largely unconscious) "'choice' to feel pain rather than suffer the painful truth" (Layton 2009: 309). One of psychoanalysis's most important insights is that this dynamic occurs even with respect to circumstances we consider negative and may explicitly claim to want to end. In short, psychoanalysis suggests, as Žižek phrases it in the epigraph to this conclusion, that attaining "freedom hurts."

To pursue such freedom nonetheless, the quintessential Lacanian injunction is to encourage subjects to "traverse the fantasy." As Brearley (2013: 160) summarizes this process, "the task of the ego is to wean itself away from its early reliance on magical and wishful thinking and painfully attempt to represent to itself what really is the case." With respect to neoliberal conservation, this would entail fully acknowledging the Real of capitalism as a self-destructive system driving us toward the brink of ecological catastrophe. And to break the cycle of melancholia and perversion, this would, of course, require consciously confronting the pain resulting from both the loss of attachment to a capitalist society of enjoyment and the recognition of the environmental devastation this society has wrought. As Mishan asserted some time ago: "The psychic cost of such a move into recognition is the cost of the move from the paranoid-schizoid toward the depressive position. The cost is the psychic pain of guilt at damage done, and the necessity of mourning of our grandiose fantasy of self-sufficiency and immortality. Without such a move we risk eco-catastrophe, because we cannot assess the true threat" (1996: 65).

DISAVOWAL OF DEATH

While within neoliberal conservation discourse it may indeed be easier to imagine the end of the world than the end of capitalism, this seeming acknowledgment of the grave existential threat posed by our mounting environmental crisis—which has in fact been interpreted as portending a sixth global extinction event or even "biological annihilation" altogether (see, e.g., Ceballos et al. 2017)—may not be so substantial as it appears at first blush. Rather, the dominant policy response to this acknowledgment embodied in neoliberal conservation and similar approaches, understood in Žižek's terms as considering the current situation "catastrophic but not serious," suggests something far more ambivalent at work here. For psychoanalysts, such ambivalence calls to mind what is considered a common human tendency to avoid acceptance of one's own future death (Becker 1973). As Becker (1973) explains, all people are ostensibly aware of the inevitable fact that they will eventually die, yet this fact, and the existential fear it provokes, are usually suppressed in the course of everyday life. Zilboorg describes this stance as follows:

> In normal times we move about actually without ever believing in our own death, as if we fully believed in our own corporeal immortality. . . . A man [sic] will say, of course, that that he knows he will someday die, but he does not really care. He is having a good time with living, and he does not think about death and does not care to bother about it—but this is a purely intellectual, verbal admission. The affect of fear is repressed. (1943: 468–471)

Rather than wholesale denial, this description speaks more to the presence of disavowal, as conceptualized in previous chapters. What analysis in these terms suggests, therefore, is that a particular form of ambivalent disavowal that the environmental crisis wrought by capitalism represents an existential threat to humanity as well as other forms of life on Earth serves to shield us from the fear of death that a deep awareness of this reality might otherwise provoke. Unable to receive full acknowledgment and expression, such fear may instead manifest itself in the growing "ecological anxiety disorder" that Robbins and Moore (2013) diagnose among environmentalists. This disavowal of death may partly explain our widespread failure to truly appreciate and hence act on knowledge of the reality of the impending biological annihilation we face—and thus to take refuge instead in fantasies of future salvation via neoliberal conservation.

THE END OF HOPE

Requisite to the process of both facing our existential fear and mourning for loss of attachment to the status quo, consequently, may be abandoning all hope for redemption within the bounds of a capitalist political economy. In *The Courage of Hopelessness*, Žižek (2017) draws on the example of a smoker who promises to quit in the future to illustrate the problem of a politics based in hope. As he explains this dilemma, "My awareness that I can stop smoking any time I want guarantees that I will never actually do it—the possibility of stopping smoking is what blocks the actual change; it allows me to accept our continuous smoking without bad conscience, so that the end of smoking is constantly present as the very source of its continuation" (Žižek 2017: ix). It is this promise of future change, in other words, that allows one to disavow one's inability to actually change in the present. In a similar way, neoliberal conservation can be seen to offer hope for capitalism's eventual transformation into a sustainable form, allowing us to continue to engage in (inevitably) unsustainable capitalist practices in the (continually extended) here and now by reassuring ourselves that these will be compensated for in a "net zero" future. As with Žižek's smoker, then, in neoliberal conservation "the possibility of change is evoked to guarantee that it will not be acted upon" (2017: x).

In addressing this dilemma, Žižek contends, "It is only when we despair and don't know any more what to do that change can be enacted—we have to go through this zero point of hopelessness" (2017: x). Hence, he concludes that "true courage is to admit that the light at the end of the tunnel is probably the headlight of another train approaching us from the opposite direction" (Žižek 2017: xi–xii). The train in this case, I have argued, is neoliberal capitalism; hence, escape from the tunnel is only attainable by traversing the neoliberal fantasy entirely in pursuit of a wholly different social reality.

More than a lack of practicable alternatives, the preceding discussion suggests, it may be a largely unconscious attachment to the contemporary capitalist order that helps to hold it in place (McGowan 2017). This raises the sobering prospect that many of us may not be nearly as willing to make the dramatic changes we know are necessary to develop a just and sustainable world as we would like to believe. From the psychoanalytic perspective advanced in this book, achieving effective change therefore requires generating the desire for pursuit of a new situation sufficient to motivate subjects to face the painful emotions and undergo the process of mourning necessary to break attachment to present circumstances and the cycle of drive it precipitates. This is the strategy Lacan captured in his famous maxim, "Don't compromise your desire!" (see de Vries 2007). As Rustin phrases this dilemma, "Moving out of the paranoid-schizoid into more depressive ways of thinking and feeling can be found too painful to endure, if there are no internalized good objects to sustain a belief in the existence of good objects outside the self" (2013: 175).

Several commentators contend that many members of the political left have indeed largely compromised their desire for radical progressive change over the past several decades (Brown 1999; Dean 2012; Fisher 2012). Thus, Dean suggests that a prominent strain of leftist thought

> has given way on the desire for communism, betrayed its historical commitment to the proletariat, and sublimated revolutionary energies into restorationist practices that strengthen the hold of capitalism. This Left has replaced commitments to the emancipatory, egalitarian struggles of working people against capitalism—commitments that were never fully orthodox, but always ruptured, conflicted, and contested—with incessant activity (like the mania Freud associates with melancholia) and so now satisfies itself with criticism and interpretation, small projects and local actions, particular issues and legislative victories, art, technology, procedures, and process. . . . For such a Left, enjoyment comes from its withdrawal from responsibility, its sublimation of goals and responsibilities into the branching, fragmented practices of micropolitics, self-care, and issue awareness. (Dean 2012: 173–174)

To counter this trend, Dean asserts, requires a "refusal to give way on desire and wallow in melancholia" (2012: 183). And for this to happen, Fisher contends, "the libidinal attractions of consumer capitalism need to be met with a counterlibido, not simply an anti-libidinal dampening" (2012: 134).

Yet if this new post-capitalist desire is merely for further unfulfillable fantasies, nothing will have been gained (McGowan 2017). After all, abstract notions of an idealized communist—or degrowth—future can become just as phantasmic as the promises of capitalist redemption they contest. And as Dean (2012) points out, perpetual failure to enact such a future can become just as much an object of attachment as the failure to redeem capitalism via neoliberal conservation that I have highlighted in this book. In dynamics such as these, consequently, post-capitalist desire may transform into a drive pursuing continual failure to attain the object in question, in a manner quite similar to the capitalist drive to which it ostensibly stands opposed.

Hence, the aim must be to instead stimulate novel forms of "post-fantasmatic" enjoyment (Byrne and Healy 2006) capable of traversing attachment to fantasy. As Gibson-Graham qualify, what is envisioned here

> is not a truly post-fantasmatic condition (since fantasy is the mode of integration of the subject into the symbolic order and the anchor of identification), but a more distanced and reflective relation to fantasy. . . . This new positioning brings a different relationship to both identity and desire—less trapped and invested, more aware of and open to possibilities of change. . . . Desire is set in motion again, though with somewhat less force, and disappointment is distanced from disillusion. (2006: 237)

In pursuit of post-capitalism, such post-fantasmatic enjoyment must be connected to a vision of "a world without exploitation; a world characterized by equality, justice, freedom, and the absence of oppression; a world where production is common, distribution is based on need, and decisions realize the general will" (Dean 2012: 203–204). And given that "capitalist subjectification, the desire it structures and incites, is individual," Dean asserts that post-capitalist desire, by contrast, "can only be collective, a common relation to a common condition of division" (2012: 191). In other words, post-capitalist desire can be understood as essentially "a collective desire for collectivity" (Dean 2012: 158), or what Gibson-Graham (2006) calls a desire for "being-in-common."

Gibson-Graham (2006: 239) outline a variety of initiatives "aimed at mobilizing desire for noncapitalist becomings" in their diverse community economies. As they explain, these were projects intended to provide participants with "opportunities to encounter each other in pleasurable ways—creating multiple spaces of engagement, offering activities and events that promoted receptivity. What took place in these spaces was the awakening of a communal subjectivity and a faint but discernible yearning for a communal (noncapitalist) economy" (2006: 239). This strategy can be understood as endeavoring to cultivate what Durkheim (1995) called a "collective effervescence" generated by group interaction, a dynamic also evoking Freud's (1962) famous "oceanic feeling" that can be further related to a more recent body of research exploring such experiences as a state of "flow" or "transcendence."[5] Such a state is experienced as intrinsically enjoyable (Csikszentmihalyi 1974) and hence encourages pursuit of further experiences promising a similar affective payback.

One of the key qualities commonly attributed to a flow state is its capacity to dissolve one's sense of "distinction between self and environment" (Csikszentmihalyi 1974: 58)—hence Freud's description of this as an *oceanic* feeling. Foucault (1991b: 48) identifies an analogous state as a "limit-experience" in which "the subject reaches decomposition, leaves itself, at the limit of its own possibility." Freud interpreted this experience as a reminder, in a sense, of a primordial state of oneness ostensibly achieved during pre-separation infancy. And Lacan suggests something similar in his distinction between *Jouissance* (uppercase) and *jouissance* (lowercase), with the former described in terms akin to Freud's oceanic feeling: as a primal sense of wholeness that subjects attempt to recapture later in life in the form of a lesser, derivative *jouissance* (see Fink 1995). Thus Covington describes of his own flow experience, "It must be close to our conception of paradise, what it's like before you're born and after you die" (1995: 169–170).

Intrinsic to flow is therefore a certain loss of individuality in pursuit of collective connection, highlighting the potential for stimulation of flow experiences as a means to indeed challenge "individualism as a barrier to collective will-formation" (Dean 2012: 196). While such (voluntary) surrender of individuality would seem to run counter to a modern liberal conception of freedom that conflates this with individual autonomy, others suggests that such "freedom" is itself a form of oppression and alienation (e.g., Lukács 1985; Savran 1998; Dean 2012). As Dean (2012: 196–197) relates, Lukács indeed deemed this "a freedom of the egoist, of the man who cuts himself off from others, a freedom for which solidarity and community exist at best only as ineffectual 'regulative ideas' (1985: 315)" By contrast, Lukács claimed, "The *conscious* desire for the realm of freedom can only mean consciously taking the steps that will really lead to it. And in the awareness that in contemporary bourgeois society individual freedom can only be corrupt and corrupting because it is a case of unilateral privilege based on the unfreedom of others, this desire must entail the renunciation of individual freedom" (1985: 315, emphasis in original). Building on this, Dean (2012: 197) thus asserts that pursuit of post-capitalism requires "the deliberate and practical subordination of self in and to a collective communist will." As Covington suggests of the flow experience, consequently, contrary to the modern equation of freedom with individuality, there may instead be "power in the act of disappearing" and "victory in the loss of self" (1995: 169–170).

A similar dissolution of self into the collective has, of course, characteristically been cultivated by authoritarian populists (on both right and left) to catalyze their own rise to power. Indeed, this may be one of the main factors explaining their frequent success in attracting large numbers of followers on the basis of often incoherent and irrational ideologies. One challenge for the future, then, is to employ similar means for opposite ends—to cultivate through bottom-up organization what might be termed an "affective commons," to complement and reinforce the spatial commons pursued via collective resource governance.

This, indeed, is what Neera Singh points to in asserting that "commons are not just shared natural resources but are also our shared affective capacities to act and respond, and these affective capacities shape encounters" with one another as well as the resources in question (2017: 767). Collective activities such as "patrolling the forest, picking up dead and dried wood, removing weeds, picking berries, and so on" thereby contribute to "draw people into affective relations with their local forests, its vegetation, and its wildlife and generate a sense of 'being-in-common' with the forest and with the other members of human community" (2017: 765). "Commons," Singh therefore concludes, "are nurtured through commoning practices that, in turn, enable us to think, feel, and act as a commoner" (2017: 767).

EMBRACING THE INFINITE VOID

Yet mobilizing post-fantasmatic, post-capitalist enjoyment in support of the commons may also require developing a different relationship with one's own desire and the subjectivity underpinning it. A Lacanian perspective, after all, understands the human subject as fundamentally constituted by an essential "lack." This is due to the fact that one's very self-consciousness is the product of a perception of separation between one's self and the surrounding environment. This self-perception, however, can only ever encompass a fraction of one's actual being, hence there remains an inevitable disjuncture between what one is and how one perceives oneself to be. As Dolar describes this dynamic, "there is a part of the individual that cannot successfully pass into the subject, an element of 'pre-ideological' and 'presubjective' *materia prima* that comes to haunt subjectivity once it is constituted as such" (1993: 75, emphasis in original). It is this essential lack that stimulates subjects' desire for objects believed capable of resolving it and thereby conferring a sense of wholeness imagined to have been experienced prior to self-awareness and separation. This renders the subject essentially an infinite void that can never be filled, but which it nevertheless strives to fill through pursuit of objects attached to fantasies that it imagines able to confer the desired completeness. And it is this same lack, of course, that capitalism is able to harness so effectively in "sustaining subjects in a constant state of desire" (McGowan 2017: 11) in order to stimulate the ever-increasing production and consumption requisite to capital accumulation. This stimulation reaches its epitome with the neoliberal "achievement-subject" described by Han (2017), bent on perpetual advancement and optimization. In this way, Lacan suggested, stimulation of "surplus enjoyment" and appropriation of "surplus value" go hand in hand (see Žižek 1989).

This understanding of the subject means that one can never be wholly satisfied through attainment of any particular object (or anything else), but only through acknowledgment, paradoxically, that total satisfaction is unattainable and hence that partial satisfaction of an infinite longing is the best one can ever hope to achieve. After all, for Lacanians, the supposed state of primordial wholeness (*Jouissance*) that subjects seek to recapture via pursuit of *jouissance* is itself considered illusory, yet another "fantasmatic construction" sustaining the misperception that "there was once a time or space before lack" (McMillan 2008: 22). This is because attaining such a state would require erasure of the very self-awareness through which it is perceived.

Thus, McGowan (2017: 13) contends, "No revolution can transform dissatisfaction into satisfaction, but this is how revolution has been conceived throughout the entirety of the capitalist epoch." In his analysis, this is indeed one of the main reasons why revolutions so commonly fail to achieve their envisioned ends. Consequently, McGowan asserts that pursuit of post-capitalism entails accepting that "there is no deeper or more authentic satisfaction that will overcome the antagonisms of society or the failures of subjectivity, despite what anticapitalist revolutionaries have traditionally promised" (2017: 14).

This resonates with Kallis's (2019a: 6) contention that pursuit of degrowth entails voluntary "establishment of self-imposed and deliberately chosen limits" to growth rather than assuming that such limits will be determined by the biophysical environment, as theorists since Malthus have characteristically done. Echoing Lacan, Kallis asserts that humans are characterized by infinite wants that will inevitably exceed available resources no matter how plentiful; hence, sustainability requires placing self-imposed limits on these wants to remain within boundaries that are socially rather than naturally defined. He therefore concludes, paradoxically, that "it is only when we begin to accept the world as abundant that we can contemplate limiting our wants and delimiting a safe space for our freedom" (Kallis 2019a: 6).

Yet the opposite goal—eliminating desire altogether—is equally untenable given that desire is a function of the subject's basic constitution. Achieving post-fantasmatic enjoyment, therefore, would entail accepting the impossibility of either achieving or escaping the inevitable allure of *jouissance*. In this way, an ephemeral oceanic feeling can still be pursued and enjoyed via collective engagement without one becoming overly attached to this experience or falling prey to the illusion that it could ever be achieved indefinitely or become entirely satisfying.

This, in turn, would allow for a certain distancing from the capitalist imperative to futilely endeavor to fill the infinite void through ever-increasing consumption and accumulation. As McGowan phrases it, "When one recognizes that no object will provide the ultimate satisfaction, one can divest psychically from the capitalist system" (2017: 40). Instead, one can pursue a different social order aimed, as the organizers of a recent climate change rally phrased it, at "Producing Less & Enjoying It More" (Gateway Greens 2008).

BEYOND DYSTOPIA

One of the main obstacles to effectively mobilizing post-capitalist desire is that there are currently few visions of an alternative world sufficiently compelling to motivate subjects to undergo the process of mourning necessary to break attachment to the status quo. Herein lies the crux of our present predicament. Assessments of environmental problems overwhelmingly depict an apocalyptic future in which depletion of natural resources will lead to either fierce competition for or strict rationing of what is left—a perspective that Swyngedouw (2010) evocatively calls portending "apocalypse forever." Both scenarios are generally pictured as quite grim and pleasureless. It is difficult for even those of us gravely concerned by ecological degradation and highly motivated to address it to be inspired by such prospects, particularly when this entails giving up a lifestyle that does in fact provide the promise (if not attainment) of *jouissance* in myriad forms. And so, while we may claim that we desire the dramatic change we know is needed, we may often secretly fear this change as well, engaging in our own disavowal concerning the depth of our commitment to the cause. Thus Lertzman highlights "the power of unconscious desires: that we may in fact want our cars and cheap flights and also want to avoid global climate-induced catastrophes" (2013: 120), generating a deep-seated ambivalence toward the change we (half-)know is needed.

One of the most urgent present challenges, therefore, is to develop a vision of a sustainable society sufficiently motivating to compel a large and increasing number of subjects to become willing to undergo the process of mourning requisite to breaking attachment to the neoliberal capitalist system currently suffocating the Earth. Yet such a vision cannot remain merely another impossible fantasy of future fulfilment. As McGowan observes, after all, "The promise of the better future is the foundation of the capitalist structure" (2017: 12). Consequently, he asserts, pursuit of post-capitalism must "break from the promise of a better future" and instead understand "the future not as a possibility on the horizon but as the implicit structure of the present" (McGowan 2017: 13). This seems to be what Fisher (2012: 136) also has in mind when he suggests that "the desire for Starbucks is the thwarted desire for communism." In Heron's (2020: 176) interpretation, this assertion invites us to "see the masses of people sitting alone in Starbucks with their laptops and coffee as participating in a sad and diminished reflection of a fuller, richer practice of being and desiring in common." In other words, the seeds of the better world we desire must be identified within the present, for instance, in the iceberg model of existing economic activity Gibson-Graham (2006) describe, the "baseline communism" that Graeber highlights, or the forms of actually existing redistribution outlined in chapter 8.

This is Wright's (2010) point as well in advocating pursuit of "real utopias." Echoing the foregoing discussion, Wright suggests that "the political conditions for progressive tinkering with social arrangements . . . may depend in significant ways on the presence of more radical visions of social transformations" (2010: 8). Yet such visions must remain within the realm of post-fantasy. As opposed to ideal utopias constituting "fantasies, morally inspired designs for a humane world of peace and harmony unconstrained by realistic considerations of human psychology and social feasibility" (2010: 5), Wright therefore conceptualizes real utopias as navigating the "tension between dreams and practice" to pursue "utopian ideals that are grounded in the real potentials of humanity, utopian destinations that have accessible waystations, utopian design of institutions that can inform our practical tasks of navigating a world of imperfect conditions for social change" (2010: 6). As Obeng-Odoom explains in his review of Wright's book, within this conceptualization "the element of utopia provides the driver and motivation to break away from the status quo, while the 'reality' supplies the ingredient necessary to 'ground' and propel the vision" (2012: 185). Or as hooks contends similarly, "To be truly visionary we have to root our imagination in our concrete reality while simultaneously imagining possibilities beyond that reality" (2014: 12). While importantly highlighting the need for a substantive, positive vision of an alternative social order to inspire progressive action, however, such prescriptions fail to sufficiently emphasize the importance of mobilizing not only imagination but also affect—desire—in order to motivate such action.

By contrast, attention to this affective dimension of progressive social action seems to be foundational to Bastani's (2019) advocacy of a "fully automated luxury communism" (FALC).[6] Bastani asserts that new advances in "seemingly disparate technologies—in automation, energy, resources, health and food" have converged to create the conditions of possibility for "a society beyond both scarcity and work" (2019: 12). Within this post-capitalist society, "any distinction between mental and physical labour would vanish, with work becoming more akin to play. This also meant a society with greater collective wealth, where all essential wants as well as creative desires are satisfied" (2019: 55–56). And this, he emphasizes, "is where luxury comes in" (2019: 56).

Reminiscent of McGowan, Bastani qualifies that "FALC is not a blueprint for a steady-state Eden—those always prove disappointing anyway. Nor is it a place beyond sadness or pain, where conflict and vulnerability are consigned to the past. Pride, greed and envy will abide as long as we do, the management of discord between humans—the essence of politics—an inevitable feature of any society we share with one another" (2019: 243). Echoing both hooks and Wright, moreover, Bastani explains that while FALC envisions a "transformation as seismic as that of the arrival of agriculture," it "demurs from idealism or an overly optimistic view of human nature, offering immediate action instead. . . . Its concrete politics consist in specific, readily identifiable demands" (243).

Even so, Bastani's proposal is not without its critics. While many take issue with its rampant techno-optimism, Mariqueo-Russell and Read highlight its promotion of luxury in particular, contending that "Bastani equates luxury with wellbeing and downplays other aspects of flourishing such as community and friendship. . . . Automation and luxury are not necessary to human wellbeing, and certainly not essential enough to it to risk devastating the only home we have, our planet" (2019: 110). Yet while Bastani's unbridled faith in the techno-fix is indeed questionable, as I read it, his emphasis on luxury is not intended to replace collective solidarity with individual indulgence in material opulence.[7] Rather, it aims to emphasize that a post-capitalist society cannot portend merely austere asceticism but must instead offer at least some potential to both stimulate and satiate desire to generate any significant widespread will to subordinate individual interests to its collective pursuit. In short, Bastani (2019: 56) insists, "Communism is luxurious—or it isn't communism."

AN AFFIRMATIVE BIOPOLITICS?

A key remaining question is whether biopower can be mobilized in support of positive transformation or whether it is merely an obstacle in the face of such transformation that must be transcended entirely. Foucault, after all, understood biopower as an inherently destructive force intimately bound up with violent racism in pitting populations against one another in competitive struggle, a perspective reinforced by both Mbembe (2003) and Dean (2010).

Yet others assert the potential to mobilize biopower differently as a positive, "affirmative" force, one "no longer over life but of life" (Esposito 2008: 157). As Lin and coauthors explain, "Affirmative biopolitics is broadly understood in this context as a way to theorize how new/different ways of living and forms of life have the potential to transform or resist modes of dominance over, or negation of, life. Thinking in terms of affirmative biopolitics means considering the generative 'force' in the so-called 'politics of life,' whereby the power of life may be reclaimed from governmental apparatuses" (2018: 886–887).

Ojakangas, for instance, insists that "violence is not hidden in the foundation of biopolitics; the 'hidden' foundation of biopolitics is love (agape) and care (cura), 'care for individual life'" (2005a:5). Hannah thus contends that "an affirmative biopower has at its core a *biophilia*, a love for living beings, that can be mobilized as a form of solidarity to help combat injustice and inequality, and to make the world a better place" (2011: 1050, emphasis in original). Echoing my argument in chapter 8, Hannah asserts that this necessitates "a *massive redistribution of the political, economic and environmental means for the self-determined fulfilment of life sideways across the globe*" (2011: 1050, emphasis in original),[8] which in turn requires "enabling new spaces of the common" (Esposito 2013: 88). Transcending the national populations central to Foucault's analyses, such an affirmative biopolitics would need to "be global and universalist, extending in principle at least to all of living humanity, and perhaps to other living beings as well" (Hannah 2011: 1050), in order to avoid a competitive struggle for *Lebensraum* precipitating racism and violence (Foucault 2007).

TOWARD A LIBERATION ENVIRONMENTALITY

An affirmative biopolitics, finally, would also need to be accompanied by cultivation of an alternative governmentality contrasting with the set of governmentalities currently dominating global politics, outlined in chapter 1. After introducing these various governmentalities in his *Biopolitics* lectures, Foucault pointed toward the possibility of an additional, alternative form, which he called a "a strictly, intrinsically, and autonomously socialist governmentality" (2008: 94) and Ferguson (2011) a "left art of government." Such a governmentality, Foucault explained, does not yet exist in widespread form and "is not hidden within socialism and its texts. It cannot be deduced from them. It must be invented' (2008: 94). Others, however, have begun to explore what this type of alternative, more "bottom-up" or "liberatory" form of governmentality—or "environmentality" when applied to the realm of environmental politics—emphasizing democratic self-governance and egalitarian distribution of resources might look like (see especially Fletcher 2010a; Singh 2013; Haller et al. 2016).[9]

An important aspect of such a liberation environmentality would be an explicit call for greater democracy and participatory decision-making in resource governance, for "forms of communication, information, and trust that are broad and deep beyond precedent, but not beyond possibility," as Ostrom and colleagues advocate in their celebration of common property regimes (CPRs) (1999: 282). And central to this would be an explicit focus on transforming our own subjectivities to bring them into alignment with the overarching philosophy we promote, in accordance with Foucault's understanding of critique as a very personal process comprising "work carried out by ourselves upon ourselves as free beings" (1984a: 47). The goal of this work, he asserted, is "not to recover our 'lost' identity, to free our imprisoned nature, our deepest truth; but instead the problem is to move towards something radically Other. . . . We must produce something that doesn't yet exist and about which we cannot know how and what it will be" (Foucault 1991b: 121).

After all, central to Hardin's (1968) Tragedy of the Commons thesis, as to neoliberal governance generally, is the assumption that humans function as rational actors concerned first and foremost with pursuing their own self-interest relative to (and at the expense of) others. It is on this basis that neoliberals assume that subjects must be compelled by external agents to act in accordance with the common good. The essential neoliberal governance strategy—to create incentive structures that encourage people to exercise their rational choice in socially desirable ways—follows fundamentally from this view (Fletcher 2010). Yet this understanding of human nature has long been contested by anthropologists, among others, who contend that actual human behavior deviates quite substantially from this caricature (see Büscher et al. 2012 for an overview of this critique). Graeber (2011), indeed, contends that only through centuries of concerted violence, both physical and conceptual, has this peculiar self-understanding become so widely accepted.

Foundational to the promotion of the commons, by contrast, is the contention that the widespread success of such regimes demonstrates that humans are in fact capable (again under certain conditions) of self-organizing to achieve (relatively) harmonious cooperation in the absence of external authority. As Ostrom and colleagues explain,

> The prediction that resource users are led inevitably to destroy CPRs is based on a model that assumes all individuals are selfish, norm-free, and maximizers of short-run results. . . . However, predictions based on this model are not supported in field research or in laboratory experiments in which individuals face a public good or CPR problem and are able to communicate, sanction one another, or make new rules. . . . Reciprocal cooperation can be established, sustain itself, and even grow. (1999: 281)

A liberation environmentality must nurture such optimistic assessments of human potential and the forms of horizontal, deeply democratic resource governance that follow from them, in this way promoting "different possibilities for relationships with each other and the non-human world" (Sullivan 2006: 128).

Singh (2013; 2015) has perhaps gone furthest thus far toward conceptualizing this type of liberation environmentality. In critiquing Agrawal's (2005a, 2005b) previous formulation of the environmentality concept, Singh asserts that it overemphasizes "political-economic rationalities," neglecting the crucial roles "of affect and everyday human practices in the environment to understand how human subjectivities and ways of relating to the biophysical environment emerge in affective relations" (2013: 196–197). Her analysis of community forestry practices in India, Singh contends, demonstrates how conservation practice "can be seen as affective labor in which mind and body, reason and passion, intellect and feeling are employed together. Through the environmental care practices entailed in 'growing forests,' villagers not only transform natural landscapes they also transform their individual and collective subjectivities" (2013: 190). This, Singh asserts, amounts to a governmentality "from below that enables transformations of life and of our humanity, and which offers challenges to neoliberal interventions that apply the logic of the market to human-nature relations. This biopower of human (and human and more-than-human) collaboration and communication opens up possibilities for a new radical politics" (2013: 197).

It is just this sort of bottom-up environmentality, guided "by the logic of gift, reciprocity, and affect" and emphasizing "the joyful and life-affirming aspects of conservation care labor" (Singh 2015: 59, 53), that a truly transformative environmental politics must cultivate. It further signals potential for this environmentality to pursue an affirmative biopolitics within which "affect plays a crucial role . . . intended as the force and collective capacity to live and (re)produce differently from the subsumption of biopower 'from above'" (Lin et al. 2018: 887).

CONCLUSION: STEPPING OUT OF THE LIGHT

A familiar parable tells of a police officer walking through an unnamed city at night when he happens upon a man intensely scrutinizing the sidewalk within the circle of light created by a nearby streetlamp (Figure 11).

"What are you doing?" inquires the police officer.

"I'm looking for my car keys," the man replies.

"Oh, did you lose them here?" the police officer asks.

"No," responds the man, "I lost them over there." He points toward a wooden bench shrouded in darkness several meters distant.

"I'm searching for my keys."

FIGURE 11. The streetlight effect. SOURCE: Peter Morville and Jeffery Callender.

"Then why are you looking for them here?" asks the police officer, perplexed.

"Because here the light is better."

The analysis developed in this book suggests that neoliberal conservation functions in just this manner: by pursuing environmental protection within the circle of light created by neoliberal capitalism.[10] Meanwhile, concealed in the shadows beyond is the object that the neoliberal conservation project studiously strives to avoid confronting directly, namely the central role of the capitalist system itself in driving the environmental degradation the project aims to redress.

Transcending capitalism will certainly not solve all of the many daunting problems confronting us.[11] But it is a good place to begin.

NOTES

INTRODUCTION: CAPITALISM ON TRIAL

1. Huwyler later moved on to help found his own "green finance boutique" Posaidon Capital.

2. Within conservation, however, this approach hardly constituted a "golden age"; on the contrary, it was highly problematic in terms of its frequent marginalization and displacement of local people, as a copious body of research has documented (see Adams and Hutton 2007). This was indeed one of the main reasons that the fortress approach has been so widely challenged and in many cases superseded by neoliberal strategies. For useful overviews of this history see Vaccaro et al. 2013 and Büscher and Fletcher 2015.

3. While this term has been employed in diverse ways by different commentators (see Flew 2011), most precisely defined it refers to the economic philosophy promoting interrelated principles of decentralization, deregulation (or more commonly reregulation from states to nonstate actors), marketization, privatization, and commodification throughout the global economy (see Harvey 2005; Castree 2008). This philosophy, advanced in the postwar period in direct challenge to the rise of the welfare state, gained prominence in the 1980s with its adoption as the basis of the Reagan and Thatcher administrations in the United States and United Kingdom, respectively, and subsequent promotion throughout the world by international financial institutions including the World Bank and International Monetary Fund (IMF) as a component of so-called "structural adjustment" programs (see especially Harvey 2005; Peck 2010a).

4. The relevant literature is by now quite extensive; for useful recent overviews see Holmes and Cavanagh 2016, Fletcher 2020a, and Apostolopoulou et al. 2021. Researchers have also described this trend using a variety of other labels including "for-profit" conservation (Dempsey 2016; Dempsey and Suarez 2016) and "Nature™ Inc" (Büscher et al. 2014). Research concerning neoliberalization within natural resource management more broadly is referred to by an even wider array of terms including *market environmentalism, green capitalism, green neoliberalism, neoliberal*

environmentalism and the *neoliberalization of nature* (see especially Heynen et al. 2007; Castree 2008, 2010; Bakker 2010).

5. Like my previous book, therefore, this one can be considered largely an exercise in studying both "up" (Nader 1969) and "across" (Fletcher 2014a), in that my research was conducted primarily with other (mostly white, male) middle-class professionals in positions of privilege either similar to or exceeding my own. For reflections on the particular positionality informing these research strategies please see the aforementioned texts.

6. This is not, consequently, a classical anthropological work of ethnographic thick description focused on the micropolitics of everyday interactions within local communities. Rather, it is primarily concerned with the overarching vision underlying formation of neoliberal conservation initiatives that are then promoted for implementation in similar ways in diverse local conditions. Attempting to trace these processes around the world and across the different scales through which they travel will inevitably entail some loss of detail and specificity concerning the local contexts in which they manifest. Particular actors (either human or nonhuman) will thus play little role in this analysis, and usually only to the extent to which they exemplify more general views. (When these are public figures, I have identified them by name; otherwise, I use pseudonyms throughout.) My hope is that this "myopia" (Laidlaw 2016) is balanced by the bird's-eye view I am thereby able to assume, allowing me to distil common patterns from disparate contexts in a way that a ground-level focus on site-specific dynamics cannot.

7. An ambitious project, it cannot help but entail significant limitations too. While I have conducted in-depth study in certain areas I have obviously not done this everywhere that neoliberal conservation operates. Hence I have relied on the published results of research conducted by colleagues in other areas to corroborate or contrast with my own findings. My analysis has thus undoubtedly overlooked the concrete nuances of policy and programming in a great many places. As a form of inevitably "partial" knowledge (Clifford 1986), moreover, my study has emphasized certain dynamics far more than others. Most centrally, important issues of race, gender, and coloniality in environmental governance, while placed at center stage by a rich body of literature in political ecology and related fields (see especially Martinez-Alier 2003; Agarwal 2010; Harcourt 2012; Harcourt and Nelson 2015; Liboiron 2021; Sultana 2021), receive little direct attention here. Fortunately, a burgeoning strand of complementary research has already begun to address these issues in the neoliberal conservation project far more effectively than I could anyway (see inter alia Loperena 2016; Collins 2019; Collins et al. 2021; Apostolopoulou et al. 2021; Gutiérrez-Zamora 2021; Thakholi 2021; Pandya 2022; and Isla 2015 for treatment in Costa Rica specifically). Similarly, while the impact of neoliberal conservation on nonhumans is of course a central preoccupation of the analysis, the active role of these nonhumans in the processes that target them—a growing focus of research elsewhere (e.g., Collard and Dempsey 2013; Barua 2016)—is not foregrounded in my discussion either.

8. Harvey (2005:19) points to "a creative tension between the power of neo-liberal ideas and the actual practices of neoliberalization that have transformed how global capitalism has been working over the last three decades." Peck (2010a: xiii) describes the history of neoliberalization as "one of repeated, prosaic, and often botched efforts to *fix* markets, to build quasi-markets, and to repair market failure" (emphasis in original). Steger and Roy (2010) document a long series of failed efforts of neoliberal policies to achieve intended results in diverse contexts, from Chile's dramatic 1982 recession following nearly a decade of aggressive liberalization through US president George W. Bush's plunging of the global economy into the 2008 crisis. Yet similar patterns have been documented even more widely. Büscher and Dressler (2007) highlight a pervasive (and increasing) gap between "rhetoric" and reality" within neoliberal conservation interventions. Carrier and West (2009) describe a similar discrepancy between "vision" and "execution" within environmental governance more generally. Of his research concerning international development projects in Lesotho, Ferguson observes that "again and again development projects . . . are launched, and again and again they fail" (1994: 8). Such failure is so pervasive, Ferguson concludes, that "for the 'development' industry in Lesotho, 'failure' appears to be the norm" (1994: 8). He adds, "There is reason to believe that this situation may not be unique to Lesotho." And indeed, similar patterns in international development have been highlighted by numerous others. Scott observes that "the history of Third World development is littered with the debris of huge agricultural schemes and new cities (think of Brasilia or Chandigarh) that have failed their residents" (1998: 3). Mascarenhas relates, "The history of trying to help those in desperate circumstances is saturated with failure" (2017: 128). Li highlights an "inevitable gap between what is attempted and what is accomplished" within international development producing a litany of "shortcomings and failures" (2007: 1). Escobar pronounces development "the last and failed attempt to complete the Enlightenment in Asia, Africa, and Latin America" (1995: 221). More extensively still, Rondinelli (1993: 1–2) explains, "If the success of development assistance from rich to poor countries is measured by the ability of bilateral and multilateral aid organizations to implement programs and projects with sustainable benefits or by their progress in strengthening the institutional capacity for developing countries to undertake their own development activities, the results have been disappointing. . . . Foreign assistance has had a lackluster record in promoting sustainable economic and social progress in developing countries over the past 40 years."

9. Similarly, Hickel (2018: 13, 23) explains of international development "failure" that "the global economic system [is] organised in such a way as to make meaningful development nearly impossible. . . . The problem is not that poor countries are having difficulty hoisting themselves up the development ladder; the problem is that they are being actively prevented from doing so."

10. Thus Li (2014: 230) relates, "Development agencies are accustomed to the criticism that their interventions only pretend to do good, but are really a cover for exploitation and domination. I do not make this assumption. I take the will to

improve seriously: I believe that many development programmers really do want to improve the world." As Li points out in her analysis of development interventions in Indonesia, "The profits to be gleaned from such schemes, if any, are modest and indirect. Indeed, many improvement schemes have no foreseeable prospect of yielding profits for anyone. If profit were the issue, no international donor or agriculture department would have invested in the rugged hills of Central Sulawesi" (2007: 9). Thus she asserts of her development "trustees": "Their intentions are benevolent, even utopian. They desire to make the world better than it is" (2007: 5).

11. Scott (1998: 6) is paradigmatic of this perspective in asserting, "Designed or planned social order is necessarily schematic; it always ignores essential features of any real, functioning social order." Consequently, "the simplified rules animating plans for, say, a city, a village, or a collective farm were inadequate as a set of instructions for creating a functioning social order." From a very different political standpoint, Rondinelli (1993: 3) largely agrees, highlighting "a major dilemma of development administration: planners and managers, working in bureaucracies that seek to control rather than to facilitate development, must cope with increasing uncertainty and complexity; but their methods and procedures inhibit the kinds of analysis and planning that are most appropriate for dealing with development problems effectively."

12. Scott (1998: 6) explains that "any production process depends on a host of informal practices and improvisations that could never be codified.... To the degree that the formal scheme made no allowance for these processes or actually suppressed them, it failed both its intended beneficiaries and ultimately its designers as well." Appreciation of this "local vernacular" confounding planners' preconceived designs is central to Escobar's (1995) analysis too. Easterly (2006) argues something quite similar (again from a very different political position) in his spirited defense of development "searchers" over "planners."

13. Thus Mosse (2004) argues that development policy is in fact never directly "implementable" because such policy is shaped more by the needs of development institutions than those of project recipients. As Mosse explains, *"Development interventions are driven not by policy but by the exigencies of organizations and the need to maintain relationships"* (2004: 651, emphasis in original). From this perspective, policy *"primarily functions to mobilize and maintain political support, that is to legitimize rather than to orientate practice"* (2004: 648, emphasis in original). Consequently, Mosse concludes, development *"projects do not fail; they are failed by wider networks of support and validation"* that shape and constrain project function (2004: 658, emphasis in original). Mascarenhas (2017) offers a similar explanation of the widespread failure of international humanitarian interventions. Likewise, in her discussion of neoliberal conservation, Dempsey concludes that the project "is still in many ways too radical and too challenging to the status quo to become mainstream" and hence is "in part foiled by economic self-interest and by contemporary concentrations of wealth and political power" (2016: 236).

14. Similarly, Asiyanbi and Lund (2020: 4) identify a dynamic of "policy persistence" within the quintessentially neoliberal REDD+ mechanism (see chapter 3),

which they define as giving "continued economic and political support to a policy in the face of overwhelming evidence that it is failing to achieve its stated objectives." Of "failed" development interventions more broadly, Ferguson (1994: 8) observes that "no matter how many times this happens there always seems to be someone ready to try again with yet another project." Despite persistent shortcomings in development projects, Li adds, "There is no sign that schemes for improvement are about to be abandoned. There are always experts ready to propose a better plan" (2007: 2). De Vries, likewise, highlights an "unfailing belief in development, given the notorious inability of governmental and non-governmental institutions to keep their promises" (2007: 26). Yet de Vries, building on Ferguson (1994), goes further to point out a particular dimension of how "failure" functions in this dynamic: "Rather than deterring the expansion of the apparatus," he asserts, "failure operates as the motor for its reproduction" (2007: 34). Similarly, Li relates, "Failures invite new interventions to correct newly identified—or newly created—deficiencies. The limits of each governmental intervention shape its successor" (2007: 19)

15. In his analysis of neoliberal "failure," for instance, Harvey asserts that neoliberal ideas have "primarily worked as a system of justification and legitimation for whatever needed to be done to achieve this goal" (2005, 19). As support for this contention, he observes that "when neoliberal principles clash with the need to restore or sustain elite power, then the principles are either abandoned or become so twisted as to be unrecognizable" (2005:19). Hickel (2018: 29–30) offers a similar analysis in arguing of international development that "the discourse of aid distracts us from seeing the broader picture. It hides the patterns of extraction that are actively causing the impoverishment of the global South today and actively impeding meaningful development. . . . Aid serves as a kind of propaganda that makes the takers seem like givers, and conceals how the global economy actually works."

16. Thus, Rondinelli (1993: iii) relates that development "administrators [are] discouraged from detecting and correcting errors."

17. See Mosse 2004; Igoe et al. 2010; Büscher 2014; Baptista 2017; Lund et al. 2017; Mascarenhas 2017; Svarstad and Benjaminsen 2017.

18. Rather than asking only whether projects succeed or fail, in other words, Li (2005: 391) advocates also investigating, "What do schemes do? What are their contradictory, messy, and refractory effects?" She cites Ferguson as productively training attention to these important issues. In his analysis of development interventions, Ferguson (1994: 20) famously asserted that "the most important political effects of a planned intervention may occur unconsciously, behind the backs or against the wills of the 'planners' who may seem to be running the show." In this way, "the outcomes of planned social interventions can end up coming together into powerful constellations of control that were never intended and in some cases never recognized" (1994: 19). The most important of these Ferguson identifies as development's tendency to extend state territorialization under the pretext of offering mere technical interventions. This stimulation of politics under the auspices of apolitical intervention, he concludes, coheres in an "unauthored resultant constellation that I call 'the anti-politics machine'" (1994: 21).

19. As defined by Foucault (1977) and adopted by Ferguson (1994), instrument-effects are consequences that are unintentional yet follow logically from a given intervention.

20. Thus, Brenner and Theodore (2002: 352) related that "while neoliberalism aspires to create a 'utopia' of free markets . . . it has in practice entailed a dramatic intensification of coercive, disciplinary forms of state intervention in order to impose market rule." Graeber (2015: 9) goes so far as to pronounces this the "iron law of liberalism" (by which he means *neo*liberalism), in terms of which "government policies intending to reduce government interference in the economy actually end up producing more regulations, more bureaucrats, and more police."

21. In Marx's classic formulation, M-C-M' represents the investment of money (M) to produce a commodity (C) that is sold for more money (M'), while M-M' (or M-M'-M" . . .) is investment of money for direct financial return (e.g., in stock and derivative markets).

22. While psychoanalysis originates from a particular (Western) context and has been critiqued for claiming a false universalism that fails to do justice to gender and geographical difference, in its Lacanian form, at least, it has also been effectively employed and adapted by feminists, queer theorists, and others to provide valuable support for projects grounded in these same dimensions of difference. See Kapoor 2020 for a useful overview of both critiques and productive application of a Lacanian approach. Thus, while psychoanalysis can never be a truly *decolonial* approach, given its grounding in the Western philosophical tradition, it does have potential (when employed conscientiously) to contribute to *anticolonial* work in terms of the distinction made by Liboiron (2021), wherein decolonization refers to Indigenous self-mobilization aiming to liberate lifeworlds from external imposition (both epistemological and material; see also Tuck and Yang 2012), while anticolonial efforts pursue the more limited aim to "not reproduce settler and colonial entitlement to Land and Indigenous cultures, concepts, knowledges (including Traditional Knowledge), and lifeworlds" in supporting decolonial work (Liboiron 2021: 27). In this sense, psychoanalysis can be part of the effort to create space for a more properly decolonial politics to develop.

23. See, e.g., Mishan 1996; Stavrakakis 1997a, 1997b; Swyngedouw 2010, 2011; Davidson 2012; Robbins and Moore 2013; Weintrobe 2013a.

24. See e.g., Kapoor 2005, 2014, 2017, 2020; De Vries 2007; Sato 2006; Sioh 2014; Wilson 2014a, 2014b.

25. Dean 2008; Layton 2009; Wilson 2014a, 2016.

26. Fletcher 2013a, 2013b, 2014c, 2015, 2018a.

27. This is certainly not to suggest that this synthesis encompasses the full range of conceptual lenses through which the neoliberal conservation project might be productively analyzed: it is merely the constellation of perspectives that I have found most useful for the particular analysis undertaken in this book. For complementary analyses conducted via critical race, decolonial, and feminist perspectives see inter alia Isla 2015; Loperena 2016; Collins 2019; Collins et al. 2021; Gutiérrez-Zamora 2021; Thakholi 2021; Pandya 2022.

28. While neither neglects either dimension entirely, of course, the two theorists' treatment of discursive and material processes, respectively, remains far less systematic than their analysis of the other.

29. Again, these are only some of the important dynamics the project can be seen to embody in its imbrication within what hooks (1994) among others calls the "white supremacist capitalist patriarchy" more broadly. For examples of other ways to approach the same phenomenon from angles that target other of its important dimensions please see the various references cited in note 27 above.

CHAPTER 1. CONCEPTUALIZING NEOLIBERAL BIOPOWER

1. As Foucault famously described this configuration, "Perhaps, too, we should abandon the whole tradition that allows us to imagine that knowledge can exist only where power relations are suspended. . . . We should admit rather that . . . there is no power relation without the correlative constitution of knowledge, nor any knowledge that does not presuppose and constitute at the same time power relations" (1977: 27).

2. See also Ahlborg and Nightingale 2018; Cavanagh 2018; Zhang 2018.

3. See, e.g., Abu-Lughod 1990; Mitchell 1990; Moore 1998.

4. Foucault actually once pointed to this dynamic himself in observing that "there is always within each of us something that fights something else" and hence suggesting the potential to analyze this competition among "sub-individuals" as well (1980: 208). Yet he never followed up on this line of inquiry.

5. Others have advanced quite similar concepts under different labels. Ponse (1976), for instance, identifies what she calls "counterfeit secrecy" in her discussion of tactics employed by lesbians to remain "in the closet," wherein both lesbians and their family/friends may participate in a "tacit negotiation of mutual pretense," a "state of silent 'collusion' between actor and audience . . . wherein both parties to an interaction know a secret but maintain the fiction that they do not know it." Similarly, Bourdieu (1997) describes an "open secret" in the practice of gift giving, which he describes as "an individual and collective self-deception," the "coexistence of recognition and misrecognition," and a "lie told to oneself."

6. In his work, Taussig identifies public secrecy in domains as diverse as the modern state (1992), shamanism (1998a), flag burning, and Zapatismo (1998b, 1999). Subsequent work has described public secrecy in Nigerian nationalism (Watts 2001), post-911 politics (Bratich 2006), radical activism (Bratich 2007), discourse concerning sexual violence during the 1971 Bangladesh war (Mookherjee 2006), and commercial adventure tourism (Fletcher 2010b).

7. For notable exceptions, see Swyngedouw 2011; Fletcher 2013a, 2013b, 2014b, 2015, 2018a.

8. As Han (2018: 66) further explains this distinction, "Violence robs its victim of any possibility of action. There is no room to maneuver. Violence annihilates space. In this sense it also differs from power, which leaves room for action. Power

does not categorically preclude action and freedom. It uses the freedom of others, whereas violence crushes it."

9. Graeber elaborates. "Most human relations—particularly ongoing ones, whether between longstanding friends or longstanding enemies—are extremely complicated, dense with history and meaning. Maintaining them requires a constant and often subtle work of imagination, of endlessly trying to see the world from others' points of view. . . . Threatening others with physical harm allows the possibility of cutting through all this. It makes possible relations of a far more simple and schematic kind ("cross this line and I will shoot you," "one more word out of any of you and you're going to jail"). This is of course why violence is so often the preferred weapon of the stupid. One might even call it the trump card of the stupid, since (and this is surely one of the tragedies of human existence) it is the one form of stupidity to which it is most difficult to come up with an intelligent response" (2015: 68).

10. Han (2018: 69) thus argues, "Violence is implemented because of lack of power. Exercising violence is the desperate attempt to convert powerlessness into power. A truly powerful ruler is not powerful through the incessant threat of violence"—indeed, it is precisely the skillful exercise of power that "ensures that rule can be exercised without violence."

11. This distinguishes Graeber's use of the term from Galtung's (1990), who does include direct violence as a foundation for structural violence.

12. While Foucault used these terms interchangeably, others have subsequently employed them in different ways, including as distinct and separate phenomena (see Cavanagh 2018). I follow Foucault's original, interchangeable usage herein.

13. Reinforcing this equivalence in subsequent work, Foucault explains that "the transition in the eighteenth century from a regime dominated by structures of sovereignty to a regime dominated by techniques of government revolves around population, and consequently around the birth of political economy" (2007: 106)

14. As an exercise of psychopower, "Neoliberalism represents a highly efficient, indeed an intelligent, system for exploiting freedom. Everything that belongs to practices and expressive forms of liberty—emotion, play and communication—comes to be exploited. It is inefficient to exploit people against their will. Allo-exploitation yields scant returns. Only when freedom is exploited are returns maximized" (Han 2015: 3). Consequently, Han, concludes, "Under neoliberalism, the technology of power takes on a subtle form. It does not lay hold of individuals directly. Instead, it ensures that individuals act on themselves so that power relations are interiorized—and then interpreted as freedom" (28).

15. Far from genuine freedom, however, this injunction to enjoy "entails a new form of subjectivation. Endlessly working at self-improvement resembles the self-examination and self-monitoring of Protestantism, which represents a technology of subjectivation and domination in its own right" (Han 2017: 30). Indeed, Han suggests, "The freedom of Can generates even more coercion than the disciplinarian Should, which issues commandments and prohibitions. Should has a limit. In contrast, Can has none" (1–2). Hence, "Although the achievement-subject deems itself

free, in reality it is a slave. In so far as it willingly exploits itself without a master, it is an absolute slave" (2).

16. According to Han, this particular relationship between neoliberalism and desire "also connects with the mode of operation of contemporary capitalism" (2017: 25). In this new era, "productivity is not to be enhanced by overcoming physical resistance so much as by optimizing psychic or mental processes. Physical discipline has given way to mental optimization" (Han 2015: 25). And this, in turn, produces a new frontier for accumulation, given that within an "immaterial" regime of production "we do not consume things so much as emotions. The former cannot be consumed without end—but the latter can. Emotions assume dimensions beyond the scope of use value. In so doing, they open up a field of consumption that is new and knows no limit" (Han 2017: 46).

17. Following Stiegler (2010), Han explains, "Biopolitics is the governmental technology of disciplinary power. However, this approach proves altogether unsuited to the neoliberal regime, which exploits the psyche above all. Biopolitics, which makes use of population statistics, has no access to the psychic realm. It can deliver no material for drawing up a psychogram of the population" (2017: 22).

18. Foucault, as previously noted, was "notoriously taciturn on the topic of the psyche" (Butler 1997: 18) due largely to his explicit opposition to Freud's positing of innate psychic drives and their ostensive repression as the basis of much human behavior (see especially Foucault 1991b), while Marx, writing in the mid-nineteenth century, lacked a sound basis for theorizing subjects' interiority in any respect.

CHAPTER 2. CONJURING NATURAL CAPITAL

1. In subsequent years, "net zero" pledges of this sort have multiplied prolifically among private-sector firms and state governments alike to become, indeed, one of the central pillars of contemporary climate politics more generally. See, for example, British Broadcasting Company [BBC] 2021.

2. As one critic complained, "Saying that they will invest more in low-carbon tech and less in oil and gas 'over time' is not a credible plan for reaching net zero." (Ambrose 2020).

3. Foucault defined conditions of possibility as "the conditions necessary for the appearance of an object of discourse, the historical conditions required if one is to 'say anything' about it" (1970: 49).

4. As Hajer (1993: 47) explains, "A discourse coalition is the ensemble of a set of story lines, the actors that utter these story lines, and the practices that conform to these story lines, all organized around a discourse."

5. In order to emphasize this commonality, I present these patterns in quite general terms, introducing specific quotations when appropriate as exemplars of a broader point of view replicated across the corpus of texts. This approach thus minimizes attention to elements of contestation, disagreement, and dissent, which are of course also omnipresent, in favor of outlining positions that most actors involved

agree upon and hold in common. Yet core elements that remain fundamentally contested or ambivalent are also highlighted.

6. The full quotation is: "Only a crisis—actual or perceived—produces real change. When that crisis occurs, the actions that are taken depend on the ideas that are lying around. That, I believe, is our basic function: to develop alternatives to existing policies, to keep them alive and available until the politically impossible becomes the politically inevitable" (Friedman 2002: xiv).

7. The concept is still in use in certain places and programs, however, and has been subject to analysis as such by a small body of research (see, e.g., Anderson et al. 2016; Wilshusen and MacDonald 2017; Cavanagh and Benjaminsen 2017).

8. See especially Holmes 2010, 2012.

9. Most neoliberals argue that regulatory actions should be restricted to interventions such as manipulating the discount rate to stabilize prices and control inflation.

10. See especially Farber et al. 2002; TEEB 2010; Goulder and Kennedy 2011 for more detailed discussion of these different methods.

11. Helm (2015) distinguishes "weak" and "strong" versions of his rule to represent these different aims.

12. This is a prime example of Scott's (1998) assertion of the need to simplify in order to render different entities equally "legible" within a centralized accounting framework.

CHAPTER 3. IMAGINING THE MARKET

1. Bioprospecting, a foundational conservation MBI listed here, seeks to develop certain NTFPs for commercial sale on medicinal or cosmetics markets in order to finance conservation of the surrounding ecosystem (see McAfee 1999; Hayden 2003; Neimark 2012). Hayden describes this as a "quintessential neoliberal strategy" in its framing of biodiversity "as a storehouse of valuable genetic resources and as a resource to be managed as an explicitly economic enterprise" (2003: 49). Yet while bioprospecting was quite popular in the 1980s and 1990s it has since largely faded from the scene. More on this in chapters 4 and 5.

2. Then UNEP Executive Director Erik Solheim, for instance, stated in the 2016 WCC's Opening Ceremony that creating a global PES program was one of his principal policy priorities.

3. In the lead-up to finalizing the SDGs, for instance, then UN Secretary General Ban Ki-Moon emphasized the need to "decouple economic growth from environmental degradation" (2014: 23) as a key ingredient of the agenda, while Sachs, a key advisor to Ban in SDG formulation, subsequently released a book endorsed by the UN SG in which he wrote regarding what he termed the new *Age of Sustainable Development*, "The end result, if successful, would be to 'decouple' growth and dangerous overuse of primary resources and ecosystems" (Sachs 2015: 218). The Sustainable Development Solutions Network led by Sachs to oversee SDG implementation

has further emphasized that "the key is for all countries, rich and poor, to adopt sustainable technologies and behaviors that decouple economic growth from unsustainable patterns of production and consumption" (in Fletcher and Rammelt 2017: 452). Decoupling has been championed by other prominent actors too. The Organisation for Economic Cooperation and Development (OECD 2014) has reiterated the importance of the concept, as has the EU in its seventh Environmental Action Program (EEA 2013). The concept has also been promoted by influential civil society organizations (CSOs), including the Breakthrough Institute (2014, 2015) and New Climate Economy (2014, 2015). All signs, in short, point to decoupling standing as a central component of the future global sustainable development agenda.

4. Named for influential economist Simon Kuznets, the Environmental Kuznets Curve predicts, controversially, that as per capita income rises within a given society, environmental impact will first increase then decrease in bell-like fashion as technology becomes progressively more efficient in converting natural resources into economic throughput (see Stern 2004).

CHAPTER 4. THE NEOLIBERAL ECOLABORATORY

1. A Google search for the phrase "Costa Rica paradise" delivered over forty million hits in March 2013.

2. This omission has been rectified to some degree by the newer water tariff (see Matulis 2013), and FONAFIFO has also recently sought to address scenic beauty services by signing an agreement with Costa Rica's Ecotourism Chamber of Commerce to promote "Climate Conscious Travel" whereby domestic tourism operators will pay to offset their clients' emissions (see Fletcher 2013c).

3. See Daniels et al. 2010 for a useful table outlining these various funding sources.

4. Program officials claim that the majority of REDD+ funds will be directed toward Indigenous communities, however, which are able to register much larger parcels than individual landowners and which were largely excluded from the benefits of many development initiatives in the past. Costa Rica's REDD Readiness Plan, consonant with World Bank requirements, was in fact drafted with Indigenous consultation and calls for creation of a REDD+ Board of Directors comprising FONAFIFO's current Board and two additional members, one drawn from "civil society" and the other representing the Association of Comprehensive Indigenous Development (ADII). Hence, Indigenous peoples, long marginalized within national politics (see Evans 1999), may be able to harness REDD+ to gain a more central position within environmental governance discussions. On the other hand, significant concerns have been raised internationally concerning the potentially negative impacts of REDD+ development on Indigenous communities generally (e.g., Sarmiento Barletti and Larson 2017).

5. Initial participants were Botswana, Colombia, Costa Rica, Madagascar, and the Philippines, subsequently joined by Guatemala, Indonesia, and Rwanda.

6. This was corrected to a degree by a 2009 law offering new tax breaks and other incentives for formally registered community-based tourism groups.

CHAPTER 5. THE ANTI-REGULATION MACHINE

1. CAT subsidies (Certificados de Abono Tributario) are tax-credit certificates given to producers of nontraditional exports. "Established in 1972 during the heyday of the social democratic model," Edelman (1999: 82) observes that "ironically, this state subsidy has been crucial to the 'success' of the new, supposedly free-market, strategy."

2. Sierra and Russman's (2006) analysis suggests, however, that while PSA had little influence on forest cover, it did facilitate the transition away from agriculture already underway in the region by helping to finance the transition for program participants, who did in fact register less land in agricultural production than nonparticipants.

3. See McAfee and Shapiro 2010; Milder et al. 2010; Vatn 2010; McElwee 2012; Milne and Adams 2012; Muradian and Gómez-Baggethun 2013; Muradian et al. 2013; Shapiro-Garza 2013; McElwee et al. 2014; Pirard and Lapeyre 2014; Gómez-Baggethun and Muradian 2015; Van Hecken et al. 2015a, 2015b; Wunder 2015; Vatn 2015.

4. See also McAfee and Shapiro 2010; McElwee 2012; Shapiro-Garza 2013; McElwee et al. 2014; Van Hecken et al. 2015b.

5. See Milder et al. 2010; Vatn 2010, 2015; Gómez-Baggethun and Muradian 2015; Wunder 2015.

6. This equation is altered in cases wherein costs in the site of conservation are less than in the site where extraction is to be mitigated, leading to neoliberal conservation's common aim to locate interventions where they can be undertaken most cheaply. This reinforces McAfee's (2012b) assertion of neoliberal conservation's fundamental reliance on and exploitation of global inequality as the basis of its function.

7. For instance, by not accounting for the emissions caused by program agents driving to PES field sites or not paying these agents enough to support their own sustainable livelihoods.

8. See, e.g., West 2006; Brockington et al. 2008; Bond 2011; Lohmann 2011; McAfee 2012a, 2012b.

9. This outcome, of course, may not be entirely unintended, for, as pointed out much earlier, the core neoliberal principle called "deregulation" is more often pursued as *re*regulation. Hence, Graeber contends of deregulation, "In ordinary usage, the word seems to mean 'changing the regulatory structure in a way that I like'" (2015: 17).

10. Dempsey and Robertson state: "While ES policy is often associated with market-based instruments, many ES policy tools with no connection to markets are being enacted. . . . Clearly, to call such ES policies neoliberal in the conventional

sense, or market-based, is misleading" (2012: 770–771). Muradian and Gómez-Baggethun suggest that some analyses of PES schemes may be "shooting a strawman by missing the point that in fact most of them are very far from following market rationales, and have an hybrid nature that can hardly be labelled as 'neoliberal'" (2013: 1119–1120). Van Hecken et al. (2015b: 64) thus urge us to "be cautious not to brand all PES initiatives as deliberate neoliberal tools serving green capitalist expansion."

11. See Dempsey and Robertson 2012; Gómez-Baggethun and Muradian 2015; Hahn et al. 2015; Van Hecken et al. 2015a, 2015b. Hahn et al., for instance, contend that "both proponents and critics to neoliberalism are making mistakes when they associate economic instruments with neoliberal frameworks, rather than assessing the actual institutions and performance" (2015: 79).

12. As the owner of a prominent private nature reserve on Costa Rica's central Pacific coast declared in an interview, "Ecological tourism is the only thing I know that really works to make the rainforest profitable."

13. See, e.g., Jackson 2011; Steinberger et al. 2013; Amate 2014; Isenhour and Feng 2016; Spash 2014; Steady State Manchester 2014; Burton 2015, 2016a, 2016b; Wiedmann et al. 2015; Isenhour 2016; Wanner 2015; Ward et al. 2016; Hickel and Kallis 2020.

14. Yet even this reported drop in extreme poverty may be overestimated, as it relies on headcount ratio statistics that may not assign sufficient weight to food prices in consumption expenditures of the poor and thus may exaggerate household purchasing power (Reddy 2008).

15. Bjerg (2014: 194) thus relates, "The total notional value of outstanding derivatives contracts in 2010 was estimated at $1.2 quadrillion, which is twenty times larger than the total value of the annual productive output of the entire world economy. (The latter figure stands at a mere $60 trillion.)"

CHAPTER 6. HOW TO FAIL FORWARD

1. A classic neoliberal scapegoat; see Dean 2008; Layton 2009.

2. See also Fine 2009; Arsel and Büscher 2012; Wilson 2014a.

3. See McAfee and Shapiro 2010; Shapiro-Garza 2013; McElwee et al. 2014; Van Hecken et al. 2015a.

4. See, e.g., Chan et al. 2007; Child 2009; Ehrenfeld 2008; Peterson et al. 2009; Redford and Adams 2009; Walker et al. 2009.

5. "Non-fungible tokens" (NFTs), which allow digital representations to be uniquely owned, bought, and sold, and other applications of blockchain (also known as Web3) technologies are part of the latest set of instruments to be included within the neoliberal conservation portfolio (although efforts exist to also employ blockchain in decidedly different ways as well). At time of writing, however, most efforts to integrate blockchain into conservation initiatives specifically remain largely speculative and uncertain concerning the extent to which they will actually

materialize in the future. For useful introductions to this discussion see Howson et al. 2019 and Stuit et al. 2022.

6. Even if, as Klein (2014) points out, global elites endorsing the project are least likely to be affected by ecological decline due to the preemptive fortifications their wealth allows them to erect (i.e., by building self-sufficient compounds in relatively remote locations like New Zealand's South Island).

7. Save in 2020 when the meetings were canceled due to COVID-19.

8. Even more recently, moreover, in the midst of the COP-21 summit, when it became clear that most of the world's nations were now committed to achieving a new global agreement and ExxonMobil had come under increasing attack from climate activists, the company reiterated a long-standing though lukewarm call for a universal carbon tax to compel the global market to begin moving away from fossil fuel dependence. Yet the implications of such a tax—which if high enough to be effective would make oil so expensive that a viable capitalist market for its purchase, as well as all of the other products tied to the price of oil, would collapse entirely—for the future of a company depending on oil production itself have not been addressed. The company calculates that to keep the planet within a 1.6-degree temperature rise would eventually necessitate a price of $2,000/ton of CO_2, translating into a cost of approximately US $20 per gallon of gasoline (Eaton and Carroll 2015), which would of course be impossible for capitalist markets to accommodate and still remain profitable.

9. Perhaps in recognition of this, in a more recent paper Farley seems to have reversed his position, now arguing that we need to move away from MBIs, even poorly functioning ones, altogether and instead pursue forms of environmental management that "promote cooperation" instead (Farley et al. 2015: 244).

10. Acknowledgments to Foster (2000) for this framing and the subsection's title.

11. See Magdoff and Foster 2011 and Klein 2014 among many others.

12. For instance, by the array of more critical conservation practitioners cited previously.

13. See Fletcher 2014b for discussion of this contradictory situation at the 2012 WCC, for instance.

14. "Our population," writes celebrity biologist E. O. Wilson (2016: 1) on the first page of *Half-Earth*, "is too large for safety and comfort." Sachs (2015: 1) agrees, arguing in the opening of his own book on sustainable development that "our starting point is our crowded planet." Meanwhile, *Life on the Brink: Environmentalists Confront Overpopulation*, brings an eclectic collection of writers together to "reignite a robust discussion of population issues among environmentalists, environmental studies scholars, policymakers, and the general public" (Cafaro and Crist 2012: back cover).

15. Impact = Population × Affluence × Technology.

16. Wijkman and Rockström (2012) call it "the forgotten problem," Alcorn (2007) "the real inconvenient truth," while various others label overpopulation the proverbial "elephant in the room." Wilson (2016) asserts that it is "still wildly

unpopular" to raise the issue. Claiming that "most environmental groups now steer clear of the subject," Lochhead (2013) writes, "For various reasons, linking the world's rapid population growth to its deepening environmental crisis, including climate change, is politically taboo." The edited volume *Life on the Brink*, finally, claims to "confront hard issues regarding contraception, abortion, immigration, and limits to growth that many environmentalists have become too timid or politically correct to address in recent years" (Cafaro and Crist 2012: back cover).

17. See Fletcher et al. 2014 for an overview of this research.

18. As an example of this logic, the organization Population Matters (formerly Optimum Population Trust) launched a program called PopOffsets in 2009 that it described as "the first project in the world that, simply and transparently, enables individuals and organizations to offset their carbon footprint by reducing carbon emissions by supporting family planning." Highlighting "the intrinsic links between increasing CO_2 emissions, climate change and the world's ever-growing population," the organization explained, "Research is indicating that investing in family planning is a cost-effective and permanent way of reducing CO_2 emissions and climate change, compared with other technological fixes—and has many other environmental benefits, and no downsides." For more discussion of this initiative, now discontinued, see Vidal 2009.

CHAPTER 7. NEOLIBERAL CONSERVATION IN RUINS?

1. The label was subsequently applied to other movements challenging aspects of neoliberal globalization, such as Occupy and elements of the so-called Arab Spring, during what Žižek (2012b) calls *The Year of Dreaming Dangerously*.

2. See McAfee and Shapiro 2010; Van Noordwijk et al. 2012; Muradian et al. 2013; Shapiro-Garza 2013; McElwee 2016.

3. See Daggett (2018) for an insightful analysis of the relationship between authoritarian populism and "petro-masculinity."

4. The authors qualify that green violence also encompasses "ideas and aspirations related to nature conservation," including "non-material aspects of violence and the manner in which violence takes social and linguistic form" (Büscher and Ramutsindela 2016: 10).

5. As he explains, "Symbolically, neoliberalism is already dead, but as a global metabolic system it remains alive, enslaved directly to the death drive of the Real of Capital" (Wilson 2016: 586).

CHAPTER 8. THERE IS NO ALTERNATIVE TO DEGROWTH

1. A common misunderstanding equates degrowth with simple economic decline or recession. Yet, as Kallis and colleagues explain, "involuntary declines are not degrowth in themselves, and countries in recession or depression are not degrowth

experiments" (2018: 294). In this sense, moments and places of crisis, economic busts, burst financial bubbles, natural disasters, and similar events have nothing to do with degrowth. Rather, degrowth can be conceptualized as a "radical political and economic reorganization leading to drastically reduced resource and energy throughput" (Kallis et al. 2018: 291).

2. See esp. Kallis 2018; Kallis et al. 2010, 2012a, 2012b, 2018, 2020; Cattaneo et al. 2012; Saed 2012; Sekulova et al. 2013; D'Alisa et al. 2014; Chertkovskaya et al. 2019; Hickel 2020; Schmelzer et al. 2022.

3. As Han asserts, within such a program, "freedom could only come from a mode of living (Lebensform) that is no longer a mode of production—indeed, from something altogether unproductive. The course our future takes will depend on whether we prove able, beyond the world of production, to make use of the useless" (2017: 51–52).

4. References are legion but include Feeny et al. 1990; Ostrom 1990; Ostrom et al. 1999; Agrawal 2003; Neves 2004.

5. Relevant references are again too many to list. For useful recent overviews see Escobar 2015 and Büscher and Fletcher 2020.

6. The literature on this is also quite extensive; key sources include Escobar 1995, 2008; Rahnema and Bawtree 1997; Matthews 2004; Ziai 2007; McGregor 2009; Kothari et al. 2019.

7. See, e.g., Akbulut et al. 2019; Nirmal and Rocheleau 2019.

8. Unlike unconditional programs, conditional CTPs require recipients to perform a certain set of actions (typically school attendance and/or health care visits) to receive payments.

9. See Standing (2017) for a useful overview of this proposal and discussion surrounding it.

10. This perspective has become quite influential within human geography and related disciplines, inspiring a large body of subsequent research, much of it advanced under the rubric of the Community Economies Collective (see http://www .communityeconomies.com). Yet it has also been criticized on a vareity of grounds, particularly in terms of its potential to impart an inflated sense of potential to ostensibly post-capitalist practices, and difficulty in distinguishing progressive forms of diverse economy from oppressive ones (e.g., Castree 1999; Kelly 2005; Samers 2005; North 2008). White and Williams (2016), on the other hand, fault the framework for not presenting this potential strongly *enough*. Meanwhile, others have taken similar forms of analysis in different directions, producing more variegated diverse economies perspectives (see Gritzas and Kavoulakos 2016 for a recent review of this growing literature).

11. While this discussion emphasizes the redistribution of monetary resources within the context of the dominant global economy, an equally important focus of discussion is the potential to move beyond money entirely as the basis for a post-capitalist societal transformation (see Nelson 2022).

12. Degrowth has of course also been critiqued as an impossible pipedream (e.g., Milanovic 2017), and hence from this perspective could also potentially be viewed

as itself an unattainable fantasy. Yet what most distinguishes it from decoupling, I maintain, is the fact that such critiques focus merely on the feasibility of degrowth within current economic and political structures rather than questioning its essential possibility. In other words, critics question whether degrowth can effectively address poverty alongside sustainability or whether it could become acceptable to policy makers, not whether it would be possible in principle to found a functional economy on degrowth principles. In this way, critics take as their parameters the current political-economic system, while proponents of degrowth argue that it is precisely this system that must transform for degrowth to become possible. Consequently, while indeed "unrealistic" within the current conjuncture (more on this framing in the conclusion), degrowth need not be considered impossible in the same manner as I and others have argued that decoupling is (that is, in terms of an essential disjuncture between economic aims and biophysical realities). Indeed, one might view the two approaches as diametrically opposed in this respect: while decoupling fits seamlessly within the dominant ideology despite being impossible in practice, degrowth is entirely the reverse—technically feasible yet politically unpalatable.

13. This is certainly not the only existing proposal for reorienting conservation to address the problematic issues highlighted in this analysis, as our book itself is at pains to make clear (Büscher and Fletcher 2020). Please refer to that text (and particularly the "Intermezzo") for extensive discussion of the wide range of similar yet distinct proposals emanating from a variety of different perspectives and organizations throughout the world to which the convivial conservation proposal is indebted and upon which it builds.

CONCLUSION: TRAVERSING THE NEOLIBERAL FANTASY

1. See, e.g., Hamilton 2003; Gibson-Graham 2006; Dufour 2008; Welzer 2011; Heikkurinen 2019; Rosa 2019; Brossmann and Islar 2020.

2. And again: "I absolutely will not play the part of one who prescribes solutions. I hold that the role of the intellectual today is not that of establishing laws or proposing solutions or prophesying, since by doing that one can only contribute to the functioning of a determinate situation of power that to my mind should be criticized. . . . Rather, I concern myself with determining problems, unleashing them, revealing them within the framework of such complexity as to shut the mouths of prophets and legislators: all those who speak *for* others and *above* others" (1991b: 157, 159).

3. See, e g., Latour 2004; Gibson-Graham 2006; Singh 2013, 2015; Lansing et al. 2015.

4. While White and Williams argue that using the term alternatives to describe these dynamics "fails to capture not only the ubiquity of such practices in everyday life, but also how those engaging in them do not see them as 'alternatives' in the sense of a second choice, or less desirable option, to capitalist practices" (2016: 1),

I would contend that the term does not necessitate this connotation, but can instead simply designate difference from the dominant discourse.

5. For an overview of this research see Fletcher 2014a: ch. 3.

6. See also Soper's (2020: 1) advocacy of an "alternative hedonism" celebrating "the enjoyment that comes with having more time, doing more things for oneself, travelling more slowly and consuming less stuff," as well as Lelkes's (2021) similar proposal for "sustainable hedonism."

7. As Bastani himself explains of his proposal, "Nothing is certain about where these technologies will end, nor whose benefit they will serve. What is discernible, however, is that a disposition can be drawn from them—if only they are allied to a political project of collective solidarity and individual happiness" (2019: 12).

8. As Hannah immediately qualifies, however, "This biopolitical programme of course raises all sorts of problems: issues of boundary definition with regard to non-human life; issues of how to conceive of the role of collective planning under 'devolved futurism' (what of 'sustainability,' for example, or climate change?); and of course issues relating to authoritative or coercive resources necessary to bring about any significant change in this direction" (2011: 1050).

9. A perspective that might also include Brenner et al.'s (2010a) "deep socialization."

10. A dynamic termed by researchers the "streetlight effect" (see Freedman 2010).

11. As highlighted in earlier chapters, for instance, capitalism's intimate imbrications with racial, colonial, and gender-based oppression and violence within the overarching white supremacist capitalist patriarchy will also require confrontation and dismantling on their own terms.

BIBLIOGRAPHY

Abu-Lughod, L. (1990). "The Romance of Resistance: Tracing Transformations of Power through Bedouin Women." *American Ethnologist* 17(1): 41–55.

Achtenberg, E. (2013). "Bolivia: The Unfinished Business of Land Reform." *North American Congress on Latin America: Rebel Currents*, April 1. http://nacla.org/blog/2013/3/31/bolivia-unfinished-business-land-reform.

Adams, W.M., and J. Hutton. (2007). "People, Parks and Poverty: Political Ecology and Biodiversity Conservation. *Conservation and Society* 5(2): 147-183.

AD Insider. (2019). "Inside Antilia, Mukesh Ambani's $2 Billion Mumbai Mansion." *Architectural Digest India*, April 19. https://www.architecturaldigest.in/content/mukesh-ambani-antilia-home-mumbai/#s-custo.

Agarwal, B. (2010). *Gender and Green Governance.* Oxford: Oxford University Press.

Agrawal, A. (2003). "Sustainable Governance of Common Pool Resources: Context, Methods, and Politics." *Annual Review of Anthropology* 32(1): 243–262.

———. (2005a). *Environmentality: Technologies of Government and the Making of Subjects.* Durham, NC: Duke University Press.

———. (2005b). "Environmentality: Community, Intimate Government, and the Making of Environmental Subjects in Kumaon, India." *Current Anthropology* 46(2): 161–190.

Ahlborg, H., and A.J. Nightingale. (2018). "Theorizing Power in Political Ecology: The Where of Power in Resource Governance Projects." *Journal of Political Ecology* 25: 381–401.

Aitken, R. (2013). "The Financialization of Micro-Credit." *Development and Change* 44(3): 473–499.

Akbulut, B., F. Demaria, J-F. Gerber, and J. Martinez-Alier, eds. (2019). *Ecological Economics* 157, special section on "Theoretical and Political Journeys between Environmental Justice and Degrowth: What Potential for an Alliance?"

Akram-Lodhi, A. H. (2013). "How to Build Food Sovereignty." Presentation at *Food Sovereignty: A Critical Dialogue*, International Conference, Yale University, 14–15 September.

Alcorn, R. (2007). "The Real Inconvenient Truth." *Californians for Population Stabilization* blog, December 5. https://capsweb.org/opinion/real-inconvenient-truth/.

Alexander, S. (2012). "Planned Economic Contraction: The Emerging Case for Degrowth." *Environmental Politics* 21(3): 349–368.

Amate, J.I. (2014). "La Desmaterialización de la Economía Mundial a Debate: Consumo de Recursos y Crecimiento." *Revista de Economía Crítica* 18: 60–81.

Ambrose, J. (2020). "BP Sets Net Zero Carbon Target for 2050." *The Guardian*, February 12. https://www.theguardian.com/business/2020/feb/12/bp-sets-net-zero-carbon-target-for-2050.

Anderson, Z.R., K. Kusters, J. McCarthy, and K. Obidzinski. (2016). "Green Growth Rhetoric versus Reality: Insights from Indonesia." *Global Environmental Change* 38: 30–40.

Angelsen, A. (2017). "REDD+ as Result-based Aid: General Lessons and Bilateral Agreements of Norway." *Review of Development Economics* 21(2): 237–264.

Anthias, P. (2018). *Limits to Decolonization: Indigeneity, Territory, and Hydrocarbon Politics in the Bolivian Chaco*. Ithaca, NY: Cornell University Press.

Apostolopoulou, E., A. Chatzimentor, S. Maestre-Andrés, M. Requena-i-Mora, A. Pizarro and D. Bormpoudakis. (2021). "Reviewing 15 Years of Research on Neoliberal Conservation: Towards a Decolonial, Interdisciplinary, Intersectional and Community-engaged Research Agenda." *Geoforum* 124: 236–256.

Apple. (2021). "Apple and Partners Launch First Ever 200 Million Restore Fund." April 15. https://www.apple.com/au/newsroom/2021/04/apple-and-partners-launch-first-ever-200-million-restore-fund/.

Arboleda, M. (2020). *Planetary Mine: Territories of Extraction under Late Capitalism*. London: Verso.

Arrighi, G. (2009). *The Long Twentieth Century*. 2nd ed. London: Verso.

Arsel, M. (2012). "Between 'Marx and Markets'? The State, the 'Left Turn' and Nature in Ecuador." *Tijdschrift voor Economische en Sociale Geografie* 103(2): 150–163.

Arsel, M., and B. Büscher. (2012). "'Nature™ Inc.': Changes and Continuities in Neoliberal Conservation and Market-Based Environmental Policy." *Development and Change* 43(1): 53–78.

Arsel, M., B. Hogenboom, and L. Pellegrini. (2016a). "The Extractive Imperative and the Boom in Environmental Conflicts at the End of the Progressive Cycle in Latin America." *The Extractive Industries and Society* 3(4): 877–879.

Arsel, M., B. Hogenboom, and L. Pellegrini, eds. (2016b). *The Extractive Industries and Society* 3(4), special issue on "The Extractive Imperative in Latin America."

Arsel, M., F. Adaman, and A. Saad-Filho, eds. (2021). *Geoforum* 124, special issue on "Authoritarian Developmentalism."

Asiyanbi, A.P. (2016). "A Political Ecology of REDD+: Property Rights, Militarised Protectionism, and Carbonised Exclusion in Cross River." *Geoforum* 77: 146–156.

Asiyanbi, A., and J.F. Lund. (2020). "Policy Persistence: REDD+ between Stabilization and Contestation." *Journal of Political Ecology* 27(1): 378–400.

Baker, T., and J. Simon, eds. (2002). *Embracing Risk*. Chicago: University of Chicago Press.

Baker-Médard, M., and J. Sasser. (2020). "Technological (Mis)Conceptions: Examining Birth Control as Conservation in Coastal Madagascar." *Geoforum* 108: 12–22.

Bakker, K. (2010). "The Limits of 'Neoliberal Natures': Debating Green Neoliberalism." *Progress in Human Geography* 34(6): 715–735.

Ban, K-M. (2014). *The Road to Dignity by 2030: Ending Poverty, Transforming All Lives and Protecting the Planet.* New York: United Nations.

Banerjee, A., and E. Duflo. (2011). *Poor Economics: A Radical Rethinking of the Way to Fight Global Poverty.* New York: PublicAffairs.

Baptista, J.A. (2017). *The Good Holiday: Development, Tourism and the Politics of Benevolence in Mozambique.* New York: Berghahn.

Barca, S., E. Chertkovskaya, and A. Paulsson. (2019). "Introduction." In *Towards a Political Economy of Degrowth*, E. Chertkovskaya, A. Paulsson and S. Barca, eds. Lanham, MD: Rowman & Littlefield.

Barua, M. (2016). "Lively Commodities and Encounter Value." *Environment and Planning D: Society and Space* 34(4): 725–744.

Bastani, A. (2019). *Fully Automated Luxury Communism: A Manifesto.* London: Verso.

Bauman, Z. (2004). *Wasted Lives: Modernity and Its Outcasts.* Cambridge: Polity.

Becker, E. (1973). *The Denial of Death.* New York: Free Press.

Beder, S. (1998). *Global Spin: The Corporate Assault on Environmentalism.* White River Junction, VT: Chelsea Green Publishing.

———. (2001). "Neoliberal Think Tanks and Free Market Environmentalism." *Environmental Politics* 10(2): 128–133.

Beggs, E., and E. Moore. (2013). *The Social Landscape of African Oil Palm Production in the Osa and Golfito Region, Costa Rica.* San José, Costa Rica: INOGO, Stanford Woods Institute for the Environment.

Bell, C.M. (1992). *Ritual Theory, Ritual Practice.* New York: Oxford University Press.

Berkes, F. (2007). "Community-Based Conservation in a Globalized World." *Proceedings of the National Academy of Sciences* 104(39): 15188–15193.

Best, J. (2014). *Governing Failure: Provisional Expertise and the Transformation of Global Development Finance.* Cambridge: Cambridge University Press.

Bhattacharya, T., ed. (2017). *Social Reproduction Theory: Remapping Class, Recentering Oppression.* London: Pluto Press.

Bidet, J. (2015). *Foucault with Marx.* S. Corcoran, trans. London: Zed.

Birch, K., and M. Siemiatycki. (2016). "Neoliberalism and the Geographies of Marketization: The Entangling of State and Markets." *Progress in Human Geography* 40(2): 177–198.

Bishop, M., and M. Green. (2008). *Philanthrocapitalism: How the Rich Can Save the World and Why We Should Let Them.* London: A&C Black.

Bjerg, O. (2014). *Making Money: The Philosophy of Crisis Capitalism.* London: Verso.

———. (2016). *Parallax of Growth: The Philosophy of Ecology and Economy.* Cambridge, UK: Polity.

Blackman, A., and R.T. Woodward. (2010). "User Financing in a National Payments for Environmental Services Program: Costa Rican Hydropower." *Ecological Economics* 69: 1626–1638.

Böhm, S., and S. Dabhi, eds. (2009). *Upsetting the Offset*. London: MayFly Books.

Bond, P. (2011). "Carbon Capital's Trial, the Kyoto Protocol's Demise, and Openings for Climate Justice." *Capitalism Nature Socialism* 22(4): 3–17.

Borges-Méndez, R. (2008). "Sustainable Development and Participatory Practices in Community Forestry: The Case of FUNDACOR in Costa Rica." *Local Environment* 13(4): 367–383.

Borras, S.M., Jr. (2008). "La Vía Campesina and Its Global Campaign for Agrarian Reform." *Journal of Agrarian Change* 8(2–3): 258–289.

Borup, M., N. Brown, K. Konrad and H. Van Lente. (2006). "The Sociology of Expectations in Science and Technology." *Technology Analysis & Strategic Management* 18: 285–298.

Bourdieu, P. (1997). "Marginalia—Some Additional Notes on the Gift." In *The Logic of the Gift*, A. Schrift, ed. London: Routledge.

Boza, M. (1993). "Conservation in Action: Past, Present and Future of the National Parks System in Costa Rica." *Conservation Biology* 12(6): 239–247.

Boza, M., D. Jukofsky, and C. Wille. (1995). "Costa Rica Is a Laboratory, Not Ecotopia." *Conservation Biology* 9(3): 684–685.

Bracking, S. (2016). *The Financialisation of Power: How Financiers Rule Africa*. London: Routledge.

Brand, U. (2012). "Green Economy—the Next Oxymoron? No Lessons Learned from Failures of Implementing Sustainable Development." *GAIA* 21(1): 28–32.

Brandon, K. (2004). "The Policy Context for Conservation in Costa Rica: Model or Muddle?" In *Biodiversity Conservation in Costa Rica*, G.W. Frankie, A. Mata, and S.B. Vinson, eds. Berkeley: University of California Press.

Bratich, J. (2006). "Public Secrecy and Immanent Security." *Cultural Studies* 20: 493–511.

———. (2007). "Popular Secrecy and Occultural Studies." *Cultural Studies* 21: 42–58.

Braun, B. (2015). "The 2013 Antipode RGS-IBG Lecture: New Materialisms and Neoliberal Natures." *Antipode* 47: 1–14.

Breakthrough Institute. (2014). *An Ecomodernist Manifesto*. Oakland, CA: Breakthrough Institute.

———. (2015). *Nature Unbound: Decoupling for Conservation*. Oakland, CA: Breakthrough Institute.

Brearley, M. (2013). "Discussion: Unconscious Obstacles to Caring for the Planet: Facing Up to Human Nature." In *Engaging with Climate Change: Psychoanalytic and Interdisciplinary Perspectives*, S. Weintrobe, ed. New York: Routledge.

Brenner, N., J. Peck, and N. Theodore. (2010a). "After Neoliberalization?" *Globalizations* 7(3): 327–345.

———. (2010b). "Variegated Neoliberalization: Geographies, Modalities, Pathways." *Global Networks* 10: 182–222.

Brenner, N., and N. Theodore. (2002). "Cities and the Geographies of 'Actually Existing Neoliberalism.'" *Antipode* 34(3): 349–379.

British Broadcasting Company (BBC). (2021). "What is Net Zero and How Are the UK and Other Countries Doing?" Science–Environment, November 21. https://www.bbc.com/news/science-environment-58874518.

British Petroleum (BP). (2020). "British Petroleum Sets Ambition for Net Zero by 2050, Fundamentally Changing Organisation to Deliver." Press Releases, February 12. https://www.bp.com/en/global/corporate/news-and-insights/press-releases/bernard-looney-announces-new-ambition-for-bp.html.

Brockett, C., and R. Gottfried. (2002). "State Policies and the Preservation of Forest Cover: Lessons from Contrasting Public-Policy Regimes in Costa Rica." *Latin American Research Review* 37(1): 7–40.

Brockington, D. (2002). *Fortress Conservation: The Preservation of the Mkomazi Game Reserve, Tanzania*. Oxford: James Currey.

———. (2009). *Celebrity and the Environment: Fame, Wealth and Power in Conservation*. London: Zed Books.

———. (2012). "A Radically Conservative Vision? The Challenge of UNEP's *Towards a Green Economy*." *Development and Change* 43(1): 409–422.

Brockington, D., and R. Duffy. (2010). "Capitalism and Conservation: The Production and Reproduction of Biodiversity Conservation." *Antipode* 42(3): 469–84.

Brockington, D., R. Duffy, and J. Igoe. (2008). *Nature Unbound: Conservation, Capitalism and the Future of Protected Areas*. London: Earthscan.

Brossmann, J., and M. Islar. (2020). "Living Degrowth? Investigating Degrowth Practices through Performative Methods." *Sustainability Science* 15(3): 917–930.

Brown, W. (1999). "Resisting Left Melancholy." *Boundary* 2 26(3): 19–27.

———. (2015). *Undoing the Demos: Neoliberalism's Stealth Revolution*. Cambridge, MA: MIT Press.

———. (2019). *In the Ruins of Neoliberalism: The Rise of Antidemocratic Politics in the West*. New York: Columbia University Press.

Bruff, I., and C.B. Tansel. (2019). "Authoritarian Neoliberalism: Trajectories of Knowledge Production and Praxis." *Globalizations* 16(3): 233–244.

Brysk, A. (2009). "The Little Country That Could: Costa Rica." In *Global Good Samaritans: Human Rights as Foreign Policy*, A. Brysk, ed. Oxford: Oxford University Press.

Bumpus, A., and D. Liverman. (2008). "Accumulation by Decarbonisation and the Governance of Carbon Offsets." *Economic Geography* 84: 127–156.

Burgmann, V. (2018). "The Importance of Being Extreme." *Social Alternatives* 37(2): 10–12.

Burton, M. (2015). "The Decoupling Debate: Can Economic Growth Really Continue without Emission Increases?" *Degrowth* blog, October 12. http://www.degrowth.de/en/2015/10/the-decoupling-debate-can-economic-growth-really-continue-without-emission-increases/.

———. (2016a). "Again and Again: Supposed Evidence for Decoupling Emissions from Growth Is Not What It Seems." *Degrowth* blog, March 28. http://www

.degrowth.de/en/2016/03/once-again-supposed-evidence-for-decoupling
-emissions-from-growth-is-not-what-it-seems/.

———. (2016b). "New Evidence on Decoupling Carbon Emissions from GDP Growth: What Does It Mean?" Steady State Manchester. https://steadystate manchester.net/2016/04/15/new-evidence-on-decoupling-carbon-emissions -from-gdp-growth-what-does-it-mean.

Büscher, B. (2010). "Anti-Politics as Political Strategy: Neoliberalism and Transfrontier Conservation in Southern Africa." *Development and Change* 41(1): 29–51.

———. (2012). "Payments for Ecosystem Services as Neoliberal Conservation: (Reinterpreting) Evidence from the Maloti-Drakensberg, South Africa" *Conservation and Society* 10: 29–41.

———. (2013). "Nature on the Move: The Value and Circulation of Liquid Nature and the Emergence of Fictitious Conservation." *New Proposals: Journal of Marxism and Interdisciplinary Inquiry* 6(1/2): 20–36.

———. (2014). "Selling Success: Constructing Value in Conservation and Development." *World Development* 57: 79–90.

———. (2018). "A review of *Enterprising Nature. Economics, Markets, and Finance in Global Biodiversity Politics* by Jessica Dempsey." *Economic Geography* 94(1): 89–91.

Büscher, B., and V. Davidov, eds. (2013). *The Ecotourism-Extraction Nexus: Political Economies and Rural Realities of (un)Comfortable Bedfellows*. London: Routledge.

Büscher, B., and W. Dressler. (2007). "Linking Neoprotectionism and Environmental Governance: On the Rapidly Increasing Tensions between Actors in the Environment-Development Nexus." *Conservation and Society* 5(4): 586–611.

Büscher, B., W. Dressler, and R. Fletcher, eds. (2014). *Nature™ Inc.: Environmental Conservation in the Neoliberal Age*. Tucson, AZ: University of Arizona Press.

Büscher, B., and R. Fletcher. (2015). "Accumulation by Conservation." *New Political Economy* 20(2): 273--98.

———. (2016). "Nature Is Priceless Which Is Why Turning It into 'Natural Capital' Is Wrong." *The Conservation*, September 22. https://theconversation.com/nature-is -priceless-which-is-why-turning-it-into-natural-capital-is-wrong-65189.

———. (2020). *The Conservation Revolution: Radical Ideas for Saving Nature beyond the Anthropocene*. London: Verso.

Büscher, B., and M. Ramutsindela. (2016). "Green Violence: Rhino Poaching and the War to Save Southern Africa's Peace Parks." *African Affairs* 115(458): 1–22.

Büscher, B., S. Sullivan, J. Igoe, K. Neves, and D. Brockington. (2012). "Towards a Synthesized Critique of Neoliberal Biodiversity Conservation." *Capitalism Nature Socialism* 23(2): 430.

Business and Biodiversity Offsets Programme (BBOP). (2018). *Working for Biodiversity Net Gain: An Overview of the Business and Biodiversity Offsets Programme (BBOP) 2004–2018*. Washington, DC: BBOP

Butler, J. (1997). *The Psychic Life of Power: Theories in Subjection*. Stanford, CA: Stanford University Press.

Byrne, K., and S. Healy. (2006). "Cooperative Subjects: Toward a Post-fantasmatic Enjoyment of the Economy." *Rethinking Marxism* 18: 241–258.

Cafaro, P., and E. Crist, eds. (2012). *Life on the Brink: Environmentalists Confront Overpopulation*. Athens: University of Georgia Press.

Cahill, D. (2014). *The End of Laissez-Faire? On the Durability of Embedded Neoliberalism*. Cheltenham, UK: Edward Elgar Publishing.

Carrier, J.G., and D.V.L. MacLeod. (2005). "Bursting the Bubble: The Socio-Cultural Context of Ecotourism." *Journal of the Royal Anthropological Institute* 11: 315–334.

Carrier, J.G, and D. Miller, eds. (1998). *Virtualism: A New Political Economy*. London: Berg.

Carrier, J.G., and P. West, eds. (2009). *Virtualism, Governance and Practice: Vision and Execution in Environmental Conservation*. New York: Berghahn.

Castree, N. (1999). "Envisioning Capitalism: Geography and the Renewal of Marxian Political Economy." *Transactions of the Institute of British Geographers* NS 24: 137–158.

———. (2003). "Commodifying What Nature?" *Progress in Human Geography* 27: 273–297.

———. (2008). "Neoliberalising Nature: The Logics of Deregulation and Reregulation." *Environment and Planning A* 40: 131–152.

———. (2013). *Making Sense of Nature*. New York: Routledge.

Cattaneo, C., G. D'Alisa, G. Kallis, and C. Zografos, eds. (2012). *Futures* 44(6), special issue on "Degrowth Futures and Democracy."

Cavanagh, C.J. (2018). "Political Ecologies of Biopower: Diversity, Debates, and New Frontiers of Inquiry." *Journal of Political Ecology* 25: 402–425.

Cavanagh, C.J., and T.A. Benjaminsen, eds. (2017). *Journal of Political Ecology* 24, special section on "Political Ecologies of the Green Economy."

Cavanagh, C.J., P.O. Vedeld, and L.T. Trædal. (2015). "Securitizing REDD+? Problematizing the Emerging Illegal Timber Trade and Forest Carbon Interface in East Africa." *Geoforum* 60: 72–82.

Ceballos, G., P. Ehrlich, and R. Dirzo. (2017). "Biological Annihilation via the Ongoing Sixth Mass Extinction Signalled by Vertebrate Population Losses and Declines." *PNAS* 114(30): E6089–E6096.

Chambers, J., K. Massarella, and R. Fletcher. (2022). "The Right to Fail? Problematizing Failure Discourses in International Conservation." *World Development* 150: 10573.

Chan, K., R. Pringle, J. Ranganathan, C. Briggs, Y. Chan, R. Ehrlich, P. Haff, N. Heller, K. Al-Krafaji, and D. Macmynowski. (2007). "When Agendas Collide: Human Welfare and Biological Conservation." *Conservation Biology* 21(1): 59–68.

Chapin, M. (2004). "A Challenge to Conservationists." *WorldWatch* 17(6): 17–31.

Chertkovskaya, E., A. Paulsson, and S. Barca, eds. (2019). *Towards a Political Economy of Degrowth*. Lanham, MD: Rowman & Littlefield Publishers.

Child, M. (2009). "The Thoreau Ideal as a Unifying Thread in the Conservation Movement." *Conservation Biology* 23(1): 241–243.

Chornook, K., and W. Guindon. (2008). *Walking with Wolf*. Hamilton, ON: Wandering Woods Press.

Clarke, J. (2017a). "The Neoliberal Writing on the Wall: Ontario's Basic Income Experiment." *The Bullet*, June 26. https://socialistproject.ca/bullet/1438.php.

Clarke, J. (2017b). "The Neoliberal Danger of Basic Income." *Ontario Coalition Against Poverty* (blog), September 18. https://ocaptoronto.wordpress.com/2017/09/18/the-neoliberal-danger-of-basic-income/.

Clifford, J. (1986). "Introduction: Partial Truths." In *Writing Culture*, J. Clifford, and G. Marcus, eds. Berkeley: University of California Press.

Cole-Christensen, D. (1997). *A Place in the Rainforest*. Austin: University of Texas Press.

Collard, R.C., and J. Dempsey. (2013). "Life for Sale? The Politics of Lively Commodities." *Environment and Planning A* 45(11): 2682–2699.

———. (2016). "Capitalist Natures in Five Orientations." *Capitalism Nature Socialism* 28(1): 78–97.

Collins, Y.A. (2019). "Colonial Residue: REDD+, Territorialisation and the Racialized Subject in Guyana and Suriname." *Geoforum* 106: 38–47.

Collins, Y.A., V. Maguire-Rajpaul, J. Krauss, A. Asiyanbi, A. Jiminez, M. Mabele, and M. Alexander-Owen. (2021). "Plotting the Coloniality of Conservation." *Journal of Political Ecology, 28*(1).

Comaroff, J. (1985). *Body of Power, Spirit of Resistance: The Culture and History of a South African People*. Chicago: University of Chicago Press.

Compas. (2007). *Learning Endogenous Development: Building on Bio-cultural Diversity*. Warwickshire, UK: Practical Action Publishing.

Cooper, M. (2010). "Turbulent Worlds: Financial Markets and Environmental Crisis." *Theory, Culture & Society* 27(2–3): 167–190.

Corson, C. (2010). "Shifting Environmental Governance in a Neoliberal World: USAID for Conservation." *Antipode* 42(3): 576–602.

Corson, C., L.M. Campbell, and K.I. MacDonald. (2014). "Capturing the Personal in Politics: Ethnographies of Global Environmental Governance." *Global Environmental Politics* 14(3): 21–24.

Costanza, R., J.H. Cumberland, H. Daly, R. Goodland, and R.B. Norgaard. (1991). *An Introduction to Ecological Economics*. New York: CRC Press.

Costanza, R., R. d'Arge, R. de Groot, M. Farber, B. Grasso, K. Hannon, S. Limburg, R. Naeem, J. O'Neill, R. Paruelo, R. Raskin, P. Sutton, and M. van den Belt. (1997). "The Value of the World's Ecosystem Services and Natural Capital." *Nature* 387: 253–260.

Costanza, R., R. de Groot, P. Sutton, S. van der Ploeg, S.J. Anderson, I. Kubiszewski, S. Farber, and R.K. Turner. (2014). "Changes in the Global Value of Ecosystem Services." *Global Environmental Change* 26: 152–158.

Covington, D. (1995). *Salvation on Sand Mountain: Snake Handling and Redemption in Southern Appalachia*. New York: Penguin.

Credit Suisse and McKinsey. (2016). *Conservation Finance from Niche to Mainstream: The Building of an Institutional Asset Class*. Zurich: Credit Suisse Group AG and McKinsey Center for Business and Environment.

Credit Suisse, WWF, and McKinsey and Company. (2014). *Conservation Finance: Moving beyond Donor Funding toward an Investor-Driven Approach*. Zurich:

Credit Suisse Group AG, WWF and McKinsey Center for Business and Environment.

Crouch, C. (2011). *The Strange Non-Death of Neo-Liberalism*. Cambridge, UK: Polity.

Cuello, C., K. Brandon, and R. Margoluis. (1998). "Costa Rica: Corcovado National Park." In *Parks in Peril: People, Politics, and Protected Areas*, K. Brandon, K. Redford and S. Sanderson, eds. Washington, DC: Island Press.

Csikszentmihalyi, M. 1974. *Flow: Studies in Enjoyment*. Public Health Service Grant Report No. RO1HM 22883-02.

Daggett, C. (2018). "Petro-masculinity: Fossil Fuels and Authoritarian Desire." *Millennium* 47(1): 25–44.

Daily, G.C., ed. (1997). *Nature's Services: Society's Dependence on Natural Ecosystems*. Washington, DC: Island Press.

Daily, G.C., and K. Ellison. (2002). *The New Economy of Nature: The Quest to Make Nature Profitable*. Washington, DC: Island Press.

Daily, G.C., P.M. Kareiva, S. Polasky, T.H. Ricketts, and H. Tallis. (2011). "Mainstreaming Natural Capital into Decisions." In *Natural Capital: Theory and Practice of Mapping Ecosystem Services*, P. Kareiva, H. Tallis, T.H. Ricketts, G.C. Daily, and S. Polasky, eds. Oxford, UK: Oxford University Press.

D'Alisa, G., F. Demaria, and C. Cattaneo. (2013). "Civil and Uncivil Actors for a Degrowth Society." *Journal of Civil Society* 9(2): 212–224.

D'Alisa, G., F. Demaria, and G. Kallis, eds. (2014). *Degrowth: A Vocabulary for a New Era*. London: Routledge.

Daly, G. (2009). "Politics of the Political: Psychoanalytic Theory and the Left(s)." *Journal of Political Ideologies* 14(3): 279–300

Daly, H.E. (2008). "A Steady-State Economy: A Failed Growth Economy and a Steady-State Economy Are Not the Same Thing; They Are the Very Different Alternatives We Face." Presentation for the UK Sustainable Development Commission, London, UK, April 24.

———. 2014. "Use and Abuse of the 'Natural Capital' Concept." *The Daly News*, November 13. http://steadystate.org/use-and-abuse-of-the-natural-capital -concept/.

Daniels, A., V. Esposito, K.J. Bagstad, A. Moulaert, and C.M. Rodriguez. (2010). "Understanding the Impacts of Costa Rica's PES: Are We Asking All the Right Questions?" *Ecological Economics* 69: 2116–2126.

Dasgupta, P. (2021). *The Economics of Biodiversity: The Dasgupta Review*. London: HM Treasury.

Davidson, M. (2012). "Sustainable City as Fantasy." *Human Geography* 5: 14–25.

Dean, J. (2008). "Enjoying Neoliberalism." *Cultural Politics* 4(1): 47–72.

———. (2010). "Drive as the Structure of Biopolitics Economy, Sovereignty, and Capture." *Krisis* (2): 2–15.

———. (2012). *The Communist Horizon*. London: Verso.

Dempsey, J. (2016). *Enterprising Nature: Economics, Markets, and Finance in Global Biodiversity Politics*. Malden, MA: Wiley Blackwell.

Dempsey, J., and M.M. Robertson. (2012). "Ecosystem Services: Tensions, Impurities, and Points of Engagement within Neoliberalism." *Progress in Human Geography* 36(6): 758–779.

Dempsey, J., and D.C. Suarez. (2016). "Arrested Development? The Promises and Paradoxes of 'Selling Nature to Save It.'" *Annals of the American Association of Geographers* 106(3): 653–671.

Descola, P. (2013). *Beyond Nature and Culture*. Chicago: University of Chicago Press.

De Janvry, A., and L. Ground. (1978). "Types and Consequences of Land Reform in Latin America." *Latin American Perspectives* 5(4): 90–112.

de Vries, P. (2007). "Don't Compromise Your Desire for Development! A Lacanian/Deleuzian Rethinking of the Anti-Politics Machine." *Third World Quarterly* 28(1): 25–43.

Deleuze, G., and F. Guattari. (1987). *A Thousand Plateaus*. B. Massumi, trans. Minneapolis: University of Minnesota Press.

Deutz, A., G.M. Heal, R. Niu, E. Swanson, T. Townshend, L. Zhu, A. Delmar, A. Meghji, S.A. Sethi, and J. Tobin-de la Puente. (2020). *Financing Nature: Closing the Global Biodiversity Financing Gap*. Washington, DC: The Paulson Institute, The Nature Conservancy, and the Cornell Atkinson Center for Sustainability.

Dickson I. (n.d.). *Embracing Failure in Conservation: Introducing a Common Language for Conservation Practitioners to Record and Discuss Learning from Failure*. Cambridge: CCI.

Dietz, R., and D. O'Neill. (2013). *Enough Is Enough: Building a Sustainable Economy in a World of Finite Resources*. San Francisco, CA: Berrett-Koehler Publishers.

Dolar, M. (1993). "Beyond Interpellation." *Qui Parle* 6(2): 75–96.

Dressler, W., B. Büscher, and R. Fletcher. (2014). "Conclusion: The Limits of Nature™ Inc. and the Search for Vital Alternatives." In *Nature™ Inc.: Environmental Conservation in the Neoliberal Age*, B. Büscher, W. Dressler, and R. Fletcher, eds. Tucson, AZ: University of Arizona Press.

Driscoll, L., C. Hunt, M. Honey, and W. Durham. (2011). *The Importance of Ecotourism as a Development and Conservation Tool in the Osa Peninsula, Costa Rica*. Washington, DC: CREST.

Duffy, R. (2016). "War, by Conservation." *Geoforum* 69: 238–248.

Dufour, D-R. (2008) *The Art of Shrinking Heads: On the New Servitude of the Liberated in the Age of Total Capitalism*. Cambridge: Polity.

Dunlap, A., and J. Fairhead. (2014). "The Militarisation and Marketisation of Nature: An Alternative Lens to 'Climate-Conflict.'" *Geopolitics* 19(4): 937–961.

Dunlap, A., and S. Sullivan. (2020). "A Faultline in Neoliberal Environmental Governance Scholarship? Or, Why Accumulation-by-Alienation Matters." *Environment and Planning E: Nature and Space* 3(2): 552–579.

Durkheim, E. (1995). *The Elementary Forms of Religious Life*. New York: Free Press.

Easterly, W. (2006). *The White Man's Burden*. New York: Penguin.

Eaton, C., and S. Carroll. (2015). "Exxon Mobil Backs Carbon Tax." *Houston Chronicle*, December 7. http://www.houstonchronicle.com/business/energy/article/Exxon-espouses-carbon-tax-amid-Paris-climate-talks-6682461.php.

Edelman, M. (1995). "Rethinking the Hamburger Thesis: Deforestation and the Crisis of Central America's Beef." In *The Social Causes of Environmental Destruction in Latin America*, M. Painter and W. Durham, eds. Ann Arbor: University of Michigan Press.

———. (1999). *Peasants against Globalization: Rural Social Movements in Costa Rica*. Stanford, CA: Stanford University Press.

EEA. (2013). *Trends and Projections in Europe 2013: Tracking Progress towards Europe's Climate and Energy Targets until 2020*. Brussels: EEA.

Ehrenfeld, D. (1988). "Why Put a Value on Biodiversity?" In *Biodiversity*, E.O. Wilson, ed. Washington, DC: National Academy Press.

———. (2008). "Neoliberalization of Conservation." *Conservation Biology* 22(5): 1091–1092.

Ekins, P. (2000). *Economic Growth and Environmental Sustainability*. New York: Routledge.

Erickson, C.L. (2008). "Amazonia: The Historical Ecology of a Domesticated Landscape." In *Handbook of South American Archaeology*, H. Silverman and W.H. Isbell, eds. New York: Springer.

Escobar, A. (1995). *Encountering Development: The Making and Unmaking of the Third World*. Princeton, NJ: Princeton University Press.

———. (2008). *Territories of Difference: Place, Movements, Life, Redes*. Durham, NC: Duke University Press.

———. (2010). "Postconstructivist Political Ecologies." In *The International Handbook of Environmental Sociology*, M.R. Redclift and G. Woodgate, eds. London: Edward Elgar Publishing.

———. (2015). "Degrowth, Postdevelopment, and Transitions: A Preliminary Conversation." *Sustainability Science* 10(3): 451–462.

Esposito, R. (2008). *Bíos: Biopolitics and Philosophy*. T. Campbell, trans. Minneapolis: University of Minnesota Press.

———. (2013). "Community, Immunity, Biopolitics." *Angelaki: Journal of the Theoretical Humanities* 18(3): 83–90.

Esteva, G. (2012). "Los Quehaceres del Día." In *Renunciar al Bien Común: Extractivismo y (Pos)Desarrollo en América Latina*, G. Massuh, ed. Buenos Aires: Mardulce.

European Commission (EC). (2018). *Study on EU Financing of REDD+ Related Activities and Results-Based Payments Pre and Post 2020*. Brussels: European Commission.

Evans, K. (2012). "It's Too Soon to Bury REDD+." *Forests News*, May 8. https://forestsnews.cifor.org/49642/its-too-soon-to-bury-redd?fnl=en.

Evans, M. (2018) "Reimaging REDD+ 10 Years On, Making Success a Reality." *Landscape News*, June 13. https://news.globallandscapesforum.org/27781/reimagining-redd-10-years-on-making-success-a-reality/.

Evans, S. (1999). *The Green Republic: A Conservation History of Costa Rica*. Austin: University of Texas Press.

Engineers Without Borders (EWB) Canada. (2017). *2017 Failure Report*. https://www.ewb.ca/wp-content/uploads/2018/08/EWB_FAILURE-REPORT_EN_03-08-2018-pages.pdf.

ExxonMobil. (2014). *Energy and Carbon: Managing the Risks.* http://cdn.exxon mobil.com/~/media/global/files/energy-and-environment/report---energy-and -carbon---managing-the-risks.pdf.

Fairhead, J., M. Leach, and I. Scoones, eds. (2012). *Journal of Peasant Studies* 39(2), special issue on "Green Grabbing."

Fanon, F. (1963). *The Wretched of the Earth*, C. Farrington, trans. New York: Grove Press.

Farber, S.C., R. Costanza, and M.A. Wilson. (2002). "Economic and Ecological Concepts for Valuing Ecosystem Services." *Ecological Economics* 41(3): 375–392.

Farley, J., and R. Costanza. (2010). "Payments for Ecosystem Services: From Local to Global." *Ecological Economics* 69: 2060–2068.

Farley, J., A. Schmitt, M. Burke, and M. Farr. (2015). "Extending Market Allocation to Ecosystem Services: Moral and Practical Implications on a Full and Unequal Planet." *Ecological Economics* 117: 244–252.

Federici, S. (2004). *Caliban and the Witch: Women, the Body, and Primitive Accumulation.* New York: Autonomedia.

Feeny, D., F. Berkes, B.J. McCay, and J.M. Acheson. (1990). "The Tragedy of the Commons: Twenty-Two Years Later." *Human Ecology* 18(1): 1–19.

Femia, J. (1975). "Hegemony and Consciousness in the Thought of Antonio Gramsci." *Political Studies* 23(1): 29–48.

Feola, G. (2019). "Degrowth and the Unmaking of Capitalism." *ACME: An International Journal for Critical Geographies* 18(4): 977–997.

Ferguson, J. (1994). *The Anti-politics Machine: 'Development,' Depoliticization and Bureaucratic Power in Lesotho.* Minneapolis: University of Minnesota Press.

———. (2010). "The Uses of Neoliberalism." *Antipode* 41(1): 166–184.

———. (2011). "Toward a Left Art of Government: From 'Foucauldian Critique' to Foucauldian Politics." *History of the Human Sciences* 24(4): 61–68.

———. (2015). *Give a Man a Fish: Reflections on the New Politics of Distribution.* Durham, NC: Duke University Press.

Fine, B. (2009). "Development as Zombieconomics in the Age of Neoliberalism." *Third World Quarterly* 30(5): 885-904.

Fink, B. (1995). *The Lacanian Subject: Between Language and Jouissance.* Princeton, NJ: Princeton University Press.

Finley-Brook, M. (2007). "Green Neoliberal Space: The Mesoamerican Biological Corridor." *Journal of Latin American Geography* 6(1): 101–124.

Fisher, M. (2012). "Post-capitalist Desire." In *What We Are Fighting For: A Radical Collective Manifesto*, F. Campagna and E. Campiglio, eds. London: Pluto Press.

Fletcher, R. (2007). "Introduction: Beyond Resistance?" In *Beyond Resistance: The Future of Freedom*, R. Fletcher, ed. New York: Nova Science Publishers.

———. (2010a). "Neoliberal Environmentality: Towards a Poststructuralist Political Ecology of the Conservation Debate." *Conservation and Society* 8(3): 171–181.

———. (2010b). "The Emperor's New Adventure: Public Secrecy and the Paradox of Adventure Tourism." *Journal of Contemporary Ethnography* 39(1): 6–33.

———. (2012a). "Using the Master's Tools? Neoliberal Conservation and the Evasion of Inequality." *Development and Change* 43(1): 295–317.

———. (2012b). "Capitalizing on Chaos: Climate Change and Disaster Capitalism." *Ephemera* 12(1–2): 97–112.

———. (2013a). "Bodies Do Matter: The Peculiar Persistence of Neoliberalism in Environmental Governance." *Human Geography* 6(1): 29–45.

———. (2013b). "How I Learned to Stop Worrying and Love the Market: Virtualism, Disavowal and Public Secrecy in Neoliberal Environmental Conservation." *Environment and Planning D: Society and Space* 31(5): 796–812.

———. (2013c). "Making 'Peace with Nature': Costa Rica's Campaign for Climate Neutrality." In *Climate Change Governance in the Developing World*, D. Held, C. Roger, and E. Nag, eds. London: Polity Press.

———. (2014a). *Romancing the Wild: Cultural Dimensions of Ecotourism.* Durham, NC: Duke University Press.

———. (2014b). "Orchestrating Consent: Post-politics and Intensification of Nature™ Inc. at the 2012 World Conservation Congress." *Conservation and Society* 12(3): 329–342.

———. (2014c). "Taking the Chocolate Laxative: Why Neoliberal Conservation 'Fails Forward.'" In *Nature™ Inc.: Environmental Conservation in the Neoliberal Age*, B. Büscher, W. Dressler, and R. Fletcher, eds. Tucson, AZ: University of Arizona Press.

———. (2015). "Blinded by the Stars? Celebrity, Fantasy, and Desire in Neoliberal Environmental Governance." *Celebrity Studies* 6(4): 457–470.

———. (2016). "Carbon, Carbon Everywhere: How Climate Change Is Transforming Conservation in Costa Rica." In *The Carbon Fix: Forest Carbon, Social Justice, and Environmental Governance*, S. Paladino and S. Fiske, eds. London: Routledge.

———. (2018a). "Beyond the End of the World: Breaking Attachment to a Dying Planet." In *Psychoanalysis and the GlObal*, I. Kapoor, ed. Lincoln: University of Nebraska Press.

———. (2018b). "License to Kill: Contesting the Legitimacy of Green Violence." *Conservation and Society* 16(2): 147–156.

———. (2020a). "Neoliberal Conservation." In *Oxford Research Encyclopedia of Anthropology*, M. Aldenderfer, ed. New York: Oxford University Press.

———. (2020b). "Diverse Ecologies: Mapping Complexity in Environmental Governance." *Environment and Planning E: Nature and Space* 3(2): 481–502.

Fletcher, R., and J. Breitling. (2012). "Market Mechanism or Subsidy in Disguise? Governing Payment for Environmental Services in Costa Rica." *Geoforum* 43(3): 402–411.

Fletcher, R., J. Breitling, and V. Puleo. (2014). "Barbarian Hordes: The Overpopulation Scapegoat in International Development Discourse." *Third World Quarterly* 35(7): 1195–1215.

Fletcher, R., and B. Büscher. (2017). "The PES Conceit: Revisiting the Relationship between Payments for Environmental Services and Neoliberal Conservation." *Ecological Economics* 132: 224–231.

————, eds. (2018). *Conservation and Society* 16(2), special issue on "Political Ecologies of 'Green Wars.'"

Fletcher, R., B. Dowd-Uribe, and G.A. Aistara, eds. (2020). *The Ecolaboratory: Environmental Governance and Economic Development in Costa Rica.* Tucson: University of Arizona Press.

Fletcher, R., W. Dressler, B. Büscher, and Z. Anderson. (2016). "Questioning REDD+ and the Future of Market-Based Conservation." *Conservation Biology* 30(3): 673–675.

Fletcher, R., W. Dressler, Z. Anderson, and B. Büscher. (2019). "Natural Capital Must Be Defended: Green Growth as Neoliberal Biopolitics." *Journal of Peasant Studies* 46(5): 1068–1095.

Fletcher, R., and C. Rammelt. (2017). "Decoupling: A Key Fantasy of the Post-2015 Sustainable Development Agenda." *Globalizations* 14(3): 450–467.

Flew, T. (2011). "Michel Foucault's *The Birth of Biopolitics* and Contemporary Neoliberalism Debates." *Thesis Eleven* 108(1): 44–65.

Fondo Nacional de Financiamiento Forestal (FONAFIFO). (2012). *Estudio de Cobertura Forestal de Costa Rica.* San José, Costa Rica: FONAFIFO.

Foster, H. (2020). *What Comes After Farce: Art and Criticism at a Time of Debacle.* London: Verso.

Foster, J.B. (2011). "Capitalism and Degrowth: An Impossibility Theorem." *Monthly Review* 62(8): 26–33.

Foucault, M. (1970). *The Archaeology of Knowledge.* London: Routledge.

————. (1972). *Madness and Civilization.* New York: Pantheon.

————. (1977). *Discipline and Punish: The Birth of the Prison.* New York: Vintage.

————. (1978). *The History of Sexuality: An Introduction.* New York: Pantheon.

————. (1980). *Power/Knowledge.* New York: Pantheon.

————. (1983). "The Subject and Power." In *Michel Foucault: Beyond Structuralism and Hermeneutics*, by H. Dreyfus and P. Rabinow. Chicago: University of Chicago Press.

————. (1984a). "What Is Enlightenment?" In *The Foucault Reader*, P. Rabinow, ed. New York: Pantheon.

————. (1984b). "On the Genealogy of Ethics." In *The Foucault Reader*, P. Rainbow, ed. New York: Pantheon.

————. (1991a). "Governmentality." In *The Foucault Effect: Studies in Governmentality*, G. Burchell, C. Gordon, and P. Miller, eds. Hemel Hempstead, UK: Harvester Wheatsheaf.

————. (1991b). *Remarks on Marx: Conversations with Duccio Trombadori.* New York: Semiotext(e).

————. (1999). "Is It Useless to Revolt?" In *Religion and Culture: Michel Foucault*, J. Carrette, ed. London: Routledge.

————. (2003). *"Society Must Be Defended."* New York: Picador.

————. (2007). *Security, Territory, Population.* New York: Palgrave MacMillan.

————. (2008). *The Birth of Biopolitics.* New York: Palgrave MacMillan.

Fraser, N. (2017). "The End of Progressive Neoliberalism." *Dissent* 2(1): 2017.

Freedman, D.H. (2010). "Why Scientific Studies Are So Often Wrong: The Street-light Effect." *Discover Magazine* 26: 1–4.

Freud, S. (1925). "Mourning and Melancholia." In *Collected Papers, Volume 4*. London: Hogarth Press.

———. (1962). *Civilization and its Discontents*. New York: Norton.

Friedman, M. (2002). *Capitalism and Freedom*. Fortieth Anniversary ed. Chicago: University of Chicago Press.

———. 2008. "Other People's Money." YouTube, December 26. https://www.you tube.com/watch?v=k2Kg2SvsI8Q.

Gal, S. (1995). "Language and the 'Arts of Resistance.'" *Cultural Anthropology* 10(3): 407–24.

Galeano, E. (1997). *Open Veins of Latin America*. New York: Monthly Review Press.

Gallopin, G. (2003). *A Systems Approach to Sustainability and Sustainable Development*. Santiago, Chile: Economic Commission for Latin America.

Galtung, J. (1990). "Cultural Violence." *Journal of Peace Research* 27(3): 291–305.

Gateway Greens. (2008). "Surviving Climate Change: Producing Less and Enjoying It More." Roundtable, June 27–29. https://gateway-greens.org/archive/2008/08 -jun27_climateroundtable.htm.

Gibson-Graham, J.K. (1996). *The End of Capitalism (As We Knew It): A Feminist Critique of Political Economy*. Minneapolis: University of Minnesota Press.

———. (2006). *A Postcapitalist Politics*. Minneapolis: University of Minnesota Press.

———. (2011). "A Feminist Project of Belonging for the Anthropocene." *Gender, Place, and Culture* 18(11): 1–21.

Global Witness. (2019). *Enemies of the State? How Governments and Businesses Silence Land and Environmental Defenders*. London: Global Witness.

Goldenberg, S., J. Vidal, L. Taylor, A. Vaughan, and F. Harvey. (2015). "Paris Climate Deal: Nearly 200 Nations Sign in End of Fossil Fuel Era." *The Guardian*, December 12. http://www.theguardian.com/environment/2015/dec/12/paris-climate -deal-200-nations-sign-finish-fossil-fuel-era.

Goldman, M. (2005). *Imperial Nature: The World Bank and Struggles for Social Justice in the Age of Globalisation*. New Haven, CT: Yale University Press.

Gómez-Baggethun, E., and R. Muradian. (2015). "In Markets We Trust? Setting the Boundaries of Market-Based Instruments in Ecosystem Services Governance." *Ecological Economics* 117: 217–224.

Google. (2021). "Wildlife Insights Helps Capture the Beauty of Biodiversity, As Well as Its Fragility." Sustainability: Environment Projects, March. https://sustainability. google/progress/projects/wildlife-insights/.

Gough, M. (2016). "Forward." In *Natural Capital Protocol*. London: NCC.

Goulder, L.H., and D. Kennedy. (1997). "Valuing Ecosystem Services: Philosophical Bases and Empirical Methods." In *Nature's Services: Society's Dependence on Natural Ecosystems,* G.C Daily, ed. Washington, DC: Island Press.

———. (2011). "Interpreting and Estimating the Value of Ecosystem Services." In *Natural Capital: Theory and Practice of Mapping Ecosystem Services*, P. Kareiva,

H. Tallis, T.H. Ricketts, G.C. Daily, and S. Polasky, eds. Oxford: Oxford University Press.

Government of Costa Rica. (2010). *REDD Readiness Preparation Proposal (R-PP)*. Forest Carbon Partnership. https://www.forestcarbonpartnership.org/system/files/documents/R-PPCostaRica%20%282a%29.pdf.

Graeber, D. (2011). *Debt: The First Five Thousand Years*. Brooklyn, NY: Melville House.

———. (2014). "On the Moral Grounds of Economic Relations: A Maussian Approach." *Journal of Classical Sociology* 14(1): 65–77.

———. (2015). *The Utopia of Rules: On Technology, Stupidity, and the Secret Joys of Bureaucracy*. London: Melville House.

Gramsci, A. (1971). *Selections from the Prison Notebooks*. Q. Hoare, trans. London: Lawrence and Wishart.

Gray, J. (1998). *False Dawn: The Delusions of Global Capitalism*. London: Granta.

Green, D. (2012). *From Poverty to Power: How Active Citizens and Effective States Can Change the World*. London: Oxfam.

———. (2013). "From Poverty to Power." Oxfam. https://frompoverty.oxfam.org.uk/.

Greenpeace. (2013). *Dealing in Doubt: The Climate Denial Machine vs Climate Science*. New York: Greenpeace USA. http://www.climateaccess.org/sites/default/files/Greenpeace_Dealing%20in%20Doubt.pdf.

Gritzas, G., and K.I. Kavoulakos. (2016). "Diverse Economies and Alternative Spaces: An Overview of Approaches and Practices." *European Urban and Regional Studies* 23(4): 917–934.

Grugel, J., and M.P. Riggirozzi. (2012). "Post-Neoliberalism in Latin America: Rebuilding and Reclaiming the State after Crisis." *Development and Change* 43(1): 1–21.

Guardiola-Rivera, O. (2013). *Story of a Death Foretold: The Coup against Salvador Allende, September 11, 1973*. New York: Bloomsbury Press.

Gudynas, E. (2011). "Buen Vivir: Germinando Alternativas al Desarrollo." *América Latina en Movimiento* 462: 1–20.

Gutiérrez-Zamora, V. (2021). "The Coloniality of Neoliberal Biopolitics: Mainstreaming Gender in Community Forestry in Oaxaca, Mexico." *Geoforum* 126: 139–149.

Habermas, J. (1975). *Legitimation Crisis*. T. McCarthy, trans. Boston: Beacon Press.

Hahn, T., C. McDermott, C. Ituarte-Lima, M. Schultz, T. Green, and M. Tuvendal. (2015). "Purposes and Degrees of Commodification: Economic Instruments for Biodiversity and Ecosystem Services Need Not Rely on Markets or Monetary Valuation." *Ecosystem Services* 16: 74–82.

Haines, H.H. (1995). *Black Radicals and the Civil Rights Mainstream, 1954–1970*. Knoxville: University of Tennessee Press.

Hajer, M. (1993). "Discourse Coalitions and the Institutionalisation of Practice: The Case of Acid Rain in Great Britain." In *The Argumentative Turn in Policy Analysis and Planning*, F. Fischer and J. Forester, eds. Durham, NC: Duke University Press.

Hall, C. (1984). *Costa Rica: A Geographical Interpretation in Historical Perspective.* Boulder, CO: Westview Press.

Haller, T., G. Acciaioli, and S. Rist. (2016). "Constitutionality: Conditions for Crafting Local Ownership of Institution-Building Processes." *Society & Natural Resources* 29(1): 68–87.

Hamilton, C. (2003). *Growth Fetish.* Crows Nest: Allen & Unwin.

Hammond, E. (2013). "Costa Rica's INBio, Nearing Collapse, Surrenders Its Biodiversity Collections and Seeks Government Bailout." *Third World Network,* April 20. http://www.twnside.org.sg/title2/biotk/2013/biotk130401.htm.

Han, B.-C. (2015). *The Burnout Society.* Stanford, CA: Stanford University Press.

———. (2017). *Psychopolitics: Neoliberalism and New Technologies of Power.* London: Verso.

———. (2018). *Topology of Violence (Untimely Meditations).* Cambridge, MA: MIT Press.

Hanlon, J., D. Hulme, and A. Barrientos. (2010). *Just Give Money to the Poor: The Development Revolution from the Global South.* West Hartford, CT: Kumarian Press.

Hannah, M.G. (2011). "Biopower, Life and Left Politics." *Antipode* 43(4): 1034–1055.

Haraway, D.J. (2016). *Staying with the Trouble: Making Kin in the Chthulucene.* Durham, NC: Duke University Press.

Harcourt, W., ed. (2012). *Women Reclaiming Sustainable Livelihoods: Spaces Lost, Spaces Gained.* London: Palgrave.

Harcourt, W., and I.L. Nelson, eds. (2015). *Practising Feminist Political Ecologies: Moving Beyond the "Green Economy."* London: Zed Books.

Hardin, G. (1968). "The Tragedy of the Commons." *Science* 162: 1243–1248.

Hardt, M., and A. Negri. (2009). *Commonwealth.* Cambridge, MA: University of Harvard Press.

Hartmann, B. (1998). "Population, Environment and Security: A New Trinity." *Environment and Urbanization* 10(2): 113–128.

Harvey, D. (1989). *The Condition of Postmodernity: An Inquiry into the Origins of Cultural Change.* Oxford: Basil Blackwell.

———. (2005). *A Brief History of Neoliberalism.* Oxford: Oxford University Press.

———. (2014). *Seventeeen Contradicitons and the End of Capitalism.* Oxford: Oxford University Press.

Hayden, C. (2003). *When Nature Goes Public: The Making and Unmaking of Bioprospecting in Mexico.* Princeton, NJ: Princeton University Press.

Heindrichs, T. (1997). *Innovative Financing Instruments in the Forestry and Nature Conservation Sector of Costa Rica.* Eschborn, Germany: Deutsche Gesellschaft für Technische Zusammenarbeit (GTZ) GmbH.

Heikkurinen, P. (2019). "Degrowth: A Metamorphosis in Being." *Environment and Planning E: Nature and Space* 2(3): 528–547.

Hellenbach, T.O. (1993). "The Future of Munkeywrenching." In *Ecodefense: A Field Guide to Monkeywrenching,* 3rd edition, D. Foreman and B. Hayward, eds. Chico, CA: Abbzug Press.

Helm, D. (2015). *Natural Capital: Valuing our Planet*. New Haven, CT: Yale University Press.

Hendrikse, R.P., and J.D. Sidaway. (2010). "Commentary: Neoliberalism 3.0." *Environment and Planning A* 42(9): 2037–2042.

Hennike, P. (2014). "Decoupling Resource Consumption and Economic Growth: Insights into an Unsolved Global Challenge." Presentation at *Fourth International Conference on Degrowth for Ecological Sustainability and Social Equity*, Leipzig, Germany, September 2–6.

Heron, K. (2020). "We Still Have a World to Win: From Capitalist Realism to Post-Capitalist Desire." *Mediations* 33(1–2): 173–180.

Heynen, N., J. McCarthy, P. Robbins, and S. Prudham, eds. (2007). *Neoliberal Environments: False Promises and Unnatural Consequences*. New York: Routledge.

Hickel, J. (2018). *The Divide: Global Inequality from Conquest to Free Markets*. New York: WW Norton & Company.

———. (2020). *Less Is More: How Degrowth Will Save the World*. New York: Random House.

Hickel, J., and G. Kallis. (2020). "Is Green Growth Possible?" *New Political Economy* 25(4): 469–486.

Hicks, C.C., A. Levine, A. Agrawal, X. Basurto, S.J. Breslow, C. Carothers, S. Charnley, S. Coulthard, N. Dolsak, J. Donatuto, C. Garcia-Quijano, M.B. Mascia, K. Norman, M.R. Poe, T. Satterfield, K. St. Martin, and P.S. Levin. (2016). "Engage Key Social Concepts for Sustainability." *Science* 352: 38–40.

Holland, T.G., G.D. Peterson, and A. Gonzalez. (2009). "A Cross-National Analysis of How Economic Inequality Predicts Biodiversity Loss." *Conservation Biology* 23(5): 1304–1313.

Holling, C.S. (1973). "Resilience and Stability of Ecological Systems." *Annual Review of Ecology and Symantics* 4: 1–23.

Holmes, G. (2010). "The Rich, the Powerful and the Endangered: Conservation Elites, Networks and the Dominican Republic." *Antipode* 42: 624–646.

———. (2012). "Biodiversity for Billionaires: Capitalism, Conservation and the Role of Philanthropy in Saving/Selling Nature." *Development and Change* 43: 185–203.

Holmes, G., and C.J. Cavanagh. (2016). "A Review of the Social Impacts of Neoliberal Conservation: Formations, Inequalities, Contestations." *Geoforum* 75: 199–209.

Holmes, G., C. Sandbrook, and J. Fisher. (2017). "Understanding Conservationists' Perspectives on the New Conservation Debate." *Conservation Biology* 31(2): 353–363.

Honey, M. (2008). *Ecotourism and Sustainable Development: Who Owns Paradise?* 2nd ed. Washington, DC: Island Press.

hooks, b. (1994). *Teaching to Transgress: Education as a Practice of Freedom*. London: Routledge.

———. (2014). *Feminism Is for Everybody: Passionate Politics*. London: Routledge.

Horkheimer, M., and T. Adorno. (1998 [1944]). *Dialectic of Enlightenment*. New York: Continuum.

Hornborg, A. (2017). "Dithering while the Planet Burns: Anthropologists' Approaches to the Anthropocene." *Reviews in Anthropology* 46(2-3): 61–77.

Horton, L.R. (2009). "Buying Up Nature: Economic and Social Impacts of Costa Rica's Ecotourism Boom." *Latin American Perspectives* 36(3): 93–107.

Howson, P., S. Oakes, Z. Baynham-Herd, and J. Swords. (2019). "Cryptocarbon: The Promises and Pitfalls of Forest Protection on a Blockchain." *Geoforum* 100: 1–9.

Huawei. (2021). "Huawei Announces Cooperation Progress with IUCN on Tech4Nature at WCC 2021." News and Events, September 7. https://www.huawei.com/en/news/2021/9/tech4nature-tech4all-iucn-wcc-nature-guardian.

Hunter, J.R. (1994). "Is Costa Rica Truly Conservation-minded?" *Conservation Biology* 8(2): 592–595.

IBISWorld. (2015). *Global Oil and Gas Exploration and Production: Market Research Report.* http://www.ibisworld/globalindustry/global-oil-gas-exploration-production.html.

Igoe, J. (2004). *Conservation and Globalization: A Study of Indigenous Communities and National Parks from East Africa to South Dakota.* Belmont, CA: Wadsworth/Thompson.

Igoe, J., and D. Brockington. (2007). "Neoliberal Conservation: A Brief Introduction." *Conservation and Society* 5(4): 432–449.

Igoe, J., K. Neves, and D. Brockington. (2010). "A Spectacular Eco-tour around the Historic Bloc: Theorising the Convergence of Biodiversity Conservation and Capitalist Expansion." *Antipode* 42(3): 486–512.

Inflection Point. (n.d.). "Our Mission." http://www.inflectionpointcm.com/our-mission.

Intergovernmental Panel on Climate Change (IPCC). (2014) *Climate Change 2014: Impacts, Adaptation, and Vulnerability.* http://www.ipcc.ch/report/ar5/wg2/.

———. (2021) *Climate Change 2021: The Physical Science Basis.* https://www.ipcc.ch/report/ar6/wg1/.

International Institute for Environment and Development (IIED). (2015). *REDD+ and the Private Sector: Tapping into Domestic Markets. IIED Briefing,* November 2015. http://pubs.iied.org/pdfs/17319IIED.pdf.

International Institute for Sustainable Development (IISD). 2016. "Coalition for Private Investment in Conservation, Natural Capital Protocol Presented at IUCN WCC." News, September 3. http:// sdg.iisd.org/news/coalition-for-private-investment-in-conservation-natural-capital-protocolpresented-at-iucn-wcc/.

International Monetary Fund (IMF). (2009). *2009 Annual Report.* Geneva: IMF.

International Union for the Conservation of Nature (IUCN). (2015). *No Net Loss and Net Positive Impact Approaches for Biodiversity.* Gland, Switzerland: IUCN.

Isla, A. (2015). *The "Greening" of Costa Rica: Women, Peasants, Indigenous Peoples, and the Remaking of Nature.* Toronto, ON: University of Toronto Press.

Isenhour, C. (2016). "Unearthing Human Progress? Ecomodernism and Contrasting Definitions of Technological Progress in the Anthropocene." *Economic Anthropology* 3(2): 315–328.

Isenhour, C., and K. Feng. (2016). "Decoupling and Displaced Emissions: On Swedish Consumers, Chinese Producers and Policy to Address the Climate Impact of Consumption." *Journal of Cleaner Production* 134: 320–329.

Jackson, T. (2011). *Prosperity without Growth: Economics for a Finite Planet*. New York: Routledge.

Jacques, M. (2016). "The Death of Neoliberalism and the Crisis in Western Politics." *The Guardian*, August 21. https://www.theguardian.com/commentisfree/2016/aug/21/death-of-neoliberalism-crisis-in-western-politics.

Jameson, F. (2003). "Future City." *New Left Review* 21: 65–79.

Jay, M. (1996). *The Dialectical Imagination: A History of the Frankfurt School and the Institute of Social Research, 1923–1950*. Berkeley: University of California Press.

Johns, D. 2014. "With Friends Like These, Wilderness and Biodiversity Do Not Need Enemies." In *Keeping the Wild: Against the Domestication of Earth*, G. Wuerthner, E. Crist, and T. Butler, eds. New York: Island Press.

Jordan, A., T. Rayner, H. Schroeder, N. Adger, K. Anderson, A., Bows, C. Le Quéré, M. Joshi, S. Mander, N. Vaughan, and L. Whitmarsh. (2013). "Going beyond Two Degrees? The Risks and Opportunities of Alternative Options." *Climate Policy* 13: 751–769.

Juniper, T. (2013). *What Has Nature Ever Done for Us? How Money Really Does Grow on Trees*. London: Profile Books.

Kaihao, W. (2018). "Cooperation: The WWF and Tech Company Intel Use Artificial Intelligence to Help with the Conservation of Endangered Amur Tigers." *China Daily*, August 4. https://www.pressreader.com/hong-kong/china-daily/20180804/282020443108617.

Kallis, G. (2011). "In Defense of Degrowth." *Ecological Economics* 70: 873–881.

———. (2018). *Degrowth (The Economy: Key Ideas)*. New York: Agenda Publishing.

———. (2019a). *Limits: Why Malthus Was Wrong and Why Environmentalists Should Care*. Stanford, CA: Stanford University Press.

———. (2019b). "Socialism without Growth." *Capitalism Nature Socialism* 30(2): 189–206.

Kallis, G., C. Kerschner, and J. Martinez-Alier. (2012a). "The Economics of Degrowth." *Ecological Economics* 84: 172–180.

———, eds. (2012b). *Ecological Economics* 84, special section on "The Economics of Degrowth."

Kallis, G., V. Kostakis, S. Lange, B. Muraca, S. Paulson, and M. Schmelzer. (2018). "Research on Degrowth." *Annual Review of Environment and Resources* 43: 291–316.

Kallis, G., S. Paulson, G. D'Alisa, and F. Demaria. (2020). *The Case for Degrowth*. New York: John Wiley & Sons.

Kallis, G., F. Schneider, and J. Martinez-Alier, eds. (2010). *Journal of Cleaner Production* 18(6), special issue on "Growth, Recession or Degrowth for Social Equity and Sustainability."

Kapoor, I. (2005). "Participatory Development, Complicity and Desire." *Third World Quarterly* 26(8): 1203–1220.

———. (2014). "Psychoanalysis and Development: Contributions, Examples, Limits." *Third World Quarterly* 35(7): 1120–1143.

———. (2015). "What 'Drives' Capitalist Development." *Human Geography* 8(3): 66–78.

———. (2017). "Cold Critique, Faint Passion, Bleak Future: Post-Development's Surrender to Global Capitalism." *Third World Quarterly* 38(12): 2664–2683.

———. (2020). *Confronting Desire: Psychoanalysis and International Development.* Ithaca, NY: Cornell University Press.

Kareiva, P., H. Tallis, T.H. Ricketts, G.C. Daily, and S. Polasky, eds. (2011). *Natural Capital: Theory and Practice of Mapping Ecosystem Services.* Oxford, UK: Oxford University Press.

Kay, C. (2002). "Why East Asia Overtook Latin America: Agrarian Reform, Industrialisation and Development." *Third World Quarterly* 23(6): 1073–1102.

Kelly, P. (2005). "Scale, Power and the Limits to Possibilities. A Commentary on J.K. Gibson-Graham's 'Surplus Possibilities: Postdevelopment and Community Economies.'" *Singapore Journal of Tropical Geography* 26: 39–43.

Keucheyan, R. (2016). *Nature Is a Battlefield: Towards a Political Ecology.* New York: Wiley.

Kiely, R. (2018). *The Neoliberal Paradox.* London: Edward Elgar Publishing.

———. (2021). "Conservatism, Neoliberalism and Resentment in Trumpland: The 'Betrayal' and 'Reconstruction' of the United States." *Geoforum* 124: 334–342.

Kiernan, M.J. (2009). *Investing in a Sustainable World: Why Green Is the New Color of Money on Wall Street.* New York: Amacom.

Kirsch, S. (2010). "Sustainable Mining." *Dialectical Anthropology* 34(1): 87–93.

Klein, N. (2007). *The Shock Doctrine: The Rise of Disaster Capitalism.* New York: Metropolitan Books.

———. (2014). *This Changes Everything: Capitalism vs. the Climate.* New York: Simon & Schuster.

Kleiner, D. (2016). "Universal Basic Income Is a Neoliberal Plot to Make You Poorer." *OpenDemocracy*, November 25. https://neweconomics.opendemocracy.net /universal-basic-income-is-a-neoliberal-plot-to-make-you-poorer/.

Konings, M. (2009). "The Ups and Downs of a Liberal Consciousness, Or, Why Paul Krugman Should Learn to Tarry with the Negative." *Ephemera* 9(4): 350–356.

Kothari, A., A. Salleh, A. Escobar, F. Demaria, and A. Acosta, eds. (2019). *Pluriverse: A Post-development Dictionary.* Oxford: Oxford University Press.

Kull, C.A., C.K. Ibrahim, and T.C. Meredith. (2007). "Tropical Forest Transitions and Globalization: Neo-liberalism, Migration, Tourism, and International Conservation Agendas." *Society & Natural Resources* 20(8): 723–737.

Laidlaw, J. (2016). "Through a Glass, Darkly." *Hau: Journal of Ethnographic Theory* 6(2): 17–24.

Lakoff, G. (2009). *The Political Mind.* New York: Penguin.

Langholz, J.A. (2003). "Privatizing Conservation." In *Contested Nature*, S.R. Brechin, P.R. Wilshusen, C.L. Fortwangler, and P.C. West, eds. Albany: State University of New York Press.

Lansing, D. (2013). "Understanding Linkages between Ecosystem Service Payments, Forest Plantations, and Export Agriculture." *Geoforum* 47: 103–112.

Lansing, D., R.C. Collard, J. Dempsey, J. Sundberg, N. Heynen, B. Büscher, W. Dressler, and R. Fletcher. (2015). Review symposium of *Nature™ Inc.: Environmental Conservation in the Neoliberal Age. Environment and Planning A* 47(11): 2389–2408.

Latour, B. (2004). "Why Has Critique Run Out of Steam? From Matters of Fact to Matters of Concern." *Critical Inquiry* 30(2): 225–248.

Layton, L. (2009). "Irrational Exuberance: Neoliberal Subjectivity and the Perversion of Truth." *Subjectivity* 3(3): 303–322.

Le Billon, P. (2021). "Crisis Conservation and Green Extraction: Biodiversity Offsets as Spaces of Double Exception." *Journal of Political Ecology* 28(1): 854–888.

Leinonen, S. (n.d.). "Unprofitable Endangered Species." Seppo.net. http://www.seppo.net/cartoons/displayimage.php?pos=-816.

Lelkes, O. (2021). *Sustainable Hedonism: A Thriving Life that Does Not Cost the Earth*. Bristol, UK: Bristol University Press.

Lemke, T. (2001). "'The Birth of Bio-politics': Michel Foucault's Lecture at the Collège de France on Neo-liberal Governmentality." *Economy and Society* 30(2): 190–207.

Lertzman, R.A. (2013). "The Myth of Apathy: Psychoanalytic Explorations of Environmental Subjectivity." In *Engaging with Climate Change: Psychoanalytic and Interdisciplinary Perspectives*, S. Weintrobe, ed. New York: Routledge.

Levine, A. (2002). "Convergence or Convenience? International Conservation NGOs and Development Assistance in Tanzania." *World Development* 30(6): 1043–1055.

Li, T.M. (2005). "Beyond 'the State' and Failed Schemes." *American Anthropologist* 107(3): 383–394.

———. (2007). *The Will to Improve: Governmentality, Development, and the Practice of Politics*. Durham, NC: Duke University Press.

———. (2010). "To Make Live or Let Die? Rural Dispossession and the Protection of Surplus Populations." *Antipode* 41 : 66–93.

———. (2014). "Anthropological Engagements with Development." *Anthropologie & Développement* 37–38–39 : 227–240.

Liboiron, M. (2021). *Pollution Is Colonialism*. Durham, NC: Duke University Press.

Lin, C.C.T., C. Minca, and M. Ormond. (2018). "Affirmative Biopolitics: Social and Vocational Education for Quechua Girls in the Postcolonial 'Affectsphere' of Cusco, Peru." *Environment and Planning D: Society and Space* 36(5): 885–904.

Liodakis, G. (2018). "Capital, Economic Growth, and Socio-Ecological Crisis: A Critique of De-Growth." *International Critical Thought* 8(1): 46–65.

Lochhead, C. (2013). "Population Growth Increases Climate Fear." *SFGate*, September 2. https://www.sfgate.com/science/article/Population-growth-increases-climate-fear-4781833.php.

Locke, H. (2014). "Green Postmodernism and the Attempted Hijacking of Conservation." In *Keeping the Wild: Against the Domestication of Earth*, G. Wuerthner, E. Crist, and T. Butler, eds. New York: Island Press.

Lohmann, L. (2009). "Neoliberalism and the Calculable World: The Rise of Carbon Trading." In *Upsetting the Offset*, S. Böhm and S. Dabhi, eds. London: MayFly Books.

———. (2011). "The Endless Algebra of Climate Markets." *Capitalism Nature Socialism* 22(4): 93–116.

Long, N. (2003). *Development Sociology: Actor Perspectives.* New York: Routledge.

Loperena, C.A. (2016). "Conservation by Racialized Dispossession: The Making of an Eco-destination on Honduras's North Coast." *Geoforum* 69: 184–193.

Lukács, G. (1985). *History and Class Consciousness.* R. Livingstone, trans. Cambridge, MA: MIT Press.

Lukes, S. (2004). *Power: A Radical View.* 2nd ed. New York: Macmillan International Higher Education.

Lund, J.F., E. Ungusia, M.B. Mabele, and A. Scheba. (2017). "Promising Change, Delivering Continuity: REDD+ as Conservation Fad." *World Development* 89: 124–139.

Lunstrum, E. (2014). "Green Militarization: Anti-Poaching Efforts and the Spatial Contours of Kruger National Park." *Annals of the Association of American Geographers* 104(4): 816–832.

———. (2017). "Feed Them to the Lions: Conservation Violence Goes Online." *Geoforum* 79: 134–143.

Lyotard, J.-F. (1993). *Libidinal Economy.* Bloomington: Indiana University Press.

MacDonald, C.C. (2009). "A Good Cause Gone Bad." *Adbusters* #81. https://www.adbusters.org/magazine/81/environment.html.

MacDonald, K.I. (2010a). "Business, Biodiversity and New 'Fields' of Conservation: The World Conservation Congress and the Renegotiation of Organizational Order." *Conservation and Society* 8(4): 256–275.

———. (2010b). "The Devil Is in the (Bio)diversity: Private Sector 'Engagement' and the Restructuring of Biodiversity Conservation." *Antipode* 42(3): 513–50.

MacDonald, K.I., and C. Corson. (2012). "'TEEB Begins Now': A Virtual Moment in the Production of Natural Capital." *Development and Change* 43(1): 159–184.

Mackey, B. (2014). "The Future of Conservation: An Australian Perspective." In *Keeping the Wild: Against the Domestication of Earth*, G. Wuerthner, E. Crist, and T. Butler, eds. New York: Island Press.

Magdoff, F., and J.B. Foster. (2011). *What Every Environmentalist Needs to Know about Capitalism: A Citizen's Guide to Capitalism and the Environment.* New York: New York University Press.

Malm, A. (2016). *Fossil Capital: The Rise of Steam-Power and the Roots of Global Warming.* London: Verso.

———. (2021). *How to Blow Up a Pipeline.* London: Verse.

Mann, C.C. (2005). *1491.* New York: Vintage.

Marcuse, H. (1966). *Eros and Civilization.* Boston: Beacon.

Mariqueo-Russell, A., and R. Read. (2019). "Fully Automated Luxury Barbarism." *Radical Philosophy* 2: 108–110.

Martinez-Alier, J. (2003). *The Environmentalism of the Poor: A Study of Ecological Conflicts and Valuation.* Cheltenham, UK: Edward Elgar.

———. (2009). "Socially Sustainable Economic De-growth." *Development and Change* 40(6): 1099–1119.

Mascarenhas, M. (2017). *New Humanitarianism and the Crisis of Charity: Good Intentions on the Road to Help.* Bloomington: Indiana University Press.

Massarella, K., S.M. Sallu, J.E. Ensor, and R. Marchant. (2018). "REDD+, Hype, Hope and Disappointment: The Dynamics of Expectations in Conservation and Development Pilot Projects." *World Development* 109: 375–385.

Matthews, S. (2004). "Post-Development Theory and the Question of Alternatives: A View from Africa." *Third World Quarterly* 25(2): 373–384.

Matulis, B.S. (2013). "The Narrowing Gap between Vision and Execution: Neoliberalization of PES in Costa Rica." *Geoforum* 41: 253–260.

Maxwell, J.C. (2000). *Failing Forward: Turning Mistakes into Stepping Stones for Success.* New York: Harper Collins.

Mbembe, J.A. (2003). "Necropolitics." *Public Culture* 15(1): 11–40.

McAfee, K. (1999). "Selling Nature to Save It? Biodiversity and Green Developmentalism." *Environment and Planning D* 17(1): 133–154.

———. (2012a). "The Contradictory Logic of Global Ecosystem Services Markets." *Development and Change* 43(1): 105–131.

———. (2012b). "Nature in the Market-World: Ecosystem Services and Inequality." *Development* 55(1): 25–33.

McAfee, K., and E.N. Shapiro. (2010). "Payments for Ecosystem Services in Mexico: Nature, Neoliberalism, Social Movements, and the State." *Annals of the Association of American Geographers* 100(3): 579–599.

McCarthy, J. (2019). "Authoritarianism, Populism, and the Environment: Comparative Experiences, Insights, and Perspectives." *Annals of the American Association of Geographers* 109(2): 301–313.

McCauley, D.J. (2006). "Selling Out on Nature." *Nature* 443(7): 27–28.

———. (2015). "Fool's Gold in the Catskill Mountains: Thinking Critically about the Ecosystem Services Paradigm." In *Protecting the Wild. Parks and Wilderness, The Foundation for Conservation*, G. Wuerthner, E. Crist, and T. Butler, eds. Washington, DC: Island Press.

McElwee, P. (2012). "Payments for Environmental Services as Neoliberal Market-Based Forest Conservation in Vietnam: Panacea or Problem?" *Geoforum* 43(3): 412–426.

———. (2016). *Forests Are Gold: Trees, People and Environmental Rule in Vietnam.* Seattle: University of Washington Press.

McElwee, P., T. Nghiem, H. Le, H. Vu, and N. Tran. (2014). "Payments for Environmental Services and Contested Neoliberalisation in Developing Countries: A Case Study from Vietnam." *Journal of Rural Studies* 36: 423–440.

McGowan, T. (2017). *Capitalism and Desire: The Psychic Cost of Free Markets.* New York: Columbia University Press.

McGregor, A. (2009). "New Possibilities? Shifts in Post-Development Theory and Practice." *Geography Compass* 3(5): 1688–1702.

McKenzie, E., F. Irwin, J. Ranganathan, C. Hanson, C. Kousky, K. Bennett, S. Ruffo, M. Conte, J. Salzman, and J. Paavola. 2011. "Incorporating Ecosystem Services in Decisions." In *Natural Capital: Theory and Practice of Mapping Ecosystem Services*, P. Kareiva, H. Tallis, T.H. Ricketts, G.C. Daily, and S. Polasky, eds. Oxford, UK: Oxford University Press.

McMillan, C. (2008). "Symptomatic Readings: Žižekian Theory as a Discursive Strategy." *International Journal of Žižek Studies* 2(1): 1–22.

McNally, D.M. (2006). *Another World Is Possible: Globalization and Anti-Capitalism*. Revised ed. Monmouth, Wales: Merlin Press.

McShane, T.O., P.D. Hirsch, T.C. Trung, A.N. Songorwa, A. Kinzig, B. Monteferri, D. Mutekanga, H.V. Thang, J.L. Dammert, M. Pulgar-Vidal, M. Welch-Devine, J.P. Brosius, P. Coppolillo, and S. O'Connor. (2011). "Hard Choices: Making Trade-offs between Biodiversity Conservation and Human Well-Being." *Biological Conservation* 144(3): 966–972.

Meadows, D.H., D.L. Meadows, and J. Randers. (1972). *The Limits to Growth*. New York: Universe Books.

Merten, D.E. (1999). "Enculturation into Secrecy among Junior High School Girls." *Journal of Contemporary Ethnography* 28: 107–37.

Middeldorp, N., and P. Le Billon. (2019). "Deadly Environmental Governance: Authoritarianism, Eco-populism, and the Repression of Environmental and Land Defenders." *Annals of the American Association of Geographers* 109(2): 324–337.

Mikkelson, G., A. Gonzalez, and G.D. Peterson. (2007). "Economic Inequality Predicts Biodiversity Loss." *PloS ONE* 2(5). E444.doi:10.1371/journal.pone.0000444.

Milanovic, B. (2011). *Worlds Apart: Measuring International and Global Inequality*. Princeton, NJ: Princeton University Press

———. (2017). "The Illusion of 'Degrowth' in a Poor and Unequal World." *Global Inequality* (blog), November 18. http://glineq.blogspot.com/2017/11/the-illusion-of-degrowth-in-poor-and.html.

Milder, J.C., S.J. Scherr, and C. Bracer. (2010). "Trends and Future Potential of Payment for Ecosystem Services to Alleviate Rural Poverty in Developing Countries." *Ecology & Society* 15(2). http://www.ecologyandsociety.org/vol15/iss2/art4/.

Miller, C. (2003). "The AMISCONDE Partnership in Costa Rica." *Journal of Sustainable Forestry* 16(1): 15–37.

Miller, P., and N. Rose. (2008). *Governing the Present*. Cambridge: Polity Press.

Miller, S.W. (2007). *An Environmental History of Latin America*. Cambridge, UK: Cambridge University Press.

Milman, O. (2020). "Trump's Push to Reopen US Risks 'Death Sentence' for Many, Experts Warn." *The Guardian*, May 6. https://www.theguardian.com/us-news/2020/may/06/trump-economy-reopen-us-experts-warning.

Milne, S., and B. Adams. (2012). "Market Masquerades: Uncovering the Politics of Community-Level Payments for Environmental Services in Cambodia." *Development and Change* 43: 133–158.

Mishan, J. (1996). "Psychoanalysis and Environmentalism: First Thoughts." *Psychoanalytic Psychotherapy* 10: 59–70.

Mitchell, T. (1990). "Everyday Metaphors of Power." *Theory and Society* 19(5): 545–577.

Moberg, M., and S. Lyon, eds. (2010). *Fair Trade and Social Justice.* New York: New York University Press.

Molina, I., and S. Palmer. (2007). *The History of Costa Rica.* 2nd ed. San José: Editorial UCR.

Monbiot, G. (2013). "The Faith in Markets Is Misplaced: Only Governments Can Save Our Living Planet." *The Guardian*, April 22. http://www.guardian.co.uk /commentisfree/2013/apr/22/faith-markets-misplaced-governments-save-planet.

———. (2014). "It's Simple. If We Can't Change Our Economic System, Our Number's Up. *The Guardian*, May 27. https://www.theguardian.com/commentisfree /2014/may/27/if-we-cant-change-economic-system-our-number-is-up.

Mookherjee, N. (2006). "'Remembering to Forget': Public Secrecy and Memory of Sexual Violence in the Bangladesh War of 1971." *Journal of the Royal Anthropological Institute* 12: 433–450.

Mooney, H. (2011). "Forward." In *Natural Capital: Theory and Practice of Mapping Ecosystem Services*, P. Kareiva, H. Tallis, T.H. Ricketts, G.C. Daily, and S. Polasky, eds. Oxford, UK: Oxford University Press.

Moore, D.S. (1998). "Subaltern Struggles and the Politics of Place: Remapping Resistance in Zimbabwe's Eastern Highlands." *Cultural Anthropology* 13(3): 344–381.

Moore, J. (2014). "The End of Cheap Nature: Or How I Learned to Stop Worrying about 'the' Environment and Love the Crisis of Capitalism." In *Structures of the World Political Economy and the Future of Global Conflict and Cooperation*, C. Suter and C. Chase-Dunn, eds. Berlin: Lit Verlag.

Mosse, D. (2004). "Is Good Policy Unimplementable? Reflections on the Ethnography of Aid Policy and Practice." *Development and Change* 35(4): 639–671.

Mowforth, M., and I. Munt. (2003). *Tourism and Sustainability: New Tourism in the Third World.* 2nd ed. London: Routledge.

Mulder, M.B., and P. Coppolillo. (2005) *Conservation: Linking Ecology, Economics, and Culture.* Princeton, NJ: Princeton University Press.

Muradian, R., M. Arsel, L. Pellegrini, F. Adaman, B. Aguilar, B. Agarwal, E. Corbera, D. Ezzine, J. Farley, G. Froger, E. Garcia-Frapolli, E. Gómez-Baggethun, and J. Gowdy. (2013). "Payments for Ecosystem Services and the Fatal Attraction of Win-Win Solutions." *Conservation Letters* 6: 274–279.

Muradian, R., E. Corbera, U. Pascual, N. Kosoy, and P.H. May. (2010). "Reconciling Theory and Practice: An Alternative Conceptual Framework for Understanding Payments for Environmental Services." *Ecological Economics* 69: 1202–1208.

Muradian, R., and E. Gómez-Baggethun. (2013). "The Institutional Dimension of 'Market-Based Instruments' for Governing Ecosystem Services." *Society & Natural Resources* 26(10): 1113–1121.

Myers, J.P., and J.S. Reichert. (1997). "Perspectives on Nature's Services." In *Nature's Services: Society's Dependence on Natural Ecosystems*, G.C. Daily, ed. Washington, DC: Island Press.

Nader, L. (1969). "Up the Anthropologist—Perspective Gained from Studying Up." In *Reinventing Anthropology*, D. Hymes, ed. New York: Pantheon.

Natural Capital Coalition (NCC). (2016). *Natural Capital Protocol*. London: NCC.

Neimark, B. (2012). "Green Grabbing at the 'Pharm' Gate: Rosy Periwinkle Production in Southern Madagascar." *Journal of Peasant Studies* 39(2): 423–445.

Nelson, A. (2022). *Beyond Money: A Postcapitalist Strategy*. London: Pluto Press.

Nelson, S. (2014). "Resilience and the Neoliberal Counterrevolution: From Ecologies of Control to Production of the Common." *Resilience* 2(1): 1–17.

Neves, K. (2004). "Revisiting the Tragedy of the Commons: Ecological Dilemmas of Whale Watching in the Azores." *Human Organization* 63(3): 289–300.

———. (2010). "Cashing in on Cetourism: A Critical Engagement with Dominant E-NGO Discourses on Whaling, Cetacean Conservation, and Whale Watching." *Antipode* 42(3): 719–741.

New Climate Economy (NCE). (2014). "Better Growth, Better Climate." http://2014.newclimateeconomy.report/.

———. (2015). "Seizing the Global Opportunity." http://2015.newclimateeconomy.report/.

Newswire. (2011). "Declaration of the Indigenous Peoples of the World at COP 17." *Newswire*, December 7. http://intercontinentalcry.org/newswire/declaration-of-the-indigenous-peoples-of-the-world-at-cop-17/.

Nilsen, A.G. (2021). "Give James Ferguson a Fish." *Development and Change* 52(1): 3–25.

Nirmal, P., and D. Rocheleau. (2019). "Decolonizing Degrowth in the Post-development Convergence: Questions, Experiences, and Proposals from Two Indigenous Territories." *Environment and Planning E: Nature and Space* 2(3): 465–492.

North, P. (2008). "Review of *A Postcapitalist Politics*." *Progress in Human Geography* 32(3): 477–481.

Obeng-Odoom, F. (2012). "Review of *Envisioning Real Utopias*." *Capital & Class* 36(1): 185–187.

O'Connor, J. (1988). "Capitalism, Nature, and Socialism: A Theoretical Introduction." *Capitalism Nature Socialism* 1: 11–38.

———. (1994). "Is Sustainable Capitalism Possible?" In *Food for the Future: Conditions and Contradictions of Sustainability*, P. Allen, ed. New York: Wiley-Interscience.

O'Hagan, E.M. (2017). "Love the Idea of a Universal Basic Income? Be Careful What You Wish For." *The Guardian*, June 23. https://www.theguardian.com/commentisfree/2017/jun/23/universal-basic-income-ubi-welfare-state.

Ojakangas, M. (2005). "Impossible Dialogue on Bio-power: Agamben and Foucault." *Foucault Studies* 2: 5–28.

Organisation for Economic Cooperation and Development (OECD). (2014). *Green Growth Indicators*. Paris: OECD.

Ortner, S. (1984). "Theory in Anthropology since the Sixties." *Comparative Studies in Society and History* 26(1): 126–166.

Ostrom, E. (1990). *Governing the Commons: The Evolution of Institutions for Collective Action*. Cambridge, UK: Cambridge University Press.

Ostrom, E., J. Burger, C.B. Field, R.B. Norgaard, and D. Policansky. (1999). "Revisiting the Commons: Local Lessons, Global Challenges." *Science* 284: 278–282.

Ostrom, E., and M. Cox. (2011). "Moving beyond Panaceas: A Multi-tiered Diagnostic Approach for Social-Ecological Analysis." *Environmental Conservation* 37(4): 451–463.

Ostry, J.D., P. Loungani, and D. Furceri. (2016). "Neoliberalism: Oversold." *Finance & Development* 53(2): 38–41.

Papua New Guinea and Costa Rica. (2005). *Reducing Emissions from Deforestation in Developing Countries: Approaches to Stimulate Action*. United Nations Framework Convention on Climate Change. http://unfccc.int/resource/docs/2005/cop11/eng/misc01.pdf.

Pagiola, S. (2002). "Paying for Water Services in Central America: Learning from Costa Rica." In *Selling Forest Environmental Services: Market-Based Mechanisms for Conservation*, S. Pagiola, J. Bishop, and N. Landell-Mills, eds. London: Earthscan.

———. (2008). "Payments for Environmental Services in Costa Rica." *Ecological Economics* 65: 712–724.

Palfrey, R., J. Oldekop, and G. Holmes. (2021). "Conservation and Social Outcomes of Private Protected Areas." *Conservation Biology* 35(4): 1098–1110.

Pandya, R. (2022). "An Intersectional Approach to Neoliberal Environmentality: Women's Engagement with Ecotourism at Corbett Tiger Reserve, India." *Environment and Planning E: Nature and Space*: 25148486221082469.

Park, J., K. Conca, and M. Finger. (2008). *The Crisis of Global Environmental Governance*. London: Routledge.

Patel, R. (2010). *The Value of Nothing: How to Remake Market Society and Redefine Democracy*. New York: Picador.

Peck, J. (2010a). *Constructions of Neoliberal Reason*. Oxford: Oxford University Press.

———. (2010b). "Zombie Neoliberalism and the Ambidextrous State." *Theoretical Criminology* 14: 104–110.

Peck, J., and N. Theodore. (2015). *Fast Policy*. Minneapolis: University of Minnesota Press.

Peck J., and A. Tickell. (2002). "Neoliberalizing Space." *Antipode* 34: 380–404.

Pellegrini, L., and A. Dasgupta. (2011). "Land Reform in Bolivia: The Forestry Question." *Conservation & Society* 9(4): 274–285

Pena, P. (2014). *The Politics of the Diffusion of Conditional Cash Transfers in Latin America*. Brooks World Poverty Institute Working Paper no. 201, University of Manchester, UK.

Perfecto, I., and J. Vandermeer. (2008). "Biodiversity Conservation in Tropical Agroecosystems: A New Conservation Paradigm." *Annals of the New York Academy of Sciences* 1134: 173–200.

Peters, M. (2008). "The Global Failure of Neoliberalism: Privatize Profits; Socialize Losses." *Global-e*, November 6. http://global-ejournal.org/2008/11/06/the-global-failure-of-neoliberalism-privatize-profits-socialize-losses/.

———. (2018). "The End of Neoliberal Globalization and the Rise of Authoritarian Populism." *Educational Philosophy and Theory* 50(4): 323–25.

Peterson, M., D. Hall, A. Feldpausch-Parker, and T. Peterson. (2009). "Obscuring Ecosystem Function with Application of the Ecosystem Services Concept." *Conservation Biology* 24(1): 113–119.

Phelps, J., E.L. Webb, and A. Agrawal. (2010). "Does REDD+ Threaten to Recentralize Forest Governance?" *Science* 328: 312–13.

Piketty, T. (2014). *Capital in the Twenty-first Century*. A. Goldhammer, trans. Cambridge, MA: Belknap Press.

Pirard, R. (2012). "Market-Based Instruments for Biodiversity and Ecosystem Services: A Lexicon." *Environ. Sci. Policy* 19–20: 59–68.

Pirard, R., and R. Lapeyre. (2014). "Classifying Market-Based Instruments for Ecosystem Services: A Guide to the Literature Jungle." *Ecosystem Services* 9: 106–114.

Polanyi, K. (1944). *The Great Transformation. The Political and Economic Origins of Our Time*. Boston: Beacon.

Polaski, S., G. Caldarone, T.K. Duarte, J. Goldstein, N. Hannahs, T. Ricketts, and H. Tallis. (2011). "Putting Ecosystem Service Models to Work: Conservation, Management, or Trade-offs." In *Natural Capital: Theory and Practice of Mapping Ecosystem Services*, P. Kareiva, H. Tallis, T.H. Ricketts, G.C. Daily, and S. Polasky, eds. Oxford, UK: Oxford University Press.

Ponse, B. (1976). "Secrecy in the Lesbian World." *Urban Life* 5(3): 313–338.

Porras, I. (2010). *Fair and Green? Social Impacts of Payments for Environmental Services in Costa Rica*. London: International Institute for Environment and Development (IIED).

Prins, G., M. Cook, C. Green, M. Hulme, A. Korhola, and E.R. Korhola. (2009) *How to Get Climate Policy Back on Course*. Institute for Science, Innovation and Policy (University of Oxford) and the LSE mackinder Programme. www.lse.ac.uk/collections/mackinderProgramme/.

Rahnema, M., and V. Bawtree, eds. (1997). *The Post-Development Reader*. London: Zed.

Rainforest Foundation UK. (2017). "Failing Forests: The World Bank's Flagship REDD+ Programme Ten Years On." News, December 11. http://www.rainforestfoundationuk.org/failing-forests-the-world-banks-flagship-redd-programme-ten-years-on.

Ramírez Cover, A. (2017). *A Political Ecology of Neoliberal Multiculturalism: Social Inclusion and Market-Based Conservation in Indigenous Costa Rica*. PhD dissertation, International Institute of Social Studies, The Hague, the Netherlands.

Rappel, I.J., and N.H. Thomas. (1998). "An Examination of the Compatibility of World Bank Policies towards Population, Development and Biodiversity in the Third World." *The Environmentalist* 18: 95–108.

Reddy, S.G. (2008). "The World Bank's New Poverty Estimates: Digging Deeper into a Hole." *Challenge* 51(6): 105–112

Redford, K.H., and W.A. Adams. (2009). "Payment for Ecosystem Services and the Challenge of Saving Nature." *Conservation Biology* 23(4): 785–787.

Redford, K.H., C. Padoch, and T. Sunderland. (2013). "Fads, Funding, and Forgetting in Three Decades of Conservation." *Conservation Biology* 27: 437–438.

Reid, J. (2013). "Interrogating the Neoliberal Biopolitics of the Sustainable Development-Resilience Nexus." *International Political Sociology* 7: 353–367.

Resnick, S.A., and R.D. Wolff. (2002). *Class Theory and History: Capitalism and Communism in the USSR.* London: Routledge.

Rival, L. (2010). "Ecuador's Yasuní-ITT Initiative: The Old and New Values of Petroleum." *Ecological Economics* 70(2): 358–365.

Robertson, M.M. (2000). "No Net Loss: Wetland Restoration and the Incomplete Capitalization of Nature." *Antipode* 32(4): 463–493.

———. (2004). "The Neoliberalization of Ecosystem Services: Wetland Mitigation Banking and Problems in Environmental Governance." *Geoforum* 35(3): 361–373.

Robinson, W.I. (2003). *Transnational Conflicts: Central America, Social Change, and Globalization.* London: Verso.

———. (2008). *Latin America and Global Capitalism: A Critical Globalization Perspective.* Baltimore, MA: Johns Hopkins University Press.

———. (2014). *Global Capitalism and the Crisis of Humanity.* Cambridge, UK: Cambridge University Press.

Robbins, P., and S.A. Moore. (2013). "Ecological Anxiety Disorder: Diagnosing the Politics of the Anthropocene." *Cultural Geographies* 20: 3–19.

Rojas, M., and B. Aylward. (2003). *What Are We Learning from Experiences with Markets for Environmental Services in Costa Rica? A Review and Critique of the Literature.* London: International Institute for Environment and Development (IIED).

Rondinelli, D.A. (1993). *Development Projects as Policy Experiments: An Adaptive Approach to Development Administration.* New York: Psychology Press.

Rosa, H. (2019). *Resonance: A Sociology of our Relationship to the World.* Cambridge: Polity.

Rose, N., P. O'Malley, and M. Valverde. (2006). "Governmentality." *Annu. Rev. Law Soc. Sci.* 2: 83–104.

Rosero, L., T. Maldonado-Ulloa, and R. Bonilla-Carrio. (2002). "Bosque y Poblacion en la Peninsula de Osa, Costa Rica." *Revista Biologia Tropical* 50(2): 585–598.

Roy, A. (2010). *Poverty Capital: Microfinance and the Making of Development.* London: Routledge.

Rustin, M. (2013). "Reply: How Is Climate Change an Issue for Psychoanalysis?" In *Engaging with Climate Change: Psychoanalytic and Interdisciplinary Perspectives,* S. Weintrobe, ed. New York: Routledge.

Saad-Filho, A. (2016). "Social Policy Beyond Neoliberalism: From Conditional Cash Transfers to Pro-Poor Growth." *Journal of Poverty Alleviation and International Development* 7(1): 67–93.

Sachs, J. (2006). *The Millennium Villages Project: A New Approach to Ending Poverty.* Washington, DC: Centre for Global Development.

———. (2015). *The Age of Sustainable Development.* New York: Columbia University Press.

Saed, ed. (2012). "Introduction to the Degrowth Symposium." *Capitalism Nature Socialism* 23(1).

Salzman, J., G. Bennett, N. Carroll, A. Goldstein, and M. Jenkins. (2018). "The Global Status and Trends of Payments for Ecosystem Services." *Nature Sustainability* 1(3): 136–144.

Samers, M. (2005). "The Myopia of 'Diverse Economies,' or a Critique of the 'Informal Economy.'" *Antipode* 37(5): 875–886.

Sánchez-Azofeifa, G.A., A. Pfaff, J.A. Robalino, and J.P. Boomhower. (2007). "Costa Rica's Payment for Environmental Services Program: Intention, Implementation, and Impact." *Conservation Biology* 21: 1165–1173.

Sandbrook, C., J. Fisher, and B. Vira. (2013). "What Do Conservationists Think about Markets?" *Geoforum* 50: 232–240.

Sandler, B. (1994). "Grow or Die: Marxist Theories of Capitalism and the Environment." *Rethinking Marxism* 7(2): 38–57.

Sapinski, J.P., H.J. Buck, and A. Malm, eds. (2020). *Has It Come to This? The Promises and Perils of Geoengineering on the Brink*. Rutgers, NJ: Rutgers University Press.

Sarmiento Barletti, J.P., and A.M. Larson. (2017). *Rights Abuse Allegations in the Context of REDD+ Readiness and Implementation: A Preliminary Review and Proposal for Moving Forward*. Bangor, Indonesia: CIFOR.

Sato, C. (2006). "Subjectivity, Enjoyment, and Development: Preliminary Thoughts on a New Approach to Postdevelopment." *Rethinking Marxism* 18(2): 273–288.

Savran, D. (1998). *Taking It Like a Man: White Masculinity, Masochism, and Contemporary American Culture*. Princeton, NJ: Princeton University Press.

Schlesinger, S.C. (1999). *Bitter Fruit: The Story of the American Coup in Guatemala*. Cambridge, MA: Harvard University Press.

Schmelzer, M., A. Vetter, and A. Vansintjan. (2022). *The Future Is Degrowth: A Guide to a World beyond Capitalism*. London: Verso.

Schmidheiny, S. (1992). *Changing Course: A Global Business Perspective on Development and the Environment*. Cambridge, MA: MIT Press.

Scott, J.C. (1990). *Domination and the Arts of Resistance*. New Haven, CT: Yale University Press.

———. (1998). *Seeing Like a State: How Certain Schemes to Improve the Human Condition Have Failed*. New Haven, CT: Yale University Press.

Sekulova, F., G. Kallis, B. Rodríguez-Labajos, and F. Schneider, eds. (2013). *Journal of Cleaner Production* 38, special issue on "Degrowth: From Theory to Practice."

Shapiro-Garza, E. (2013). "Contesting the Market-Based Nature of Mexico's National Payments for Ecosystem Services Programs: Four Sites of Articulation and Hybridization." *Geoforum* 46: 5–15.

Shade, L. (2015). "Sustainable Development or Sacrifice Zone? Politics Below the Surface in Post-neoliberal Ecuador." *The Extractive Industries and Society* 2(4): 775–784.

Shaw, G. (2016). "Going into Business for Wildlife Conservation." *Stanford Social Innovation Review*, April 12. https://ssir.org/articles/entry/going_into_business_for_wildlife_conservation?s=03#bio-footer.

Shaw, I.G., and M. Waterstone. (2019). *Wageless Life: A Manifesto for a Future beyond Capitalism*. Minneapolis: University of Minnesota Press.

Sierra, R., and E. Russman. (2006). "On the Efficiency of Environmental Service Payments: A Forest Conservation Assessment in the Osa Peninsula, Costa Rica." *Ecological Economics* 59: 131–141.

Silva, E. (2003). "Selling Sustainable Development and Shortchanging Social Ecology in Costa Rican Forest Policy." *Latin American Politics and Society* 45(3): 93–127.

Simmel, G. (1950). *The Sociology of Georg Simmel*. K. Wolff, trans and ed. London: Free Press.

Simpson, R.D. (2004). "Conserving Biodiversity through Markets: A Better Approach." *PERC Policy Series* PS-32: 1–28.

Singh, N.M. (2013). "The Affective Labor of Growing Forests and the Becoming of Environmental Subjects: Rethinking Environmentality in Odisha, India." *Geoforum* 47: 189–198.

———. (2015). "Payments for Ecosystem Services and the Gift Paradigm: Sharing the Burden and Joy of Environmental Care." *Ecological Economics* 117: 53–61.

———. (2017). "Becoming a Commoner: The Commons as Sites for Affective Socio-nature Encounters and Co-becomings." *Ephemera* 17(4): 751–776.

Sioh, M. (2014). "Manicheism Delirium: Desire and Disavowal in the Libidinal Economy of an Emerging Economy." *Third World Quarterly* 35(7): 1162–1178.

Sklair, L. (2001). *The Transnational Capitalist Class*. Oxford: Blackwell.

Sloterdijk, P. (1988). *Critique of Cynical Reason*. Minneapolis: University of Minnesota Press.

Sorkin, A.R. (2016). "A New Fund Seeks Both Financial and Social Returns." *The New York Times*, December 19. https://www.nytimes.com/2016/12/19/business /dealbook/a-new-fund-seeks-both-financial-and-social-returns.html.

Soper, K. (2020). *Post-growth Living: For an Alternative Hedonism*. London: Verso.

Soto, M.M. (2010). "Ticos Protegerán Bosques con Tarjeta Bancaria y Ecomarchamo." *La Nacion*, November 21. http://www.nacion.com/2010-10-22/AldeaGlobal /NotaPrincipal/AldeaGlobal2563315.aspx.

Spash, C.L. (2014). *Better Growth, Helping the Paris Cop-Out? Fallacies and Omissions of the New Climate Economy Report*. Vienna: University of Economics and Business. SRE-Discussion 2014/04.

Spelhaug, J. (2018). "Cloud Computing and AI Help The Nature Conservancy Dive Deeper into Conservation." Microsoft, April 19. https://blogs.microsoft.com /green/2018/04/19/the-nature-conservancy-case-study/.

Springer, S. (2016). "The Violence of Neoliberalism." In *The Handbook of Neoliberalism*, S. Springer, K. Birch, and J. MacLeavy, eds. New York: Routledge.

Standing, G. (2017). *Basic Income: And How We Can Make It Happen*. New York: Penguin.

Stavrakakis, Y. (1997a). "Green Ideology: A Discursive Reading." *Journal of Political Ideologies* 2: 259–279.

———. (1997b). "Green Fantasy and the Real of Nature: Elements of a Lacanian Critique of Green Ideological Discourse." *Journal for the Psychoanalysis of Culture & Society* 2: 123–132.

———. (2007). *The Lacanian Left: Psychoanalysis, Theory, Politics.* Edinburgh: University of Edinburgh Press.

Steady State Manchester. (2014). "Less Levity Professor Stern! Economic Growth, Climate Change and the Decoupling Question." https://steadystatemanchester .net/2014/09/21/less-levity-professor-stern-economic-growth-climate-change -and-the-decoupling-question/.

Steger, M.B., and R.K. Roy. (2010). *Neoliberalism: A Very Short Introduction.* Oxford: Oxford University Press.

Steinberg, P.F. (2001). *Environmental Leadership in Developing Countries: Transnational Relations and Biodiversity Policy in Costa Rica and Bolivia.* Cambridge, MA: MIT Press.

Steinberger, J.K., F. Krausmann, M. Getzner, H. Schandl, and J. West. (2013). "Development and Dematerialization: An International Study." *PloS One* 8(10): e70385.

Steiner, A. (2011). "Forward." In *Decoupling Natural Resource Use and Environmental Impacts from Economic Growth.* Nairobi: UNEP.

Stem, C., J. Lassoie, D. Lee, and D. Deshler. (2003). "How 'Eco' Is Ecotourism? A Comparative Case Study of Ecotourism in Costa Rica." *Journal of Sustainable Tourism* 11(4): 322–347.

Stern, D.I. (2004). "The Rise and Fall of the Environmental Kuznets Curve." *World Development* 32(8): 1419–1439.

Stern, N., S. Peters, V. Bakhshi, A. Bowen, C. Cameron, S. Catovsky, D. Crane, S. Cruickshank, S. Dietz, and N. Edmonson. (2006). *Stern Review: The Economics of Climate Change.* London: Her Majesty's Treasury.

Stern, N. (2012). "Forward." In *Corporation 2020: Transforming Business for Tomorrow's World*, by P. Sukhdev. Washington, DC: Island Press.

Stiegler, B. (2010). *Taking Care of Youth and the Generations.* S. Barker, trans. Stanford, CA: Stanford University Press.

Stiglitz, J.E. (2008). "The End of Neoliberalism?" *Project Syndicate*, July 7. http:// www.project-syndicate.org/commentary/stiglitz101.

Stuit, A., D. Brockington, and E. Corbera. (2022). "Smart, Commodified and Encoded: Blockchain Technology for Environmental Sustainability and Nature Conservation." *Conservation & Society* 20(1): 12–23.

Sukhdev, P. (2011). "Three-Dimensional Capitalism." *The Guardian*, July 4. https:// www.theguardian.com/sustainable-business/blog/three-dimensional-capitalism -market-economy.

———. (2012). *Corporation 2020: Transforming Business for Tomorrow's World.* Washington, DC: Island Press.

Sullivan, S. (2006). "The Elephant in the Room? Problematizing 'New' (Neoliberal) Biodiversity Conservation." *Forum for Development Studies* 33(1): 105–135.

———. (2013a). "Banking Nature? The Spectacular Financialisation of Environmental Conservation." *Antipode* 45(1): 198–217.

———. (2013b). "After the Green Rush? Biodiversity Offsets, Uranium Power and the 'Calculus of Casualties' in Greening Growth." *Human Geography* 6(1): 80–101.

———. (2018). "Making Nature Investable: From Legibility to Leverageability in Fabricating 'Nature' as 'Natural Capital.'" *Science & Technology Studies* 31(3): 47–76.

Sultana, F. (2021). "Political Ecology 1: From Margins to Center." *Progress in Human Geography* 45(1): 156–165.

Sunderlin, W.D., E.O. Sills, A.E. Duchelle, A.D. Ekaputri, D. Kweka, M.A. Toniolo, S. Ball, N. Doggart, C.D. Pratama, J.T. Padilla, and A. Enright. (2015). "REDD+ at a Critical Juncture: Assessing the Limits of Polycentric Governance for Achieving Climate Change Mitigation." *International Forestry Review* 17(4): 400–413.

Svarstad, H., and T.A. Benjaminsen. (2017). "Nothing Succeeds Like Success Narratives: A Case of Conservation and Development in the time of REDD." *Journal of Eastern African Studies* 11(3): 482–505.

Svarstad, H., T.A. Benjaminsen, and R. Overå. (2018). "Power Theories in Political Ecology." *Journal of Political Ecology* 25: 350–363.

Swyngedouw, E. (2010). "Apocalypse Forever? Post-Political Populism and the Spectre of Climate Change." *Theory, Culture & Society* 27(2–3): 213–232.

———. (2011). "The Trouble with Nature: Ecology as the New Opium for the Masses." In *The Ashgate Research Companion to Planning Theory*, J. Hillier and P. Healey, eds. Aldershot, UK: Ashgate.

Tallis, H., and S. Polaski. (2011). "Assessing Multiple Ecosystem Services: An Integrated Tool for the Real World." In *Natural Capital: Theory and Practice of Mapping Ecosystem Services*, P. Kareiva, H. Tallis, T.H. Ricketts, G.C. Daily, and S. Polasky, eds. Oxford, UK: Oxford University Press.

Taussig, M.T. (1992). *The Nervous System*. New York: Routledge.

———. (1998a). "Crossing the Face." In *Border Fetishisms*, P. Spyer, ed. New York: Routledge.

———. (1998b). "Viscerality, Faith, and Skepticism: Another Theory of Magic." In *In Near Ruins*, N. Dirks, ed. Minneapolis: University of Minnesota Press.

———. (1999). *Defacement: Public Secrecy and the Labor of the Negative*. Stanford, CA: Stanford University Press.

Tercek, M.R., and J.S. Adams. (2013). *Nature's Fortune: How Business and Society Thrive by Investing in Nature*. New York: Basic Books.

The Economics of Ecosystems and Biodiversity (TEEB). (2008). *The Economics of Ecosystems and Biodiversity: An Interim Report*. http://doc.teebweb.org/wp -content/uploads/Study%20and%20Reports/Additional%20Reports/Interim %20report/TEEB%20Interim%20Report_English.pdf.

———. (2010). *Mainstreaming the Economics of Nature: A Synthesis of the Approach, Conclusions and Recommendations of TEEB*. http://teebweb.org/publications /teeb-for/synthesis/.

The Nature Conservancy (TNC). (2020). *The Nature of Innovation: 2019 Annual Report*. Washington, DC: The Nature Conservancy.

Thiam, T. (2016). "Foreword." In *Conservation Finance from Niche to Mainstream: The Building of an Institutional Asset Class*. Zurich: Credit Suisse and McKinsey Credit Suisse Group AG and McKinsey Center for Business and Environment.

Thakholi, L. (2021). "Conservation Labour Geographies: Subsuming Regional Labour into Private Conservation Spaces in South Africa." *Geoforum* 123: 1–11.

Thompson, E.P. (1993). *Customs in Common.* New York: New Press.

Thrift, N. (2005). *Knowing Capitalism.* London: Sage.

Timmermans, F., A. Steiner, and S. Dixson-Declève. (2021). "Net Zero Is Not Enough—We Need to Build a Nature-Positive Future." *The Guardian,* October 28. https://www.theguardian.com/environment/2021/oct/28/net-zero-is -not-enough-we-need-to-build-a-nature-positive-future-aoe.

Tomšič, S. (2016). *The Capitalist Unconscious: Marx and Lacan.* London: Verso.

Tsing, A.L. (2000). "Inside the Economy of Appearances." *Public Culture* 12(1): 115–144.

———. (2015). *The Mushroom at the End of the World: On the Possibility of Life in Capitalist Ruins.* Princeton, NJ: Princeton University Press.

Tuck, E., and K.W. Yang. (2012). "Decolonization Is Not a Metaphor." *Decolonization: Indigeneity, Education & Society* 1(1): 1–40.

Turnbull, D. 2014. "Exon to World: Drop Dead." Oil Change International press release, March 31. http://priceofoil.org/2014/03/31/exxon-world-drop-dead/.

Turnhout, E., K. Neves, and E. de Lijster. (2014). "'Measurementality' in Biodiversity Governance: Knowledge, Transparency, and the Intergovernmental Science-Policy Platform on Biodiversity and Ecosystem Services (IPBES)." *Environment and Planning A* 46(3): 581–597.

United Nations (UN). (2014). *Millennium Development Goals Update 2014.* New York: United Nations.

United Nations Environment Programme (UNEP). (2009). *Global Green New Deal—A Policy Brief.* Nairobi: UNEP.

———. (2011a). *Decoupling Natural Resource Use and Environmental Impacts from Economic Growth.* Nairobi: UNEP.

———. (2011b). *Towards a Green Economy: Pathways to Sustainable Development and Poverty Reduction.* Nairobi: UNEP.

———. (2014). *Decoupling 2: Technologies, Opportunities and Policy Options.* Nairobi: UNEP.

United Nations Environment Programme Finance Initiative (UNEPFI). (2012). *The Natural Capital Declaration.* https://www.unepfi.org/fileadmin/documents/ncd _booklet.pdf.

United Nations World Tourism Organization (UNWTO). (1998). *Ecotourism, Now One-Fifth of Market.* Madrid: UN World Tourism Organization.

———. (2018). *World Tourism Highlights 2017.* Madrid: UNWTO.

United States Agency of International Development (USAID). (2012). "Tropical Forest Conservation Act (TFCA) Program Descriptions: Costa Rica." http:// www.usaid.gov/our_work/environment/forestry/tfca_descs.html#Costa_Rica.

United States Department of State. (2012). "Seventy Years of U.S. Development Assistance." http://photos.state.gov/libraries/costarica/19452/pdfs/development _assistance.pdf.

Vaccaro, I., O. Beltran, and P. Paquet. (2013). "Political Ecology and Conservation Policies: Some Theoretical Genealogies." *Journal of Political Ecology* 20(1): 255–272.

Vandermeer, J., and I. Perfecto. (2005). *Breakfast of Biodiversity: The Political Ecology of Rainforest Destruction*. 2nd ed. Oakland, CA: Food First Books.

Van den Hombergh, H.G.M. (2004). *No Stone Unturned: Building Blocks of Environmentalist Power versus Transnational Industrial Forestry in Costa Rica*. Amsterdam: Dutch University Press.

Van Hecken, G., J. Bastiaensen, and F. Huybrechs. (2015a). "What's in a Name? Epistemic Perspectives and Payments for Ecosystem Services Policies in Nicaragua." *Geoforum* 63: 55–66.

Van Hecken, G., J. Bastiaensen, and C. Windey. (2015b). "Towards a Power-Sensitive and Socially-Informed Analysis of Payments for Ecosystem Services (PES): Addressing the Gaps in the Current Debate." *Ecological Economics* 120: 117–125.

Van Hecken, G., V. Kolinjivadi, C. Windey, P. McElwee, E. Shapiro-Garza, F. Huybrechs, and J. Bastiaensen. (2018). "Silencing Agency in Payments for Ecosystem Services (PES) by Essentializing a Neoliberal 'Monster' into Being: A Response to Fletcher & Büscher's 'PES Conceit.'" *Ecological Economics* 144: 314–318.

Van Noordwijk, M., B. Leimona, R. Jindal, G.B. Villamor, M. Vardhan, S. Namirembe, D. Catacutan, J. Kerr, P.A. Minang, and T.P. Tomich. (2012). "Payments for Environmental Services: Evolution toward Efficient and Fair Incentives for Multifunctional Landscapes." *Annu. Rev. Environ. Resour.* 37(1): 389–420.

Vatn, A. (2010). "An Institutional Analysis of Payments for Environmental Services." *Ecological Economics* 69(6): 1245–1252.

———. (2015). "Markets in Environmental Governance: From Theory to Practice." *Ecological Economics* 105: 97–105.

Vidal, J. (2009). "Rich Nations to Offset Emissions through Brith Control." *The Guardian*, December 3. https://www.theguardian.com/environment/2009/dec/03/carbon-offset-projects-climate-change.

Vivanco, L.A. (2006). *Green Encounters: Shaping and Contesting Environmentalism in Rural Costa Rica*. New York: Berghahn.

Von Weizsäcker, E., and A. Khosla. (2011). "Preface." In *Decoupling Natural Resource Use and Environmental Impacts from Economic Growth*. Nairobi: UNEP.

Walker, S., A. Brower, T. Stephens, and W. Lee. (2009). "Why Bartering Biodiversity Fails." *Conservation Letters* 2(4): 149–157.

Wanner, T. (2015). "The New 'Passive Revolution' of the Green Economy and Growth Discourse: Maintaining the 'Sustainable Development' of Neoliberal Capitalism." *New Political Economy* 20(1): 21–41.

Ward, J.D., P.C. Sutton, A.D. Werner, R. Costanza, S.H. Mohr, and C.T. Simmons. (2016). "Is Decoupling GDP Growth from Environmental Impact Possible?" *PLOS ONE* 11(10): e0164733.

Watt, R. (2021). "The Fantasy of Carbon Offsetting." *Environmental Politics* 30(7): 1069–1088.

Watts, M.J. (2001). "Violent Geographies: Speaking the Unspeakable and the Politics of Space." *City & Society* 13: 85–117.

Wealth Accounting and Valuation of Ecosystem Services (WAVES). (n.d.a). "About Us." https://www.wavespartnership.org/en/about-us.

———. (n.d.b). "Natural Capital Accounting." https://www.wavespartnership.org/en/natural-capital-accounting.

———. (n.d.c). "Costa Rica." https://www.wavespartnership.org/en/costa-rica.

Weedon, C. (1987). *Feminist Practice and Poststructuralist Theory*. Oxford: Basil Blackwell.

Weintrobe, S., ed. (2013a). *Engaging with Climate Change: Psychoanalytic and Interdisciplinary Perspectives*. New York: Routledge.

———. (2013b). "Introduction." In *Engaging with Climate Change: Psychoanalytic and Interdisciplinary Perspectives*, S. Weintrobe, ed. New York: Routledge.

Weinzettel, J., E.G. Hertwich, G.P. Peters, K. Steen-Olsen, and A. Galli. (2013). "Affluence Drives the Global Displacement of Land Use." *Global Environmental Change* 23(2): 433–438.

Weld, M. (2016). "Opinion: Sadly, Malthus Was Right. Now What?" *Montreal Gazette*, February 14. https://montrealgazette.com/opinion/columnists/opinion-sadly-malthus-was-right-now-what.

Wells, M.P., and K. Brandon. (1992). *People and Parks: Linking Protected Area Management with Local Communities*. Washington, DC: World Bank.

Welzer, H. (2011). *Mental Infrastructures: How Growth Entered the World and Our Souls*. Berlin: Heinrich Böll Foundation.

West, C. (2016). "Goodbye, American Neoliberalism. A New Era is Here." *The Guardian*, November 17. https://www.theguardian.com/commentisfree/2016/nov/17/american-neoliberalism-cornel-west-2016-election.

West, P. (2006). *Conservation Is Our Government Now: The Politics of Ecology in Papua New Guinea*. Durham, NC: Duke University Press.

White, R.J., and C.C. Williams. (2016). "Beyond Capitalocentrism: Are Non-Capitalist Work Practices 'Alternatives'?" *Area* 48(3): 325–331.

Wiedmann, T.O., H. Schandl, M. Lenzen, D. Moran, S. Suh, J. West, and K. Kanemoto. (2015). "The Material Footprint of Nations." *Proceedings of the National Academy of Sciences of the United States of America* 112(20): 6271–6276.

Wijkman, A., and J. Rockström. (2012). *Bankrupting Nature: Denying our Planetary Boundaries*. London: Routledge.

Wilderness Conservation Society (WCS). (2020). "Failure Factors: Sometimes the Most Important Thing to Know, Is Knowing What Leads to Failure." https://programs.wcs.org/failurefactors/.

Wilkie, D., K. Stevens, and R. Margoluis. (2019). "Failure Factors: Sometimes the Most Important Thing to Know Is What Did Not Go as Planned (Commentary)." *Mongabay*, November 13. https://news.mongabay.com/2019/11/failure-factors-sometimes-the-most-important-thing-to-know-is-what-did-not-go-as-planned/.

Wilkinson, R., and K. Pickett. (2010). *The Spirit Level: Why Equality Is Better for Everyone*. London: Penguin UK.

Willers, B. (1994). "Sustainable Development: A New World Deception." *Conservation Biology* 8(4): 1146–1148.

Williams, R. (1977). *Marxism and Literature*. Oxford: Oxford University Press.

Wilshusen, P.R., and K.I. MacDonald. (2017). "Fields of Green: Corporate Sustainability and the Production of Economistic Environmental Governance." *Environment and Planning A* 49(8): 1824–1845.

Wilson, B.M. (1994). "When Social Democrats Choose Neoliberal Economic Policies: The Case of Costa Rica." *Comparative Politics* 26(2): 149–168.

Wilson, E.O. (2016). *Half-Earth: Our Planet's Fight for Life*. New York: WW Norton & Company.

Wilson, J. (2014a). "The Shock of the Real: The Neoliberal Neurosis in the Life and Times of Jeffrey Sachs." *Antipode* 46(1): 301–321.

———. (2014b). "Fantasy Machine: Philanthrocapitalism as an Ideological Formation." *Third World Quarterly* 35(7): 1144–1161.

———. (2016). "Neoliberal Gothic." In *Handbook of Neoliberalism*, S. Springer, K. Birch, and J. MacLeavy, eds. London: Routledge.

———. (2021). *Reality of Dreams: Post-neoliberal Utopias in the Ecuadorian Amazon*. New Haven, CT: Yale University Press.

Wilson, J., and M. Bayón. (2017). "The Nature of Post-neoliberalism: Building Biosocialism in the Ecuadorian Amazon." *Geoforum* 81: 55–65.

Wolff, R.D. (2012). *Democracy at Work: A Cure for Capitalism*. Chicago, IL: Haymarket Books.

World Bank. (2015). *The State of Social Safety Nets 2015*. Washington, DC: World Bank.

———. (2016). "Accounting Reveals that Costa Rica's Forest Wealth is Greater than Expected." News, April 13. https://www.worldbank.org/en/news/feature/2016/05/31/accounting-reveals-that-costa-ricas-forest-wealth-is-greater-than-expected.

World Business Council for Sustainable Development (WBCSD). (2010). *Vision 2050: The New Agenda for Business*. Geneva: WBCSD.

World Commission on Environment and Development (WCED). (1987). *Our Common Future*. Oxford, UK: Oxford University Press.

World Wildlife Fund (WWF). (2020). *2019 Consolidated Financial Statements and Independent Auditor's Report*. Amsterdam, Netherlands: WWF.

Wright, E.O. (2010). *Envisioning Real Utopias*. London: Verso.

———. (2019). *How to Be an Anticapitalist in the Twenty-First Century*. London: Verso.

Wunder, S. (2007). "The Efficiency of Payments for Environmental Services in Tropical Conservation." *Conservation Biology* 21(1): 48–58.

———. (2015). "Revisiting the Concept of Payments for Environmental Services." *Ecological Economics* 117: 234–243.

Yates, J., and K. Bakker. (2014). "Debating the 'Post-neoliberal Turn' in Latin America." *Progress in Human Geography* 38 (1): 62–90.

Yurchak, A. (2013). *Everything Was Forever, Until It Was No More: The Last Soviet Generation*. Princeton, NJ: Princeton University Press.

Zhang, Q. (2018). "Managing Sandstorms through Resettling Pastoralists in China: How Multiple Forms of Power Govern the Environment at/across Scales." *Journal of Political Ecology* 25: 364–380.

Ziai, A. (2007). *Exploring Post-Development: Theory and Practice, Problems and Perspectives*. New York: Routledge.

Zilboorg, G. (1943). "Fear of Death." *Psychoanalytic Quarterly* 12: 465–475.

Žižek, S. (1989). *The Sublime Object of Ideology*. London: Verso.

——. (1992). *Looking Awry: An Introduction to Jacques Lacan through Popular Culture*. Cambridge, MA: MIT Press.

——. (1993). *Tarrying with the Negative*. Durham, NC: Duke University Press.

——. (1994). "Introduction: The Spectre of Ideology." In *Mapping Ideology*, S. Žižek, ed. London: Verso.

——. (1997). *The Plague of Fantasies*. London: Verso.

——. (1999) *The Ticklish Subject: The Absent Centre of Political Ontology*. London: Verso.

——. (2000). "Da Capo Senza Fino." In *Contingency, Hegemony, Universality*, E. Laclau, J. Butler, and S. Žižek, eds. London: Verso.

——. (2001). "The Rhetorics of Power." *Diacritics* 31: 91–104.

——. (2006). *Interrogating the Real*. New York: Bloomsbury Publishing.

——. (2007). *Slavoj Žižek Presents Mao: On Practice and Contradiction*. London: Verso.

——. (2008). *In Defense of Lost Causes*. London: Verso.

——. (2009a). *The Parallax View*. Cambridge: MIT Press.

——. (2009b). *First as Tragedy, Then as Farce*. London: Verso.

——. (2010). *Living in the End Times*. London: Verso.

——. (2012a). *The Pervert's Guide to Ideology* [documentary film]. S. Fiennes, Director. New York: P Guide Productions/Zeitgeist Films.

——. (2012b). *The Year of Dreaming Dangerously*. London: Verso.

——. (2017). *The Courage of Hopelessness: Chronicles of a Year of Acting Dangerously*. London: Penguin UK.

Z/Yen. (n.d). "Policy Performance Bonds." Sustainability. https://www.zyen.com /research/research/sustainability/policy-performance-bonds/.

INDEX

accounting: capital, 72; for ecosystem services, 113, 115; for natural capital, 71
accumulation, 7–8, 12, 41, 75, 77, 79, 89, 133, 142–44, 153–54, 173–75, 181, 184; capital, 12, 41, 75, 141, 179, 195, 222; capitalist, 15, 172; continual, 175, 205; excessive, 130; expanded, 41, 181; non-consumptive, 13; primitive, 133, 196; of resources, 202; sustainable, 11, 172
achievement-subject, 32, 222, 238n15
activities: economic, 68, 190; extractive, 125, 177; productive, 125; profit-seeking, 129
actors, 3–5, 7, 40, 46, 49, 144, 152, 158, 202; nonstate, 4, 105, 231n3; powerful, 129, 163; rational, 61, 74, 228
agenda, 12, 44–45, 52, 79, 151, 161, 178, 201
agreement, Coasean-type, 78–79
agriculture, sustainable, 5, 78–79
agroforestry, 104
aid: development, 207; results-based, 126
alternatives, 190–91, 193, 195, 197–201, 203, 205, 207, 209, 211, 213–14, 218, 247n4
Anderson, Inger, 3, 50
anti-regulation machine, 9–10, 116–17, 119, 121, 123, 125, 127, 129, 131, 133, 135, 137, 139, 141, 143
approach, 3–4, 8, 14, 45, 67–68, 70, 72, 153–54, 198, 200–201, 203; market-based, 94, 150
appropriation, 181, 196–97, 222
Arrighi, Giovanni, 142–43
Arsel, Murat, 172
art, 29, 31, 146, 218

assessment, benefit-cost. *See* benefit-cost analysis
asset, 3, 53, 55, 64, 74, 129, 134, 159; capital, 45; class, 70, 82, 144; economic, 63; natural, 53, 69, 73
assistance, development, 233
attachment, 30, 35, 162, 215, 217, 219
automation, 225–26

Bakker, Peter, 53, 58–59, 67, 173
bank, 2, 142, 194, 205
basic income, 194, 201
Bastani, Aaron, 225, 248n7
benefit-cost analysis, 65, 150
benefits, 53–54, 58, 61–62, 64–65, 71, 73–74, 76, 128, 134–35; aggregate, 71; concrete, 160; conservation, 77, 191; ecological, 132; ecotourism, 135; environmental, 77, 121, 133, 135, 245n18; global, 134; long-term, 196; to nature, 84; social, 73; sustainable, 233
biodiversity: banking, 4, 85; global, 165; loss, 143, 149, 166, 191–92; preservation, 92, 118; program, 47, 73; protection, 115, 150; value of, 62
biopolitical, 37, 188–89, 248n8
biopolitics, 28, 30–31, 34, 36, 65, 168, 185, 188, 226, 239n17; neoliberal, 35, 37, 57, 88, 188. *See also* biopower
biopower, 17, 27–31, 34–37, 226, 229; affirmative, 226; exercise of, 28, 30, 34–35; neoliberal, 16–17, 36–37. *See also* biopolitics

bioprospecting, 78, 80, 100, 118, 134, 149, 151, 206, 240n1

biosphere, 166–67

blockchain, 151, 243n5

Bolivia, 173–74, 208

bond, green, 83, 151

Bono, 12

Borges-Méndez, Ramon, 106

Boza, Mario, 91, 93–94, 98, 101

Breitling, Jan, 131

British Petroleum (BP), 38–40, 47, 89

Brockington, Dan, 3, 42, 52, 59, 79, 84, 163, 210

Bruntland Commission, 43–44, 85

Büscher, Bram, 9, 12, 75, 77–82, 127, 150, 153–55, 164, 182

business, 40, 49, 61–62, 69, 71–74, 76–77, 83, 100, 144, 146, 169; accounting, 55; agenda, 50; case, 69, 72; model, 39, 72, 78

Business and Biodiversity Offsets Programme (BBOP), 79–80

business-as-usual, 138

calculation, benefit-cost, 33–34, 37, 132, 144. *See also* benefit-cost analysis

Cambridge Conservation Initiative (CCI), 170

capacity, 11, 18–19, 40–41, 43, 45, 81–82, 88, 95, 134, 140, 149–50, 206, 212

capital, 52–55, 59, 65–67, 69, 77–78, 181, 185–88, 190, 195, 200, 208; circulating, 143; extractive, 179; fictitious, 184; financial, 53, 67, 188; fixed, 80; general circuit of, 142; global, 206; liquid, 82; misallocation of, 55; natural, 65, 71, 77, 127; social, 53, 58, 67, 72

capitalism, 11–13, 15, 29–30, 77, 84, 88, 162, 164–65, 167, 180, 184–88, 195, 202, 204–5, 215–19; casino, 142; cognitive, 181; consumer, 218; contemporary, 30, 239; fictitious, 80, 141; global, 7, 164, 167, 185, 201, 233; industrial, 88, 202; neoliberal, 13, 127, 154, 214, 217, 224, 230; nineteenth-century, 32; sustainable, 16; three-dimensional, 55

capitalist, 67, 76, 175, 183, 185, 204–5, 217, 223

carbon, 38–39, 83, 89, 132, 148

care, 94, 216, 226

Carrier, James, 61, 127, 135

Castree, Noel, 77

celebrity, 163

Centre for International Forestry (CIFOR), 126

ceremony, 162–63

change, 69–70, 76, 86, 92, 164, 169, 187, 200, 204, 217, 219, 224; cultural, 170; economic, 172; fundamental, 33; radical, 195, 203, 213, 218; socioeconomic, 157; structural, 198

Clarke, John, 201–2

clients, 61–62

climate change, 45, 75–76, 81, 132, 135, 157, 166–67, 179, 245n18; anthropogenic, 92, 134; economics of, 167; governance of, 47

coherence, 15, 23, 52, 151, 155, 205

commodification, 4, 74, 133, 143–44, 159, 175, 195, 231n3

commodities, 5, 68, 74, 79–80, 97–99, 141, 236n1; marketing of, 142; production of, 12, 115, 140

common pool resources, 196

common property regimes (CPRs), 195–96, 227–28

commons, 43, 196, 221, 228

communism, 218, 224, 226

communities, 6, 74, 77, 106, 160, 205, 220, 226; indigenous, 241n4

compliance, 18, 26–28, 111, 183

conditional cash transfer (CCT), 200

conditions of possibility, 39–40, 89, 214, 225

conservation, 12, 46–47, 57, 75–76, 79–80, 89, 91–92, 99–101, 111–12, 115–16, 122–23, 147–50, 170, 172–73, 175, 177–81, 185–87, 192–93; accumulation by, 75, 184; biodiversity, 1, 3, 100, 103, 118, 135, 149; capitalist, 76; community-based, 42, 206; finance, 50, 118, 144; for-profit, 231n4; fortress, 98, 123; global, 143, 151; incentivized, 124, 131, 136; investment for, 89; market-based, 123; movement, 3; neoliberal, 4–17, 36–37, 51–52, 65–68, 72–75, 79–82, 84, 88–89, 116–18, 126–34, 143–46, 148–55, 158–60, 162–65, 170–72, 177–81, 183–88, 215–17, 230,

232n7; outcomes, 82, 123; policy, 1, 67, 76, 164, 205; projects, 82; resource, 58, 75; strategy, 101, 135, 149; tropical, 94; value of, 80

conservation areas, 91, 101

conservation-as-development, 49

conservation biologists, 6, 149

conservation-extraction nexus, 79, 116, 122–23, 128, 175

Conservation International (CI), 1, 51

conservationists, 64, 68, 76–77, 97, 99, 143–44, 147, 151, 154–55, 163–64, 168, 170; international, 174; neoliberal, 78; wildlife, 144

conservation organizations, 3, 89, 147, 206; conventional, 73; prominent, 150

consumers, 30, 62, 68, 80, 104, 107–8, 133, 139

contracts, 108, 128

contradiction, 111, 127, 132, 154, 161, 170, 184, 214

control, 18, 61, 68, 128, 152, 155, 188, 195

Convention on Biological Diversity (CBD), 44

convergence, 46, 138, 198

conversion, 52, 65, 79

corporations, 44, 68, 70–74, 76, 147, 181

Correa, Rafael, 173–175

Costanza, Robert, 43, 46, 48, 54, 63, 74, 158

Costa Rica, 5–6, 90–100, 102, 104, 106, 110–16, 118–25, 128–32, 134–35, 191; conservation, 92; development, 96, 119; environmental management, 97; national parks, 93; neoliberalization, 95; REDD+, 112–13; state agents, 100

cost-benefit calculation. *See* benefit-cost analysis

costs, 62–64, 69, 71–74, 76, 118, 122, 126, 129, 133–35, 138, 215–16; environmental, 123, 125–26, 133, 140, 154; input, 73; negative, 72; social, 73, 133, 195; true, 64

counter-neoliberalization, 175

countries, 3, 5–6, 91–97, 99–102, 108, 112, 114–16, 118–20, 122, 131, 137–38, 196–97; developing, 85, 137; high-income, 146, 192–93; industrialized, 138; lower-income, 192; low-income, 193; middle-income, 132; wealthy, 168

Covington, Dennis, 220–21

creation, 55, 58, 72–73, 75, 77, 85, 109, 111, 130, 132, 141–42

Credit Suisse, 2, 50–51, 67, 73

crisis, 30, 41, 44, 48, 120, 183, 208, 213, 240n6; accumulation, 41, 213; economic, 4, 11, 159, 173, 183, 186; environmental, 216; global, 41, 69

critics, 5, 10, 39, 52, 95, 153, 156, 158, 239n2, 243n11, 247n12

critique, 12, 15, 36, 43–44, 93–94, 148–51, 153–54, 159, 162, 164, 210–11, 214, 228

cynical reason, 24, 35, 158

damage: economic, 196; environmental, 79, 125, 127

Dasgupta, Partha, 165–67

Dean, Jodi, 30–31, 33–34, 36, 161, 185, 188, 205, 218–21, 226

death, 31, 34, 146; disavowal of, 216–17; drive, 187, 245n5

debt, 142; service, 95

decisions: collective land use, 131; resource allocation, 158

decolonial, 14, 236n22

decolonization, 197, 236n22

decoupling, 12, 86–89, 136–42, 145, 151, 158, 160–61, 184, 209, 240n3, 246n12; absolute, 86, 89, 136–37; impact, 86, 136–37; relative, 89, 136–37, 141–42; resource, 86; sustainable, 138

defeat, 128–29, 131

deficiency, 15, 149, 151, 160, 170, 172

deforestation, 98, 112, 115, 131

degrowth, 13, 16, 190–91, 193–95, 197–99, 201, 203–5, 207, 209–10, 219, 223, 245n1, 246n12

dematerialization, 12, 87, 89, 141, 184

Dempsey, Jessica, 5, 7, 9, 36, 40, 81–82, 133, 136, 150, 153–54, 160, 234n13

denial, 9, 24–25, 185, 216

deregulation, 34, 142, 231n3, 242n9

design, 10–11, 53, 76, 105–6, 129, 137, 200

desire, 23, 25–26, 30, 33, 35, 87, 89, 187–88, 215, 218–25; collective, 219; communist, 218; post-capitalist, 218–19

development, 5, 7, 45–46, 49, 54–55, 75–77, 80, 82, 92, 97, 114–15, 126, 172, 183,

development (*continued*)
233nn8,9,10, 234nn11,12,13,
235nn14,15,18; community-based, 102,
206; conventional, 75, 198; goals, 44, 138;
human, 44; indicators, 140; initiatives,
241n4; interests, 123; international, 6,
10, 96, 169; interventions, model, 40,
174; neoliberal, 173, 199; objectives, 55,
175; paradigm, 45; social, 42, 119; sustainable, 43–46, 51, 55, 85, 94, 113, 151,
153, 161, 240n3; uneven, 128, 196
disavowal, 23–27, 30, 35–36, 158–59, 164,
166, 168, 185, 189, 212, 214–17, 224
discipline, 19, 28–29, 32
discourse, 8, 13–14, 19, 21, 40, 63, 72, 168;
environmental, 167–68; neoliberal, 34, 59
disjuncture, 25, 125, 127
diversity, 149, 194
domination, 18–19, 186, 233n10, 238n15
Dressler, Wolfram, 127, 213
drive, 18, 30–31, 36, 58, 132, 184–85, 187–88,
213, 215, 218–19. *See also* death, drive

EarthFirst!, 202–3
economic: activities, 65, 86, 114, 138–39;
growth, 12, 15, 34–35, 37, 84–88, 135–36,
140–42, 145, 160–61, 178, 184; value,
80–81, 86–87, 129, 140, 142, 149, 186
economics: capitalist, 30; development, 167
Economics of Ecosystems and Biodiversity,
The (TEEB), 48, 50, 54–55, 61–63
economists, ecological, 43, 52, 64, 130, 154,
164
economy, 45, 59, 62, 73, 76, 85, 87, 139–40,
153, 156, 159–60, 162, 173–74, 192–93,
204–5; capitalist, 11, 13, 41, 88, 167, 195,
209; community, 204, 219; global, 12,
37, 140, 142, 145–46, 177, 184, 207;
market, 8, 130, 158; neoliberal, 145, 205;
steady-state, 193; sustainable, 70; world,
138, 142, 184
ecosystem, 2, 43, 45, 52–54, 58, 67, 91–92,
149, 158, 192
ecosystem services, 46–48, 54–56, 61–64,
67, 71, 74–75, 107–9, 114–15, 148, 154,
160; benefits of, 49, 62; global, 47–48
ecotourism, 4–5, 14, 78–81, 92, 100, 114–15,
118, 129, 132, 134–35, 151

Ecuador, 173–75, 177
Edelman, Marc, 95, 97, 119–21, 191
efficiency, economic, 132
elites, 19, 129, 147; capitalist, 7
emissions, 38–39, 112–13, 125, 157, 168;
global, 156
Emissions Trading Scheme (ETS), 135
emotion, 33, 35
employees, 72, 150
energy, 39, 77, 86, 92, 101, 114, 135, 137, 139,
193, 225
environment, 2, 41, 44–45, 58, 63, 68, 101,
189, 192; natural, 54, 59, 174
environmental: degradation, 42, 55–56, 62,
68, 128, 130–31, 134, 167–68, 191–93;
governance, 97, 102, 113, 119, 122, 127,
177, 181; management, 94, 97; organizations, 51, 100, 202; performance, 83;
policy, 5–6, 14, 97, 122; politics, 14, 204,
227, 229; protection, 57, 62, 94, 98,
119–22, 141, 145, 171–72, 179, 181, 183;
regulation, 4, 77; services, 4, 74, 104,
106–7; sustainability, 11, 13, 46, 178
environmentalism, 13, 165, 171, 232; neoliberal, 13, 49, 75
environmentalists, 1, 217
environmentality, 227, 229; liberation,
227–29
Escobar, Arturo, 14, 52, 174, 197–99, 233n8,
234n12
Evans, Sterling, 91–94, 99–101
evidence, 4, 9, 15, 65, 134, 138–39, 151–52,
154, 157–58, 160–61, 170
expansion, 72, 95, 99, 106, 110, 115, 118–19,
123, 139, 142–43, 148; agricultural, 98;
capitalist, 185; global, 140
expectations, 70, 159–60, 162–63
experience, 15, 18, 23, 30, 53, 101, 170–71,
220, 223
expertise, 73
explanations, 6–7, 9, 14–15, 166
export, 100, 192
extraction, 79–80, 115–16, 122–25, 129–30,
139–40, 174–75, 177–78, 180–81, 184,
235n15; capitalist, 189; resource, 4, 172, 179
extractive: imperative, 173–74; industries,
79, 116, 118, 122–23, 125, 173, 184
ExxonMobil, 157, 244n8

fad, 151, 153

failure, 6–10, 30, 108–10, 147, 151, 153, 156, 161–62, 168–72, 180, 185, 187–89, 219, 233nn8,9, 235nn14,15,18; celebration of, 169; in conservation, 170, 180; consistent, 149; continual, 171, 219; of market logic, 161; of neoliberal mechanisms, 149, 172; in practice, 162; project, 170; widespread, 8, 144, 151, 170, 172, 183, 217

faith, 136, 152, 160–61, 170, 226

false consciousness, 18–20, 24

fantasy, 9, 14–16, 23–26, 159, 161–62, 178, 180, 185, 209, 215–17, 219, 222, 224; decoupling, 184; of free trade, 161; neoliberal, 186, 221, 223, 227; traversing the, 215

farce, 155, 159

Farley, Joshua, 158, 244n9

fear, 216–17

Ferguson, James, 7, 10, 140, 199–201, 227, 233n8, 235nn14,18; 236

fetishization, 170

finance, 9, 69, 89, 107, 113, 124, 127, 148, 177, 180, 184; conservation, 175; development, 206–7; nonmarket, 118, 127

financialization, 12, 141–43, 159, 181, 184

flow, 220–21

Fondo Nacional de Financiamiento Forestal (FONAFIFO), 103, 105–8, 110, 112–13, 241n2

food, 53–54, 77, 81, 158, 162, 168, 225

forest: management, 103; products, 114

Forest Carbon Partnership Facility (FCPF), 112

forestry, 5, 79–80; sustainable, 78, 103

forests, 45, 53, 55, 77, 91, 94, 99, 103, 113–15, 120–21, 221

Foucault, Michel, 8, 10, 13–15, 17, 19–20, 24–29, 31–35, 39, 59–61, 188–89, 210–12, 226–28, 236n19, 237nn1,4, 238nn12,13, 239nn3,18

freedom, 7, 31–32, 36, 188–89, 215, 219–21, 223, 238nn8,14,15, 246n3

Freud, Sigmund, 215, 220, 239n18

Friedman, Milton, 213, 240n6

FUNDECOR, 105–6, 112

funding, 98, 101, 105, 108, 118, 125–26, 128, 131, 135, 144, 150, 152, 175–77

funds, 52, 68, 103, 105, 107–10, 112, 118, 125, 139, 173, 175–77

game, 57, 60, 161, 212

Gesellschaft für Technische Zusammenarbeit (GTZ), 104

Gibson-Graham, J. K., 204–5, 219

gift, 229, 237n5

Global Environment Facility (GEF), 1, 4, 51, 108

Global Witness, 173, 182

governance, 30, 33, 36, 41, 43, 61, 109, 111, 124, 131, 174, 176, 181; environmental, 42; neoliberal, 66, 79

government, 27, 29, 31, 34, 44–45, 67–68, 74–75, 99, 101–2, 107, 109, 111, 113, 129–30, 201; United States, 1–2, 69, 96

governmentality, 15, 28–29, 31–32, 227, 229; neoliberal, 34

Graeber, David, 26–27, 59, 130, 182, 184, 205, 228, 236n20, 238nn9,11, 242n9

Gramsci, Antonio, 18, 20, 26

Green Economy, 45–46, 48, 50, 86, 151

greenhouse gas (GHG), 156, 185

gross domestic product (GDP), 68, 86, 95, 100, 114, 140–41, 166

growth, 2, 4, 13–14, 16, 58, 84–85, 87–88, 133, 135, 139–42, 145, 180, 184–85, 195, 205–6; contemporary, 167; economic, 12, 58, 84, 119, 145, 175, 193; green, 85, 87–88, 114, 136, 139, 141, 151; nonmaterial, 87; physical, 86–87; sustainable, 77, 85

Haraway, Donna, 172, 212–13

Harvey, David, 7, 41–42, 80, 121, 139, 141–42, 233n8, 235n15

hegemony, 18, 26, 40, 213–14; capitalist, 204

Helm, Dieter, 53–55, 64–65, 85, 240n11

Hickel, Jason, 139, 184, 233n9, 235n15

Honey, Martha, 92, 100–101, 135

Honolulu, 1–2

hooks, bell, 225, 237n29

hopelessness, 217

Hunter, Robert, 94–95, 99, 115

ideology, 15, 18–21, 24–26, 35–36, 162, 164–65, 187, 210, 215; neoliberal, 153, 186

illusion, 23, 141–42, 223

imaginary, 23–24, 142, 187
imagination, 225, 238n9
impact, 68, 71–72, 79–80, 86, 89, 136–37,
    153, 155, 158, 166, 168, 185, 192; ecological,
    65, 89, 185; environmental, 12, 51, 62,
    72–73, 86–87, 89, 115, 126, 142, 145, 186
incentives, 31, 55, 71, 96, 99, 106, 129, 131,
    133; economic, 131
income, 46, 53, 84
individual, 6, 31, 57, 59, 74, 84, 152, 228
inequality, 84, 126, 128, 132, 168, 191–93,
    195–97, 227; global, 141, 242n6; impact,
    166
Inflection Point Capital Management
    (IPCM), 70, 82
initiatives, 4, 7, 11, 16, 48, 50–51, 107, 111,
    114, 169–70, 175–77, 205, 207–8;
    market-based, 4, 51
innovation, 85, 87–89, 139, 160–61, 169;
    technological, 87–88
instrument-effects, 10, 236n19
instruments: economic, 243n11; financial,
    83, 151
integrated-conservation-and-development
    project (ICDP), 42, 120, 206
intellectuals, progressive, 212
Intergovernmental Science-Policy Platform
    for Biodiversity and Ecosystem Services
    (IPBES), 47–48
International Institute for Environment
    and Development (IIED), 81, 126
International Monetary Fund (IMF), 95,
    97, 146–47, 192, 196, 231n3
International Union for the Conservation
    of Nature (IUCN), 1, 42, 44, 47, 49–51,
    61, 71, 147, 150
intervention, 7–8, 31, 34, 59–60, 101, 108, 118,
    123, 137, 233n10; neoliberal, 1, 153, 229
investment, 1–2, 12, 39, 69–70, 76, 81–83,
    89, 91, 139–40, 142–43, 236n21; private,
    2–3, 49, 51; private sector, 75
investors, 2, 40, 69–70, 75, 77, 83, 130, 144,
    206
Isla, Ana, 94

Jevons Paradox, 137–38
jouissance, 15, 25, 30, 35, 162–63, 209, 215,
    220, 222–24

Kallis, Giorgos, 37, 139, 184, 193–95, 208,
    223, 245n1
Kapoor, Ilan, 30, 214, 236n22
Kareiva, Peter, 48–49, 55, 76
Klein, Naomi, 41, 213, 244n6
knowledge, 26, 36, 217, 236n22, 237n1
Konings, Martijn, 212

Lacan, Jacques, 14–15, 23, 25, 30, 35–36, 187,
    214, 220–22
lack, 15, 121, 127, 135, 154, 170, 174, 182, 190,
    218, 221–22
land, 77, 99, 101, 103, 107, 109, 120–21, 124,
    126, 191, 193, 195, 208; marginal, 121
Langholz, Jeffrey, 101
language, 58, 154
Lansing, David, 128
Latin America, 72, 95, 173, 178, 182–83, 192,
    197
law, 55, 75, 103, 107
Le Billon, Philippe, 79, 182
legislation, 44, 99, 103
Li, Tania, 233n10, 235nn14,18
liberalism, 34, 188–89, 236n20; classic, 60
liberals, 59–60
Liboiron, Max, 236n22
life, 30–31, 34, 37, 54, 87, 185, 216, 220,
    226–27, 229
lifeworlds, 204, 236n22
logic, 7, 16, 59, 129, 153, 159, 161, 168, 188,
    229, 245n18
Lohmann, Larry, 129, 132
loss, 30, 55, 62, 73, 75, 80, 149, 155, 215, 217,
    220
love, 226
lucrative, 83, 122, 125, 180
Lukács, Georg, 220
Lukes, Steven, 17–18

management, natural resource, 92, 131, 231n4
market: capitalization, 106; economics, 186;
    exchange, 124, 136; failure, 56, 68, 82,
    117, 119, 161, 233n8; forces, 60, 122, 130;
    free, 147; funding, 125, 148; logic, 4–5,
    7, 161, 189; mechanisms, 107, 109, 113,
    117, 120, 123, 129, 133, 147, 150, 189, 206;
    transactions, 136, 205, 124, 135; volun-
    tary offset, 81, 113, 118

market-based instrument (MBI), 4, 67, 78, 115, 118, 121–23, 125–27, 149–50, 155, 242n10, 244n9; conservation, 81, 179

market-based mechanism, 123, 127, 150. *See also* market-based instrument

marketization, 61, 183, 231n3

marketplace, 62–63

market players, 108, 147, 177

markets, 4, 10–11, 58–61, 65–71, 73–75, 77–81, 83, 108–10, 117–18, 124–27, 133–34, 143–44, 150, 177, 188–89, 191; bond, 142; capital, 70; capitalist, 12, 62, 129, 133, 244; carbon, 46–47, 108, 113, 126, 129, 132, 134, 149; commodity, 133; competitive, 131, 134; conservation, 74, 81, 83, 154; derivative, 142, 236n21; economic, 58–59; environmental, 72, 83; financial, 12, 70, 82, 142; free, 10, 130, 142, 158, 172, 184, 191, 236n21; global, 83, 135, 143, 174, 177, 244n8; international, 98, 126; investment, 50, 74; private, 67; profitable, 4, 11; self-regulating, 107, 109; self-sustaining, 107, 143

Marx, Karl, 14–15, 19, 25, 35, 159, 236n21, 239n18

Marxism, 6, 13

Marxists, 7–9, 13, 36, 153, 159, 205

mask, 17, 19, 21, 24, 94

material, raw, 54, 142, 174, 177

Matulis, Brett, 110–11, 128

McAfee, Kathleen, 126–28, 242n6

McCarthy, James, 178–79, 181–82

McCauley, Douglas, 150

measurement, 52, 62–63, 154

mechanism, 11, 59–60, 67, 81, 102, 104, 110, 112, 126–27, 131–32, 135, 206, 208; capitalist, 185; conservation-based finance, 177; economic, 77; fortress conservation, 176; neoliberal, 10, 132, 172, 178, 183

melancholia, 215, 218

militarization, 183

Millennium Ecosystem Assessment (MEA), 47–48

mining, 78, 153; sustainable, 153–54

MIRENEM, 101, 103

money, 64, 70, 112, 142–44, 162, 180, 190, 194, 208, 236n21, 246n11

Mosse, David, 9, 234n13,

mourning, 215–18, 223–24

National Biodiversity Institute (INBio), 100, 134

natural capital, 16, 46–47, 52–55, 58, 61–62, 65, 67, 71, 74–75, 179, 187–88; accounting, 48–49, 71–72, 78, 113, 142; stocks, 65; valuation, 47–48, 148, 151, 165

Natural Capital Coalition (NCC), 54, 72

Natural Capital Declaration, 48, 52, 54–55

Natural Capital Project (NCP), 48–49, 51, 160

Natural Capital Protocol, 49, 54, 63, 72, 78

natural resources, 43, 82, 179, 181; non-renewable, 54; protected, 119; shared, 221. *See also* resources, natural

nature, 15, 17, 33, 35, 53, 57–59, 61–65, 67, 69, 71, 74, 76, 84, 182–83; human, 57, 225, 228; liquid, 82; marketisation of, 183; neoliberal, 131, 200; neoliberalization of, 232n4

Nature Conservancy, The (TNC), 3–4, 48–49, 51, 73, 99, 102, 150, 202

neoliberal: governance, 10, 37, 63, 123, 131, 161, 200, 228; principles, 42, 111, 116; project, 33, 41, 67, 189; reforms, 96, 119, 142, 178, 181

neoliberal conservation: evolution of, 12; interventions, 10, 130, 162; mechanisms, 11, 126, 149; policies, 127, 187; promotion of, 146, 155; proponents of, 9, 67; rollout of, 6, 95; vision, 52, 56, 87, 89, 94. *See also* conservation, neoliberal

neoliberalism, 3–5, 7–8, 10, 31–34, 36–37, 41–42, 60–61, 84, 111, 119–21, 146–47, 174–75, 183, 185–89, 200–202, 238n14; authoritarian, 178–81, 183, 185; green, 94, 101

neoliberalization: ambivalent, 97, 106; green, 99, 115; intensified, 94, 110; variegated, 117

neoliberals, 11, 31, 33, 41, 60–61, 110–11, 120, 122–23, 127–28, 131, 162, 165, 181, 183, 185–86

net zero, 38, 217

neutrality, carbon, 40, 89

nongovernmental organizations (NGO), 4, 6, 92, 101, 112, 115, 120, 174, 197. *See also* organizations, nongovernmental
nonhumans, 232n6

obedience-subject, 32
object, sublime, 187
O'Connor, James, 142–43
offset, 39, 79, 81, 89, 110, 122, 125, 137, 180, 245n18
offsetting, 79, 89, 125
opportunities, 71, 76–77, 84, 91, 169, 191, 219
order, symbolic, 23, 186, 219
organizations, 1, 3, 6, 40–41, 45–46, 49–51, 102, 105–6, 134, 136, 147, 150–51, 169–70; nongovernmental, 3, 4, 101, 113. *See also* conservation organizations
Ostrom, Elinor, 227
overpopulation, 165–68

Pagiola, Stefano, 102–3, 108, 124
Pago por Servicios Ambimentales (PSA), 103–12, 115, 117–18, 120, 122, 124–26, 128, 242n2
paradise, 92, 220
park, 45, 91–92, 99
participant, 1, 69, 128, 152, 162–63, 219
Partido Liberación Nacional (PLN), 97
payment for ecosystem services (PES), 4–5, 74, 78–79, 81–82, 124, 126, 130–31, 149, 151, 155, 158, 196, 201
payment for environmental services. *See* payment for ecosystem services
payments, 4, 74, 78, 81, 100, 104–7, 118, 120, 125–26, 159, 175
Peck, Jamie, 5, 42, 147, 152–53, 165, 183, 200, 233n8
performance, economic, 38, 72
person, 27, 54, 158, 166, 171
philanthropy, 74–75
planet, 11, 47, 55–56, 69, 76–77, 156, 166, 207, 226, 244n8
planners, 6, 8, 234n11, 235n18
planning, 7, 39, 42, 89, 96, 235nn14,18; family, 166, 245n18
pleasure, 15, 25, 215
Polanyi, Karl, 59, 80, 119

policies, 2, 5, 112, 116, 122, 125, 131–32, 151–52, 161, 167, 229–30; carbon control, 132; development, 234n13; free-market, 119, 128; international, 13, 206; neoliberal capitalist, 196; state, 5, 99
political ecology, 14, 17, 19, 36, 232n7
population, 28–29, 31, 34, 37, 84, 166, 238n13, 239n17, 244nn14,15,16; global, 166–67
post-capitalism, 204, 209–10, 219, 221–22, 224
postdevelopment, 198
post-neoliberalism, 173, 177–78
poststructuralism, 6–9, 13, 36, 41
poverty, 85, 88, 107, 119–20, 128, 167, 190, 196, 200, 202; alleviation of, 58, 141, 145, 201; reduction of, 128, 138, 140–41, 195, 206
power, 15, 17–20, 23–27, 29, 31–36, 152, 158–59, 183, 186, 196, 199–200, 211–12, 224, 226, 237nn1,8, 238nn10,14; disciplinary, 28–29, 31–33, 239n17; exercise of, 20, 26, 29; modern, 28, 32; neoliberal, 31, 34; political, 179, 234n13; relations, 32, 211, 237n1, 238n14; sovereign, 28
power/knowledge, 19
preservation, 65, 99, 104, 115, 126, 188
price, 52, 56, 62, 64, 67, 73, 79, 83, 96, 98, 133, 169; signals, 63, 78–79
principle, user pays, 104, 108, 111
problems, environmental, 11, 58, 76, 125, 133, 211, 223
production: agricultural, 120, 192, 207, 242n2; capitalist, 159, 181, 184; commodity, 12; conventional, 125–26
profits, 11–12, 55, 57, 73, 75, 123, 125–26, 129–30, 133, 140–41, 143–44, 159–60, 234n10; sustainable, 12
program, 4, 102–4, 107–11, 117–19, 124–26, 128, 195, 197
projects, development, 7, 9, 102, 160, 177, 182, 233n8, 235nn14,18
property, 158–59, 195, 204
protected areas, 3, 80, 92, 101, 115, 182
psychoanalysis, 13–14, 36, 159, 162, 188, 209–10, 214–16, 218, 236n22; Lacanian, 9, 13, 23, 26. *See also* Lacan, Jacques
psychopower, 26, 32, 34, 238n14

rationality, 29

Real, 286; of capital, 15, 181, 186–88, 245n5; of nature, 15

reality, 10, 12, 16, 18–21, 24–25, 27, 107, 109–10, 124–27, 133, 136–37, 186, 213–14, 216–17; social, 24, 61, 186, 217

recession, 41, 181, 233n8, 245n1

reciprocity, 158, 229

redistribution, 109, 124, 127, 195–97, 201, 207–8, 246n11; intentional, 208

reduced emissions through avoided deforestation and forest degradation (REDD+), 78, 81–82, 112–13, 115, 126–27, 131, 135, 144, 148–49, 151, 155, 206

reforestation, 99, 103–4

reform, 96, 101–2, 174, 179, 202–3; land, 197, 208

regime, 173–75, 179, 181, 200, 228; common property, 195–96, 227; neoliberal, 34

regulation: state, 10, 154, 162, 188; direct, 10, 37

research, 5–6, 40, 91, 122, 125, 190, 196, 205, 207

resilience, 149, 169

resistance, 4, 19–20, 23, 42, 48, 117, 173, 183

resource: control, 4, 105; extraction, 12–13, 79, 89, 101, 123, 174, 180, 192; productivity, 87

resources, 58, 60, 65, 67, 86, 121, 124–26, 128–29, 131, 138, 180, 182, 184, 194–96, 206–7; immaterial, 86; natural, 52–53, 55, 58, 62–63, 67–68, 76–77, 80, 100–101, 113, 121–23, 128, 131, 141, 144, 173–75; in situ, 135–36, 206

responsibility, 102, 111, 127, 134, 200, 218

revenue, 2, 107–8, 110, 122, 124, 126, 128–29, 175, 177, 180, 206–7

revolution, 58–59, 199, 201, 222

risk, 65, 71–72, 83–84, 147, 167, 188–89, 226

Sachs, Jeffrey, 85, 240n3, 244n14

Sánchez-Azofeifa, Arturo, 103–4, 107–8

Schmidheiny, Stephen, 44

science, 53, 154, 160, 179

Scott, James, 18–19, 214, 233n8, 234nn11,12, 240n12

secrecy, public, 20–21, 23–24, 35, 157, 164–65, 167, 214, 237n6. *See also* secret, public

secret, 20–21, 24, 237n5; public, 21, 24, 165, 186

sector, private, 2, 55, 67–69, 73, 75, 105, 126, 144

security, 28, 36, 83, 188–89; economic, 72, 191

self, 33, 218, 220–21

self-interest, 57, 74, 228

services, 52–54, 59, 62–65, 69, 71, 74, 77, 81–82, 103–4, 106–7, 114, 117, 119, 158, 166

Singh, Neera, 221, 227, 229

socialism, 165, 196, 227

social movements, 197–98, 203

societies, 10, 21, 23, 57, 59, 61, 63, 71, 73, 95–96, 178, 180, 191–92, 225; high-income, 41, 43, 193; low-income, 40, 206–8; post-capitalist, 225–26; Western, 28

solutions, 56, 62, 76, 161, 171, 184–85, 201, 211, 247n2

sovereign, 29, 31

space, 59, 61, 64, 148, 152, 164–65, 170, 182, 213, 219, 222

stakeholders, 58, 111, 113, 144, 196

state, 8, 10, 45, 47, 59–61, 64, 94, 96–97, 105, 107, 119–20, 123, 129–30, 172, 174; neoliberal, 111; sovereign, 29

Stavrakakis, Yannis, 35

Steinberg, Paul, 98–100, 131

Steiner, Achim, 45, 50, 85–86

stocks, 32, 52, 54, 76, 113, 142, 187–88

Ston Forestal, 121

strategy, 5, 25, 28, 68, 70, 77, 80, 100, 121–23, 141, 143, 202, 204; conservation, 56; market-based, 5, 119

structural adjustment, 95, 97, 101–2

subjectivation, 25, 238n15

subjects, 18–20, 25–26, 28, 30–32, 34–36, 116, 166, 214–15, 218–20, 222–24, 228; neoliberal, 33, 186

subjugation, 31

sublime object. *See* object, sublime

subsidies, 67, 103–4, 107, 109, 124, 200–202, 206

success, 5, 9–10, 17, 30, 36, 87, 92, 162, 164, 169–70, 233n8

Sukhdev, Pavan, 52–55, 63, 68–69, 71, 73, 75–76, 83, 85, 87–88

Sullivan, Sian, 52, 61–62, 70, 79, 82–83, 85, 197, 228

superego, 33
support, political, 179, 234n13, 235n14
sustainability, 13, 44, 56, 69–70, 77–78, 88,
   154, 168, 223, 247n12, 248n8
Sustainable Development Goals (SDGs),
   12, 85, 151, 166, 240n3
Sustainable Development Solutions
   Network (SDSN), 88, 160, 240n3
symbolic, 23–24, 165, 180
symptoms, 15, 23, 25, 185, 187
system, 27, 84, 103, 106, 139, 142–43, 184,
   186, 195, 201, 204–5; complex, 43

Taussig, Michael, 20–21, 23–24, 27, 157,
   164, 214, 237n6
tax, 74, 107–8, 111, 244n8; revenues, 109,
   202
Tercek, Mark, 49, 68–69, 71, 73–74, 77, 84
trade, 4, 58–59, 75, 80, 124–25, 136–37,
   143–44, 148, 177, 179, 192; free, 130, 161,
   165
traditional ecological knowledge (TEK),
   198
transformation, 7, 156, 174, 199, 210, 213,
   217, 225–26, 229; economic, 97
transition, 36, 140–41, 183, 195, 242n2
truth, 9, 19–21, 25, 29–30, 154, 157

Ugalde, Alvaro, 91–92
United Kingdom (UK), 156
United Nations Environment Programme
   (UNEP), 1, 46, 48, 50–51, 53–55, 77,
   86–88, 136–42, 160
United Nations Framework Convention on
   Climate Change (UNFCCC), 44, 46,
   112, 155, 157–58
United Nations World Tourism Organiza-
   tion (UNWTO), 135
United States Agency of International
   Development (USAID), 96, 102, 105
universal basic income (UBI), 200–201,
   208–9
use, sustainable, 55–56, 75
utopia, real, 224–25

valuation, 58, 63–65, 74, 188; economic,
   46–47, 52, 58, 63–64, 66, 73, 159

value, 7–8, 36–37, 52, 54–56, 58–59, 62–67,
   71–72, 74, 76, 80–82, 86–87, 114–16,
   140–42, 187–88; absolute, 64; dematerialized, 88; of ecosystem services, 56, 64,
   74; intrinsic, 63, 158, 175; monetary, 52
van den Hombergh, Helena, 120–21
van Hecken, Gert, 124–25, 200, 243n10
violence, 4, 26–27, 31, 161, 182–83, 189, 200,
   226–27, 237nn6,8, 238nn9,10,11, 248n11;
   direct, 26–27, 31, 183, 238n11; green, 183,
   245n4, structural, 27–28, 238n11
vision, 55, 58–59, 61, 67, 70, 73, 75–76,
   81–82, 87, 89, 91, 126–27, 130, 223–25
voluntary carbon market (VCM), 81

water, 52, 54, 77, 83, 86, 110, 114, 137, 158
Wealth Accounting and Valuation of
   Ecosystem Services (WAVES), 48,
   113–14
Weintrobe, Sally, 25
Wildlife Conservation Society (WCS), 49,
   51, 170
workers, 41, 68, 201, 208
worker self-directed enterprise (WSDE),
   208
World Bank, 1, 4, 43, 48, 50–51, 95, 97,
   102–3, 108–10, 112–15
World Business Council for Sustainable
   Development (WBCSD), 44, 47–48,
   50–51, 62, 64, 70, 73, 76, 87–88
World Conservation Congress (WCC),
   1–2, 4, 6, 42, 47–49, 69, 147, 152,
   162–63, 244n13
World Conservation Strategy, 42–43
World Forum on Natural Capital
   (WFNC), 48, 50
World Parks Congress, 6, 135
World Resource Institute (WRI), 51
world-system, 51
World Wildlife Fund (WWF), 3–4, 48–51,
   68, 150

Yasuní-ITT, 175–76

Žižek, Slavoj, 14–15, 23–27, 30, 33, 158–59,
   161–62, 164–65, 167, 185–87, 210, 212,
   214, 217

Founded in 1893,
UNIVERSITY OF CALIFORNIA PRESS
publishes bold, progressive books and journals
on topics in the arts, humanities, social sciences,
and natural sciences—with a focus on social
justice issues—that inspire thought and action
among readers worldwide.

The UC PRESS FOUNDATION
raises funds to uphold the press's vital role
as an independent, nonprofit publisher, and
receives philanthropic support from a wide
range of individuals and institutions—and from
committed readers like you. To learn more, visit
ucpress.edu/supportus.

www.ingramcontent.com/pod-product-compliance
Lightning Source LLC
Chambersburg PA
CBHW020826270326
41928CB00006B/454